The Collapse and
Recovery of Europe,
AD 476–1648

ALSO BY JACK L. SCHWARTZWALD

*The Ancient Near East, Greece and Rome:
A Brief History* (McFarland, 2014)

*Nine Lives of Israel: A Nation's History through the Lives
of Its Foremost Leaders* (McFarland, 2012)

The Collapse and Recovery of Europe, AD 476–1648

Jack L. Schwartzwald

McFarland & Company, Inc., Publishers
Jefferson, North Carolina

LIBRARY OF CONGRESS CATALOGUING-IN-PUBLICATION DATA [new form]

Names: Schwartzwald, Jack L., 1958– author.
Title: The collapse and recovery of Europe, AD 476–1648 / Jack L. Schwartzwald.
Description: Jefferson, North Carolina : McFarland & Company, Inc., Publishers, 2016. | Includes bibliographical references and index.
Identifiers: LCCN 2015038586| ISBN 9781476662305 (softcover : acid free paper) | ISBN 9781476622576 (ebook)
Subjects: LCSH: Europe—Politics and government—476–1492. | Europe—Politics and government—1492–1648.
Classification: LCC D131 .S36 2016 | DDC 940.1—dc23
LC record available at http://lccn.loc.gov/2015038586

BRITISH LIBRARY CATALOGUING DATA ARE AVAILABLE

© 2016 Jack L. Schwartzwald. All rights reserved

No part of this book may be reproduced or transmitted in any form or by any means, electronic or mechanical, including photocopying or recording, or by any information storage and retrieval system, without permission in writing from the publisher.

Front cover image: *Death of King Gustav II Adolf of Sweden at the Battle of Lützen* by Carl Wahlbom, 1855 (National Museum, Sweden)

Printed in the United States of America

*McFarland & Company, Inc., Publishers
Box 611, Jefferson, North Carolina 28640
www.mcfarlandpub.com*

Table of Contents

Preface 1

Section I
City of the World's Desire
Byzantium
3

Section II
City of God
Medieval Europe
65

Section III
City of Man
The Renaissance, Reformation and Thirty Years' War
145

Notes 219
Bibliography 236
Index 243

Preface

The present work takes up the thread of Western civilization where its companion volume—*The Ancient Near East, Greece and Rome: A Brief History*—left off; namely, with the fall of the Western Roman Empire. The collapse of that empire in the late 5th century AD marked the disintegration of order and security in Western Europe. It would require the trial and error of 1,200 years before a successor system of political organization—the nation-state—finally emerged to fill the void.

This work is the story of these 1,200 years. Like its companion, the book is divided into three sections. Section I, *City of the World's Desire*, chronicles the history of the Eastern Roman Empire, commonly called Byzantium, which for a thousand years after Rome's fall considered itself the empire of the "Romans" still. In spite of this glaring case of misidentification—for Byzantium's main cultural elements were not Roman, but Hellenistic, Christian and Asiatic—the empire of the Byzantines endured for a millennium on its own merits before succumbing to foreign conquest. Section II, *City of God*, covers the history of Western Europe—Rome's orphaned child—during this same millennium as it sought to reconstruct the universal empire it had lost. This grand object—pursued first and foremost by the Catholic Church—was never truly in reach, however, and the dream of "Rome resurrected" died with the passing of the Middle Ages, leaving the question of Europe's ultimate political organization unanswered. It was in the ensuing period—from the end of the Hundred Years' War (1453) to the Treaty of Westphalia (1648)—that the nation-state, after centuries in development, was finally crowned as the definite successor to Rome. *City of Man*, the saga of the nation-state's final triumph, comprises the third and last part of our story. Once again, the emphasis of each section is on political and military history, but each concludes with a segment titled "Societal Achievements," which concentrates on the cultural and scientific accomplishments of the era under study.

Effort has been taken to present the subject matter of this volume concisely and in a tone that will appeal to undergraduate college students and general readers alike. In pursuing this end, much inspiration has been taken from Will and Ariel Durant's 11-volume *Story of Civilization*, H. G. Wells' *Outline of History* and Edward Gibbon's *Decline and Fall of the Roman Empire*, all of which similarly sought to combine a comprehensive approach to history with a presentation style that would appeal to a broad audience. With today's emphasis on diversity, one is more likely to encounter courses on "World History" than on "Western Civilization" in college curricula. As this was not the case as recently as three decades ago when courses in Western Civilization were ubiquitous, the author is indebted to several textbooks from that earlier era, chief among them the 5th edition of Brinton, Christopher and Wolff's *A History of Civilization* (1976), C. Harold King's *A History of Civilization* (1964) and Wallbank and Taylor's *Civilization, Past and Present* (1954).

The extensive historical collections at the libraries of Brown University and the University of Rhode Island provided a bounty of source materials for this survey. Several primary source anthologies were also consulted, with J. H. Robinson's two-volume *Readings in European History*, Ross and McLaughlin's *Portable Medieval Reader*, Frederic A. Ogg's *Source Book of Medieval History* and Eugen Weber's *The Western Tradition, From the Ancient World to the Atomic Age* leading the list.

I am again indebted to the many family members, friends and colleagues who provided encouragement during the preparation of this volume. First mention, as always, goes to my wife, Cheryl, followed closely by our two cats, Cody and Crosby (my indefatigable research assistants). Sincere thanks are also owed to my mother Frankie and sister Ann (both educators), and father Joe, for their proofreading labors and to my co-workers at South County Hospital for the wonderful work environment created by their support and friendship.

Section I

City of the World's Desire
Byzantium

At the outset of the 1st century AD, the Roman Empire's chief strategic ambition was to advance its defensive boundary on the German frontier to the line of the River Elbe. The realization of this goal promised a dual advantage in removing the dangerous salient in the existing border (formed by the junction of the Rhine and the Danube rivers) and in markedly reducing the length of the frontier that required defense.[1] In AD 9, however, a Roman army of three legions commanded by Publius Quinctilius Varus was lured into ambush in the Teutoburger Forest and annihilated. In consequence, the Elbe scheme became impracticable for lack of manpower, causing Augustus (Rome's first emperor), to bang his head on the wall in despair, crying, "O, Quinctilius Varus, give me back my legions!"

It was not until the AD 160s that Rome was again in a position to press toward the coveted boundary, but this time a plague contracted by soldiers on the Parthian front made its way westward to decimate the western legions. The manpower shortage this time was so acute that the stoic emperor, Marcus Aurelius, had to fill out the Roman ranks with gladiators, slaves and units of his own Praetorian Guard just to keep the Germans at bay.[2]

Rome would have its victories after this date—Claudius II's decimation of the Goths at Nish (AD 269) and Julian the Apostate's victory against the Alemanni at Strassbourg (AD 357) serve as ready examples. But the Elbe remained out of reach, and the failure to secure it set the stage for unceasing tribulation and periodic catastrophe. An instance of the latter occurred in AD 251 at Abrittus, where the Ostrogoths trapped a Roman army on boggy ground and cut them to pieces, killing the Emperor Decius (whose corpse was forever lost in the mire). Similarly, at Hadrianopolis in AD 378, the cavalry of the Visigoths defeated Rome's infantry so decisively that the legion ceased to be a viable military formation.

At the time of the Teutoburger disaster in AD 9, the parliamentary tradition of the Germanic tribes consisted of gathering around one's chieftain, growling disapproval when angry and clapping spears together when pleased.[3] In AD 410, these same tribesmen, led by the Visigoth Alaric the Bold, sacked Rome. Many a distraught Roman attributed this calamity to the abandonment of the old Roman gods, for Rome was now a Christian empire. But the Christian case was ably defended by St. Augustine, Bishop of Hippo, who replied that the world was a battleground between the "City of God," whose flock adhered to the timeless truths of Christianity, and the "City of Man," whose followers had abandoned the teachings of Jesus for the transient pleasures of the secular world. Christians should not falter in their faith in this troublous time, he argued, but take renewed comfort, for "the City of God abideth forever, though the greatest city of the world has fallen in ruin."[4]

The Visigoths soon withdrew, and Rome survived to win another notable victory—this one *in league* with the Germanic tribes against Attila the Hun at Châlons (AD 451). But four years later the capital was sacked again by the Vandals (who proved themselves worthy of their name's place in history in the process), and in AD 476 the last Western emperor, Romulus Augustulus, was dethroned by the Germanic chieftain, Odoacer.

The eastern half of the empire, based in Constantinople, was still intact, and for a time a *modus vivendi* was achieved between Zeno (the eastern emperor) and Odoacer, with the latter agreeing to rule in cooperation with the Roman senate. But the relationship was a strained one and to prevent further encroachments by the German, Zeno bribed a neighboring people, the Rugians, to invade Italy. Odoacer defeated the Rugians before they could cross the frontier and the Rugian king and queen were beheaded in a public spectacle.[5]

Zeno, meanwhile, had become entangled in the east with two rival Ostrogothic chieftains, Theodoric and Strabo.[6] The trio tried every combination: Zeno and Theodoric against Strabo, Theodoric and Strabo against Zeno, and finally Zeno and Strabo against Theodoric. In the end, none of these arrangements proved satisfactory, and the chance of some different accommodation among the three was ruined when Strabo achieved the rare equestrian feat of being thrown from his horse onto the point of an upright spear.[7] Strabo's death only rendered the quarrel between Theodoric and Emperor Zeno more acute. But at length, the latter hit upon the highly agreeable suggestion that Theodoric conquer Italy. The emperor hoped thereby to kill the proverbial two birds with one stone, ridding himself of Odoacer while removing the troublesome Theodoric to a more distant locale.

Theodoric clashed with Odoacer on the Isonzo near the Venetian border and again on the Adige near Verona. Both encounters resulted in victory for the Ostrogoth—the slaughter being sufficient in the latter to populate the Adige with corpses.[8] Odoacer retreated to Ravenna. Unable to starve him out after a two-year siege, Theodoric feigned exhaustion with the struggle and proposed peace and partition of the peninsula. Then, at the banquet convened to celebrate the accord, he drew his sword and cleaved Odoacer in two lengthwise, thereby completing his victory (AD 493).[9]

Despite the violence of this usurpation, Theodoric was familiar with the ways of civility. He had spent much of his youth as a hostage in Constantinople, and owing to that happenstance, Italy would experience a rudimentary renaissance under his tutelage. By betrothing his sister and daughters to the motley collection of barbarian princes on his frontiers and by personally marrying a sister of Frankland's King Clovis, he secured his borders, and brought peace to the beleaguered Italians. Hoping to fuse Gothic and Roman society into one, Theodoric cooperated with the Roman Senate, supported the agricultural activities of small farmers, saw to the draining of marshes and to improvements in roads and harbors, and resumed the old "bread and circuses." Although he was himself an adherent of the heretical Arian creed, he forbade the persecution of Catholics or Jews. He promoted education—his eminent subjects, Cassiodorus and Boethius, produced a litany of writings destined to influence Medieval thought for centuries. He died in AD 526, after fostering peace and stability for three decades. It would be unjust to censure him until his final years, when the resolution of a longstanding schism between the pope in Rome and the eastern patriarchs at Constantinople made him (as a heretic Arian) fear for his throne.[10] Thenceforth, he played the tyrant—torturing and executing a group of senators accused of treasonous correspondence with the Eastern Roman Empire.[11]

As he left no son, Theodoric's throne passed to his eight-year-old grandson, Athalaric, under the regency of the boy's mother (i.e., Theodoric's daughter), Amalasuntha. The regent attempted to provide the boy with a formal education, but found him an unwilling pupil. When, in exasperation, she slapped him for his persistent misbehavior, he complained to the Gothic nobility, who promptly protested to the regent that their king was being raised in a manner unbecoming of a Goth. To rectify the matter, the nobles took over as Athalaric's custodians, with the result that the boy died at sixteen from alcoholism, womanizing and other "becoming" pursuits.[12]

Although relations with her son had not been cordial for several years, Athalaric's death left Amalasuntha in the awkward position of "regent without a prince." In an attempt to ease her predicament, she married an avaricious cousin, Theodahad, who was thus crowned king. But the union was an imperfect one. Theodahad had Amalasuntha imprisoned on an island on a lake in Tuscany, where, in short order, she was surprised in her bath by a strangler.[13]

Unfortunately for Theodahad, Amalasuntha had had more than one iron in the fire prior to her untimely death—including an offer to hand over the whole of Italy to the Eastern emperor in return for his support. As it happened, the emperor's legions had lately completed the reconquest of Carthage and Sicily, and the emperor himself, Justinian I, was most eager to extend his hegemony to the Italian mainland, thus to regain the city of Rome for the empire that still bore that fair name. To Justinian, the murder of Amalasuntha seemed ample pretext to proceed with what he had intended to do in any event.

The Eastern Roman Empire

At the end of the 5th century AD, it was not clear that the Eastern Roman Empire would survive the fall of her Western sister for ten years, much less for nearly 1,000. During the reign of Leo I (AD 457–474), the Germanic tribes bade fair to do in the East what they were doing in the West. Aspar, a Germanic chieftain, had bullied his way into the post of master of soldiers and was plotting to make his son the emperor's heir. The threat was averted when Leo recruited into his army a strong contingent of Isaurian troops from Anatolia—among them, the future emperor, Zeno, whom we have already met. Aspar and his son were duly murdered at court, but for the performance of this service, the Isaurians exacted a heavy price. Openly disdained as rustic foreigners by the capital populace, they nonetheless gained predominance in the government. Zeno's seven-year-old son was named Leo's heir, and when the child died in the year of his accession (AD 474), the throne passed to Zeno himself, who ruled on the strength of his Isaurian constituency (AD 474–491).[14]

In AD 491, Zeno died and his widow, bowing to the will of the capital citizenry, chose a local noble, Anastasius I, as husband and emperor. Cast from power, the Isaurians resorted to civil war only to be defeated in a great battle at Cotyaeum.[15] The situation remained precarious, however, as the empire faced attack on its western flank from the Bulgarians[16]—one of three major Hunnic tribes that had emerged from the chaos following the death of Attila. The Bulgarians destroyed one Roman army in AD 493 and inflicted heavy losses on another nine years later. To allay the threat, Anastasius oversaw the construction of a 41-mile defensive rampart stretching from the Black Sea to the Sea of Marmora.[17] Further east, Anastasius fought a five-year war with Persia, which ended in a seven-years' truce buttressed by the construction of a fortress at Daras blocking the usual route of Persian invasion.[18]

On the domestic front, Anastasius reformed the currency, and by cutting expenditures as well as taxes, he returned the empire to a stable economic footing. To the distress of the Orthodox, however, the emperor betrayed a strong tendency toward the Monophysite heresy, which imparted but one "nature" to Jesus (human and divine, united) in contradistinction to the Orthodox two (human and divine, separate). At the Council of Chalcedon (451), the Orthodox view had prevailed. But the controversy would not end, and caught in the middle, a succession of emperors tried alternately to enforce the council's ruling or to affect a workable compromise. Capitalizing on the discontent surrounding Anastasius' policy, the soldier Vitalian attempted to usurp the throne in the name of orthodoxy. His rebellion lasted five years, but after obtaining several victories, Vitalian was decisively beaten in a naval confrontation near the capital (AD 518).

Later that year, Anastasius died without heir, whereupon a large sum of money was delivered to the count of the palace guard to secure the throne for a favored pretender named Theocritus. But after pocketing the cash, the count—an illiterate peasant named Justin who had risen to his current station by serving with distinction in the wars of Anastasius—paraded a series of unacceptable candidates before the senate until the latter, fearing imminent intervention by some usurper or other if they did not make a choice, insisted that Count Justin mount the throne himself. After the customary protestations that the notion had never crossed his mind, Justin bowed to the "senate's will" and embarked on a nine-year reign (518–527).[19]

The new emperor cemented his authority by renouncing the Monophysitism of his predecessor and embracing orthodoxy. The decision won him unified ecclesiastical support, the adherence of the old rebel, Vitalian,[20] and a reconciliation with the pope in Rome—the last having been mediated by Justin's gifted nephew, Peter Sabbatius. When Justin succumbed to an old battle wound in 527, the throne passed to the selfsame Peter (ruled, 527–565), now known as "Justinian" in reverence to the uncle who had adopted him as heir.[21]

A year earlier, Justinian had effected a change in the law forbidding men of senatorial rank from wedding common actresses[22] and had taken as his bride Theodora, formerly (if the hostile court historian, Procopius, is to be believed) Constantinople's most celebrated courtesan and veteran of a stage show in which trained geese lured forth by grains of barley joined her in a lewd act that no other actress (or goose) has ever thought of doing again.[23] The rehabilitation of this delicate creature was completed by Justinian's accession to the throne, so that, in Gibbon's phrasing, "The prostitute, who, in the presence of innumerable spectators, had polluted the theatre of Constantinople, was adored as a queen in the same city."[24]

As emperor, Justinian dreamed of restoring the Western Empire by military conquest—"his designs," says Professor Bury, "reached to Gaul, if not to Britain"[25]—and, pursuant to this lofty enterprise, he raised taxes on Constantinople's estate owners. It was a marvelously unpopular decision. The groaning aristocracy sought to forestall the emperor's intended expedition by exaggerating the Persian threat to the realm's eastern frontier. Even worse, hordes of peasants, ruined by the new taxes, descended upon the capital to look for handouts.²⁶ The city was thus transformed into a veritable tinderbox, and the spark that set it ablaze was a riot at Constantinople's sporting arena—the Hippodrome.

The Hippodrome played host to Byzantium's famed chariot races, wherein charioteers clad in team uniforms of green or blue served as the direct ancestors of today's sports heroes. The fans, however, were a breed apart from their modern counterparts. Far from confining themselves to cheers and boos, they divided themselves along political lines—the Blues favoring an aristocratic agenda, the Greens (tainted by the Monophysite heresy²⁷) that of the commoners. Thus, the Hippodrome served as a popular parliament, and even the emperor was expected to ally himself with one color or the other. On mounting the throne, however, Justinian forswore his former allegiance

Justinian the Great, from a Byzantine mosaic at the Basilica of San Vitale, Ravenna, Italy (© Depositphotos.com/Patrick Guénette).

to the Blues and stood aloof. The decision was greatly resented, and when the emperor attended the rehearsal for the Ides of January races in AD 532, the partisans of the Greens voiced their discontent, shouting out that they were the victims of oppression. Taken aback, Justinian instructed his crier to answer, "Be mute, ye Jews, Samaritans, and Manichaeans!" The Greens replied that their emperor was a tyrant, a liar and a murderer. "Do you despise your lives?" came the response from Justinian's crier, whereupon the Blues, seeing a chance to regain the emperor's favor, chased the Greens from the stadium.²⁸

The streets now erupted in deadly factional violence. Justinian's police arrested the chief perpetrators, seven of whom—representatives of both parties among them—were sentenced to execution.²⁹ Five of the condemned promptly met death by decapitation or hanging. The last two—one Blue and one Green—being conducted to the gallows, survived when the ropes used to hang them broke. They were ushered to the safety of a monastery, but the emperor refused to entertain pleas on their behalf. Two days later, when he again attended the Hippodrome races, he haughtily ignored the crowd's repeated petitions for mercy. Enraged by his recalcitrance, the factions shouted, "Long live the humane Greens and Blues!" indicating thereby that they were now united against their monarch.³⁰ As the signal of revolution, they adopted the rallying cry, "*Nika*" ("Conquer"), and their chants were succeeded by rioting in the streets.³¹ Churches, government buildings and a hospital full of patients were consumed in flames.³² Surrounded in his palace, the emperor considered abdication. But his wife—now chaste and accustomed to being empress—bade him stand his ground. Regaining his composure, Justinian summoned the era's leading general: Belisarius.

Although he was not yet thirty, Belisarius had already made a name for himself on the Persian frontier. Serving as master of soldiers at Daras in AD 530, he had received a missive from his Persian opposite which stated that he (the Persian) intended to bathe in Daras the next day and that the Romans should therefore ready his bath.[33] On the heels of this impolite battle summons a Persian force appeared on the horizon that outnumbered Belisarius' army by nearly two to one. Far from preparing a bath, however, Belisarius prepared his ground. The center of his line, protected by a defensive trench, was positioned further from the enemy than were the wings. An attack on his center would thus have to pass between the wings, where it would be vulnerable to counterattack on both flanks. The only viable targets in the Roman line were thus the wings (which were also protected by defensive trenches). On the first day of battle, the Persians attacked the Roman left and drove it back. Belisarius, however, had placed contingents of Hunnic cavalry on either side of this wing, and their onslaught into the Persian flanks drove the latter into a disorderly retreat. On day two, the Persians tried their luck on the Roman right and bade fair to drive it from the field. This time, they were struck in flank and put to rout by infantry and cavalry from the Roman center. Hence, by narrowing the enemy's tactical choices, and by positioning his light cavalry so that they were able to attack the enemy in flank as the latter pressed forward, Belisarius beat the odds and emerged with a stunning victory.[34]

Two years later, at the Hippodrome, his tactics were rather less nuanced. Repelled at the entrance to the royal box, where the rioters were crowning a pretender to the throne, Belisarius' troops stormed the stadium's side entrances and proceeded to butcher thirty thousand *Nika* rioters where they stood.[35] Amidst the pandemonium, a few souls reached the exits alive only to find the outlets guarded by the troops of Narses, Justinian's eunuch, who finished them off with equal rapacity.[36]

With his power thus confirmed, Justinian set to work in earnest on his extraordinary quest to reunite the empire. An "Everlasting Peace," negotiated with Chosroes, the Persian king of kings, secured his eastern frontier, and left his army free for duty in the West. Carthage was chosen as the staging ground. The city's Vandal king, Hilderic, had made friendly gestures to Byzantium only to be overthrown by his rival, Gelimer, who was openly hostile. Citing this usurpation as his pretext, Justinian dispatched Belisarius to North Africa with an armada bearing five thousand cavalry and ten thousand foot.

Things went awry immediately. The armada's bread stores had been inadequately baked prior to departure, and at mealtime, the legionaries sat down to a lump of "moldy paste."[37] Belisarius obtained new provisions, but once back at sea, his riotous sailors threatened to mutiny if they encountered the Vandal fleet. Taking them at their word, Belisarius put in at the nearest port, and proceeded overland toward Carthage. En route, his troops broke ranks and plundered the locals. Belisarius rebuked them, saying that their mission depended on the goodwill of the populace—an advantage that would surely be forfeited if the Byzantines mimicked the brutality of the Vandals.[38]

After a prolonged coastline march, battle was finally joined on the eastern approaches of Carthage. Gelimer had the upper hand in men, but he divided his forces in a badly coordinated attack, and the Vandal detachments were defeated in detail. By day's end, Belisarius was victorious. The gates of Carthage were thrown open and the Byzantine commander dined at a table prepared earlier in the day for the Vandal king (AD 533).[39]

Only Gibbon's penchant for dry humor could fashion this campaign "the last contest between Rome and Carthage," or Belisarius "the third Africanus." In any event, there was still much to do. Italy, Sicily and Spain had yet to be conquered.[40] Belisarius chose Sicily as his immediate objective. Technically, the island was already his. It had been presented to the Vandals by the Goths as part of a wedding dowry before Belisarius' African campaign, and as the Vandals had now been defeated, the Byzantine captain claimed it as spoils of war. At Panormus, he backed his claim with an unusual naval tactic: Using pulleys attached to the topmasts of his galleys, he hauled aloft rowboats filled with archers, who unloosed their missiles downwards onto the city ramparts.[41] Sicily fell to the conqueror. He set his sights next on the Ostrogothic kingdom of Italy. And what more chivalrous pretext for invasion could there have been than the pitiable epistle from poor strangled Amalasuntha begging succor from Belisarius' master, Justinian.

To avenge the murder of Theodoric's daughter, Belisarius crossed from Messina to Rhegium and advanced to the gates of Naples, which capitulated after four hundred Byzantine soldiers stole into the city via its aqueduct in the pitch of night. Fleeing for his life, Theodahad, the cousin, husband and murderer of Amalasuntha, was deposed and murdered by his own disgruntled soldiers, while faraway Rome happily received a Byzantine garrison and proclaimed themselves the willing subjects of Emperor Justinian.

Thus, just sixty years after the abdication of Romulus Augustulus, a Byzantine force of five thousand men had retaken Rome (AD 536). The story, however, does not end there; for a Gothic army of 150,000 warriors promptly descended from Ravenna to invest Belisarius' minuscule Roman garrison. The general prepared himself for the onslaught as best he could—stocking the city with Sicilian corn, and improving its defenses.[42] Roman youths were conscripted to help man the walls, and Hadrian's mausoleum was converted into a fortress. As the Goths approached with their scaling ladders, battering rams and siege engines, Belisarius made himself present at every vulnerable spot, encouraging the troops, and drawing their applause by skewering the attackers with arrows shot from his own bow. At his command, a concentrated fire was directed against the teams of oxen bringing up the Gothic siege towers so that the structures sat useless at a distance.[43]

Belisarius' tactics were sufficient to produce a standoff, but the siege continued. With his supplies running out, the general appealed to Justinian for reinforcements. These were sent in piecemeal contingents, and though they were hardly numerous, they seemed to magnify their numbers by arriving at different sites, and by advancing from different directions. Anxious to arrange peace, the Goths offered to abandon all claim to Sicily in return for a Byzantine withdrawal from Italy. "The emperor is not less generous," Belisarius answered scornfully; "in return for a gift which you no longer possess: he presents you with ... sovereignty of the British Island."[44]

The Goths had clearly lost the initiative, and when news arrived that the town of Rimini, deep in Gothic territory, had fallen to a Byzantine cavalry force, they struck camp and fled—many drowning in the Tiber in a panicked crossing of the Milvian Bridge.[45] Belisarius pursued them to Ravenna. Unfortunately, the emperor was now concerned that the enormity of his vassal's success might translate into a bid for the throne.[46] As a result, he dispatched the disagreeable eunuch, Narses, to keep him in bounds. The two generals butted heads immediately, and after eking out one final triumph—the capture of Ravenna by a ruse—Belisarius was recalled (AD 539).

Neither success nor unswerving loyalty was proof against a jealous emperor. Out of necessity, Justinian commissioned his great captain to combat the Persians who, after seven years, had tired of an "Everlasting Peace" and renewed the war under Chosroes. But no sooner had Belisarius brought the conflict to a successful conclusion than he found himself in imminent danger of execution. The Empress Theodora had long despised the popular general, and now falsely accused him of conspiring with other officers over the imperial succession while Justinian, a victim of plague, clung tenuously to life (AD 542).[47] When the emperor recovered, Belisarius was informed that his miserable person had only been spared because Antonina (Belisarius' wife) was a favorite of the empress.[48]

Without Belisarius' guiding presence, the empire's fragile Western conquests began to unravel. The peoples of Africa rebelled against Justinian's oppressive taxes. They were put down in an effusion of blood, but soon afterwards, the Goths of Italy rallied to the banner of a rising prince named Totila and attempted to reconquer the peninsula. Amidst their ranks were many native Italians who had had quite enough of Byzantine corruption and haughtiness. Totila and his Goths besieged Rome, whose perfidious governor played the war-profiteer rather than tend to the city's defense. He monopolized the food stores of his own people—selling supplies at scandalous prices to the wealthier citizens while the poor sustained themselves on rodent flesh and inedible vegetation.[49] Again the emperor turned to Belisarius, who reappeared in Italy in 544, but with too small a force to relieve the capital. Totila captured the city in 546, and then launched a campaign into southern Italy. Belisarius astutely let him go, and wrested Rome from the garrison he had left behind. After a successful defense of the city, however, he was recalled to Constantinople, leaving Rome's stunned defenders to defect back to Totila (548).

In the same year, Justinian's beloved Theodora died of cancer, throwing the monarch into profound mourning. Italian affairs were left to languish for four years, during which time a bitter religious controversy erupted between the papacy and the Eastern patriarchs. The latter, at the urging of Justinian, were attempting to bridge the chasm between Monophysitism and orthodoxy. Far from succeeding, the leading patriarchs managed to get themselves excommunicated.[50] Only in 552 did Justinian again turn his attentions to his Western Empire. This time, however, he passed over the trusty Belisarius, and dispatched Narses to Italy—supplying the favored eunuch with the adequate troops and funding that he had always withheld from his talented general. Narses engaged Totila at Tagina, near Rome, where the Gothic King was defeated and slain (552). Teias, the next Gothic King, challenged the eunuch on the banks of the Sarnus, where he, too, met defeat and death (553). The Goths were prepared to give up the fight, but in their moment of despair, the Franks and Alemanni arrived from Germany to succor them. A last battle was fought at Casilinum, where Narses destroyed the triangular Franco-Germanic phalanx in a double envelopment modeled on Cannae and Marathon (554). For his victories, he was made "exarch," or chief governor, of Italy—a post he filled for fifteen years.

While the flower of the Byzantine army remained with Narses in Italy, Constantinople was imperiled by the invasion of a new host of barbarians. In his far-flung imperial adventures, Justinian had not discerned that the true threat to his empire lay neither in Asia nor in Italy, but on the banks of the Danube.[51] When Theodoric ruled Italy, the latter boundary had been ably defended, but now the Gothic power was broken, and the Byzantines lacked the manpower to guard the border for themselves.[52] Beyond the barrier, great popular migrations were taking place. In the winter of 559, the Bulgarians crossed the frozen Danube. The rampart of Anastasius proving no obstacle, the host marched to the very walls of Constantinople, accompanied by another nomadic people, the "Sclavonians"—a forest-dwelling people whose primitive timber huts, in Gibbon's estimation, could not be compared "without flattery ... to the architecture of the beaver."[53] The new peril provided Belisarius with a last opportunity for glory. At his disposal were a mere 300 veterans and 3,500 reservists (whose job, hitherto had been to lock and unlock the capital's gates). Belisarius concealed the latter in the woods flanking his chosen field of battle. The invaders pressed forward to get at his veterans only to be harassed by a barrage of arrows on either flank. The veterans then put them to rout without the loss of a single man.[54]

Alas, it is an enduring truth that no good deed goes unpunished. Another success recommended another persecution from Justinian. In 562, the fifty-seven-year-old Belisarius was preposterously accused of conspiring to murder the eighty-year-old emperor, and was imprisoned for a period of seven months before the ridiculous accusation was dropped. He died at sixty in the same year as his master (AD 565).

The conquests of Belisarius and Narses produced no lasting result. Rather than strengthen the empire, the destruction of the Vandal power in Africa and the Gothic power in Italy destroyed the buffer that had existed against enemies further afield.[55] Far more enduring than these military achievements was a new imperial law code. Under Justinian, a committee of legal experts headed by the jurist Tribonian reviewed all existing edicts dating to, and including, the Hadrianic Code of the second century AD. After removing contradictory and outdated material, the compilers published the *Codex Justinianus* (529). They followed this work with the so-called *Digests*, a catalog of legal opinions from the annals of ancient Rome, and the *Institutes*, which served as a text for aspiring lawyers (530–533). Although Tribonian was accused of doctoring some of the laws in return for bribes prior to publication, the *Codex*, *Digests*, and *Institutes* laid the foundation of our modern Western legal system.

The reign was also notable for lavish spending on the part of the emperor, who saw to a multiplication of roads, bridges, aqueducts and fortifications, which did more to bankrupt his sprawling empire than to secure it. The Church of St. Sophia dates to Justinian, whose architects rebuilt it in all of its present splendor after its precursor was destroyed in the *Nika* riots. Even Justinian's illicit importation of silkworm eggs from China—an action that gave rise to a long-profitable industry—could not replenish what war and architecture had taken from the treasury.

Before we leave Justinian's reign, we need to mention the great plague that ravaged the empire in 542. Procopius, Justinian's court historian, chronicled the epidemic. We shall let him describe it:

> About the same time was a Plague, which almost consumed mankind.... It began among the Egyptians of Pelusiam, and spread ... through the world, as by set journeys and stages.... In the second year of it, it came to Byzantium ... where it was my fortune then to reside....
>
> [Most victims] suddenly became feverish.... Their body changed not color, nor was hot ... [so] that neither the sick, nor the physician feeling his pulse apprehended danger. But to some the same day, to some the next ... there rose a *Bubo*, not only in the groin ... but in the [armpits], under the ear, and in other parts....

At first few died ... then died five thousand every day, then 10,000 and more. In the beginning, men took care to bury each his own dead.... But in the end, all was confusion: Servants were without Masters; and rich men wanted servants to attend them; and many houses were empty. So that diverse [people] for want of acquaintance lay long unburied.... And now in the afflicted city were no trades or shops to be seen.[56]

It had been an early visit of the Black Death, and before it was over, many of the dead had been carted across the water to the fortress of Galata, where the towers were unroofed and crammed full of corpses before being closed over again.[57] As noted above, the emperor himself was afflicted, though he managed to recover. But death cannot be put off forever, and Justinian finally did expire at age eighty-three (565), bequeathing to his nephew, Justin II, a depleted treasury and territories that his overextended armies could not hope to defend.

Under Justin II, Byzantine power began to recede. In 568, the fierce "Long-beards," or Lombards, ravaged northern Italy, and when Byzantine arms sustained an additional reverse at the hands of the Persians at the opposite end of the empire—losing the strategic border fortress of Daras—Justin lost his sanity. On the advice of his wife, Empress Sophia, he abdicated in favor of Tiberius, his captain of the guards and adoptive son.[58] Abandoning the wasteful spending habits of his predecessors, the new emperor lessened the tax burden on his subjects. Sadly, a bowl of overripe mulberries cut short his meritorious reign. In 582, his posthumous son-in-law,[59] Maurice, a general with a record of impressive victories in the ongoing war with Persia, succeeded him.

Maurice and Phocas

So acute and manifold was the military threat during the reign of Maurice (582–602) that it became necessary to codify the empire's military strategy. The resulting work, the *Strategicon*—attributed to Maurice himself, but perhaps only commissioned by him—served as the standard text on military matters for three centuries. Having learned hard lessons from earlier wars with the Huns, the core of the army was now composed of armored cavalrymen equipped with the composite bow and the lance—coincidentally, the same equipment used by the Parthians with such devastating effect against the Romans at the battle of Carrhae in 53 BC.[60] The adoption of the stirrup and a rigorous training regimen helped compensate for a lack of innate skill at horsemanship,[61] and loyalty was ensured by minimizing the number of foreign auxiliaries in the ranks, which were instead filled out with native levies—of whom the Isaurians appear to have been the best fighters.[62]

For the first eight years of Maurice's reign, the new army had to contend with the Persian threat. But in AD 590, the Persian great king was unseated in a palace coup, and in the ensuing struggle over the succession, Maurice's army rendered decisive aid to Chosroes II, the eldest son of the deposed monarch. To reciprocate, Chosroes returned the fortress of Daras, and maintained a liberal peace with the empire. The respite allowed Maurice to overhaul his provincial administration by designating Carthage as the provincial capital or "exarchate" of Africa, and Ravenna as the capital of Italy.[63] Each exarchate was entrusted to an "exarch" or provincial governor who was vested simultaneously with civil and military authority (a dual responsibility that would be expanded upon in the administrative "theme" system of the next century).[64]

With his eastern and western flanks secure, Maurice was finally free to attend to a long-smoldering threat in the Balkans. The neighborhood had been bad enough when the Lombards were there. But the Danube basin was now the preserve of the ill-mannered Avar tribe, who raised alarms in Constantinople by capturing the old Roman city of Sirmium in 581. Maurice sought to buy them off with an annual tribute of 80,000 gold coins, but the greed of the avaricious enemy was not easily sated. Their "chagan," or chieftain, demanded in turn the delivery of an elephant from the royal zoo, a couch forged from gold, and finally a 20,000-coin increase in his annual subsidy.[65] The first two petitions were granted, but the third was refused, whereupon the chagan burst across the Save to seize Belgrade. Unwilling to tolerate such brazenness, Maurice prepared to strike back.

Not since the reign of Theodosius I (AD 379–395) had a Roman emperor led an army in the field, and Gibbon applauds Maurice's bold foray at the head of his troops.[66] But ill omens—consisting of a violent storm, a solar eclipse and the birth of deformed child in a village on the line of march[67]—unnerved the emperor and convinced him to cease his exertions after an advance of just seven miles. The army went on without him, first under the banner of his brother, Peter (whose attempt to secure a water supply ended in defeat on the banks of the Helibacia), and then under an able officer named Priscus, who drove the Avars back across the Danube.

The plight of the army of the Danube was not an easy one, and the emperor's attitude rendered it all the more difficult. When the chagan captured 12,000 imperial troops, the pennywise Maurice allowed them to perish rather than hand over the modest ransom that would have saved them. Worse still, he informed his legions that henceforth they would be billed for their arms and provisions, and that they would have to spend the winter foraging in Avar territory to avoid placing a burden on the state.[68] The exasperated soldiery rebelled against this decree, and nominated an ordinary centurion named Phocas (ruled 602–610) to lead them. On reaching the capital, the usurper put Maurice to death most cruelly after making him a captive witness to the execution of his four sons. As the boys were murdered, says Theophylact, Maurice cried out, "Thou art just, O Lord! and thy judgments are righteous"; and when the family's wet nurse nearly managed to save the emperor's infant by substituting her own, Maurice insisted that the real child be brought forward rather than compound the crime with the blood of an uninvolved innocent.[69] Maurice's wife was spared at first, but when she conspired to avenge her family, she and her three daughters were decapitated.[70]

The accession of Phocas was a catastrophe. While the new emperor decorated the Hippodrome with the heads of real or imagined rivals, the Avars ravaged the Balkans. At the same time, Chosroes II invaded the empire on the pretext of avenging his murdered patron, Maurice (603). By 608, a Persian army had appeared at the gates of Chalcedon, just across the straits from Constantinople. Terrified by the onslaught, the aristocracy begged Heraclius, the elderly exarch of Carthage, to save the commonwealth before Phocas brought it to ruin.[71] Too old to come in person, Heraclius dispatched his son and namesake to Constantinople at the head of a strong naval force (610). The populace welcomed their rescuer with delirious shouts of joy uttered in barely passable Latin, which was falling out of usage in the East in favor of Greek.[72] Dragged forth in chains and thrown at the feet of Heraclius, Phocas was challenged to acquit himself. Offering no defense, he asked contemptuously, "Wilt thou govern better?" The tone was unsuited to his predicament. He was beaten and decapitated on the spot.[73]

The Heraclian Dynasty

Despite the enthusiasm with which he was received, the younger Heraclius could do little to stem the tide of disaster. Antioch (611), Syria (613) and Palestine (614) fell to Persia in rapid succession, and the True Cross was carted off into captivity. By 615, the tents of the enemy were again seen across the Bosphorus at Chalcedon, and, a year later, the fall of Egypt relieved the emperor and his people of their grain supply.

It was no better on the western frontier, where the Avars had advanced into Thrace, almost to the gates of the capital. At length, Heraclius concluded that the nation's calamities were not his problem, and announced that he would return to Carthage. Just as he was about to embark, however, the patriarch of Constantinople rebuked him for abdicating his duties, and convinced him to remain at his post. The decision spawned a dynasty that would endure for four generations.

For the first twelve years of his reign, Heraclius could not mount so much as one counterattack against the chastisers of his realm. Slowly, however, he nurtured the empire's strength. By apportioning imperial lands to his provincial subjects in return for a pledge of hereditary military service, the emperor was able to raise new levies. The severing of the Egyptian grain supply had forced an end to the corn dole, and faced with starvation, the capital's freeloaders likewise enlisted.[74] There were no funds in the treasury to outfit the new recruits, but Chosroes unwittingly resolved this impasse by dispatching a scornful letter to the empire—as insulting to Jesus as it was to Heraclius (whom the Persian monarch called a "vile and insensate slave"). Upon publication of this missive, the churches of Constantinople placed their accumulated treasure (the last source of revenue in the state) at the emperor's disposal to be minted into new coinage.[75] By AD 622, all was in order and a fleet of galleys emerged from the capital's harbor carrying the emperor and his new legions. Rather than make for the Asian shore, however, the galleys rowed westward down the straits and out of sight. In light of their former victories, the startled Persians looking on from Chalcedon may have viewed the scene as an act of desertion, but they were soon undeceived. Sailing along the coast of Asia Minor, Heraclius put in unopposed at Issus—the old battleground of Alexander the Great in Cilicia—where the natural defenses allowed him leisure to drill his new army. Before the year was out, he had lured a Persian force into the Taurus Mountains and destroyed it.[76] In 623, he occupied Armenia, and a year after that he crossed into Mesopotamia. Chosroes sent three armies against him, but the dauntless emperor drove them off. Greatly alarmed, Chosroes staged a diversion—joining the Avars in a dual siege of Constantinople in hopes of forcing Heraclius to retreat (626). The emperor, however, had reinforced the capital with 12,000 elite troops and a corps of engineers practiced in the art of siege defense. Although the city relied upon an external water source, it was unavailing to cut her aqueducts—for within her walls was an underground complex of cisterns housing a nearly inexhaustible water reserve. (The largest of these reservoirs was the so-called "Cistern of 1001 Columns." Built during the reign of Justinian, and boasting domed ceilings with myriad arches, it had a surface area of 2800 square meters—spacious enough for a relaxing boat ride.[77]) Unable to make headway against the walls, the Avars attempted an amphibious assault involving the transport of a large Persian force from Chalcedon. But in the midst of the operation the galleys of the Byzantines intercepted the primitive canoe-navy of the Avars, routing it so disastrously that the entire siege was abandoned.[78]

One year later, the decisive clash occurred at Nineveh in Mesopotamia (627). Once the capital of ancient Assyria, the site was nothing more than a barren desert when the rival armies collided. Of the ensuing eleven-hour battle, we possess no reliable description. Theophanes Confessor reports that Heraclius, riding at the head of his troops, slew three assailants while sustaining only an inconsequential wound on the lip.[79] At battle's end, the Persians were routed. On hearing the news at Dastagerd, Chosroes gathered his concubines and escaped in disgrace to Ctesiphon, the Persian capital. There, he was dethroned and killed by his son, Siroes, who made peace with the empire.

Before returning to Constantinople where the euphoric citizenry proclaimed him the equal of Scipio (628), Heraclius detoured to Jerusalem to restore the True Cross to its proper home.[80] Unfortunately, it was to be his last triumph, for a new power was poised to divest him of the fruits of his victories.

The Rise of Islam

Islam, which means "surrender (to God)," had its origins in the Arabian town of Mecca. The town had long been a religious center of sorts, where pilgrims paid homage to a meteorite—the mysterious arrival of which, at some unspecified point in antiquity, had prompted the superstitious inhabitants to revere it as a god. In time, the stream of idolaters arriving to worship the esteemed rock became a great source of profit to the city, but its fortunes—and those of the world at large—were to change with the coming of Mohammed.

Born destitute in AD 570, and orphaned as a child, Mohammed was taken under the care of an uncle who introduced him to caravan life. From this early experience, the youth obtained enough business acumen to draw the attention of a rich widow named Kadija. The two were soon married, and Mohammed, now financially secure, turned increasingly to spiritual contemplation. In his view, the superstitious traditions of his fellow townsmen acquitted themselves unfavorably when compared with the lofty monotheism of the Jews residing in neighboring Medina. But Judaism was not a religion of proselytization, while Byzantine Christianity, the other local monotheistic religion—was so immersed in doctrinal minutia as to be incomprehensible to a people still struggling with the origin of meteorites.[81]

According to Muslim tradition, the dilemma required the intercession of Archangel Gabriel, who appeared to Mohammed in a vision and revealed the truth. Thus, in AD 610, Mohammed became the prophet of a new religion. He preached to the locals about Allah, the one true God, who accepted his suppliants into a great brotherhood of equals in this world and into paradise in the next. To join, one merely had to believe. There were no domineering priests, and no tedious conversion rituals, for Allah could see directly into the soul of the true believer.

Because Mecca's income depended on its meteorite-god and a continuing influx of pagans, the town fathers gave a cool reception to the new creed of their wayward son. Nor could they countenance his popularity in neighboring Medina, where many idolaters had become attracted to his teachings. Medina was a major outpost on the caravan trail between Mecca and Syria, and could not be made home to a rival theology.[82] A careful consideration of risks and benefits recommended the speedy apprehension and murder of the new prophet, but before the resolution could be carried out, Mohammed fled to Medina, arriving on September 20, 622. The Muslim calendar dates itself to this event, which is celebrated in the annals of Islam as the "*Hegira*" or "journey."

Now fifty-one, Mohammed found himself the leader of a growing enterprise. To be sure, his treasury was empty, but owing to the ongoing revelations of Allah this impediment was quickly surmounted. It was revealed to the messenger that the time of one's death is preordained, and that to die in the service of God is to gain immediate entry into Heaven. The venerable words had an immediate effect. According to Gibbon: "The intrepid souls of the Arabs were fired with enthusiasm ... and the death which they had always despised became an object of hope and desire.... The first companions of Mahomet advanced to battle with a fearless confidence: there is no danger where there is no chance: they were ordained to perish in their beds; or they were safe and invulnerable amidst the darts of the enemy."[83]

This law of "*Kismet*," or predestination, convinced Mohammed's flock to arm themselves without trepidation. At Badr, several hundred Musulmans surprised a Meccan caravan, casting the unbelievers from their camels, and appropriating their goods in the worthy cause of Allah (AD 623). Understandably outraged, the people of Mecca took up arms in retaliation. At Uhud, Mohammed was lured into battle against a superior force. A group of Jewish soldiers offered their assistance, but were turned away as unbelievers. In the ensuing clash, the Muslim army was taken in flank. Fighting amidst the confusion, the prophet was wounded three times. A false report announced his death, and some of the faithful took to their heels, but Mohammed, still alive, felled one of his assailants with a spear and led the remainder of his flock to the safety of a nearby hilltop from which they could not be displaced.[84]

The battle—a tactical defeat, but a strategic draw—was followed by several years of desultory fighting, before Mecca raised a force of ten thousand men to extinguish the flame of Islam once and for all. At the time, Mohammed had a following of but three thousand men in arms, so, on the sole approach to the city, he constructed a protective ditch—something that had never been seen in sandy Arabia.[85] According to H. G. Wells, the Meccans complained bitterly to those standing in array behind the obstacle, but received no satisfactory reply.[86] For three weeks they remained outside Medina, making fruitless charges and challenging the defenders to come out and fight like men, before a torrential rain intervened to dampen their zeal. Finally, as they could see no way of breaching the fortification, they withdrew in a huff (AD 625).

Mohammed's message now spread inexorably. The Jews of Koraidha, rather favoring their own one true God, rejected Islam and were put to the sword without mercy, while hordes of converted idolaters swelled the ranks of the new religion. In 629, 10,000 Muslims occupied Mecca and imposed a compromise peace: It was ordained that Mecca would be the pilgrimage site for Islam, and that Muslims in prayer would bow their heads in her direction. In return, her people were to smash their pagan idols and take up the cause of Allah.

Henceforth, Arabia was the fount of Islam. The word went forth—"There is no God but Allah, and Mohammed is his Messenger"—and the desert peninsula, which had defied conquest through the ages, was now subdued at a blow by the fanatical following of the new prophet. Nor did Mohammed intend to halt at the Arabian frontier. He perceived all too well the fatigue of the two empires to his north. Byzantium (as we shall henceforth refer to the Eastern Roman Empire[87]) and Persia had exhausted one another in their decades-long struggle, and even as Heraclius bore the True Cross back to Jerusalem (628), the envoys of Mohammed delivered ultimatums to the emperor and the Persian great king, notifying them that they must submit to Allah. Heraclius sent the ambassadors back to Arabia laden with gifts, but Chosroes ripped up the written message and threw it in the faces of the envoys. On hearing of this insult, the prophet issued a prophetic rebuke: "It is thus that God will tear the kingdom, and reject the supplications of Chosroes."[88]

By AD 630, Islam was poised to expand in the fashion of a whirlwind. Alas, Mohammed was not fated to witness the triumphant march. He died, aged sixty-two, in AD 632, and was succeeded by his longtime friend, Abu Bekr, who thus became the first "caliph" (i.e., "successor"). Scarcely had Abu Bekr declared a worldwide *jihad*, however, before he also succumbed (634). Thus it was left to the next caliph, Omar I, to carry out the prescribed conquests. In 636, this new leader launched simultaneous offensives against the Byzantines and Persians. The former contest was decided at the Yarmuk River, where the Muslim forces, led by the great general, Khalid, routed a Byzantine army in the midst of a sandstorm.[89] There is confusion in the sources as to whether the Byzantine cavalry—composed partly or wholly of Christian Arabs—defected to Khalid to make the outcome a foregone conclusion,[90] or whether they actually drove the Muslim right from the field. According to the latter version, the Muslim fugitives were berated by their women (who had accompanied the army and were stationed in the rear) until they returned to the battle-line.[91] In the meantime, the remaining Arab defenders had improvised a rampart by grounding their camels.[92] Impeded by this obstacle, the Byzantine assault lost its momentum, whereat the Arabs—presumably buoyed by the return of their fugitives—staged devastating countercharges on both flanks to precipitate a general rout. Fleeing the slaughter, many hapless Byzantines rushed headlong into the Yarmuk, thinking it fordable, only to drown in its depths.[93] Afterwards, a disheartened Heraclius sent the True Cross to Constantinople[94] and abandoned Jerusalem to the advancing Muslims (or "Saracens"—meaning "easterners"—as the Byzantines called them). The Holy City fell after a one-year siege (637). On gaining entry, Caliph Omar demanded to see the site of the destroyed Jewish Temple so that he could erect a Muslim house of worship in its place.[95] Left defenseless by the emperor, Antioch capitulated the following year.

At the same time, another Muslim army struck westward into Egypt, seizing Memphis as a base of operations (638). From there they advanced on Alexandria. Heraclius, now close to death, failed to act, and the city fell after a fourteen-month siege (642). Truth or calumny relates that the city had again acquired a formidable library, and that the Saracen general on the scene inquired of Caliph Omar what ought to be done with its priceless volumes. Omar is said to have replied: "If these writings of the Greeks agree with the book of God, they are useless, and need not be preserved; if they disagree, they are pernicious, and ought to be destroyed."[96] Thus, a third collection of irreplaceable Alexandrian volumes was supposedly lost to posterity—consumed as kindling to warm the baths of the city's conquerors.[97]

Persia, meanwhile, was suffering an even worse fate. In 637, the Persian general, Rustam, engaged an army of Muslims at Kadessia. The battle was in its fourth day when Rustam decided to settle the issue by unloosing his war elephants. Unfortunately, one of the beasts sustained an injury and went berserk. The rest took this as their cue to stampede, and after rushing to-and-fro between the two armies, fate or Allah led them back amongst their own ranks.[98] Rustam sought safety in flight. But the Arabs pursued and decapitated him—bearing his head back to the battlefield on a lance, so that his unseeing eyes might witness the final overthrow of his legions.[99] On hearing the news, the Great King Yezdegerd (a grandson of Chosroes) fled the capital at Ctesiphon and became a fugitive. After an odyssey of fifteen years, he crossed the Oxus and Jaxarta near India, obtained financial backing from the Chinese emperor, and raised an army of Turks with which to cross back into Persia. Sadly, the Turks mutinied and killed him en route (651), and with his death, the Persian Empire expired.[100]

Unlike the hapless Persians, the Byzantines at least managed to survive. Everything from Syria to Tripoli had fallen into Arabian hands, but an internecine battle over the Islamic succession now supervened to save the empire. In 644, Caliph Omar was assassinated. Most of the faithful anticipated the accession of Ali, the son-in-law and trusted disciple of Mohammed. But the caliphate was given over instead to Othman—a member of Mecca's aristocratic Omayyad clan. The luxury-loving Omayyads had resisted the prophet at the time of the *Hegira*, and the devout still held them in contempt for it. Thus, when Othman began doling out government offices to his oligarchic cronies, he precipitated a violent schism, pitting those who believed that Ali was the sole legitimate claimant (i.e., the "Shiites") against those who accepted the status quo (i.e., the "Sunnites"). After prevailing for eleven turbulent years, Othman was assassinated by a mob of religious fanatics, and Ali seized the caliphate (655). The result was civil war. In 656, Othman's former adherents were defeated in the so-called "Battle of the Camel,"[101] but they soon rallied to the standard of a warlord named Moawiyah, and the ferocious conflict resumed. Exasperated by the unending struggle, a party of religious zealots resolved to eliminate both leaders. In 661, an assassin plunged a poisoned dagger into Ali's skull,[102] but Moawiyah escaped death, and reclaimed the caliphate for the Omayyads.

These violent disturbances served to slow, but not to arrest, the march of Islam. It would, therefore, be reasonable to assume that Byzantium's attention was riveted upon its progress. Instead, the new emperor, Constans II, the youthful grandson of Heraclius, involved himself in a renewed dispute between the pope and patriarch as to whether Christ had one nature or two (AD 648). After hearing both sides of this urgent question, he solved the controversy by outlawing all further discussion of the matter. The pope, refusing to shut his mouth, was abducted and sent to the Crimea to die of neglect. The schism, however, had encompassed five years, and by the time Constans bothered to look southwards again, the caliphate had built a navy for itself in the dockyards of Alexandria.

Hitherto, the Taurus Mountain Range had served as a bulwark against the Saracens—never mind the Bosphorus beyond—but now the Saracens possessed the option of an assault by sea. In 654, the new Islamic armada seized Rhodes—the island's long-fallen bronze Colossus being sold to a Jewish trader who employed a herd of camels to haul off the pieces.[103] A year later, Emperor Constans confronted the Saracens at Lycia with the Byzantine fleet. The "Battle of the Masts" ended in a crushing victory for the Muslims, and Constans only managed to save himself by exchanging costumes with one of his retinue—the son of an imperial trumpeter, who was hacked to death while the emperor made good his escape.[104]

The catastrophe left the coast of Asia Minor at the mercy of the Islamic fleet. Ever the pragmatist, Constans rounded up thousands of Slavs and forced them to move to Anatolia—there to impede the progress of the advancing foe. He then abandoned Constantinople and moved his court to Sicily in hopes of directing the war from Syracuse (662). Alas, he was not popularly received in his new refuge: Six years after his arrival, one of the locals knocked him unconscious with a bathing vase and drowned him in his tub (668).[105] Prior to his demise, however, the emperor had instituted a new system of military districts called *themes*, which effectively placed the Balkans and Asia Minor under martial law.[106] To provide the themes with adequate troops, his son and successor, Constantine IV Pogonatus ("the Bearded"), expanded the policy of exchanging land for hereditary military service. (The government found that it could not lose by this policy even in peacetime, since the soldiers increased the state's agricultural output and represented a valuable source of tax revenue when they returned to their plows as free peasants between campaigns.[107])

Unable to defeat the Arabs in a pitched battle, the thematic armies arrayed themselves in unassailable fortresses, and resorted to a scorched-earth attrition war.[108] While the theme system failed to halt the Muslims at the frontier, it provided Byzantium with a disciplined and loyal army. Thus, in 674, when the Arab fleet, under Caliph Moawiyah, besieged Constantinople, it came up against a garrison of steadfast soldiery. The siege dragged on for five summers, during which time internecine squabbling and a first encounter with "Greek Fire" (of which we shall soon hear more) progressively eroded the Muslim resolve. At length, the attack was abandoned with the loss of 30,000 men.

Most scholars hail the victory over Moawiyah as an epoch-making event, without which the subsequent history of Europe would have been indistinguishable from the history of Islam.[109] At the opposite extreme of the empire, however, the story was less inspiring. During the reign of Heraclius, the Spanish coast had fallen to the Goths since there had been no troops available to defend it. Likewise, the Lombards had continued their encroachments in Italy, and the Arabs had pressed ahead in North Africa. In 698, the latter seized Carthage despite the dispatch, from Constantinople, of an imperial relieving army augmented by a throng of Spanish Goths who shared a common interest in arresting the Islamic tide. Within ten years, the Arabs subdued the native Moors and seized the entire North African coastline, from Egypt to the Atlantic.

Meanwhile, Constantine IV had died (685), and the throne had passed to his son, Justinian II. Whether out of piety or to show that he ruled in Jesus' name, the new emperor minted coins with Jesus' image on the obverse and his own image consigned to the reverse.[110] To provide recruits for his army, Justinian advanced into Slavic Thrace and brought back 30,000 unwilling draftees. When he tried to employ them in a new war against the Arabs, however, they defected to the enemy, and his army suffered a crushing defeat (692). At home, he promulgated a new "Farmer's Law" which extended and codified the traditional Heraclian practice of parceling out lands to small farmers in return for military service. But in doing so, he alienated the property-grasping aristocracy just when the tax burden of his wars was provoking the hostility of everyone else.[111] At last, in an atmosphere of mounting discontent, Justinian was cast from his throne and mutilated by the amputation of his nose—hence his appellation, "Rhinotmetus," meaning "the noseless" (695). Such a deformity ought to have made him forever ineligible for the throne, but a decade later, he was reinstated with the assistance of the king of the Bulgars, whom he repaid with the title of "Caesar" and a large amount of cash. Gaining entrance to the capital via an abandoned aqueduct, he hauled the two pretenders who had ruled in his absence into the Hippodrome and watched the chariot races with his feet resting on their necks.[112] They were subsequently executed.

But Justinian was even less popular now than he had been previously, and after instituting a six-year reign of terror that wasted the resources of the empire he was again deposed—the usurpers thinking it prudent this time to amputate his entire head. The revolution likewise claimed Justinian's six-year-old son, Tiberius, who had taken refuge in a church. Although they found him clutching the altar and displaying a piece of the True Cross, his pursuers dragged him forth and murdered him without hesitation, thus extinguishing the Heraclian dynasty which had ruled the empire for 101 years (711).[113]

The Isaurians and the Iconoclast Controversy (717–802)

Philippicus Bardanes, the usurper of Justinian's throne, was himself deposed after a short and unsatisfactory reign. He was succeeded by Anastasius II, who received the diadem in 713 amidst rumors of a Saracen onslaught that would dwarf the efforts of Moawiyah. Bracing himself for the worst, Anastasius repaired the capital's walls, filled her granaries to the brim, and concocted a scheme to burn the timber stores which the Saracens were hoarding along the Syrian coast for the construction of a new fleet.

Brilliantly conceived, Anastasius' plan was found wanting in execution. The raid made it no further than Rhodes before the imperial marines mutinied and murdered their commander, Deacon John. Returning to the capital, they deposed Anastasius and elevated an incapable revenue collector named Theodosius (715).[114] The Syrian timber, meanwhile, was employed for its intended purpose. By 717, a Saracen fleet numbering 1,800 vessels had put to sea, and even Theodosius' most ardent supporters realized that it would take more than a revenue collector to keep them at bay. The puppet emperor was therefore asked to abdicate to make room for a new dynasty—the Isaurian (717–820)—whose first claimant, Leo III, assumed control of the threatened city in March of 717.

Some have speculated that the Saracens were complicit in Leo's elevation, and hoped to make him an agent of their designs.[115] If so, they misjudged their man. Five months after Leo's accession, eighty thousand Saracens commanded by Moslemah, brother of the reigning caliph, were transported across the Hellespont at Abydos to invest Constantinople's great western wall. Presently, they were joined by the Arabian fleet, which gave the appearance of a forest approaching on the water.[116]

On a map, the city of Constantinople resembles the head of a dog with the nose and muzzle facing to the right (i.e., eastwards). The entrance to the Bosphorus—the narrow straits leading to the Black Sea—separates the "nose" from the coastline of Asia Minor further east. Above the "muzzle," to the north, is another narrow waterway—the Golden Horn, which flows out of the Bosphorus to form the city's natural harbor. In the period of which we are speaking, the harbor was protected in time of danger by a chain stretching from the top of the "nose" northwards to the town of Galata on the harbor's opposite coast.

On the southern side of the city, beneath the "muzzle," lies a larger body of water—the Sea of Marmora, which stretches from the Bosphorus westwards to the Hellespont or Dardanelles (the straits leading to the Mediterranean). The western side of the city is the

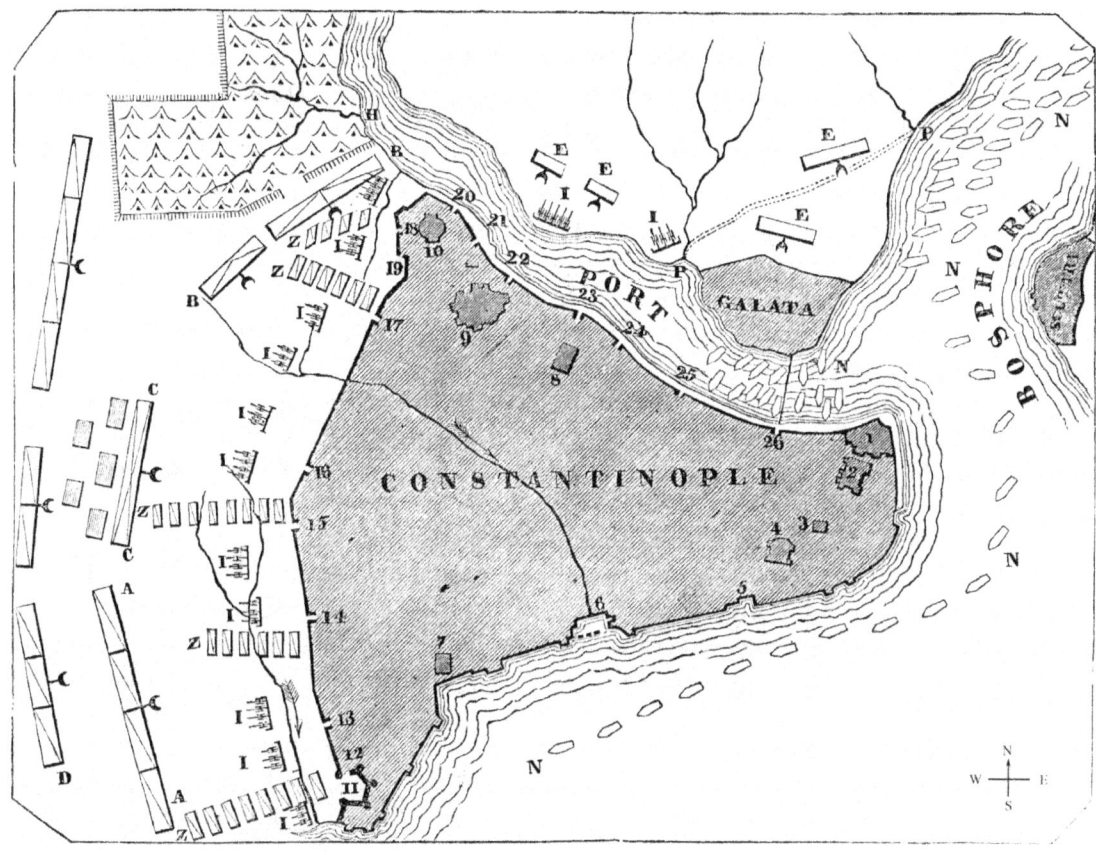

City map of Constantinople. Note the resemblance of the city's outline to the head of a dog (© Depositphotos.com/Antonio Abrignani).

only side not encompassed by water and thus in need of manmade fortifications. To protect this approach, Constantine the Great built a wall stretching from the Golden Horn in the north to the Sea of Marmora in the south. Over the ensuing 100 years the city expanded well beyond this barrier. Consequently, during the reign of Theodosius II in the 5th century, a new and much longer wall had to be constructed further west. The outline of the newer wall stretching once more from the Golden Horn in the north to the Sea of Marmora in the south traces out the dog's ear, the back of its head and the nape its neck. Of this wall the 1911 *Encyclopædia Britannica* says, "here was a barricade 190–207 ft. thick, and 100 ft. high, with its several parts rising tier above tier to permit concerted action, and alive with large bodies of troops ready to pour ... missiles of death ... upon a foe."[117]

Nothing in the Saracen armory could breach such a barrier, so unless another way could be found to enter the city, the matter would have to be settled by siege. While deploying their naval forces, however, the Arabs could not help but notice that the chain guarding the Golden Horn was unattached. Suleiman, the commander of the fleet, must have thought this a great piece of good fortune, for if the harbor could be taken, the city's much less formidable northern wall could be stormed. Hardly had this thought occurred to him, however, before a Byzantine squadron emerged from the harbor and set his fleet ablaze.

It was the work of Byzantium's secret weapon, "Greek Fire"—a mixture containing a volatile gas known as naphtha, which ignited on exposure to the air. According to Gibbon, it produced "a fierce and obstinate flame, which not only rose in perpendicular ascent, but likewise burnt with equal vehemence in descent or lateral progress; instead of being extinguished, it was nourished and quickened by the element of water; and sand, urine, or vinegar, were the only remedies that could damp the fury of this powerful agent."[118] Callinicus, a chemist and engineer who defected to the Byzantine court from Heliopolis in Muslim Syria, is credited with developing the recipe, which is still imperfectly understood today. For four centuries, the composition remained a jealously guarded secret before the Muslims finally generated their own supply, and employed it against the Christian Crusaders.

The flames were delivered in myriad ways. A packet of arrows, rigged to separate in the air, might incinerate several targets at once; the substance could be poured from fortress ramparts onto enemy scaling ladders and siege engines or hurled in breakable containers from one ship to another at sea; or, to lend special horror, it could be jettisoned as a molten liquid from a copper gargoyle's head mounted on a ship's prow.[119]

Their fleet destroyed, the stunned Arabs attempted to besiege the city by land, but a winter of heavy snows reduced them to chilly starvation. In the spring more ships and supplies arrived, but most of the rowers were Christian galley slaves from Egypt[120] who thought it a much better idea to fight alongside their co-religionists than to be burnt by liquid fire. Consequently, they defected to Leo with half the fleet. Meanwhile, Leo's skill at negotiation (or bribery) had purchased the cooperation of the Bulgars, who raided the Saracen camp and massacred 22,000 siege-weary Musulmans. Rumors of further Christian reinforcements prompted Moslemah's decision to withdraw after a 13-month struggle (718).[121]

Once again, Byzantium had served as the shield of Europe against Islamic encroachment. With the threat now allayed, the empire turned its attention to a matter of more lasting import—religious controversy. Whether patriarch or commoner, no one could get as minute in matters of doctrine as the Byzantines. Zealous believers had been at each other's throats since the 4th century when St. Gregory of Nyssa complained, "If you ask change for your money, you get a lecture on the difference between the Father and the Son. If you ask the price of a loaf of bread, the baker will tell you that the Father is more than the Son. If you ask if the bath is ready, the reply is that the Son is born of nothing!"[122] As we have seen, the 5th century bore witness to the great debate over the nature of Christ and the nature of Jesus as he existed on earth. The Monophysites held that these natures were one and the same, while the pope favored two separate natures, with Christ being divine and Jesus human. The question was taken up at the Council of Chalcedon (451), which declared the latter opinion orthodox. All attempts at a compromise formula went for naught: "Monenergism"—the view that Jesus was indeed of two natures but imbued with a single energy—was tried without success; and in its wake, "Monotheletism"—conceding the Savior's dual nature, while attributing to both the same single will—was laughingly anathematized as a most amusing heresy.

Under Leo III and his Isaurian successors, however, a new quarrel erupted: the "*Iconoclast*" or "image-breaking" controversy. Sculptures and paintings on religious themes, along with holy relics, had become widespread throughout the empire. In the West, the papacy pointed to their appeal amongst potential converts, while in the East, they were held in great favor by the monastic orders. But the emperors of the Isaurian Dynasty saw their use

Section I: City of the World's Desire

Page from a 12th century medieval manuscript authored by John Skylitzes, currently housed at the Biblioteca Nacional de España in Madrid. The upper illustration shows Byzantine cavalry at war. The lower shows the use of Greek Fire (Wikimedia Commons).

as a return to idolatry. In their view, the faithful were becoming so devoted to the adoration of icons that they were forgetting that it was Jesus himself—and not his image—that was divine. Icon defenders denied this assertion, arguing that imagery was not idolatry because Christ had revealed Himself to mankind in human form. To depict His image was thus to pay homage to Him. To outlaw His image was to reject His very incarnation.[123]

Leo, however, was not to be dissuaded. In 726, he ordered the destruction of the icon of Jesus that adorned the bronze gate leading to the imperial palace. Aghast, the populace rioted. A mob gathered at the gate, and shook the ladder of the emperor's workmen until the hapless laborers plummeted to the street. News of these goings-on reached the Cyclades fleet, which promptly mutinied and sailed for the capital with the intention of casting Leo out of office. But on attempting to force the harbor, the armada was set ablaze with Greek Fire, and the expedition's leader, an image-defender named Kosmas, was decapitated.[124] Through it all, Leo persisted with his policy of icon destruction (i.e., "iconoclasm"). In 730, he issued an edict calling for the destruction of all icons across the empire. Pope Gregory II cried heresy, and his successor, Gregory III, threatened excommunication against anyone who complied with the decree. In retaliation, Leo wrested Sicily, southern Italy and Greece from the papal sphere and gave their bountiful revenues to the patriarch of Constantinople.

Leo died in 741, but the iconoclast campaign continued under his son and successor, Constantine V "Copronymus" (i.e., "christened in dung"—an appellation supplied by his detractors who secretly mocked him for having defecated at his baptism).[125] Within a year, the new emperor was unseated by a revolt in the *Opsikion* Theme—the same regiment that had overthrown Anastasius II a generation earlier. But a number of other themes rallied to Constantine's cause. He was reinstated in 743 amidst much hacking off of limbs and putting out of eyes—punishments that had been sanctified by law during Leo's reign by the publication of a new legal manual entitled the *Ecloga*.[126] The bloodletting was cut short, however, by an outbreak of bubonic plague that claimed so many victims that the capacity of Constantinople's cemeteries was overwhelmed and the dead had to be dumped into empty cisterns pending the establishment of new burial grounds (747).[127]

By this time, new perils had arisen on the frontier. The Arab front was quiescent. By the mid–740s, the Mohammedans had suffered a series of reverses at the hands of the Byzantines—most notably at Akroinos (739). The setbacks discredited the Arab-dominated Omayyad nobility, and provoked a bloody civil war that ended in their overthrow by the more cosmopolitan Abbasids. Hitherto, the Arab aristocracy had enjoyed exclusive control of all governmental offices, but the Abbasid victory laid these posts open to Muslims of all races and classes.[128] In 750, the last eighty Omayyad nobles submitted to the rule of their black-robed adversaries, who invited them to a banquet in Damascus as a show of reconciliation. When the guests arrived, however, "the laws of hospitality were violated by a promiscuous massacre." Says Gibbon, the hosts fell upon the Omayyads with swords. A carpet or board was placed atop the gasping victims, a meal was laid out, "and the festivity of the (Abbasids) was enlivened by the music of their dying groans."[129]

While the Muslims dined, the Byzantines were at war in the West. In 751, the Lombards seized Ravenna, prompting Pope Stephen II to seek protection from Pippin, King of the Franks, rather than from the hostile, iconoclastic emperor in Constantinople. This momentous decision—which we will discuss in further detail in the next section—effectively terminated Byzantine rule in central Italy, but owing to war in the Balkans, the Byzantines scarcely noticed it. During his reign, Emperor Constantine fought no less than nine campaigns against the vexatious Bulgar king, Teletzes; and though he won the battles, he never quite managed to hurl the enemy back across the Danube. His victory at Anchiolos (763) stunned the Bulgars into ten years of inactivity, but rather than use the respite for peace and recuperation, Constantine embarked upon a new campaign against the icons. Targeted for suppression on this occasion were the image-hoarding monasteries. The buildings were plundered and appropriated for public use, while individual monks were hideously tortured. Eyes are alleged to have been put out, noses cut off, faces set alight with flammable oil, and men hurled alive into the sea after being tied up in sacks weighed down with stones. (If the hostile Theophanes is to be believed, many of these torments were inflicted by Constantine's own hand.)[130] Luckily for those yet to be victimized, the war with the Bulgars resumed in 772, and Constantine died on campaign against them three years later.

Leo IV, Constantine's son and successor, harried the Arabs out of Asia Minor with a scorched earth policy (779),[131] but succumbed shortly afterwards to a chronic illness. As his son, Constantine VI, was not yet of age, his beautiful barbarian widow, Irene, became regent (780).

Although her generals won some notable victories for her in the Balkans, Empress Irene is best known for her decision to support the use of images. It was a bold departure from the policy of her Isaurian predecessors, and though it made her popular with the orthodox, it provoked mutinies in the iconoclast themes. More than this, it diverted her attention from the Arabs, who promptly bowled over a Byzantine army in Asia Minor and pressed on to the Bosphorus (782). Without the means to strike back, Irene was forced to purchase the enemy's withdrawal with a large tribute payment. Although the victorious general, Harun al-Raschid—i.e., "Aaron the Upright," son of the reigning caliph—honored the agreement and withdrew, the Byzantines would soon cross swords with him again, much to their detriment.

For the time being, however, Irene was free from the Arab threat. She decided, therefore, to convene an ecumenical council in hopes of ending the iconoclast schism. The council's deliberations were promptly interrupted by a group of iconoclast soldiers who burst in on the proceedings with swords unsheathed, but after friendly troops were summoned from the countryside, the council reconvened and officially declared an end to iconoclasm (786).

Christ the Saviour (Pantokrator), a 6th-century encaustic icon from Saint Catherine's Monastery, Mount Sinai (Wikimedia Commons).

Unfortunately for Irene, her talentless son, Constantine VI, had now come of age (787), and the elevation of this impressionable mediocrity threatened to undo the empress' program. For three years, she continued her personal rule in violation of the law, but in 790 the army rallied to her son and deposed her. This, however, proved unavailing. Irene had schooled the boy in ineptitude, and once enthroned he was unable to devise his own policy. Regaining his trust with constant protestations of motherly fealty, Irene convinced her son to restore to her much of her former influence (792). She repaid this kindness by setting about his ruination. At her bidding, the boy blinded the general who had deposed her, in consequence of which he lost the support of the soldiery. By encouraging him in an unsanctioned divorce, she put him at odds with the church.[132] Meanwhile, the one policy he devised on his own—the resumption of the iconoclast policy of his forefathers—made him unpopular with the masses.[133] By 797, the empress-dowager felt confident enough to strike. Her co-conspirators seized the emperor and brought him to the same bedchamber where she had borne him.[134] There he was deposed and blinded so that he could never again challenge her authority.

Irene's subsequent effort to reign alone cannot be counted a success. After five turbulent years as sole ruler, she was ousted by her own ministers while contemplating a wedding proposal from Frankland's Charlemagne, whom the pope had just crowned emperor of the West (802). Their nuptials would have reunited the Eastern and Western Empires and legitimized their respective titles and positions. But before she could render a decision, she was overthrown and banished to the isle of Lesbos.[135] She died there within the year, while her son lived on as a blind monk through four more reigns.[136]

Rule of the Usurpers (802–820)

The Isaurian Dynasty was now at an end. The usurper, Nicephorus I (ruled, 802–811), formerly Irene's treasurer, seized the throne. As one of his first acts, the new ruler penned an epistle to Harun al-Raschid, informing the Saracen that he must no longer expect the usual Byzantine tribute payment. Indeed, said the missive, he would have to repay what he had hitherto received. The letter was particularly ill-timed if Nicephorus meant to back it up by force, for Irene had severely compromised the effectiveness of the army by purging it of its iconoclast officers. Likewise, she had bankrupted the treasury in buying off the empire's enemies and in cutting taxes on the oligarchic supporters of her religious policy.[137] A short time after sending his letter, Nicephorus received it back with the following annotation: "In the name of the most merciful God, Harun al Raschid, commander of the faithful, to Nicephorus, the Roman dog. I have read thy letter, O thou son of an unbelieving mother. Thou shalt not hear, thou shalt behold, my reply."[138] The caliph's legions proceeded to decimate the emperor's armies in Asia Minor, and to purchase a respite from these thrashings, Nicephorus had not only to reinstate the tribute, but to pay an additional three gold coins per year as a personal tax to the caliph.[139]

Harun remained the bane of the empire until his death in 809. But afterwards, a succession crisis threw the caliphate into chaos, leaving Nicephorus free to attend to other matters. While he was preoccupied with the Saracens, the Bulgars had renewed their depredations in the Balkans. Nicephorus now repaid them in kind. In 809, he sacked the

Bulgar capital. Two years later, he embarked on a more ambitious (and ruthless) campaign. Ignoring pleas for negotiation, he set the Bulgar king's wooden palace ablaze, while his men callously tossed infant Bulgars into threshing machines.[140] Forced to fight, the Bulgars turned the tables by trapping the imperial army in a ravine. The emperor seems now to have gone mad with despair. He refused to come out of his tent,[141] and moaned to his attendants: "Alas! Alas! Unless we could assume the wings of birds, we cannot hope to escape."[142] Three days later, the Bulgars stole into the Byzantine camp and murdered Nicephorus in his asylum.[143] Panic swept the army. The cavalry fled at a gallop—riding headlong into a nearby river where most of them drowned.[144] The uncouth Bulgars, meanwhile, decapitated Nicephorus' corpse and presented his head to their king, Krum, atop a lance. Krum later had the skull scraped clean and coated with silver, to be used as a beverage goblet on festive occasions. (When ambassadors arrived from Constantinople to discuss peace terms, Krum poured a refreshing libation into it and bade them drink.[145])

Nicephorus' death was not widely lamented. He had alienated the church and aristocracy by revoking the tax breaks they received from Irene.[146] Theophanes, who hated him because he was an iconoclast, thought that he had missed his calling as a herder of pigs; while Gibbon tells us that, "the advantage of his death overbalanced, in the public opinion, the destruction of a Roman army."[147] His son, Staurakios, wounded in the neck, had been borne to safety in a litter by a small party of survivors. Although he had as much right to the throne as any other usurper's son, he was now quadriplegic, and could scarcely live, much less rule. Thus, despite his protests, the regalia of office were snatched from his flaccid grip and given to his brother-in-law, Michael I Rhangabé (811), a puppet of the orthodox clergy.[148]

Michael's first priority was to deal with the Bulgars, who had now captured the imperial port of Mesembria on the Black Sea. His soldiers, however, refused to fight, and when his wife, Empress Procopia (the daughter of Nicephorus), sought to sway them with a motivational speech, the chauvinistic soldiery became openly hostile.[149] At Versinikia, outside Adrianople, the entire right wing of the army abandoned the emperor on the field of battle. The remaining troops were routed, and Michael had to flee back to Constantinople where he immediately abdicated in favor of Leo the Armenian, the mutinous commander of the very troops who had betrayed him (813). There followed an episode of pure theatre. Leo feigned refusal of the throne. Michael the Phrygian, his secret co-conspirator, brandished a sword at him, saying that he must rule or die. The false choice was accepted with false reluctance, and Leo was crowned to the naïve acclamations of the capital populace.

Within days of Leo's accession, Krum advanced to the gates of Constantinople (813). A peace parley ensued in which Leo attempted to ambush the Bulgar, but Krum escaped and plundered the countryside. A few months later, Leo gained a face-saving victory near Mesembria with a nocturnal surprise attack. The Bulgarian dead were interred at a site called the "Mountain of Leo," which the Bulgarians superstitiously avoided ever after.[150] Even still, the merits of Leo's triumph might have been doubtful had Krum not died of a cerebral hemorrhage before he could renew the contest.

In religious matters, Leo earned the nickname "Chameleon" owing to a deft attempt to solve the iconoclast dilemma by allowing images to remain in the churches while decreeing that they must be hung high enough on the wall so that the faithful could not touch them as objects of reverence.¹⁵¹ Ultimately, however, the competing parties forced his hand, and at a general council, he came down on the side of the iconoclasts (815). In the aftermath, a few recalcitrant clergymen were banished (among them the historian Theophanes, who died soon after).¹⁵²

While Leo restored discipline to the army and reformed the courts and tax code, his former accomplice, Michael the Phrygian, grumbled that he had not received adequate recompense for his part in elevating the emperor to his throne. He voiced his dissatisfaction to all who would listen, and when he was censured for it, he conspired to employ in earnest the sword he had used as a stage-prop at Leo's accession. Alert to the plot, Leo had him arrested and laid plans to incinerate him in the imperial bathhouse furnace. But from death row, Michael hatched a new conspiracy. On Christmas Day, his henchmen drew their swords on Leo in the middle of a church service. Mistaking their man, they hacked the hapless priest to bits. Seizing the only weapon at hand—a large metal cross—Leo put up a formidable defense until the assailants severed his arm and felled him with repeated blows. He died next to the communion table.¹⁵³

The Phrygian Dynasty & the End of Iconoclasm (820–867)

The latest in a succession of usurpers, Michael the Phrygian—known also as "the Stammerer" (although his actual speech impediment seems to have been a lisp)¹⁵⁴—ascended the throne while still in leg irons, because no blacksmith could be found to remove them prior to his sudden enthronement on Christmas morning. Despite this inauspicious start, the new ruler was destined to found a dynasty. His reign opened with a serious challenge from a former comrade-in-arms named Thomas "the Slav" (or "the Cappadocian") who raised the banner of rebellion in 822. Supported by a throng of outcasts—some of them disaffected Slavs who had been forced to relocate to Asia Minor¹⁵⁵—he ravaged the Anatolian themes and marched on Constantinople in an attempt to usurp the throne.

Until he reached the walls of the capital, Thomas carried everything before him. But thereafter, the fates would not cooperate. During the reign of Nicephorus I, it had been foretold that of Leo, Michael and Thomas—all of whom were then army officers—two would one day seize the throne while the third would die in the attempt. The fulfillment of this prophecy could no longer be deferred. Twice Thomas' ill-disciplined army endeavored to storm the capital and twice they were thrown back. The imperial fleet then destroyed Thomas' naval transports in the straits, cutting off the rebel's communications with Asia Minor, while a marauding Bulgar army invaded Thrace, to threaten the lands Thomas' army required for forage. An attempt to drive off the marauders ended in a defeat in the open field, which was closely followed by a second defeat at the hands of the emperor. Put to flight, Thomas was captured at Arcadiopolis and dragged back to the capital, where he was paraded through the streets draped over a donkey with his hands and feet severed until he bled to death (824).¹⁵⁶

The damage caused by his rebellion, however, had been extensive. Many small farmers in Asia Minor were ruined through pillaging, and the patrician class began buying up their lands with impunity—a trend that threatened the military foundation and the tax-base of the empire.[157] The Arabs took advantage of the enfeebled monarchy to seize Crete (826), Sicily (827), and much of what remained of Byzantine Italy, leaving only Venice in imperial hands.[158] The rest of the Italian peninsula was now either Saracen, Frankish or Lombard. Thus, as Michael's reign drew to a close (829), the conquests of Justinian the Great were all but undone.

To prop up the legitimacy of his dynasty, Michael recalled the daughter of Constantine VI from a nunnery, and took her as his bride. Moreover, he had long-since crowned Theophilus, his eldest son from a previous marriage, as co-emperor. Hence, at his death, the succession went smoothly, and for the first time since the death of Constantine V (775), the throne passed peaceably from father to son.

A stickler for jurisprudence, Theophilus I (ruled, 829–842) executed the assassins of Leo V (though that assassination had placed his father on the throne), tore down his brother-in-law Petronas' house because it was in violation of the building codes and fairly reimbursed a man whose stolen horse had been presented to the emperor as a gift.[159] On the other hand, he decreed that all his male subjects must wear their hair cut short (since he himself was balding), conducted religious matters in the manner of an iconoclastic bigot,[160] and unjustly ordered the decapitation of his friend and brother-in-law, Theophobus, owing to a febrile deathbed suspicion that the latter might usurp the throne from his son and heir.

No stranger to the battlefield, the new emperor campaigned vigorously against the Arabs. But when he burnt the town of Zapetra, the familial home of the caliph, the latter responded in kind. An army of 130,000 Saracens bearing the inscription "Amorion" on their shields marched to the town of Amorion (the home of Theophilus' forefathers in Phrygia) and burnt it just as surely[161]—a fiasco that earned the emperor his cognomen, "the Unfortunate."

Under Theophilus, iconoclasm had its last great renaissance, but at his death his wife, Theodora, finally put the controversy to permanent rest. While she served as regent for their son, Michael, she convened the Ecumenical Council of 842, which restored the use of images once and for all. At the same time, however, the council confirmed the emperor's supremacy over the patriarchate. Many historians believe that this was no coincidence— arguing that since the inception of the controversy the iconoclasts had been intent on smashing not the images but the power of the patriarchs.[162] Stated in another way, the patriarchs and the orthodox religious party had won the battle for the icons but had lost a war in which they scarcely knew they were engaged.

Still, the end of Iconoclasm was not without spiritual dividends. According to Ostrogorsky, the orthodox victory released the Byzantine Church from its image-decrying oriental bondage, and set it up as a westernized "Greek" alternative to the "Roman" Church in the ongoing contest to convert the Slavs.[163] Indeed, the Slavs of the Peloponnesus were converted to the Byzantine creed while Theodora still reigned, and the Moravians and Bulgars followed suit during the reign of her son.[164]

On attaining the age of sixteen (856), Michael III, "the Drunkard,"[165] ordered the execution of his mother's chief minister and forced the empress to end her regency. He subsequently spent most of his reign cheering on the blue faction at the Hippodrome. On one occasion, he even refused to receive news of a barbarian invasion because its timing conflicted with the chariot races.[166] Yet some incursions could not be ignored—the arrival of a plundering Russian fleet in the Sea of Marmora (860) being a striking example. Consequently, Michael entrusted the maintenance of the imperial frontiers to his gifted uncle, Bardas, whom he elevated to the office of Caesar, and who won for him several stunning victories.

Although the emperor accompanied Bardas on many of his campaigns, he fancied himself a comedian and much preferred reveling with his court buffoons—the favorite activity of whom was to roam the streets of the capital in the garb of the patriarch and his retinue chanting clownish songs to the melodies of the psalms.[167] Among this merry entourage was a Thracian horse-tamer named Basil, who was known as "the Macedonian."[168] Basil so ingratiated himself with Michael that the emperor conspired with him in the assassination of Uncle Bardas, whom Basil dispatched with a most unsporting sword-thrust to the back.[169]

By 866, Basil had risen to the lofty rank of co-emperor—an office he discharged so proficiently that Michael's suspicions were aroused. Fearing an inevitable fall from favor, Basil burst into the royal chambers with a cadre of fellow conspirators after a dinner party. A first sabre stroke severed the hands of the bleary-eyed emperor, who cried out so loudly that the flustered assassins thought the guards would be alerted. But the latter interpreted the noise as mere drunken revelry and did not come.[170] Satisfied that they were safe, the murderers plunged a sword into the emperor's heart, thereby ending the dynasty of the Phrygians and inaugurating that of the Macedonians at a blow (867).

The Macedonian Dynasty (867–1057): The Empire Reaches its Zenith

Although Basil had been without scruple in seeking power, Gibbon tells us that once on the throne "he ruled with the wisdom and tenderness of a parent."[171] The first Macedonian's achievements were manifold. In foreign affairs, his generals won such signal victories against the Saracens that Byzantine arms appeared again on the distant Euphrates. His armies also reoccupied the southern Italian port of Bari (876), whence they were able to recapture control of Calabria (i.e., the Italian heel), which Basil renamed "Longobardia." At home, the buildings and churches of Constantinople were refurbished, while the exchequer was put back on stable footing by improved tax collection and by restraints placed on the greedy landlords of Asia Minor. The Latin legal code compiled three and a half centuries earlier by Justinian was revised and translated into Greek. (A further revision, entitled *Basilica*, was published in sixty volumes during the reign of his son.) The rebellious and iconoclastic "Paulician" heresy (whose adherents, professing to be the orthodox followers of Saint Paul, had established an independent mini-state at Tephrike on the Saracen frontier) was utterly eradicated (878); and Basil celebrated its extinction by firing three arrows into the severed head of its leader, Chrysocheir. But in 879, Basil's much-loved eldest son, Constantine, died unexpectedly, and afterwards, the emperor seems to have ruled as a reclusive madman until, in the nineteenth year of his reign, his belt was ensnared by the antler of a berserk stag during the hunt. Before his retainers could disentangle him, he had received mortal wounds (886).

Basil's reign laid the foundation for Byzantium's greatest dynasty. His son and successor, Leo VI "the Philosopher" (ruled, 886–911), not only published the *Basilica*, but also a new military manual, the *Tactica*, which served as the basic textbook of Byzantine warfare for centuries to come. Under Leo's system, cavalry led the attack, followed by sixteen ranks of infantry. The first rank of foot soldiers faced their shields to the front to form a forward wall, while those behind clasped theirs overhead to protect against enemy missile fire. Last came the bowmen, firing over the heads of their advancing comrades until the rival armies closed.[172] Marching into the fray alongside the men were the army chaplains, who sustained the courage of all with reminders of God and the Cross.[173] In their train came an ambulance corps, which received a gold coin for each successful rescue of a wounded soldier.[174]

Failing to produce an heir with a succession of three wives, Leo married a concubine who bore him a son though it was against his own conjugal laws to do so. As the patriarch would recognize neither the marriage nor the heir, Leo was placed in the odd position of appealing to the pope to have his son legitimized. While he was thus occupied, the affairs of state were delegated to his corrupt chief minister, Stylian Zautses, whose chief accomplishment was to precipitate an unnecessary war with the recently Christianized Bulgars. Traditionally, the Bulgars had shipped their commercial wares directly to Constantinople via the Black Sea, or had sent them by a short land route through the main Bulgar market towns. Zautses turned the entire enterprise over to his own cronies, who raised the tariffs on Bulgarian goods, and forced Bulgarian traders to stop at the imperial tax offices in Thessalonica—a remote, hazardous and (for the Bulgars) profitless detour. Their pleas for redress being ignored, the irate Bulgars took up arms, defeated a Byzantine army and cut off the noses of the survivors.[175] In a decidedly Byzantine riposte, Leo bribed the distant Magyar tribe to attack the Bulgars from the rear, thereby inducing their retreat. But two can play at that game: Symeon, the Bulgar king, bribed the terrible Pechenegs of the Russian steppe to attack the Magyars. The latter fled headlong into the Pannonian plain where they founded Hungary, while the Bulgars renewed their assault on the empire. Only when the Byzantines revoked the tariff and agreed to pay a large annual tribute was peace finally secured (896).

Military adversity stalked the author of the *Tactica* for the remainder of the reign. In 904, a Saracen fleet sacked Thessalonica in reprisal for imperial encroachments in Armenia. In retaliation, Leo dispatched a fleet to retake Crete (911). But after a failed siege of the island, the fleet was ambushed and destroyed by the Saracen navy. The emperor died shortly thereafter, leaving the throne to his son Constantine VII Porphyrogenitus.

The appellation "Porphyrogenitus" means "born in the purple," and if we accept literally the idea that Constantine was an emperor from birth, he reigned for fifty-four years without ruling during any of them (905–959). Until he was six, his father held the imperium. In his seventh year it passed to his uncle, the profligate Alexander, who planned to castrate the youth, but died before he could do so.[176] Then came a regency headed by Nicholas, the patriarch of Constantinople. But Nicholas was deposed after attempting to betroth the emperor to a daughter of the Bulgar king, Symeon—a union that would have secured the peace, but at the cost of rendering Symeon undesirably influential at the Byzantine court. Nicholas was replaced by Constantine's mother, Empress Zoë Carbonopsina, who at least seemed to have had the boy's best interests at heart. She and her eunuchs held sway for five years. But in 917, the Pechenegs reneged on a newly signed alliance, leaving the imperial army to be routed by the Bulgars at Anchiolos near the Black Sea. According to one chronicler, the dead were so numerous that their bones were still piled up on the field a century later.[177] Utterly discredited, Zoë was ousted by her naval commander, Romanus Lecapenus.

Romanus betrothed his daughter, Helena, to the emperor, and was for a time content with the title "Father of the Basileus." But the rank ultimately proved insufficient to his ambition. Consequently, he elevated himself, as Romanus I, to the position of co-emperor. Three of his sons were similarly honored so that, between them, they might optimally assist Constantine with the affairs of state. Thanks to the helpful Lecapenus clan, the legitimate emperor was relieved of the burden of government for no less than two and a half decades (919–944), during which time he composed a number of literary treatises, including the definitive study of Byzantine court protocol.

There were numerous attempts to unseat Romanus during this period, including one by an imposter masquerading as a member of the powerful Ducas clan. Defeated and punished by the amputation of his hand, the false "Constantine Ducas" assumed a new appendage made of brass, attached a sword to it and tried again. This time Romanus captured him and burned him alive.[178] Meanwhile, King Symeon had again placed the capital under siege (924). In a private interview, Romanus addressed the crisis by shaming the barbarian for spilling the blood of his fellow Christians and then bribed him to withdraw. Since the walls of Constantinople were impregnable anyway, Symeon was easily swayed. He withdrew his forces from Thrace, and redeemed his Christian reputation by returning to his own dominions where a large annual tribute now awaited him.

Freedom from the Bulgarian threat allowed for a successful concentration of forces against the Saracens on the eastern frontier, where the Byzantine general, John Kurkuas, won such signal victories as to be hailed as a new Trajan or Belisarius.[179] Unfortunately, the entire army and navy were still occupied in that theatre when, in 941, the Russians decided to make their second descent on the capital. En route, they raided the Byzantine coast, burning or crucifying the Christian inhabitants and hammering nails into the skulls of captured monks.[180] When the Russians appeared off the coast of the capital, fifteen obsolete galleys were the only ships that the Byzantines had at hand. Summoned out of retirement, the ships were refitted to expel "Greek Fire" in every direction. (Previously only the prow had been so equipped.)[181] Thus renovated, the galleys sailed into the midst of the hostile fleet and let loose their conflagration. Scores of Russians dove overboard to escape the flames, only to be carried into the deep by the weight of their armor. Some burnt like torches even as they drowned owing to the inextinguishable naphtha.[182] The roasting of their lead ships (and sailors) convinced the horrified Russians to retreat. They reached Bythinia, which they pillaged, but when they withdrew, they sailed straight into the main Byzantine fleet (which had now returned from the East) and were piteously destroyed.

Co-Emperor Romanus had now reigned for twenty-two successful years. After three more, however, he was toppled and dispatched to an island monastery by his treacherous sons who desired power for themselves. The usurpers quickly found that their conspiracy had neither the support of the people nor of their own sister, Helena, the loyal wife of Constantine, the true emperor. Apprehended while dining, they were delivered to the very same monastery to which they had sent their father. Romanus welcomed them with a hearty display of pretended joy, saying how wonderful it was that they would think to visit him in his retirement.[183]

Constantine might now have ruled by his own hand, but the gentle monarch deferred instead to the authority of his wife.[184] While she steered the course of government, the emperor dedicated himself to the authorship of a handbook for his son on how to rule. It stands as a remarkably instructive work for an author with no practical experience in such matters. But the son in question, Romanus II (reigned, 959–963), seems not to have benefited from his father's counsel. Gibbon notes of this young successor that "the hours which (he) owed to his people were consumed in strenuous idleness. In the morning he visited the circus; at noon he feasted the senators; the greater part of the afternoon he spent in the sphaeristerium, or tennis-court, the only theatre of his victories; from thence (after hunting wild boar) he ... returned to the palace, proudly content with the labors of the day."[185] After four years of this exertion, he died—perhaps poisoned by his ambitious wife, Theophano, a barkeep's daughter whom he had insisted on marrying. He left two sons as heirs, Basil II (976–1025) and Constantine VIII. The former would boast the greatest reign in the history of the empire, but at his father's death he was just five years old, and it was not yet his time to rule.

Toward the end of Constantine VII's reign, the Muslim caliphate fractured in pieces amidst internecine warfare,[186] while the Byzantine army rebounded under the leadership of two capable generals: Nicephorus Phocas, who gained a stunning victory in Asia Minor in 958, and his nephew, John Tzimisces, who recaptured the stronghold of Samosata on the Euphrates a year later. Under Romanus II, the former captain embarked on the reconquest of Crete. In Saracen hands since 826, the island was the scourge of Byzantine shipping. Twice in the previous half century, the emperors of the Macedonian Dynasty had attempted to dislodge the piratical Muslims, but both efforts had ended in catastrophe. Happily, Nicephorus was more enterprising than his forebears. After landing, he moved his army overland to besiege the capital of the island at Candia (960). The siege progressed slowly, and the Byzantines had to endure the harsh winter of 961 with supplies that scarcely eclipsed those available to the defenders. But the arrival of fresh provisions in the spring reanimated their resolve. A Muslim relieving army was defeated in the field and the heads of the slain were displayed on spears before the walls of Candia.[187] Then, in March, Nicephorus presided over the successful storming of the city. The victory was attended by a cruel bloodletting. The Muslim garrison was massacred, the women raped and the children transfixed and held aloft on lances.[188]

Nicephorus, the "White Death of the Saracens,"[189] was now the toast of the army—though not of Romanus II and Theophano who regarded his popularity as a threat. Without the courtesy of granting him a "triumph," they harried him from the capital to command the armies of the eastern theatre. But with the death (or murder) of Romanus II in 963, Empress Theophano needed a guardian for her two underage sons, and Nicephorus was recalled to Constantinople.

The laurels withheld from the conquering hero while Romanus II lived were now repaid with interest. Nicephorus gained a diadem—reigning as co-emperor with the two boys entrusted to his care (963). He also gained the hand of Theophano. But his six years on the throne witnessed a steady decline in his popularity. True, he was a loyal guardian to his stepsons. Indeed, he has been described as "one of the most virtuous men and conscientious sovereigns that ever occupied the throne of Constantinople."[190] True, too, he waged successful campaigns against the Saracens—capturing Tarsus, their stronghold in Asia

Minor, and Cyprus, just off the coast. In Gibbon's view, the "skill and perseverance" displayed by the Byzantine soldiery in these campaigns, made them worthy of the name "Romans."[191] But the taxes the emperor collected in support of his victories were burdensome. To make amends, Nicephorus allowed the aristocracy a free hand in buying up the property of small farmers in distress—a concession that fanned a long-smoldering social problem into flame by swelling the ranks of the dispossessed, and imbuing them with a hatred both of the "Powerful" (as the exploitive aristocracy was popularly known) and of the emperor who catered to their interests.[192]

A rugged soldier, Nicephorus slept on the floor of the palace even when he was emperor[193]—a shining example of military etiquette that kept him popular with his army if not with his bride. In 968, he laid preparations for the liberation of Antioch, which had been in Muslim hands since AD 640. A lieutenant named Burtzes was placed in command with instructions to await the emperor's arrival before storming the city. Acting on intelligence provided by his spies, however, Burtzes captured a strategic tower along the city wall by escalade, and after a delay of three days, a reluctant fellow officer named Peter came to his assistance to complete the taking of the city. Nicephorus dismissed both officers for insubordination thus accruing a great deal of umbrage. To protect himself from the mounting unrest, he converted the imperial palace into a fortress. But one rival was too well connected to be kept at bay. His nephew, John Tzimisces was a talented general who believed he should be named heir to the throne (something that Nicephorus would not consider out of loyalty to the sons of Romanus II).[194] He was, in addition, Theophano's secret lover. Attended by a dozen henchmen—among them the vengeful Burtzes—Tzimisces was raised in a basket to a palace window by Theophano's ladies-in-waiting on December 10, 969. Proceeding to the emperor's quarters, the assassins roused Nicephorus from his sleep and cruelly beat him to death while he piteously cried, "Oh God! Grant me thy mercy!"[195] Theophano wantonly exhibited the victim's severed head at the palace window.[196]

A successful soldier in addition to being a regicide, Tzimisces was the obvious successor, but Polyeuctus, the patriarch of Constantinople, refused to crown him unless he offered up his co-conspirators as scapegoats for Nicephorus' murder and did away with the scheming Theophano. Condemned to a remote nunnery established in the reign of Nicephorus, the irate empress rained blows upon the head of the court chamberlain, Basil Lecapenus—a eunuch and bastard son of Romanus I, who had dreamed up the sentence as an especial insult—decrying him (correctly) as the illegitimate offspring of a Scythian mother.[197] Tzimisces' coronation followed directly.

The new emperor faced an immediate military crisis. The frugal Nicephorus had terminated the tribute owed by treaty to the Bulgars. Then, to keep the latter occupied, he had bribed the Russians to make a diversionary assault on their rear (965). The diversion was more successful than anticipated. By the time Tzimisces gained power, the Russians had overrun Bulgaria, and were advancing into Thrace to threaten Adrianople (969). Unwilling to leave the capital with his throne insecure, Tzimisces deputed command to a trusted officer, Bardas Sclerus. Upon encountering the Russians, Sclerus feigned retreat to lure their vanguard into ambuscade. As soon as this was accomplished, he wheeled to confront the main Russian army near Arcadiopolis.[198] The result was a rout. The Russians fled back to Preslav (the occupied Bulgarian capital), where they were defeated again—this time by Tzimisces, who now felt secure enough to venture out in person.

Surrounded and starving on the banks of the Danube, the Russian Prince, Svyatoslav was surprised to receive lenient terms, including safe passage and a supply of corn for his famished army. But his withdrawal was well worth the purchase price, for it left the greater prize of an undefended Bulgaria in Byzantine hands. Symeon's once-proud kingdom was now an imperial province. (The unlucky Svyatoslav never made it home. The Pechenegs ambushed and killed him en route.[199])

With his northern flank secure, Tzimisces turned against the Saracens. In his first campaign, he drove deep into Mesopotamia. A second outing, in 975, netted him Damascus and Beirut. These were astounding gains, but Tzimisces did not live to enjoy them. On his way home, he rode through a vast stretch of Byzantine territory being used only for grazing. Inquiring of his retinue why such large tracts were not being put to better use, he was told that the lands were the private holdings of the court chamberlain, Basil Lecapenus, who had greatly enriched himself while the emperor was away on campaign. In astonishment, Tzimisces declared that he was not so much emperor as a eunuch's mercenary. He would have done better to conceal his resentment, for the court chamberlain had spies everywhere. Before Tzimisces could reach the capital, he had been served a cup of poison by one of the chamberlain's agents. He entered Constantinople in extremis and died soon afterwards at the age of fifty-one.[200]

With Tzimisces' death, Basil Lecapenus was the most powerful official in the state. Ineligible for the throne owing to his incapacity for procreation, he was nonetheless in a position to act as regent for Basil and Constantine, the young sons of Romanus II. He was not, however, the sole candidate for the job. Bardas Sclerus, the victor of Arcadiopolis, commanded the loyalty of the heavy infantry. Lecapenus removed him from command and made him governor of distant Mesopotamia. Far from preempting a rebellion, the act provoked one. Seizing eastern Anatolia, Sclerus laid plans to march on the capital. To combat the menace, the court chamberlain commissioned an army under Bardas Phocas, the nephew of Nicephorus II. Sclerus defeated Phocas twice—at Amorium and Basilica Therma—and was in the midst of defeating him for a third time at Pancalia on March 24, 979, when Phocas, in despair, rode within shouting distance and challenged the rebel to single combat. Keen to witness this spectacle, the rival armies ceased their exertions. It was generally held of Phocas that he could kill a man with a single blow.[201] Rather than give him the chance to prove it, Sclerus spurred his horse at close range and struck his rival in the head before he was ready. This seemingly sound strategy failed in its intended effect, however, for it did not take into account the lesser-known fact about Phocas—namely, that he could take as well as he could give. With the vibrations of his helmet still ringing in his ears, Phocas delivered a swift and terrible riposte. Sclerus, most authorities agree, was unconscious before he hit the ground. His soldiers gathered him up, still woozy, and took to their heels.

From 979 until 986, Basil Lecapenus ruled the empire as regent for the rightful heir, Basil II. In the latter year, however, his eager young ward attained his majority and packed the eunuch off to a monastery (the now traditional destination for a retired member of the Lecapenus clan). The youthful emperor faced an immediate crisis to the north where the resurgent Bulgars had reclaimed their independence under an upstart prince named Samuel. Basil's initial attempt to subdue them ended in disaster. His army was ambushed in the Bulgarian mountains at a site known as Trajan's Gate (986). Limping back to the capital in defeat, Basil learned that Bardas Phocas had staged a rebellion with the backing of the officer corps and the great magnates of Asia Minor.²⁰² To retain his throne, the emperor had to seek an outside alliance, which he obtained by betrothing his sister, Anna, to the pagan Prince Vladamir of Russia. The pact was sealed with the barbarian's conversion to Orthodox Christianity—a decided step up from his former faith, which entailed ritual human sacrifice.²⁰³

With the help of his hardy Russians, Basil defeated Phocas at Chrysopolis, and pursued him to Abydos on the Hellespont (989). With no way out, Phocas attempted a personal charge against the emperor. En route, however, he changed course, ascended a hillock, climbed off his horse and lay down beside it.²⁰⁴ It was the universal opinion of all spectators that this was a very peculiar thing. Phocas himself was never able to render an explanation since by the time anyone reached him he was stone dead—of what exactly, no one can say with certitude. Just prior to the charge his cupbearer gave him a libation, and the possibility of poison has been raised,²⁰⁵ although modern historians scouring the primary sources have concluded variously that it was a seizure, stroke or heart attack.²⁰⁶ In any event, the fallen pretender's corpse was hewn into bits, and the head was presented to Basil.²⁰⁷ (The example set thereby was not lost on that other renegade, Bardas Sclerus, who agreed to terms later in the year.)

The defeated aristocracy was now made to pay for its disloyalty. The scandalous agrarian policy of Nicephorus II was reversed, and the "Powerful" were ordered to return all estates expropriated from the peasantry since 944—the year in which Romanus Lecapenus, a staunch protector of the peasants, had been overthrown. No recompense was allowed either for the properties or for upgrades made on them in the intervening years. Additionally, the aristocrats were made to assume the tax bills of peasants who could not meet their obligations.²⁰⁸

Firmly seated in power, Basil set out to avenge the embarrassment of Trajan's Gate. The renewed contest with the Bulgar king, Samuel, absorbed the better part of twenty years before a decisive encounter was finally fought at Cimbalongus (the "Long Plain")²⁰⁹ in the valley of the Strymon (1014). There, the Bulgar army was annihilated, and 14,000 prisoners fell into the hands of Basil, who administered a gruesome punishment. The captives were divided into groups of one hundred. Of these, ninety-nine were deprived of their sight, while the hundredth retained one eye so that he could guide the others home. Samuel is said to have died of despair on beholding their wretched fate. His nation once more became a Byzantine province, while Basil, now known as "Bulgaroktonos"—the "Bulgar Slayer"—spent his last ten years enacting surprisingly humane policies to assimilate its population.

The Decline of the Monarchy and the Time of Troubles (1025–1081)

By the time of Basil's death in 1025, another victory—at Cannae (1018)—had restored imperial authority even in southern Italy. Byzantium now possessed territory and prestige she had scarcely known since the reign of Justinian the Great. What she lacked was a worthy claimant to the throne. Basil had neither married nor produced an heir. He was succeeded, therefore, by his brother, Constantine VIII, a profligate and paranoid sixty-four year-old who (in theory) had been co-emperor for the entire reign, and who now spent his leisure poking out the eyes of suspected political enemies with hot iron rods.[210]

In order to ensure the succession, Constantine invited a patrician named Romanus Argyrus to marry his daughter Zoë. Romanus politely refused on the grounds that he was already married. But on being "informed that blindness or death was the second alternative,"[211] he bemoaned his fate to his wife who shaved off her hair and entered a nunnery without another word. Two days later, Constantine died and Romanus embarked on a highly unprofitable reign. After a brief foray onto the battlefield led to a disastrous ambush in Syria, Romanus squandered the imperial revenues on the last thing Constantinople needed: another church. State obligations required that he produce an heir. But Zoë was forty-eight at the time of their nuptials, and, fatiguing of a hopeless labor, Romanus diverted his attentions to a younger mistress. The empress responded by taking a paramour of her own—and by arranging the murder of her worthless husband, whose near-lifeless body was discovered in the imperial bath. Removed to a nearby couch, Romanus expired within minutes.[212]

Zoë wed her youthful lover the very next day, and elevated him to the throne as Michael IV. Celebrated as the handsomest man in Constantinople, the new emperor suffered from epileptic seizures—the sight of which was so distressing that a curtain had to be placed around the throne on public occasions to be drawn at the first hint of an episode.[213] Although Michael refused to be dominated by the empress, he does appear to have been a willing tool of his brother and chief minister, John the "Orphanotrophos" (i.e., "Minister of Charities"). The empire was now under siege from a variety of quarters, but John, who was utterly corrupt, had the keen ability to ignore all that while focusing his attentions solely on increasing the state revenue from which he was enriching himself.

Sicily's Muslim raiders were at this time the bane of Byzantine commerce, having seized the baton once held by the pirates of Crete. Accordingly, an army was commissioned to recapture the Sicilian island, which had been in Saracen hands for more than two centuries. Commanded by George Maniakes, the governor of Byzantine Italy, and composed of rude Norse mercenaries,[214] the army stormed Messina (1038), and then advanced on Syracuse, which fell in 1040.

But John the Orphanotrophos viewed Maniakes' victories with a jaundiced eye. The general was a scion of the agrarian "Powerful," whose political clout had rebounded since the death of Basil II. With the army's support, the Powerful had reanimated their policy of land usurpation, converting droves of Anatolia's free peasants into feudal serfs.[215] Between their military victories and their growing estates, it seemed only a matter of time before the Powerful would vie for leadership of the state. Hence, when Maniakes quarreled with the emperor's brother-in-law, Stephen, who possessed the rank but not the attributes of an admiral, finally striking the latter a blow for his incompetence, the Orphanotrophos recalled the general to Constantinople and charged him with treason.[216] The selfish decision spelt disaster for the empire. Left in the lurch, Maniakes' Normans returned to Italy and extracted, by murder and rapine, what they felt was due them for their toils in Sicily.[217] The war effort in Sicily collapsed, and all of southern Italy fell prey to rebellion—Byzantine rule in the peninsula being confined to a few coastal strongholds, most notably, the port of Bari (1040–1043).

At almost the same moment, the Orphanotrophos provoked a rebellion among the Bulgars by forcing them to pay taxes in cash rather than in agricultural produce (as was their custom).²¹⁸ As cash was a rare commodity among the Bulgars, they rallied to the standard of Peter Delyan, an illegitimate relative of the great Bulgar king, Samuel (1040). Owing to the arrest of Maniakes, Michael IV could not trust his aristocratic officers to quell the revolt. Consequently, the emperor took personal command of the army, despite the fact that he was terminally ill with dropsy. Before battle could be joined, however, a rival Bulgar pretender named Alousianus took up a kitchen knife and divested Delyan of his eyes and nose.²¹⁹ The new pretender initially sought to continue the war. But when his first attack on the Byzantine camp was repulsed, he had second thoughts, and negotiated a secret agreement with the emperor. At the next encounter, he rode to the safety of the Byzantine lines, leaving his befuddled army to be crushed. Michael returned to the capital in triumph but was so swollen from disease, that his plight could no longer be kept secret. Convincing the Empress Zoë to adopt his no-account nephew (also named Michael) as his successor, the emperor retired to a monastery where he dropped dead after half a day (1041). He had reigned just seven years and was not yet thirty.

Michael V Calaphates was unable to sustain his uncle's dynasty. A half-year into his reign, he attempted to exile his adoptive mother, Empress Zoë. The result was a wave of deadly riots. Michael Psellus, the chief chronicler of the period, was on the porch of the imperial palace when the uprising began, and was alarmed to hear what sounded like the hoof beats of stampeding horses. It was, instead, the footfalls of the mob.²²⁰ The rioters ran amok for two days, demolishing property and taking thousands of lives. The emperor, who had sought refuge in the Studite Monastery, was dragged out and delivered to a deputation of the imperial guards. To the cheers of the rioters, the guardsmen held him down and gouged out his eyes with a hot iron poker—his entreaties for mercy and his efforts to wriggle free proving fruitless. Such was the penalty for an upstart son of a ship-caulker ("caulker" being the origin of his nickname "Calaphates") who dared to unseat the lawful empress.

Zoë was reinstated and reigned briefly in conjunction with her sister, Theodora. But growing jealous of her sister's abilities and popularity (both of which eclipsed her own), the empress overturned this arrangement in favor of a third marriage. Her choice fell upon the exiled aristocrat, Constantine IX Monomachus. On the upside of the balance sheet, Constantine would preside over the reopening of the University of Constantinople and its famous law school (1045). Likewise, he repulsed a Russian sea raid against the capital—assisted, to be sure, by a fortuitous storm that smashed the enemy ships against the rocky coast. (In the ensuing days, fifteen thousand Russian corpses would drift ashore.)²²¹ A number of prisoners were also taken, whose right hands were amputated and displayed as trophies on the capital ramparts.²²²

But on the whole, the ledger on Constantine tilts decidedly toward the negative. The new ruler cavorted openly with the granddaughter of Bardas Sclerus—appearing in public with the accommodating Zoë on one arm, and "the Sclerena," as she was known, on the other. Additionally, he so indulged his allies in the commercial party (the leading faction at court) that he provoked two separate military revolts in a period of four years. The first was that of George Maniakes who had been restored to his command in Italy. While Maniakes was away on campaign, the emperor turned a blind eye to the antics of Romanus Sclerus—the brother of the Sclerena—who proceeded to elope with Maniakes' wife and property in Anatolia.²²³ Unable to obtain satisfaction, the irate general raised the banner

Constantine IX (left) and Empress Zoe (right) seated alongside Jesus in a mosaic of Hagia Sophia, Istanbul (© Depositphotos.com/Pavle Marjanovic).

of rebellion and engaged the emperor's forces at Ostrovo (1043). The imperial army was utterly routed. But with the battle won, Maniakes foolishly exposed himself in the front ranks and was thrust through with a lance. His severed head was borne back to the capital and displayed on a pole atop the Great Theatre.[224]

The court clique next went after Leo Tornikius, a patrician and provincial governor with connections to the emperor's estranged sister, Euprepia. Without justification Tornikius was made to relinquish his properties and assume a monk's habit. The persecution drove him to rebel, and his revolt reached the very walls of the capital (1047). To raise an army, the unprepared emperor emptied his dungeons and enlisted the city's rabble-rousers. Tornikius' veterans massacred these ragamuffins outside the city walls. But Tornikius missed his opportunity to occupy the city, and later, when he dodged a catapulted stone in a particularly cowardly way, his army lost faith in him. Abandoned to his fate, he was captured and blinded.[225]

Another plot to unseat the emperor arose within his own retinue. The court jester, Boïlas, was a man of ability who, when not eliciting the laughter of the emperor, managed certain imperial affairs. His facility at these tasks convinced him of his own merit and he was soon discovered in a plot to usurp the throne. Constantine seems to have thought it another joke, for he retained the man as his jester.[226]

Thus, in haphazard fashion, Constantine managed to cling to power. Far from strengthening the nation, however, his triumph enfeebled it. There was no effort now to reestablish a healthy free-peasantry as Basil II had attempted to do. Rather the battle had degenerated into a contest between the monarchy's commercial/civil party and the Powerful's military/feudal party for control of the state.[227] Having won, Constantine lavished gifts on his favorites in the civilian party until the treasury was all but depleted. To make good the loss, the emperor debased the currency, deprived the military of funding and allowed the soldiery of the frontier themes of Asia Minor to abandon their military duties in return for an annual cash payment to the treasury.[228]

Towards the end of Constantine's reign, the patriarch of Constantinople, Michael Ceroularius, provoked a schism with the papacy. The Schism of 1054 supposedly arose owing to minute theological differences, but the real issue was a turf war in southern Italy, where the adventurous Normans had usurped the revenue-rich properties of the Byzantine church, and placed them under papal jurisdiction.[229] Ceroularius not only demanded their return, but cast insults at the pope. A cardinal was dispatched from Rome to negotiate, but the talks deteriorated, and Ceroularius was declared excommunicate.

Emperor Constantine descended into his grave soon thereafter, and since Zoë (d. 1050) was already dead, the civil party frantically turned to the empress' retired sister, Theodora, in an effort to maintain its hold on the government (1055). The last of the Macedonian line, she reigned but two years before her death brought the battle between the civil party and the Powerful to the fore again. The commercialists, with Theodora's deathbed blessing, managed to place one last pawn on the throne in the person of Michael VI Stratioticus. But Stratioticus provoked an armed rebellion by browbeating the realm's leading military officers at an Easter ceremony, and after a bloody battle at Nicaea in which the rebels were victorious, the Powerful enthroned their own candidate: the able general, Isaac I Comnenus (1057).[230]

All would have been well had the Powerful been happy with their own choice. But Isaac was more soldier than aristocrat, and his effort to raise enough capital to restore the strength of the army was universally resented.[231] Despite an important victory over the marauding Pechenegs who broke across the Danubian frontier, the new emperor lost the support of the aristocracy. Simultaneously, he incurred the wrath of the indolent courtier class by revoking the stipends they had enjoyed under previous emperors,[232] and lost the backing of the church and the populace by quarreling with the patriarch, Ceroularius (who had helped him to power).

Amidst the discontent, Isaac contracted a chronic illness that sapped his strength. He abdicated in 1059, and died as a monk at the Studion Monastery in 1061. His successor was Constantine X Ducas—an ineffectual aristocrat who skimped on the army in order to finance the effete amusements of the civil party. By the end of his reign (1067), the military was in an advanced state of decay, and the empire was under threat east and west. The Normans, who had never forgiven the empire for abandoning them in Sicily, continued to encroach on Byzantium's last remaining strongholds in Italy, seizing Otranto in 1068. Likewise, there were stirrings within Islam. The Abbasid Caliphate, which had been in decline for a century, was locked in a duel with the rival Fatimids of Egypt who had overrun much of Syria. Seeking a protector, the reeling Abbasids turned to a neighboring Turkish tribe known as the Seljuks.

At this hour, the Byzantines might well rue their decision to disband the armies of the Asian frontier to finance the capital's profligate spending.[233] But they had also done something very much worse. A treaty dating to the reign of Basil II had ended the independence of the venerable state of Armenia at the eastern extremity of Asia Minor. The agreement, however, was not immediately acted upon, and the hardy Armenians remained the motivated clients of the empire in guarding the eastern frontier. The accession of Constantine IX Monomachus ruined this beneficial arrangement, for that emperor forced the Armenians to submit to the terms of the treaty (1045). Armenia's defense was now in the hands of the emperor and the latter proved a very negligent steward. In 1048, the Seljuk chieftain, Ibrahim Inal, crossed the Armenian border and burnt the rich city of Arzen.[234]

During the reign of Constantine X Ducas the calamities multiplied. In 1064, Ani, the Armenian capital, fell to the Seljuk sultan, Alp Arslan, the "valiant lion," who subsequently carried his depredations into the themes of Asia Minor until he was called away to deal with the troublesome Fatimids. In his absence, his emirs spread slaughter through Cappadocia and Phrygia, depopulating entire districts.[235]

Constantine X Ducas died in 1067, and in this crisis, his widow, Eudocia, chose an able general, Romanus IV Diogenes, to serve as emperor and consort (1068). Romanus worked tirelessly to restore army morale, and then set out to the eastern frontier to reverse the Seljuk tide. In the course of three campaigns, his motley collection of mercenaries reclaimed all but Armenia, forcing Alp Arslan's incompetent emirs to retire across the Euphrates.[236] In 1071, Romanus breached the Armenian frontier, and captured the fortress of Manzikert. A few miles beyond, however, lay the entire Seljuk army, commanded by Alp Arslan himself, who had now returned to the Byzantine theatre with 40,000 mounted archers.[237]

Romanus was caught in a compromising position. Nearly half his force was stationed twenty miles distant and played no role in the key battle. Even worse, some of the Turkic recruits under his direct command defected to the enemy. Nevertheless, he refused to parley, and attacked with his forces arrayed in a large phalanx. The Turkish cavalry retreated. The phalanx could not keep pace with them, and after a chase lasting several hours, Romanus had no choice but to retire to his camp. As his army executed its U-turn, however, it was thrown into a panic by a sudden charge of the enemy horse. Quick action by the imperial reserve might have forestalled disaster, but Romanus had entrusted these troops to the untrustworthy Andronicus Ducas, a nephew of the deceased Constantine X Ducas and a bitter political rival. Andronicus pronounced the battle lost. His troops cried out to Romanus' men to run for their lives and then left them to their fate.[238]

There ensued a general massacre in which brave Romanus was wounded and captured. Alp Arslan graciously released him on the promise of a large ransom and annual tribute, but en route to Constantinople, the beleaguered emperor learned that the Ducas clan had dethroned him, and that his agreement with the sultan would not be honored. An attempt to reclaim the imperium by force yielded a pitiful result. Twice defeated by the usurpers of his throne, Romanus surrendered on a promise of safety only to be maliciously blinded and left to die of his wounds.[239] He had already sent his personal assets to the sultan with the message, "As emperor I promised you a ransom of a million and a half. Dethroned, and about to become dependent on others, I send you all I possess as a proof of my gratitude."[240]

The Comnenian Dynasty: Resurgence and Collapse (1081–1185)

Manzikert was a catastrophe. In its aftermath, the Byzantines were able to protect neither Asia Minor—heretofore the chief source of their revenue and soldiery—nor their holdings in southern Italy. Bari fell to the Normans before the year was out, thus ending Byzantium's Italian tenure, and the ensuing decade witnessed a general collapse closer to home. Fuming over the unpaid tribute promised by Romanus, Alp Arslan pressed into Asia Minor. At Berzem, a prisoner caught him with his guard down and murdered him (1072), but under his son, Malek Shah, the Seljuks advanced all the way to Chrysopolis on the Bosphorus (1079).[241] By this time, the veteran soldier, Nicephorus Botaneiates (ruled, 1078–81), had seized the throne from the incompetent Michael VII Ducas (ruled 1071–78).[242] But Botaneiates' three-year reign did nothing to halt the march toward disintegration. Consequently, in 1081, Alexius I Comnenus—an estate-holder, one of the Powerful, and a participant in Botaneiates' coup—decided to make his own bid for the throne. A protégé of the powerful Ducas family to whom he was tied both by marriage and adoption, he was already a popular general at twenty-four. Thus, when his rebel army broke into the capital and ran amok, the demoralized Botaneiates agreed to abdicate.

The state of the empire was gloomy in the extreme. There was no front that was not under siege, but the most pressing trouble spot was the Adriatic. Having expelled the Byzantines from southern Italy with his victory at Bari a decade earlier, Robert Guiscard, the Norman Duke of "Apulia" (formerly Byzantine "Longobardia"), decided in the year of Alexius' accession that it would be a simple matter to seize the entire Byzantine Empire. Accordingly, he set sail for the strategic Balkan port of Durazzo, which then commanded the road between Epirus and Constantinople. Alexius bribed the Venetians to intercept him, but while these talented sailors hindered his crossing, they could not prevent it. Frantic, Alexius made peace with the Turks, emptied the garrisons of Asia Minor, and rode at the head of a makeshift army to relieve his threatened Adriatic port. Durazzo held out until he arrived owing to the valor of the local commander, George Palaeologus, who continued to direct affairs even after being shot in the head by an arrow. (As the most learned available wound specialist could not dislodge the missile, he left it embedded in Palaeologus' skull, merely breaking off the shaft.[243]) Guiscard brought up a huge siege tower filled with five hundred knights, but from the ramparts Palaeologus rammed a strong beam against the tower's drawbridge before it could be lowered so that the invaders were unable to cross over to the walls. Greek Fire then incinerated the tower—the luckiest of Guiscard's men fleeing out the bottom, while most jumped to their deaths or perished in the flames.

It was at this juncture that Alexius arrived with a polyglot army of 70,000 men, many of whom—dispossessed Italians and Anglo-Saxon refugees from the battle of Hastings (AD 1066, see Section II)—had an axe to grind with the Normans.[244] Their reckless charge nearly put the Norman right wing to rout. But the tables were turned by Guiscard's wife Gaita—a truly frightening woman whose awful war cries served to rally her husband's wavering men.[245] Alexius' vanguard was cut to pieces—the escapees seeking sanctuary in a nearby church, which the Normans promptly set aflame. Alexius himself fought bravely, lopping off the arm of one attacker, and narrowly evading the spear-thrust of another by reclining backwards on his horse. (The spear grazed his forehead and tore off his helmet.[246]) Abandoned by his Dalmatian and Turkish mercenaries, Alexius withdrew from the field, and retreated to Thessalonica with the Norman horde hot on his heels.

No longer able to oppose the Normans directly, Alexius resorted to bribery to get others to do so. His largesse kindled uprisings against Guiscard's rule across southern Italy and induced Henry IV of Germany to besiege Rome. The policy forced Guiscard's hand.

Returning to Italy, he quashed the revolts in the south and marched to the assistance of the pro–Norman pope, Gregory VII, in Rome. Henry IV fled at his approach, but hardly was Pope Gregory reinstated at the Lateran before Guiscard's ill-mannered troops provoked the local citizenry to riot. By the time calm was restored, the Normans had torched a quarter of the city (1084).

Guiscard now recrossed the Adriatic (eluding the Venetians a second time), and would have renewed the war had he not succumbed to typhoid during the epidemic of 1085. His death, however, brought no respite to Alexius, who had other enemies with whom to contend. In the Balkans, the Pechenegs defeated the emperor twice (1086 and 1088) before an overwhelming Byzantine victory at Libernion Hill put an end to their incursions (1091).[247] At the opposite end of the empire, the death of the great sultan, Malek Shah (1092), prompted an imperial bid to recover Asia Minor, which the Turks had indecorously renamed the "Sultanate of Roum" (i.e., "of Rome"). To canvass Western support for his intended campaign, Alexius sent delegates to the Catholic Church Council at Piacenza (1095). Instructed to offer an end to the Schism of 1054 as a quid pro quo for western aid, the delegates sought to embellish their case by reminding the assembled prelates of sporadic atrocities committed against Christian pilgrims in Seljuk-controlled Jerusalem. Horrified by the gruesome details, Pope Urban II convened an emergency council at Clermont, and declared a Crusade to hurl the Muslims out of the Holy Land. What followed belongs to the story of Medieval Europe. Suffice to say that the fighting men of the West answered the pope's entreaty by the horde. Byzantium found herself inundated with overzealous crusaders, and far from battling the Turks, the Byzantine army had all it could do to keep their guests from plundering Constantinople.

At length, the apprehensive Byzantines shuttled the pope's legions across the Bosphorus to the Asiatic shore—politely reminding them not to kill or rape anyone until they encountered the Turks. It was half hoped that the crusaders would be annihilated. Instead, they marched from victory to victory. At Nicaea—capital of the Sultanate of Roum—the Turkish defenders lost hope when a column of Franks appeared brandishing the heads of the city's anxiously expected reinforcements atop their spears (1097). Rather than wait for the crusaders to storm the fortifications, the Nicaeans surrendered to the emperor, allowing entry to a detachment of Byzantines who had approached on boats from the side of the city abutting Lake Ascania. Grumbling at this *fait accompli*, the crusaders moved on, defeating a Turkish army at Dorylaeum (1097), before capturing Antioch (1098) and sacking Jerusalem (1099). Their commanders had sworn an oath not to usurp territories claimed by the Byzantines, but to the emperor's chagrin once victory was won, the holy warriors did as they pleased.

Despite such friction, Alexius recovered a good portion of Asia Minor as a result of this First Crusade. His conquests were capped by a victory over the Turks at Philomelion (1116), which gave him uncontested control of all provinces northwest of that site. In all, the first of the Comneni reigned for thirty-seven years, bringing much-needed stability to an empire that had seen more than a dozen rulers in the preceding half-century.[248] But the effort to restore even a modicum of discipline and military strength to the wavering state had necessitated doubtful expedients. Taxation was sharply increased and the currency was debased—so much so that the new coins were not trusted in Europe and much Mediterranean trade was lost to the rising maritime states of Italy.[249] Moreover, due to a lack of volunteers, the emperor had had to fill out his legions by impressment,[250] and his habit of attaining short-term advantages through dissimulation—an art he had reduced to a science[251]—won him many enemies. Thus, when he died in 1118, Alexius was astoundingly unpopular for a man of such accomplishment.

Alexius' wife, Irene, contrived to place the husband of their eldest child, Anna Comnena, on the throne, but at the emperor's insistence, the succession passed to Anna's younger brother, John II Comnenus. Unhappy with this verdict, Anna intrigued to reverse it, but her treason was unmasked, and she was compelled to retire to a convent where she composed the famous *Alexiad*, a history of her father's reign. John, meanwhile, distinguished himself by enacting benevolent reforms. He abolished the death penalty, and by his clemency won the nickname "John the Good." On the imperial frontiers, he expelled the Turks from the coastline of Asia Minor, and very nearly recovered Antioch from the grasping hands of the crusaders. He might have done still more, but on a hunting expedition he clumsily sliced his own hand with a poison-tipped arrow while being charged by a wild boar.[252] He died soon after, having reigned for twenty-five years (1143).

Manuel I Comnenus, John's son and successor, was an enthusiastic militarist who possessed very little aptitude for anything else. An unnecessary war with Roger, the ruler of Norman Sicily, resulted in the sacking of Thebes, whose silk workers were carried off by the victorious Normans. When Manuel subsequently defeated Roger by capturing his base of operations on Corfu, he neglected to demand the return of these artisans. Roger promptly put their talents to work in Sicily on more generous terms than they had enjoyed in Thebes, thus usurping the lucrative silk trade.[253]

In his next conflict, Manuel defeated the Serbians single-handedly on the banks of the River Drin by charging their general and (after exchanging blows) grasping the latter's sword arm until he could be taken prisoner. There followed a war with Hungary in which Manuel captured Sirmium and Dalmatia—gains that were confirmed when Andronicus Kontostephanos, the emperor's most trusted officer, obtained a decisive victory over the Hungarians at Zeugmin. (Although the lances employed by the Byzantines in this last victory were ineffective against the heavy armor of the Hungarians, the lancers found their secondary weapon, the mace-at-arms, to be very suitable for smashing Hungarian helmets.[254]) A naval war with Venice also ended in triumph, but owing to other crises, Manuel failed to revoke the odious commercial privileges that had allowed the Venetians to undersell Byzantine merchants (to the latter's ruin) since the reign of Alexius I.

Neither these victories, nor another at Antioch against the unruly crusader states, procured any lasting advantage for the empire, and in the meantime, Manuel neglected the one theatre where he might have achieved something of lasting value. At the outset of his reign, the Seljuk-controlled portions of Asia Minor were in a state of chaos owing to rivalry among the Turkish emirs. Prompt action might have regained the entire province for the empire, but absorbed in his other wars, Manuel failed to exploit this opportunity. Not until 1176—after the sultanate had revived itself under the capable leadership of Kilij Arslan II (1156–92)—did Manuel perceive his oversight and initiate a campaign in this theatre. Almost immediately, he sustained a decisive defeat near Myriocephalus, where his army was caught in ambuscade.[255]

Manuel died in 1180, after a reign of thirty-seven years. His victories had raised Byzantine prestige considerably, but had exhausted the treasury.[256] Moreover, he had let slip Byzantium's last best hope of reclaiming the fountainhead of her strength (i.e., Asia Minor), and he had left the succession in chaos. For an extended period, an incestuous affair with his niece, Theodora, caused him to forget his obligation to produce an heir. Late in life, he wed Princess Maria of Antioch, the daughter of a crusader, who bore him a son—Alexius II. But as Alexius was only eleven years old when he mounted the throne, his mother, Princess Maria, found herself serving as regent in a foreign land. Besides being hated for her "Latin" (i.e., Western European) origins—which associated her in the popular mind with the equally hated Italian merchants and mercenaries who daily enriched themselves in the capital—she was woefully unsuited to the demands of ruling an empire (or even of choosing a minister capable of doing so in her name).[257] In short order, popular discontent erupted into mob violence. Residing in the capital at this time was a large population of Venetians who were still enjoying the commercial privileges granted to them a century earlier by Alexius I Comnenus for the support they had rendered to him in his war against Robert Guiscard. As noted, Manuel I had neglected to revoke, or at least amend, these privileges—so ruinous to Byzantium's own commerce—when he defeated the Venetian fleet.

Widely regarded as alien profiteers, the Venetians became a ready target for the rioters. They were attacked indiscriminately, and either murdered or shackled and sold as slaves to the Turks.[258] With the regency powerless to uphold the law amidst this chaos, an anti–Western member of the Comnenus clan—the boy-emperor's uncle, Andronicus Comnenus—was called to the capital by popular acclaim. Part opportunist, part adventurer, Andronicus had been imprisoned twice for plotting against the throne when Manuel was emperor. In both instances, he pulled off escapes worthy of Monte Cristo. In between, he served successively under Kievan princes, Latin kinglets, and Turkish emirs, seducing princesses all along the way. Finally, after providing the most convincing assurances that he was a reformed man, he was repatriated and appointed governor of Pontus in Asia Minor. He was still there when the people of Constantinople summoned him to supplant the hated regency of Alexius' mother.[259]

Although the intention was to make him regent in Maria's place, Andronicus usurped the throne. Maria was falsely charged with treason and strangled—a procedure that was soon afterwards successfully repeated upon her son (1183). In celebration of these achievements, Andronicus is said to have kicked the youth's lifeless corpse, shouting: "Thy father was a *knave*, thy mother a *whore*, and thyself a *fool!*"[260]

Despite his cruelty, the new emperor was at first popular. He took stern measures against corruption, mandating that his minions must behave or die.[261] He rid the realm of the hated tax-farmers who had gorged themselves at the public trough, and subdued the Powerful in a reign of terror.[262] But even as he tightened his hold on the capital, the frontiers began to slip away. With the Venetian navy no longer barring the route, the Normans resumed their quest to capture Constantinople. Led by the king of Sicily, William the Good, they sacked Thessalonica (1185), and advanced toward the capital where Andronicus was still persecuting his political rivals.

It was at about this juncture that the citizenry ceased celebrating their ruler's knack for brutality and chose to rally to one of his intended victims. Isaac Angelus, who years earlier had deposited Andronicus at Manuel's feet after one of his arrests,[263] was now targeted for death. Instead, he slew the executioner sent against him, thereby sparking a mass uprising against Andronicus' rule. The emperor attempted flight, but was apprehended aboard the imperial galley, and dragged back to the capital. There, says Gibbon, Isaac Angelis "abandoned the criminal to the numerous sufferers, whom he had deprived of a father, a husband or a friend. His teeth and hair, an eye and a hand, were torn from him, as a poor compensation for their loss; and a short respite was allowed, that he might feel the bitterness of death."[264] Before he expired, his head was doused with boiling water, and he was hung upside down for another round of torment,[265] prompting him to cry, "Lord have mercy upon me!" and "Why will you bruise a broken reed?"[266]

The Angeloi Dynasty and the First Sack of Constantinople (1185–1204)

Unfortunately, even the most bloodthirsty of the Comnenians, was better suited to rule than the new usurper. According to Gibbon, "Isaac slept on the throne, and was awakened only by the sound of pleasure."[267] His civil administration was corrupt to the core. Offices were sold to the highest bidder. Taxes fell heaviest on the provincials, but rather than repair the roads or take provision for the defense of the frontier, Isaac frittered away the revenues at court.[268] At the outset of his reign, an able Byzantine commander named Alexis Branas defeated the Normans at Mosynopolis (1186). But Isaac feared Branas as a potential rival and replaced him with two incapable generals, one of whom was blind. These incompetents promptly lost the island of Cyprus, and the appointment of another blind general, this time to the Balkan command, led to defeat in that theatre where Bulgaria, Wallachia and Serbia sought simultaneously to throw off the Byzantine yoke. Two attempts to redeem the latter situation—at Berrhoa (1190) and Arcadiopolis (1194)—were repulsed with great violence, and in the meantime, Alexis Branas raised the banner of rebellion and marched on the capital. With the loss of his throne seemingly imminent, Isaac took solace in public prayer, but his brother-in-law, the crusader, Conrad of Montferrat, roused him from this inertia by declaring that, "swords and lances were the means Heaven would use if Isaac's crown was to be saved, not priests and processions."[269] Conrad attacked Branas at the gates of the capital, defeated him and delivered his head to the emperor.

In 1189, Germany's Holy Roman Emperor, Frederick Barbarossa, desirous of participating in the Third Crusade, contracted with Isaac to march through Byzantine territory, with the understanding that supplies would be made available to his army at reasonable rates. On arriving, however, he found that Isaac had reneged on the bargain without cause. Encountering a succession of obstacles to his army's progress, Frederick unloosed his men on the local populace whose safety was only restored when Isaac agreed to honor his initial accord.

After ten years of inept rule, Isaac was finally deposed and blinded by his own brother, Alexius III (1195). Alexius, however, was cut from even weaker cloth. At his coronation, his horse took an immediate dislike to him and would not let him mount. When, with great difficulty, the emperor climbed into the saddle anyway, the horse bucked with such violence that the emperor's crown and then the emperor himself toppled to the ground.[270]

The boasts of Alexius' eight-year reign were that he bribed the menacing Holy Roman Emperor, Henry VI, not to attack him (1196), that he meted out new trade concessions to the Venetians (1198), and that he presided over the loss of Bulgaria (1201).[271] His downfall was sealed by the escape of his nephew, Alexius, son of the deposed Isaac Angelus. Alexius fled to the West, where he learned that a Fourth Crusade, being fitted out in Venice, was badly strapped for cash (1203). It did not take much to convince the crusaders to alter their itinerary and set course for the Byzantine capital. In return for their help in retrieving his father's throne, Alexius promised to end the Schism of 1054, and to alleviate their monetary woes with a large subsidy.

Thus, the Fourth Crusade set off, not for the Holy Land, but for Constantinople. The Byzantine navy had been neglected to the point of rot,[272] and nothing stood in the way of the crusader-laden armada as it sailed through the Bosphorus into the Golden Horn. First ashore was the blind octogenarian, Henry Dandolo, Doge of Venice and unofficial leader of the expedition. The unready capital was taken by storm—the ramparts being breached by scaling ladders and by drawbridges lowered onto the tops of the walls from the masts of the larger ships.[273] Alexius the usurper fled with the public funds, and was succeeded by his predecessor—the blind, suffering Isaac Angelus who was liberated from his jail cell to reassume the imperial regalia. His son was elevated to rule by his side as Alexius IV (July 1203).

Unfortunately, it soon became apparent that the young Alexius had promised the crusaders rather more than he could deliver. Nor was the populace keen to help him fulfill his obligations—particularly after the crusaders torched a large swath of the city in a botched attempt to set fire to a local mosque. In disgust, the citizenry rallied to a new usurper—Alexius V Ducas, surnamed "Murzuphlus" owing to his imposing eyebrows. The hapless Isaac Angelus was hurled back into his dungeon to die, his son was strangled, and the new emperor revoked the promises they had made to the invaders.

To this point, the crusader army had been waiting impatiently outside the city. When they learned of the coup, they stormed the walls only to be turned back by the able preparations of Alexius V. Sadly, a second and more determined assault proved successful, and once over the ramparts, the crusaders ransacked everything in sight. Two new fires reduced vast tracts of the city to ash.[274] Valuables were everywhere plundered or destroyed. Irreplaceable library materials were burnt, bronze statues dating to the era before Jesus were melted down to mint coins,[275] and the Venetians made off with the gilded horses of the Hippodrome—sending them back to Venice to adorn the Cathedral of St. Mark's, where they remain to this day.[276] Alexius V fled, but was later captured and made to climb the one hundred-and-fifty-foot Pillar of Theodosius from which he was hurled to the street.[277] To cap off the festivities, the crusaders elevated their own candidate, Baldwin of Flanders, as the first Latin emperor of Byzantium. The populace was stunned. In Byzantine eyes, the New Rome had finally gone the way of the old—brought low by the barbarians of the West.

The Latin Empire and the Byzantine Successor States (1204–1261)

Greece, Thessaly and Constantinople were now in Latin hands, but the remaining provinces, east and west, were divided into three Byzantine successor states: The Empire of Nicaea in Western Asia Minor (ruled by an Angeloi pretender), the Despotate of Epirus (ruled by a descendant of the Comneni and Ducas) and the Empire of Trebizond, on the southern shore of the Black Sea (ruled by the grandsons of Andronicus Comnenus).

The conquerors of Constantinople promptly won the universal hatred of their new subjects by attempting to force Roman Catholicism upon them. Yet the first blow to their hegemony came from without. Tsar Kaloyan of the Bulgars (the self-anointed "Roman-Slayer"[278]), whose envoys had been treated contemptuously by the new regime, surveyed the general mayhem within the once great empire, and deemed the moment opportune for an invasion of Thrace. Baldwin advanced to Adrianople to oppose him, but was lured into an ambuscade and taken prisoner (1205). He died soon afterwards in a Bulgar dungeon. The next emperor, Henry of Flanders (1205–1216), managed to hold things together for a decade or so, even making some modest inroads into Asia Minor, but after his death it became a foot race between Nicaea and Epirus to see who could regain Constantinople for the Greeks. Theodore Ducas Angelus got the Epirots off to an early lead in this contest by seizing Thessalonica, and defeating a Latin Army at nearby Serres (1224). But his impressive progress came to a grinding halt at Klokotnika, where he was defeated and captured by the Bulgars (1230).[279] Afterwards, the Empire of Nicaea stole ahead of everybody, thanks, on the one hand, to the capable leadership of John III Vatatzes (ruled, 1222–1254), and, on the other, to the timely arrival of a new barbarian horde.

It so happened that the Mongols of Asia were just now making their presence felt in the Balkans and in Asia Minor (1241). As luck would have it their encroachments wrought havoc with the Bulgars and Turks without causing the Greeks the slightest inconvenience. As a result, Vatatzes was able to concentrate all of his military resources against the sundry rivals competing for the Byzantine inheritance. In the early 1240s, he expelled the Latins from their foothold in Asia Minor, and then advanced into Europe, where, in wars with the Latins and Epirots, he occupied Thessalonica and a large fragment of Macedonia (1246).

Vatatzes was as just and prudent a ruler as had been seen in two centuries. To supply his armies, he taxed the idle luxuries of the aristocracy rather than impose new levies on the working poor. He disdained frivolity, limiting his court expenditures to the profits of his private estate, which he turned into the very model of what might be achieved in agriculture. He reanimated the tried-and-true, if long-defunct, practice of parceling out farmland in return for hereditary military service, and he received into his realm as grateful subjects many Greeks in flight from the enforced Catholicism of the Latin Empire.[280]

At his death (1254), he left an able, but epileptic, heir, Theodore II, who died of his disease after a reign of just four years (1258). The throne thus fell to Theodore's eight-year-old son, John IV, prompting a scramble for the position of regent. Emerging victorious from this contest was an able army officer named Michael Palaeologus.

During the reign of John Vatatzes, Palaeologus had been charged with treason, and as no verdict could be reached in court, it was decreed that the matter would be settled by ordeal. Palaeologus was instructed to prove his innocence by grasping a hot iron globe. He protested that though innocent of the charge he was nonetheless a sinner whose hand would certainly be burned. A bishop in attendance corrected him, saying that faith and a clear conscience would protect him from injury, whereat Palaeologus, with feigned piety, bade the priest take the globe with his own hand, from which he would faithfully receive it. After due reflection on this answer, the charge was dropped and Palaeologus was reinstated in the army where he served with distinction.[281] His service as regent would require a different adjective. Within a year of his appointment, he had arranged his own coronation as co-emperor while his tender ward was sequestered away and neglected. (The usurpation was confirmed on Christmas Day, 1261, when the boy was cast into a dungeon with his eyes put out.)[282]

In the meantime, Michael II of Epirus, attempted to halt the advance of the Nicaean Empire by forming a coalition with Manfred of Sicily and William of Villehardouin, the prince of Achaia. Their little coalition marched eastward toward Thessalonica, but the respective leaders did not trust one another, and after a series of desertions, their army was utterly defeated at Pelagonia by John Palaeologus, the brother of the usurper (1259). Fleeing the field in haste, William of Villehardouin donned a disguise and attempted, without success, to conceal himself in a haystack, where he was found and betrayed by his teeth (the ugliness of which was a fundamental element of his fame).[283]

Michael VIII Palaeologus was now positioned to bid for the final prize: the recapture of Constantinople, which under Latin rule had been reduced to a penniless ghetto wherein the reigning monarch, Baldwin II, was constrained to sell the lead from the roof of his palace to finance his household.[284] In July 1261, Michael VIII's vanguard reached the gates of the capital under the command of Alexius Strategopoulos whom the emperor had appointed caesar. But as this force was small and without siege engines, it was despised by the Latins, who attempted a counterblow by embarking on the galleys of their Venetian allies to capture the Black Sea island of Daphnusia. Strategopoulos immediately recognized the folly of this decision and dispatched a chosen party of soldiers to make their way into the undefended city under cover of darkness. Directed to the bricked-over golden gate by a loyal Greek of the capital, the commandos worked through the night. By dawn, a breach had been made, and Strategopoulos' entire force had squeezed into the city. The Greek populace supported them to a man, and within hours Constantinople was in Byzantine hands.

Summoned emergently from Daphnusia, the Latin armada arrived to find itself dispossessed. After embarking the city's Latin and Venetian refugees, it set sail for the West.[285]

The Palaeologi and the Final Fall (1261–1453)

Michael VIII Palaeologus had by no means won back, in 1261, the empire that had been lost in 1204. Much of the capital still lay in ruins dating to the initial Latin assault. The Empire of Trebizond on the Black Sea coast remained independent, and large portions of Epirus, Thessaly and Greece were in the hands of hostile princelings.[286] As the restored empire had no navy to speak of, the Aegean was controlled by the Venetians and Genoese who thus dominated the capital's commerce. Nor did this commerce retain its former preeminence. Prior to the crusades, all Mediterranean trade had flowed through Constantinople, but since the establishment of the crusader kingdoms, Italian ships had begun to bypass the Byzantine capital in order to trade directly with the ports of the Levant from Syria to Egypt. The Italian maritime states thus supplanted Byzantium as the font of Mediterranean commerce.[287]

In sum, the empire was a shadow of its former self—and new storm clouds were gathering on the horizon. Scarcely had the Latin Empire fallen before the Sicilian king, Manfred of Hohenstaufen, conceived his own plan to conquer Byzantium. Before he could act, however, Manfred was unseated by Charles of Anjou, the brother of the king of France (1266). This was no advantage to the Byzantines, however, for Charles likewise had set his sights on Constantinople, and unlike Manfred, he had the blessing of Pope Clement IV. Michael VIII responded by approaching Pope Clement with yet another of Byzantium's offers to mend the Schism of 1054 between the Greek and Roman Churches. This seemed, on the face of it, a very good way of depriving Charles of papal support. But Clement had never accepted the overthrow of the Latin Empire,[288] and he refused to discuss the matter other than to demand Byzantium's unconditional surrender to the Roman creed. Charles, meanwhile, completed his preparations, and was ready to set sail when a storm suddenly destroyed his fleet (1270).

By this time, Pope Clement was dead (d. 1268). His successor, Gregory X (reigned, 1271–1276), invited Michael to send delegates to the Council of Lyons (1274), but in the end, he, too, insisted on nothing less than abject acceptance of Roman Catholicism.[289] This left Michael in a quandary. He was willing to accept Catholicism personally, but the Byzantine rank-and-file were not. Indeed, after the experience of the Latin conquest, Michael had all he could do to convince his subjects that Catholics were even Christian.[290] The issue, however, could no longer be put off. With Charles again on the point of sailing, Michael resorted to a policy of forced conversion. It failed miserably—driving scores of outraged ecclesiastics to seek asylum in Epirus or Thessaly. Worse still, Pope Gregory died in 1276, and the talks stalled entirely until the accession of Nicholas III (pontiff, 1278–1281), who demanded on-site verification of popular compliance with the Roman creed[291]—a dismal development indeed, since any confirmatory evidence Michael might contrive to put forward was unlikely to hold up under close scrutiny.

Pope Nicholas soon died, too, whereat Charles of Anjou rendered all discussion moot by installing his own puppet, Pope Martin IV (1281). While Charles fashioned a new expeditionary force with which to attack Byzantium, Pope Martin ceased negotiations and excommunicated the emperor. By the spring of 1282, Anjou was ready, but at the last instant his project was overthrown by the Sicilian populace who resented the taxes he had imposed to pay for his proposed expedition. At Vespers on the day after Easter, 1282, the citizens of Palermo rose up and massacred their Angevin garrison. The revolt soon engulfed the entire island—the flames being stoked by the arrival of Spanish troops under Peter III of Aragon, a son-in-law of Manfred of Sicily, who now put himself forward as the heir of the deposed ruler. The rebellion proved fatal to the hopes of Charles of Anjou. He withdrew to southern Italy, and died three years later, without ever realizing his Byzantine aspirations (1285).

Thus, owing to his own good luck—or at least to the bad luck of Charles of Anjou—Michael VIII Palaeologus could boast a generally successful reign. Cooperation with the Venetians and Genoese produced an increase in the empire's commerce, and a modest reconstruction project was initiated to repair damages in the capital.[292] Byzantine generals had driven back the Sicilians, the Serbs, the Bulgars and the hostile princelings of Greece and Thessaly during a series of battles, and Michael had then arranged dynastic marriages to keep the peace.[293] In 1280, Charles of Anjou had been repulsed at Berat in his attempt to march overland to Constantinople, and the Sicilian Vespers, which ruined him completely, had been provoked by Byzantine bribes.[294] If the cost of these successes had not bankrupted the treasury, the future might actually have held promise.

But Michael's successor, Andronicus II (ruled 1282–1328), was a poor judge of priorities, who relieved the empire's budgetary distress by doing without the luxury of an army or navy. A thousand cavalrymen were charged with guarding the entire Turkish frontier, while a meager two thousand stood watch in Europe.[295] Additionally, the emperor refused to pursue Michael VIII's unpopular negotiations with the papacy, thus destroying any hope of a Western rapprochement. Consequently, the empire entered upon a long period of calamity. In 1302, Andronicus' "army" lost a battle in Bythinia to a certain Othman—the leader of an obscure Turkish tribe that had established itself in Asia Minor. A ruthless aggressor, Othman was a fair-minded prince who provided security to his minions regardless of religion. Early in his career, he won renown for deciding (justly) in favor of a Christian involved in a court case against a Muslim.[296] By the end of Andronicus' reign, Othman's "Ottomans" not only rose to predominance amongst the Turks, but with the exception of a few well-fortified towns, they hurled the Byzantines out of Asia.[297]

Meanwhile, in Europe, the Serbs and Bulgars were as restive as ever, while the Venetians and Genoese, in their unending rivalry for commercial supremacy, periodically turned the Bosphorus into a war zone. From Europe and Asia dispossessed Byzantines flocked to the capital, where overcrowding and food shortages resulted in price gouging and black marketeering.[298] The situation was so desperate, that the grandson of the emperor was heard to complain: "How different is my situation from that of the son of Philip! Alexander might complain, that his father would leave him nothing to conquer: alas! my grandsire will leave me nothing to lose."[299]

To protect his flagging interests, Andronicus hired a force of Catalan mercenaries, but this merely stirred up a new cauldron of mayhem. The Catalans defeated the Turks twice in Asia Minor, and broke their siege of Philadelphia. But afterwards, they robbed, raped and otherwise exploited the very Greeks whom they had been hired to assist. Unable to get rid of them, Andronicus hired an Alan mercenary (whose son had been killed in a clash with the Catalans) to assassinate the Catalan leader, Roger de Flor, at a banquet in Adrianople (1305). Enraged by this act, the Catalans embarked on a war of revenge. Brushing aside the shoestring Byzantine forces sent to oppose them, the "Grand Company" (as de Flor had styled them) sacked town after town, engaging in wanton massacre and plundering the countryside until nothing was left. The survivors of these assaults were brought to the Grand Company's base at Gallipoli, which thus became a bustling slave market. De Flor's assassin was tracked down and killed at the Bulgarian frontier. Only in 1309, when the Catalans espied an opportunity to seize Athens from its Frankish princeling, did the Grand Company finally depart.[300]

Following the death of Andronicus' son in 1320, the emperor's grandson and namesake, Andronicus III (ruled 1328–1341) became heir-apparent to the throne. But in seeking to murder a rival suitor in a quarrel over a woman, the younger Andronicus accidentally involved himself in the killing of his own brother, and since he showed no remorse, the emperor disowned him and fixed the succession on another relative. There followed a devastating civil war—or more precisely, three civil wars—the last of which resulted in total victory for the grandson who managed to sneak into the capital under cover of darkness to seize the throne (1328).

Unlike his grandfather, Andronicus III understood the importance of having an army. Indeed, he promptly assembled one for a belated effort to halt the momentum of the Ottoman Turks who were now besieging Nicaea (1329). The ensuing battle was inconclusive, but casualties were such that the Byzantine army had to withdraw. Unfortunately, with the emperor among the wounded, the retreat was bungled and the army was routed, leaving the

Ottomans free to reduce the few bastions remaining to the Byzantines in Asia Minor.[301] (Although Orkhan, the Ottoman sultan, allowed the Byzantine inhabitants to depart with their belongings if they so desired, most chose to remain, finding that they enjoyed less oppressive governance and taxation under the Turks.[302]) In 1338, the Ottoman vanguard reached the Bosphorus.

Still, Andronicus' reign was not bereft of accomplishment. At home, he reformed the courts and refurbished the army; and while he lost territory in a protracted war with Serbia, his forces reconquered Epirus, Thessaly, Chios and Lesbos.[303] His premature death in 1341 was therefore regrettable—all the more so because it heralded new competition over the succession. The lawful claimant was Andronicus' son, the nine-year-old John V Palaeologus (ruled 1341–1391), but he was relegated to the status of pawn while the nation was torn asunder by another civil war. The chief combatants in the new contest were John Cantacuzenus, the loyal servant of the deceased Andronicus III, who had the young emperor's best interests at heart,[304] and Alexius Apokaukos, High Admiral of the lowly Byzantine fleet, who had the boy in his clutches and pretended to be his defender. The former was sincere, the latter an opportunist, but in the eyes of the impoverished populace the millionaire Cantacuzenus seemed the villain—the latest magnate to seek control of the government on the battleground of their homes and fields.[305] Aristocrats were made the targets of popular uprisings in Constantinople, Thessalonica and Adrianople, and Cantacuzenus was chased onto foreign soil, where he had to petition mercenary support first from the Serbs and then from the Ottoman Turks (whose emir married Cantacuzenus' daughter and confined her to his bridal harem).[306] The entry of the Turks into Europe at Cantacuzenus' invitation, says Gibbon, decided the victory for Cantacuzenus, and delivered "the last and fatal stroke in the fall of the Roman empire" at one and the same time.[307] (Truth be told, both sides employed Turkish mercenaries, and since funds were lacking to pay them, both sides allowed the Turks to seize the partisans of their rivals to sell in the slave markets of Asia.[308])

In 1345, Cantacuzenus captured Adrianople with the aid of his Turkish allies, prompting the wretched Apokaukos to accelerate his reign of terror against the aristocrats of the capital. So many were arrested that the High Admiral had to renovate the palace of Constantine to create the requisite number of dungeons—a project in which he was keenly interested and which he enjoyed inspecting. Unfortunately for him, on one of his inspections he intruded upon the inmates (who were allowed to roam the building freely while awaiting the renovation of their rooms) as they were discussing how their imprisoner must die if they were ever to have a chance of freedom. One may imagine the awkwardness of the moment, but as Apokaukos had come without his bodyguards, the inmates availed themselves of the opportunity to club him to death and impale his head on the prison ramparts.[309] The fallen admiral's marines took a ghastly revenge, killing innocent inmates along with the guilty, but the initiative now lay with Cantacuzenus, and the war was brought to a favorable conclusion after the customary nocturnal breach of the capital walls (1347). The victor granted a general amnesty, and assumed the purple as John VI (ruled 1347–1354). The rightful heir—John V Palaeologus—nominally ruled with him in a subordinate capacity.

The fruits of victory were sparse indeed. The treasury was so depleted that the crowns used in the dual coronation of John V and John VI were adorned with fake jewels.[310] The nation had been in no position to weather the effects of another civil war, but the damage wrought was soon to be dwarfed by a new disaster. Within months of Cantacuzenus' accession, Genoese sailors arrived from the Black Sea port of Kaffa bearing the Black Death. A third (or more) of the population perished by this epidemic, and in the midst of this misery Byzantium ceased to be a significant player on the world stage.[311] The Serbian king, Stephen Dushan, who had already seized Macedonia during the civil war, now plucked Epirus and Thessaly from Byzantium's faltering grasp. Had he possessed a navy, he would have seized Constantinople itself.[312] All that remained to the Byzantines now were the capital, the adjoining province of Thrace, and the isolated outposts of Thessalonica and the Morea (i.e., the Peloponnesus). To solidify his hold on these table scraps, Cantacuzenus appointed John V governor of Thessalonica, and dispatched his own two sons to Thrace and the Morea.

But truth be told, the Byzantines were not even masters of their own house. The Genoese trading station at Galata, just across the Golden Horn, possessed a near monopoly on imports—and on the customs receipts that came with them. In an effort to recapture this revenue, Cantacuzenus cut the tariff rate on goods shipped directly into Constantinople. The Genoese retaliated by sinking the inferior Byzantine fleet, and then celebrated their victory by catapulting a huge stone into the capital from Galata.[313] Three years further on, Genoa provoked a war with Venice by attempting to corner the market on Black Sea trade. The Byzantines were drawn in against their will on the side of Venice, and the Bosphorus played host to a major naval engagement between the Venetian and Genoese fleets. The battle raged for an entire day, littering the water with corpses and shattered vessels. But the contest was inconclusive, the Venetians withdrew, and Byzantine commerce remained squarely beneath the Genoese thumb.

In the meantime, the young John V Palaeologus grew impatient with his mentor, Cantacuzenus, and initiated a new civil war from Thrace. It was an indulgence Byzantium could ill afford. In order to preserve his station, Cantacuzenus had to import Turkish mercenaries into Europe for the second time. He kept his throne, but the Ottomans were now uncomfortably adept at crossing the straights. Hence, when a devastating earthquake hit Thrace in 1354, they crossed over uninvited, and established a permanent settlement—their first in Europe—on the ruins of Gallipoli. Soon, the surrounding countryside was in Turkish hands; and while the landed magnates suffered mightily, the peasantry seems not to have minded its liberation from the empire's feudal labor obligations and oppressive taxation.[314] In the capital, the invasion was regarded as a catastrophe. The mob proclaimed openly for the rebellious John V, and forced Cantacuzenus to abdicate. He withdrew to a monastery where, over the course of a thirty-year retirement, he composed his memoirs (1354).

John V Palaeologus was now sole ruler of Byzantium—a ravaged nation with an empty treasury. The palace was a poorhouse—even the royal jewels had been pawned—and misadventure was the sole companion of its new occupant. John traveled far and wide in a futile search for allies to support him against his hostile neighbors. Twice he was held prisoner in foreign lands: first by his enemies in Bulgaria, and later by his creditors in Venice. He was transiently overthrown by his eldest son, Andronicus IV, and only narrowly missed being deposed for good by his grandson. In 1369, he traveled to Rome and embraced Roman Catholicism, but even this failed to win him any substantive support. And all the while the new sultan, Murad I, led the Ottoman Turks on a continuing advance through Byzantine territory. Thrace fell to them piece by piece, starting with Philipopolis and Adrianople

(1362). In 1371, a victory on the Maritza broke the power of Serbia. Bulgaria swore fealty to the Sultan, and two years later, John and his nominally independent empire did the same (1373). The Serbs alone attempted to throw off the Turkish yoke. On June 28, 1389, Murad met them on the famed "field of blackbirds"—Kossovo. At the outset of the clash, a Serb noble, feigning defection, stabbed the sultan to death. But Murad's son, Bajazet, claimed the sultanate on the field of battle, ordered the strangulation of his younger brother to prevent rival claims, and cut the Serbs to pieces.

When John V died brokenhearted in 1391, one could scarcely step outside the capital without treading on Turkish soil. Byzantium had preserved her hold on the Peloponnesus, but Thessalonica fell to the Turks in 1387, and this had been followed by the greatest humiliation of all. At the command of Bajazet, the emperor was compelled to dispatch his own troops to assist in the Ottoman siege of Philadelphia—the last Byzantine-held city in Asia (1390). In 1393, Bajazet annexed Bulgaria and occupied Nicopolis on the Danube. This was rather too alarming for the Christian West to bear. While Bajazet backtracked to besiege Constantinople itself (1394), the states of Europe finally sprang to action—dispatching an army of 100,000 crusaders along the Danube toward Nicopolis. But if Byzantine spirits rallied at the news of an army that "proudly boasted that if the sky should fall they could uphold it on their lances,"[315] they flagged again when Bajazet put the crusaders to rout. ("Marvellously [sic] displeased," by his own high casualties, the sultan had hundreds of defenseless prisoners "slain and hewen [sic] all to pieces without mercy" after the battle.[316])

How Byzantium Was Temporarily Saved by an Asiatic Horde ... and Then Met Its Doom

With his capital on the brink of starvation, Manuel II, the new Byzantine Emperor (ruled 1391–1425), toured the courts of Europe in an effort to obtain succor (1399). Despite a series of regal welcomes and an almost universal profession of sympathy, his appeals were everywhere rejected. It seemed that the fate of the venerable empire was sealed.

All this changed, however, when Tamerlane the Great and his Mongol horsemen galloped into Asia Minor from the east (1402). The Mongols had originated in the steppes between China and Siberia around 1200 AD. Their founder and greatest leader—the illiterate prince, Genghis Khan—was born clasping a blood clot from his mother's womb in his fist,[317] and celebrated his first victory by flinging seventy vanquished rebels into individual cauldrons of boiling water.[318] In 1210, Genghis invaded China, breaching the Great Wall and affecting a difficult siege of Peking, which held out grimly until a mine blew the imperial palace to smithereens (1214). Six years later, Genghis demolished the Kismian Dynasty of Persia with a masterful ruse. While diversionary attacks tied down the Persian defensive fortress line from the front, Genghis took a third of the army around the enemy left flank, stole through the "impassable" Kizyl Kum Desert and emerged to deliver the deathblow from behind at Samarkand (1220).[319] In 1227, he fell from his horse sustaining mortal injuries. By this time, his empire extended to the northern coast of the Black Sea, and in the succeeding years, his brilliant general, Sabutai, pressed forward into Europe. Moscow, Kiev and Cracow were burnt, and at Lignitz a combined army of Poles and Teutonic knights was so disastrously defeated that, according to Gibbon, the victorious Mongols were able

Section I: City of the World's Desire

to fill "nine sacks with the right ears of the slain."[320] The Hungarians were similarly routed at Mohi. Buda and Pest were razed. Bulgaria was raided, and the horde made overtures toward Vienna. In the attendant panic a preposterous rumor identified the Mongols as the ten lost tribes of Israel conjured by the Jews in a bid to take over the world. Violent anti-Jewish pogroms ensued across Europe,[321] and, amidst the butchery, it was scarcely noted that the Mongols had withdrawn as rapidly as they had come. Their tactics, it seems, were unsuited to the European terrain, and the poverty of Hungary and Poland held forth little promise of plunder. Besides, the horde had to attend the coronation of a new khan since the old one, Ogedei, had drunk himself to death (1241).[322]

When it finally ceased expanding, the Mongol empire stretched from the Pacific to Poland in the north, and from northern India to the border of the Arabian Peninsula in the south. Egypt, too, would have succumbed had her Mameluke sultan not defeated the Mongol general, Ketboga, to stem the tide (AD 1260). It has long been fashionable to denigrate this vast empire as the haven of bloodthirsty savages but the Mongols actually won their battles on the basis of supreme military organization and strategic genius. In planning their campaigns, they employed a sophisticated spy network. The Venetians, for example, betrayed information about Europe in return for military aid against their Genoese competitors.[323] Mongol tactics were fully rehearsed and could be carried out with split-second timing on the field of battle. Skirmishers were sent forward as an initial impediment to the approaching enemy. Archers and javelin throwers then unloosed their missiles to sow disorder. Typically, by the time the Mongol heavy cavalry moved forward, the beleaguered foe could no longer defend itself. Each maneuver was signaled by black and white flags, which could be seen from afar and guaranteed a degree of coordinated movement that could never have been attained using orders delivered by messenger.[324] To reduce casualties, the soldiers were supplied with silk tunics to wear under a protective jerkin. An arrow entering the body would be encompassed by the silk, and could be drawn out again with minimal friction and tissue damage by placing outward tension on the tunic.[325]

The Mongols made keen use of the terror inspired by their name. To undermine the courage of their next adversary, they advertised their every atrocity.[326] After Lignitz, says Gibbon, "the remote nations of the Baltic ... trembled at the approach of the Tartars (i.e., Mongols), whom their fear and ignorance were inclined to separate from the human species."[327] Genghis' grandson, Kublai Khan (ruled, 1251–1294), completed the conquest of China, and might have taken Japan had two successive Mongol fleets not perished by storm en route.

Under Kublai, Mongol civilization enjoyed its zenith. The Mongols displayed an avid thirst for knowledge. Tolerance was shown to all faiths, and Asia was opened to travelers from the West, of whom the best known is Marco Polo. The Mongols might even have been Christianized had the pope not tried to demote them in status to a papal fief as part of the negotiation. But after the death of Kublai, the massive empire collapsed under its own weight, and as we return to the story of Byzantium in 1402, we are only concerned with one of it fragments: the so-called "Jagatai Khanate" of Turkestan, whence Timur the Lame (Tamerlane) made his appearance in the Ottoman rear. A soldier who rode at the head of his troops, Tamarlane had twice received sword blows to his helmet that might have proved fatal to another.[328]

In dispelling the myth that the Mongols were savages, Tamerlane makes a poor example.

At Herat, he buried 2000 prisoners alive, and at Siwas, another 4000.[329] He severed the heads of entire conquered armies and piled them into skull-pyramids, including one of 70,000 at Ispahan—these being (to paraphrase Wells) his chief contribution to architecture.[330] His methods may have been crude, but Tamarlane was never beaten on a field of battle. After subduing Persia (1381), he defeated the rival Kipchak Khanate of southern Russia, and then overran northern India (1398). Only at the age of sixty-three did he again turn his attention to the West. His troops entered regions claimed by the Ottomans, and when the Mongol standard was raised on the Euphrates, Tamarlane received a harshly worded letter of complaint from the sultan. But the Mongol was not easily deterred. In 1402, he crossed into Asia Minor and engaged the Ottoman army at Ankara (Angora). According to Gibbon his forces numbered 800,000 as against 400,000 under Bajazet. The numbers are clearly inflated—likely by an order of magnitude—but suffice to say that it was a formidable contest. The outcome, however, was never in doubt. Before a sword had been unsheathed, Bazajet's Kipchak cavalry—fully a quarter of his entire force—defected to Tamerlane rather than cross swords with their racial kinsmen.[331] The remaining Ottoman cavalry was put to rout, leaving the defenseless infantry to be encircled and butchered. Bajazet was captured and placed in an iron cage, whence he beheld his wife's employment as a naked cupbearer to the conqueror.[332] By one account, the vision provoked him to beat his head against the bars until he died.[333]

Tamerlane now advanced to the Bosphorus where the Christians at Constantinople and the Ottomans at Gallipoli joined together to oppose him. The Khan requested a navy from each of them in turn, claiming that he needed it to attack the other, but neither party would be duped by such shenanigans.[334] At length, Tamerlane lost interest and retired from Ottoman territory. He died in 1405, at the opposite end of his empire, poised to conquer China. Without him, the Mongol threat evaporated.

For the Byzantines, Tamerlane's career had been a godsend. Dead Bajazet left four sons to contest the succession. Fuller says that if the Byzantines had capitalized on this confusion to capture Adrianople, they might have cast the Turks back into Asia.[335] Instead, they chose to negotiate with Bajazet's eldest son, Suleiman, who desired Byzantine support to bolster his position in the Ottoman war of succession. Suleiman's terms were liberal. He returned Thessalonica and a portion of the Black Sea coastline to the empire, and released the emperor from his state of vassalage. In return, he asked only that Adrianople be recognized as the capital of his sultanate (consisting of the Turkish dominions in Europe). Unfortunately, this happy arrangement was violently terminated in 1411, when Suleiman was strangled in his bath by the henchmen of his brother Musa. Musa was anti–Byzantine to the bone, but his reign was mercifully short. In 1413, he was dethroned and executed by a third brother, Mehmet I, who was assisted in his rise to power by the Byzantines, and who reinstated a benevolent policy toward them.

Mehmet ruled until his death in 1421, whereupon the sultanate passed to his son, Murad II (1421). Made dizzy by the whirlwind of successions, the Byzantines blundered and supported a rival candidate. Murad retaliated by investing Constantinople and Thessalonica simultaneously. The former survived owing to its stout walls; but in spite of being handed over to the protection of Venice, the latter was overthrown after a seven years' siege.

Emperor Manuel finally died in 1425 after a reign of thirty-four years. Fearing imminent disaster at the hands of the Turks, his successor, John VIII Palaeologus (ruled 1425–

1448) took the drastic step of negotiating an end to the Schism of 1054 at the Councils of Ferrara and Florence (1437–1439). In a ceremony held in the Florence Cathedral, he converted to the Roman faith.[336] As usual, however, the citizens of Constantinople would have no truck with Catholicism. They reproached the emperor bitterly for his folly. But even as they did so, John had reason to believe that he had attained his object. For the pope was preaching a new crusade.

Hungary was now alive to the Turkish threat. Realizing that their nation was next in line to be overrun, the Hungarian knights answered the papal summons, and reeled off a series of victories under the able generalship of John Hunyadi (or "Jancus the Wicked" as Turkish parents styled him to frighten their misbehaving children.[337]) Supported by the Serbs and Wallachians, they advanced to capture Nish and Sofia (1443). With fires to put out elsewhere, Sultan Murad proposed a ten-year truce leaving the crusaders in control of the areas they had occupied. The crusaders swore their acceptance of these terms on the Bible only to be reminded by Cardinal Julian Cesarini, the pope's man on the spot, that crusades were meant to end in victory, not in negotiated settlements. Julian's stirring oratory compelled the hesitating warriors to resume their advance. They proceeded, therefore, to the Black Sea port of Varna where they intended to rendezvous with the Christian fleet. Instead, they were greeted by the legions of the Turkish sultan. Murad besought Jesus to punish those who had broken an oath sworn on the Christian Bible, and put the crusaders to a merciless rout (1444).[338] King Ladislas of Hungary was decapitated, and his head, still adorned by its helmet, was displayed atop a pike.[339] Hunyadi was more fortunate. He survived to fight the Turks again—first at Kossovo (1448) where he lost, and then at Belgrade (1456) where he won a heroic and unexpected victory.[340]

Murad, meanwhile, took vengeance on John VIII Palaeologus, whose ill-considered church union had helped spawn the crusade. The Ottoman legions invaded Greece, piercing the not-particularly-effective Hexamilion Wall, which the Byzantines had built across the Gulf of Corinth to protect the Peloponnesus. In the ensuing campaign, sixty thousand of the emperor's subjects were rounded up and enslaved.[341]

Alamo on the Bosphorus

Safe behind her ramparts, Constantinople had withstood the wrath of Murad for the better part of three decades. But in 1451 the sultan was succeeded by his indefatigable nineteen-year-old son, Mehmet II, who was determined to make himself master of the Byzantine capital, ramparts or no. As his first act, Mehmet built a Turkish fortress on the European shore of the Bosphorus, just five miles away from the capital. He named the edifice "*Boghza Kesen*"—"the Throat Cutter"—which can't have been any great comfort to the Byzantines.[342] A cannon cast by his artillery engineer (a Hungarian defector named Urban) was emplaced on the walls, and by the sultan's decree all passing ships were compelled to halt for inspection. The Venetians ignored the summons. Two of their ships raced through the straits unharmed, but a third was splintered and sunk by Urban's cannon. Her crew were recovered from the water and beheaded, with the exception of her captain who was impaled on a stake and left to decompose beside a roadway.[343]

Mehmet next entrusted Urban with the task of casting a cannon powerful enough to breach the hallowed ramparts of the capital. It was the element that had been missing from all previous sieges. The artillery piece was dutifully constructed and tested at Adrianople, and according to Gibbon, "The explosion was felt or heard in a circuit of a hundred furlongs [i.e., ~12 miles]: the ball, by the force of gunpowder, was driven above a mile; and on the spot where it fell, it buried itself a fathom deep [i.e., 6 feet] in the ground."[344] Over the ensuing two months the gun was dragged 150 miles to the gates of Constantinople, where the sultan was busy assembling an army of over 100,000 men. Under Islamic law, Mehmet was required to offer the Christians their lives and property if they willingly surrendered. The citizenry refused, and the siege of Constantinople was inaugurated on April 6, 1453. Two minor fortresses outside the walls were rapidly reduced, and the prisoners, seventy-six in number, were impaled on stakes in full view of the city's defenders.[345]

Inside the capital, which was protected by a double set of walls and a ditch 100 feet deep, Constantine XI, the successor of John VIII, took a survey to see how many of his citizens were available to fight. Constantinople had once boasted over one million inhabitants. But the Black Death, and civil and foreign war, had long since taken their toll. It now held less than fifty thousand souls, and of these Constantine could count on no more than 4900 native citizens and 2000 foreign nationals (mostly from the West) to man his walls.

Luckily, even with Urban's big gun, the Turkish batteries were slow to make headway. The Ottomans attempted to fill the capital's outer ditch with debris. The Christians thwarted them by firing missiles, arrows and musket balls from the ramparts, and by sallying out at night to clear out the ditch and repair damage to the walls. Employing a siege tower with a great wooden turret, the Turks gained a foothold on the rampart. But the defenders drove them back, and contrived to obliterate the hulking monument in the dark of night by tumbling powder kegs into the ditch beneath it.[346] Hopes were raised further on April 20 when a small convoy of Genoese ships fought their way through the Turkish blockade and put in at the Golden Horn. The massive chain, stretching from Galata to the harbor of Constantinople, was lowered to give entry to the privateers, and raised again to exclude their pursuers. If supplies and reinforcements could continue to filter in by this method, the chain might yet prove to be the weak link in Mehmet's assault.

But the sultan now called upon his engineers to accomplish a remarkable feat. At his order, they constructed a two-mile plank road between the Bosphorus and the Golden Horn in the open country to the north of the suburb of Galata. Atop this, they placed a rudimentary railway of wooden beams. What came next was scarcely to be believed. Enraged by the Genoese blockade run, Mehmet had his minions remove seventy Turkish vessels from the former body of water and transport them overland, mounted on wheeled runners, to the latter. Part of the journey was uphill and required the use of windlasses and oxen, but the exploit was accomplished in a single day.[347] On April 22, 1453, the last safe harbor in the capital ceased to be safe.

Alarmed to discover the trespassing vessels in the Golden Horn, the Byzantines launched a nocturnal sea raid on April 28th, but the mission failed abysmally, and forty sailors fell into Turkish hands. When Mehmet had these unfortunates executed before the city walls, Constantine defiantly led two hundred and sixty Turkish prisoners onto the ramparts, and had them beheaded.[348]

But with his fleet in control of the Golden Horn, Mehmet was able to place artillery in previously inaccessible areas, thus exposing new sections of the walls to artillery fire. The rate of destruction now began to outpace the Christian abilities of repair. A black cloud of gloom settled over the city, leaving but one ray of hope. Venice had promised to dispatch fifteen galleys to the beleaguered capital earlier in the year. To investigate the progress of this relief force, twelve Venetian sailors in Turkish garb boarded a vessel flying the enemy pennon, slipped past the Ottoman navy and made for the Aegean. Three weeks later, on May 23, it returned—barely outrunning a squadron of Turkish pursuers—to report that an extensive reconnaissance of the Aegean had failed to produce any evidence of the promised reinforcements. It was most unlikely that a relief force was coming. Rather than save themselves the sailors had felt honor-bound to return to the hopeless confines of the capital to inform the emperor.[349]

When darkness descended on May 28th, a premonitory hush engulfed the Turkish camp as the sultan rested his troops for the final assault. Lanterns were set out before every Muslim tent and aboard every ship to brighten the night sky in anticipation of victory. Within the city, the defenders exchanged tearful farewells. Constantine attended a final Church service, then stopped at his palace where he entreated the forgiveness of his beleaguered friends and servants who wept as he set off for the battlements.[350]

Portrait of Mehmet II by Gentile Bellini, 1480 (Wikimedia Commons).

Mehmet's attack commenced at the uncivilized hour of 1:30 a.m. on May 29th. The first wave consisted of the dregs of his army, whose sole mission was to exhaust the strength and ammunition of the defenders. The Byzantines bravely repulsed them, but in so doing, they choked the citadel's protective ditch with corpses, thus providing better footing for the crack Turkish forces of the second wave.[351] For four hours, seven hundred Genoese soldiers commanded by Giovanni Giustiniani defended a breach made in the walls while the sultan rotated fresh troops in and out of the fray. Then disaster struck: The brave Giustiniani sustained an arrow wound in the face.[352] The emperor begged him to remain at his post, but the Genoese commander insisted on being carried out of the action. At the same instant, shouts were raised that the Turks were within the walls. Inexplicably, the Circus Gate, far to the north, had been left unlocked and unguarded, and the Turks had broken in. Constantine rushed to the scene hoping to re-secure the entryway, but by the time he arrived the situation had already degenerated. The area was inundated with Turkish troops.

Returning to Giustiniani's position, the emperor found that the Genoese had departed the field with their commander, and that the remaining Greek defenders were in the process of being annihilated. Fearful of being captured alive, the emperor is said to have shouted, "Cannot there be found a Christian to cut off my head?"[353] (It is difficult to imagine that anyone close enough to have heard such a remark could have lived to report it, but it is equally difficult not to pass it on to the reader. In any event, the request proved unnecessary. Constantine went down fighting with a few loyal companions—among them an oddball Spanish grandee who was convinced that he was the emperor's cousin.)

Mehmet would not rest until Constantine's body had been identified. A fugitive emperor might serve as a rallying point for some future attempt to recover the city. George Saphrantzes, who witnessed the siege and its aftermath, reports that Turkish soldiers searched through piles of heads and bodies, sponging blood from the faces, until they came upon a corpse clad in boots marked with the imperial insignia. The corpse's identity is not universally accepted. Some chroniclers say that Constantine had removed his regalia prior to the final death struggle.[354] In any event, the Turks struck off the head, placed it atop a lance and paraded it from city to city across the Ottoman Empire. (The body, in contrast, they buried with reverence at a site marked thereafter by an eternal flame.[355]) Mehmet proceeded on his horse into the church of St. Sophia, where, in the words of C. W. C. Oman, he "bade a mollah [sic] ascend the pulpit and repeat there the formula of the Moslem faith. So the cry that God was great and Mohammed his prophet rang through the dome where thirty generations of patriarchs had celebrated the Holy Mysteries, and all Europe and Asia knew the end was come of the longest tale of Empire that Christendom has yet seen."[356]

Murder and mayhem were the initial gifts of the Turkish victory. The luckiest inhabitants got aboard the Venetian and Genoese galleys that were preparing to break out of the Golden Horn. The rest faced indiscriminate butchery before the Turks realized that more might be gained by the possession of live prisoners who could be sold as slaves. Meanwhile, the pillaging invaders emptied the city of all articles of value. Many of the churches were desecrated, artwork was destroyed, and whole libraries were burned. But this only tells part of the story. Mehmet labored hard during his lifetime to repopulate and improve the city, which was thenceforward to serve as his capital. Commerce and industry revived under his leadership, and languishing sections of the city were rebuilt. By the time of his death, the population had increased to four times its level at the time of the siege, and included large Christian and Jewish communities living under the sultan's protection. While many of the new inhabitants had been forcibly resettled, large numbers came voluntarily on a promise of liberal treatment.[357] Under Ottoman rule, Constantinople regained a vigor not seen since the reign of Basil the Great—but it had necessitated the extinction of an empire to bring the city—now called Istanbul—back to life.

Societal Achievements

The West had done remarkably little to save Constantinople from its fate, and for centuries—perhaps to assuage their own guilt—European scholars expressed disdain for the civilization of Byzantium, as if to suggest that it had not been worth saving. Their assessment is unfair.[358] To be sure, the Byzantine saga is wrought with episodes of intrigue, of eyes being put out, of usurpations, of bribes and expedient alliances, but one need only cite the politics of the Renaissance to see that Byzantium possessed no monopoly on deceit or foul play. Moreover, to dwell on these negative factors is to ignore the overarching fact that, as one historian has put it, "For almost a thousand years … the Byzantine Empire was the seat of a civilization that outshone all others, a civilization as brilliant as any in the Middle Ages…."[359]

Surrounded by water on three sides and nestled snugly behind fortifications on the fourth, Byzantium's capital city, Constantinople, had been the "city of the world's desire"—the marvel of humankind. Situated on the Bosphorus, it became the world's commercial emporium in a way that Rome had never been. For nearly a millennium, the Byzantine coin, the *nomisma*, stood as the standard currency of the Mediterranean.[360]

This is not to say that Byzantium lacked peculiarities. She considered herself the daughter of Rome, but she was hardly the inheritor of the classical tradition. The conventions she preserved were imperial rather than republican. The trappings of Oriental despotism, pioneered in the old empire during the reign of Diocletian, were elevated, at Constantinople, to the level of an exact science. During public ceremonies, courtiers could not touch the emperor or even open their mouths to speak.[361] Foreign dignitaries were obliged to kneel thrice on approaching the throne,[362] and documents pertaining to foreign affairs were consigned haughtily to the "Bureau of Barbarians."[363] Nor were the Byzantines above employing a cheap gimmick or two if it would enhance their emperor's aura of majesty. According to the Western bishop, Liudprand, the imperial throne was ensconced in a jungle of mechanized animals—robotic chirping birds and roaring lions—while the throne itself, quite mysteriously, could be raised or lowered when those in audience were in the act of bowing so as to overawe them when they looked up again.[364]

Because the Byzantines were imbued with the notion that the wrong theological decision could ruin the chance of getting to heaven for everyone, minutia of religious doctrine occupied every mind—from that of the emperor down to the man in the street.[365] More than once, violent grassroots rioting erupted over questions that, in the West, might have been confined to priestly debate.

Throughout their history, the Byzantines clung tenaciously to the illusion that theirs was the "Roman" empire. In their liturgy, Asia Minor was "Romany" and the Byzantine court took it as a diplomatic affront when a papal legation arrived bearing papers addressed to the "Emperor of the Greeks."[366] (As Liudprand tells it, the embassy could not even state its purpose before the Byzantine courtiers shouted them down and hurled them into jail, promising to apprise the emperor of their felonious paperwork.[367])

The court's affectations notwithstanding, Constantinople simply was not, and could not be, Rome. Even her language differed—Latin having given way to Greek by the 7th century.[368] Despite this, any careful analysis reveals that there is much to admire about Byzantium, and that the civilization the Byzantines built stands on its own merit. Indeed, Western Civilization owes the Eastern Empire a double debt of gratitude, for Byzantium may rightly be credited with saving the Western way of life in two respects. Had she not withstood the initial onslaught of Islam at the turn of the 8th century, Europe would have been caught between two great Muslim pincers, and we might today be obliged to bow toward Mecca to pay homage to Allah. We are also indebted to the Byzantines for the preservation of our cultural heritage. The works of the ancient Greeks—and the Greek language itself—were all but lost to the medieval West. But Byzantium preserved the classical works in their original form, and her scholars were intimately familiar with them. At the time she composed her *Alexiad*, Anna Comnena had already studied the ancient Greek historians, the Greek myths and Homer.[369] In the city's last days, the patriots of the capital, imbued with historical knowledge, invoked the names of Themistocles, Pericles and Epaminondas to fire the fighting zeal of their brothers against the conquering Turks.[370]

The lost classics of ancient Greece first reappeared in Western Europe via contacts with the Arabs, but the original and accurate Greek versions possessed only by the Byzantines did not arrive until centuries later.[371] Many of them were brought by the stream of Byzantine scholars seeking refuge in the West amidst the Turkish advance of the 15th century. Had they not come with their manuscripts and expertise in Greek many classical works would have been forever lost with incalculable consequences for humankind.

Byzantium likewise preserved and organized Roman jurisprudence in the form of Justinian's *Codex* and *Digests* and Leo's *Basilica*. This knowledge, too, would make its return to the West (in this case as early as the 11th century) to be studied at the great law school in Bologna, whence it exerted a decisive influence on the European legal tradition.[372] Russia, Hungary and the Baltic States are similarly indebted to the Byzantines. Byzantine annalists recorded the early histories of these peoples, while Orthodox missionaries developed the Slavic (i.e., "Cyrillic") alphabet and taught them to read and write.[373] In civilizing effect, notes one historian, Byzantium fulfilled the role in the Slavic world that Catholic Rome fulfilled in the Germanic.[374]

Nor was Byzantium deficient in the arts. In architecture, the Byzantines were known for placing circular domes on square buildings. This may sound like a bad idea, but the beautiful Church of St. Sophia in Constantinople—today a mosque and museum in modern Istanbul—speaks for itself. The engineering solution required for this building style was the "pendentive" base, wherein footings are placed atop each of the corners of the square building to provide support. As these footings ascend, they widen and curve inwards so that the inner surface forms a quarter-circle at the top. The four quarter-circles thus formed meet to create a circular base parallel to the top of the building upon which a circular dome can be constructed.[375] St. Vitale, in Ravenna, does not feature the round dome, but it does boast the famous mosaics of Justinian and Theodora. Mosaicism achieved its height as an art form in Byzantine hands.[376] Other notable examples of the genre are on display at St. Mark's in Venice, which is also the site of one of the most famous examples of Byzantine sculpture—the gilded bronze horses taken from the Hippodrome during the Fourth Crusade.

Medieval Islam has likewise had a bad press in the West. We have already reported Islam's alleged (and doubted) culpability in dealing the final deathblow to the Alexandrian Library. More certain is the destruction of a library of Greek scientific and philosophic works in Baghdad as posing a threat to faith.[377] Yet Islam's history in the medieval period, particularly through the year 1200, is not one of destruction of knowledge. Quite the contrary, indeed, for the Muslim intellect—particularly during the reign of the Abbasids at Baghdad—was more inquisitive than that of the contemporary West. As the science historian, Charles Singer notes, the epicenter of learning during the 11th and 12th centuries lay not in Europe but in the caliphate.[378] Having imported "Arabic" numerals and the zero from India, they made great advances in algebra and trigonometry, which were then passed on to the West—mainly through the works of the great mathematician Al-Khwarizmi (780–850) in Latin translation.[379]

Arabian chemists, such as Jabir and Rhazes, did much to further the experimental method—though much of their effort was expended not altogether productively in alchemy (i.e., the impossible science of transmuting base metals into gold). Rhazes (844–926) was the best-known physician of the Arab world. He wrote a celebrated treatise on smallpox, and performed an intriguing experiment to select a site for a new hospital—suspending pieces of meat throughout Baghdad, and laying his foundation on the site where the meat was best preserved after a period of exposure.[380] As late as 1395, his work was so revered in the West that his *Comprehensive Book* on medicine stood alongside just eight other texts in the medical library at the University of Paris.[381]

While less famous than Rhazes, Avicenna (980–1037), nonetheless won the epithet "prince of physicians." His work, the *Canon of Medicine*, summarized Greek medicine, but added a significant body of original Arabic innovations, including his own notion that the goal of medical therapy was the restoration of normal processes that had been disordered by disease.[382] In physics, Al-Hazen was centuries ahead of the West in the science of optics; while in art, the Islamic aversion to reproduction of the human form brought forth the "arabesque" geometrical design popularly employed for architectural decoration.

Thanks to the Nestorian Christians of Syria, Arabic culture had access to Syrian translations of the works of Aristotle and Plato, and the subsequent Arabic commentary on these tomes was so noteworthy that by the 13th century, Western scholars preferred Arabic translations of Greek works to the versions available in their own monastic libraries.[383] In medicine, the Nestorian Christian Hunayn Ibn Ishaq (John, son of Isaac) translated the works of Galen and Hippocrates into Arabic, and Nestorian Christians ran the medical school at Nisibus in Syria,[384] thus contributing much to the establishment in the Arab world of the best hospitals of the medieval period.[385]

Finally, we may note that with Egyptian papyrus shut out from the West by the advance of Islam, the Arabs provided a better substitute. After the battle of Talas (751), they learned the manufacture of paper from the Chinese. In contradistinction to their reputation for destroying libraries, they employed the paper for the writing of books. The spread of bookstores and libraries accelerated apace, with more than a hundred booksellers and thirty-six public libraries being established in Baghdad alone.[386] Medieval Arab literature boasts the *Rubaiyat of Omar Khayyam* and the *Arabian Nights*. (The latter is the story of Scheherazade who stopped an Arabian potentate from killing each of his brides after the wedding night by enchanting him with a different story for 1001 nights in a row.)

Significantly for our story, the Arabs passed their knowledge of paper manufacture on to the West where, by the end of the medieval period, the stage was set for an intellectual revolution—one in which the new paper would be essential.[387] For in the same decade as the fall of Constantinople, Johann Gutenberg of Mainz was in the process of introducing the printing press. Before we embark on that story, however, we must visit medieval Western Europe.

Section II

City of God
Medieval Europe

In AD 554, the Roman army of Italy commanded by Narses, the faithful eunuch of Justinian the Great, prepared to do battle with the invading Franks, who had entered Italy on the pretext of assisting the defeated Goths. The rival forces were drawn up at Casilinum, near Capua. Just hours before the fight, however, Rome's Herul allies deserted the field after one of their number was summarily executed for insubordination and murder. The center of the Roman battle line, composed of infantry (of whom the Heruls had comprised a significant fraction), was therefore denuded of troops—a circumstance that seemed to favor the Franks who had deployed in an inverted "V" formation with the object of driving a wedge through that point in the Roman line.

When battle was joined, the Roman center was indeed pierced in two by the vertex of the Frankish onslaught, but the broken halves of the infantry fought on, engaging the flanks of the advancing "V" to slow its momentum. As the fighting raged, Narses ordered his cavalry (which were positioned on either flank) to face about and wheel in behind the Roman infantry, from where they employed their composite bows to fire arrows across the field—those on the Roman right targeting the backs of the Franks embroiled with the infantry on the Roman left and those on the left doing the same against the Franks contending with the infantry on the Roman right.[1] The Franks, who possessed neither helmets nor armor,[2] were greatly vexed by these arrows, the origin of which seemed a complete mystery to them since the mounted Roman archers were hidden from view behind the clashing infantry.

The deathblow was not long in coming. Convinced by one of their chieftains that a chance of glory should not be thrown away, the fugitive Heruls suddenly reappeared on the field and smashed into the vertex of the Frankish formation. Encompassed and surrounded, the Franks were cut to pieces with scarcely five of their number escaping the field alive. Roman casualties are said to have numbered no more than eighty.[3]

The Roman victory at Casilinum united the Italian peninsula under the rule of Justinian just as it had formerly been united under Theodoric the Ostrogoth. It was the last unity Italy would know for 1,300 years.[4] Appointed exarch, Narses ruled the peninsula efficiently if severely for the remainder of Justinian's reign. But his loyalty made no impress on Justinian's successors, Justin II and Empress Sophia. On receiving complaints from the Italian populace regarding the eunuch's strict rule and onerous taxation, Empress Sophia crudely impugned Narses' masculinity, declaring that the eunuch "should leave to *men* the exercise of arms, and return to his proper station among the maidens of the palace...."[5] Narses retired in a huff, first to Naples (567), and later (at the pope's invitation) to Rome, where he lived to the age of ninety-five (574), long enough to behold the ruination of Italy.

Narses' successor, the untested Longinus, proved inept in matters of defense. The Lombard tribe, or "Long-beards," had already menaced the empire from their home in the Balkans. In 568, they stormed into northern Italy, which Longinus had not seen fit to garrison. The invaders might have overrun the entire peninsula had it not been for a lover's spat between their king, Alboin, and his war bride, Rosamond, whom he had taken as spoils of war in a prior victory over the Gepids. The skull of Cunimund, Rosamund's father, plated over in gold, enjoyed an honored position at Alboin's table, where it was employed as a drinking goblet. In the swell of his Italian victories, Alboin demanded that Rosamond partake in the army's celebration by drinking a toast from it. She obeyed this cruel summons, but swore revenge. Soon after, her spear-bearing co-conspirators burst into Alboin's sleeping quarters and stabbed the king to death after he deflected their initial blows with a footstool. His corpse was interred beneath a palace staircase,[6] and while the Lombards paused at the Po in confusion over the succession, Rosamond escaped to Ravenna with her paramour.[7]

The Lombards soon renewed their advance, and though they were unable to reduce the peninsula's coastal strongholds, their menacing presence was keenly felt in the central regions of the Italian boot. By the twilight of the 6th century, Rome and its environs had descended increasingly into a wilderness of barbarism and desolation, whose inhabitants, in Gibbon's description, "shut or opened their gates with a trembling hand, beheld from the walls the flames of their houses, and heard the lamentations of their brethren who were coupled together like dogs, and dragged away into distant slavery beyond the sea and the mountains."[8]

Catholicism Ascends

The task of reversing this trend toward ever-diminishing civilization must have seemed beyond attainment, but there still existed in Italy one institution suited to the challenge. The Catholic Church already possessed a ready-made hierarchy of authority, starting at the local level with the parish priest, and ascending to the city level (or "diocese") headed by a bishop, and then to the provincial level (or "archdiocese") headed by an archbishop. Above all of these stood the Bishop of Rome or "Pope," who headed the Church, and was assisted in his decision-making by a ministerial body known as the College of Cardinals and by the Church's own legal system, known as Canon Law. Taken together, it was a formidable administrative machine, erected upon the Roman model and materially supported by the collection of "tithes" (i.e., "tenth part" or 10 percent tax on profits) at the parish level, and by a bustling agricultural industry run by the Church on its own extensive properties.[9]

But the advantages held by the Church were not purely monetary and administrative. The clergy were among the best-educated men in Europe, and as new states took form on the ruins of the Roman Empire, secular rulers were wont to hire them as councilors.[10]

There was also the issue of spiritual authority. In chaotic times, the Christian faithful are wont to take solace from the tradition, popular at the time of the early Christian persecutions, that if one's earthly existence is to be bereft of happiness, then hopes must be centered on salvation and the promise of a happy afterlife.[11] This perception virtually guaranteed the Catholic Church's hold on the faithful since it, and it alone, could administer the sacraments—the series of sacred ceremonies "required" for entry into God's Kingdom.[12]

Beyond the horizon, of course, the vast majority of barbarians were not Christian, and of those who were, many were not Catholic. But the Church had an answer for this too, for it possessed in its monastic orders a readymade legion of ambassadors.[13] By the time of Rome's fall, monasticism already had a long and storied history. The first Christian monks simply withdrew from secular affairs for the purpose of living a more pious and contemplative life. Unfortunately, over time the movement came to be dominated by a rabble of disreputable hermits who rivaled one another in their asceticism. It is generally agreed that this useless competition was won hands down by one Simeon Stylites of Syria, who climbed up a sixty-foot pillar and managed to stay there for thirty consecutive years.[14]

In the 6th century, however, monasticism metamorphosed and returned to its original purpose of serving God. The change was precipitated by a code of behavior devised by one Benedict of Nursia (i.e., St. Benedict, AD 480–543). Known as the Monastic or "Benedictine" Rule, the code renounced fanatical asceticism, arguing that sufficient homage could be paid to the Lord through sincere piety and hard work alone. The Rule set reasonable standards for pious behavior, and gave specific, practical advice for dealing with the myriad stumbling blocks the average monk was likely to encounter in daily life. Prior class distinctions were erased on admission to the order, and all goods were held in common.[15] Benedict's first cadre of followers found him too exacting, and endeavored to poison him.[16] Surviving the attempt, he founded the famed monastery at Monte Cassino, southeast of Rome, whence his philosophy came to dominate monasticism throughout the West.

With Italy's monasteries filled with exemplary individuals whose code of behavior set a worthy example for potential converts, the stage was set for the accession of a remarkable pope, Gregory the Great—the first monk ever to hold the office. The descendant of a former pope, Gregory had been born into the aristocracy. But it was spiritual wealth that he cherished most, and he used his worldly riches to found a number of monasteries. Thereafter, he lived a happy life of piety until he was forced, against his will, to leave his chosen abbey and serve as papal envoy to the Byzantine court (AD 579–586). All hopes of returning to the cloister were dashed when the reigning pontiff succumbed to plague, and the reluctant Gregory was named to succeed him (AD 590).

From the pulpit, Gregory raised the spirits of Rome's fretful citizenry. His tireless efforts to ease suffering found expression in theological treatises and consoling letters to those in spiritual distress. His charity provided food and clothing to Rome's poorer elements, and his introduction of Gregorian chant into church services soothed the apprehensions of his flock. Thanks to his nimble diplomacy, Rome was spared the worst excesses of the Lombards at a time when little aid was forthcoming (and little advice was sought) from Constantinople.

But Gregory's vision extended beyond the confines of Christendom. He was determined that his monks should carry the Catholic message abroad. In the twilight of the 6th century, he set his sights on distant Britain. By then, as it turns out, many of Britain's Anglo-Saxon inhabitants were already Christian—having been converted by Irish proselytizers in the preceding decades. But the Irish practiced their own brand of Christianity, and Pope Gregory wanted them to have the authentic product. In AD 597, Gregory's monks converted

King Ethelbert of Kent to the Roman faith, and convinced him to allow the establishment of a Catholic archbishopric at Canterbury.[17] Seven decades later, at the Synod of Whitby (664), Northumbria likewise adopted the Roman creed, thus making Catholicism the dominant religion on the island.

The first fruit of these successes was what has come to be known as the Northumbrian Renaissance[18]—an explosion (at least for that period) in literature, art and architecture, whose leading spirit was the Venerable Bede (AD 673–735), the epoch's preeminent scholar. Author of the *Ecclesiastical History of England*, in which he set the precedent of using the birth of Jesus as a gauge for dating historical events,[19] Bede was one of the earliest thinkers to regard the Earth as a sphere, and to perceive the relationship between the cycles of the moon and our earthly tides.[20] By Bede's time, England's Benedictines had a firm enough footing to begin sending their own missions to the European continent, where they found a willing audience in a kingdom of axe-throwing tribesmen—the very Franks whom Narses had defeated at Casilinum.

The Rise of the Franks

The Franks had been Catholic since the reign of King Clovis (AD 481–511), the founder of Frankland's "Merovingian" dynasty (so-named after Clovis' grandfather Merowig who fought alongside the Romans against Attila the Hun).[21] Born into the uncouth wing of the pagan faith, Clovis initially attended church only on plundering raids with his army. On one such outing, his troops carried away the local bishop's favorite vase. A church envoy requested its return. Clovis replied that if his soldiers would grant it to him in addition to his usual share of booty, he would gladly hand it over. But when he put the issue to his barbarous minions, one of them angrily struck the vase with his battle-axe, shouting that even the king could not claim more than his fair share. Clovis returned the vase (in pieces) to the bishop's envoy, and said nothing further at the time. On a subsequent review of his troops, however, he approached the soldier who had rebuked him, seized his equipment and threw it on the ground, saying that its condition was unbefitting of a warrior. Then, when the soldier leaned over to pick up his scattered weaponry, Clovis embedded an axe in his skull.[22]

If any of Clovis' soldiers ever had another complaint against their king, it is not recorded. After the incident of the vase, the only person who dared vex Clovis was his wife, Clotilda, a Catholic princess from Burgundy, who seems to have pestered the unfortunate man incessantly in an effort to convert him to Christianity. Her persistence paid off in the baptism of their first son. But the infant soon died,[23] stifling further debate for a year or two until Clovis, facing certain defeat on the field of battle, tearfully implored Jesus to intercede. In moments, the fortunes of battle changed from looming disaster to stunning victory.[24] Subsequently, Clovis became the first German prince to accept Roman Catholicism, convincing three thousand of his warriors to do likewise.

The baptism made Clovis popular with the Church, but it had no immediate effect on his manners. He offered an alliance to a neighboring prince, provided the youth would assassinate his own father and rule in his place. The prince did so, and when Clovis' agents arrived to congratulate them, he displayed to them a chest filled with his father's usurped treasure. The envoys suggested admiringly that he sink his hands into the coffer of coins to assess its depth. When the prince bent over to do so, the envoys embedded an axe in his skull—the oldest Frankish trick in the book perhaps, but not less effective than before. They then made off with the chest.

Identical consideration was given to the other Frankish princes—all related to Clovis by virtue of being descended from Merowig. Lest they rival him for pre-eminence in Frankland, Clovis had them all put to death, and when no relatives outside his immediate family were known to have survived, he suddenly bewailed their demise saying: "Woe is me! who am left as a traveller amongst strangers, and who have no longer relatives to lend me support in ... adversity." (According to Gregory of Tours, however, this fine piece of melodrama was merely a ploy to lure other relatives out of hiding so that he could murder them, too.)[25]

Beginning with his first victory—over a relic of the Roman army in northern Gaul (486)—Clovis extended his realm from its base in Belgium to

Saint Gregory the Great (© Depositphotos.com/ Zvonimir Atletić).

the Spanish frontier. Following the example of Julian the Apostate, he chose Paris (then a consummately protected island on the Seine) as his capital.[26] Through the haze of history, such handiwork might naturally be mistaken for the earliest birth pang of France. But the nursling was stillborn; for when Clovis died at age 45 (AD 511), he made no attempt to preserve Frankland's unity. Instead, he followed Frankish custom and divided the kingdom amongst his four sons. Knowing the temperament of the father, it is hardly surprising that dynastic squabbles ensued immediately, with his heirs hoodwinking, swindling and betraying one another until only the youngest, Clothar I, was left. Unfortunately, Clothar survived but three years after reuniting the realm—barely enough time to strangle a rebellious son and to incinerate his daughter-in-law and granddaughters alive alongside the corpse.[27] Then, expressing disbelief at his *own* untimely demise, he repartitioned the realm amongst his four remaining boys. Of this brood, one died early, but the other three, assisted by their wives, exterminated one another with such dexterity that it had to be left to one of their progeny to kill off the sole survivor—the aged Queen Brunhilde (the contemporary and benefactress of Pope Gregory the Great) who was "tied by the hair, one foot and one arm to the tail of an unbroken horse, that carried her away, and dashed her in pieces as he galloped and kicked..." (AD 613).[28]

It is sobering to note that these were the "good" Merovingians. After the death of Brunhilde, we are grimly told that the race degenerated. The reign of Dagobert (629–639), who had three wives and a good many more mistresses, may be counted a success of sorts owing to his efforts to develop a regular law code based in tradition.[29] But otherwise, the hand at the rudder was feeble, and Frankland began to founder along linguistic lines—East-Land, or Austrasia, being left to the barbarian German speakers of the northeast, and New-Land, or Neustria, to the Romanized Latin speakers of the southwest.[30] At times, we hear also of a Middle Kingdom called Burgundy, between the Loire and the Rhone. Over these domains, the so-called *fainéant* (i.e., "do-nothing") Merovingians reigned for 115 more years, occasionally interrupting their primary pursuit—namely, growing hair of impressive length—to parcel out shreds of their ever-diminishing crown lands in a vain effort to retain the political support of the nobility. In all, twelve different Merovingians reigned in this interval, "without" (in Guizot's estimation) "deserving in history more than room for their names."[31] (Alas, in this volume, we haven't room even for that.)

That any order was maintained at all under such circumstances was owed to the king's chief civil officer—the *major domus* or "mayor of the palace." This post had originally belonged to the ranking servant of the king's household, but as the Merovingians grew less competent, they began relying on them for advice. From there it was but a short step to the deputing of authority to these helpful individuals, with the logical end result that the Merovingians were increasingly reduced to the role of puppets by the very men who had formerly served as their butlers-in-chief.[32] Indeed, the mayoral power became so great during this period that the course of Frankish history was changed under the stewardship of two notable mayors. The first of these, Austrasia's Pippin of Heristhal, reunited Frankland by defeating the Neustrian mayor at the Battle of Tertry (687). He also campaigned against the pagan Frisians of the Dutch seacoast, whom he sought to convert to Catholicism. (It was Frankland's desire to convert the Frisians that prompted them to invite the Benedictine monks of Northumbria to come as missionaries. The Benedictines ultimately established a famous monastery at Fulda, and henceforth were to play an important role in fostering an alliance between the palace mayors and the papacy.[33])

The second of our important mayors was Pippin's son, Charles, known to history as Charles "Martel" (i.e., Charles "the Hammer"). Charles was actually Pippin's bastard, and was thus passed over in the mayoral succession in favor of a legitimate grandson. But as the grandson was still a tot, the Frankish nobles staged a rebellion in hopes of increasing their autonomy. Summoned to quash the revolt by the Austrasian party (which stood to lose if the rebellion was successful), Charles usurped the mayoral office for himself.

History, however, reveres Charles Martel as something more than the restorer of Frankish tranquility. Poised on the African side of the Mediterranean Straits at this time was the still-expanding world of Islam. In AD 711, a Berber chieftain named Tariq crossed over to Spain, landing beneath the rock that still bears his name: "Gebel al-Tariq" or "Gibraltar."[34] Within two decades, Spain's Visigothic kingdom had been wiped out, and the Muslims stood at the Pyrenees. In 732, they breached this barrier, led by Abd-ar-Rahman—an able general and statesman who was adored by the soldiery for his career of prolific victories.[35] Duke Eudes of Aquitaine, a renegade Frankish nobleman, met the Muslims at the frontier, but was put to rout with loss of his dukedom. Although he hadn't obeyed a mayor of the palace in his life, Eudes appealed to Charles Martel for support.

Seeing the common peril, Charles assented to Eudes' plea. The army of Frankland surprised Abd-ar-Rahman and his booty-laden forces between Tours and Poitiers. After a week-long standoff, the Muslims attempted to break the Franks with an all-out attack. But the Frankish phalanx stood "firm as a wall,"[36] and amidst the clang of weaponry came the shouted rumor that a party of Franks was looting the Arab baggage train. The Muslims began to desert by the squadron to safeguard their spoils. Abd-ar-Rahmen exhorted them to remain and press the attack; and, riding into the fray, he gave them a worthy example. But the Franks surrounded him, and thrust him through with their spears, thus precipitating a general flight.[37] Afterwards, the Muslims not only abandoned the field and their camp, but Frankland itself.

For his victory in the Battle of Tours, Charles is credited with saving Christendom.[38] Indeed, it was here that he gained his nickname "Martel." But the clergy of Frankland resented him for his efforts. To defeat the Muslims, he had usurped church properties from unwilling bishops, and had doled them out to the nobility who used the proceeds to outfit themselves as mounted knights. On account of these usurpations, says Gibbon, the churchmen of subsequent generations had "a pleasant vision of the soul and body of Charles Martel burning, to all eternity, in the abyss of hell."[39]

When Charles died in 741, his two eldest sons, Carloman and Pippin the Short, succeeded him as Mayors. By this date, the Merovingian King, Theordoric IV, had already been dead for four years, and Charles had never got round to replacing him. But perceiving a degree of restlessness amongst the natives, Carloman and Pippin deemed it wiser to fill the royal vacancy than to rest on the laurels of their illustrious father. Thus occurred the elevation of Childeric—the third of that name to occupy the royal seat, and the stupidest of the bunch.[40] For the mayors, it was an inspired choice. Raised from obscurity, Childeric would blossom into the most obscure member of the Merovingian line—a veritable rubber stamp for mayoral policy.

Of the ruling brothers, Carloman preferred a pious to a political life, but he remained at his post long enough to assist Pippin in the subjugation of their rebellious step-brother, Grifo, before retiring to found a monastery on Mt. Oreste. Even then, however, he could not find the peace he desired, for Frankish nobles on pilgrimage to Rome invariably intruded upon him to exchange greetings.[41] At length, he relocated to the less accessible Monte Cassino in order to avoid these nettlesome interruptions. Pippin, meanwhile, held firm the reins of government; and following a decade of successful rule, it occurred to him that he might now safely dispense with Childeric III, the nonentity he had himself enthroned. For, as Einhard informs us, Childeric "had nothing that he could call his own beyond this vain title of King, and the precarious support allowed by the Mayor of the Palace.... When he had to go abroad, he used to ride in a cart, drawn by a yoke of oxen, driven peasant-fashion, by a ploughman; he rode in this way to the palace ... and he returned home in like manner."[42] While it is true that Childeric received foreign ambassadors and proclaimed policies "as if on his own responsibility," the words he spoke "were, in fact, suggested to him, or imposed upon him."[43]

In order to legitimize his intended coup, Pippin turned to the papacy. In 751, he asked Pope Zacharias (741–752) whether it was fitting for the king to possess the throne when he was nothing more than a puppet, or whether it might be more appropriate for the mayor to sit there since he actually wielded all the power. Pippin's inquiry could not have been more timely; for Italy was just then being overrun by the Lombards, whose king, Aistulf, had threatened to decapitate every Roman with the same sword if they refused to capitulate.[44] Unhappy with these alternatives, Zacharias hoped to obtain Frankish support to protect the interests of the Holy See. As matters stood, Rome was under nominal Byzantine suzerainty. But little succor could be expected from the iconoclast emperors of the East, with whom a succession of popes had recently quarreled. Moreover, Byzantine power in the peninsula was clearly on the wane. Indeed, the Lombards had sacked Byzantium's provincial capital at Ravenna in the very year of Pippin's query.[45] Accordingly, Zacharias decided in favor of the mayor.

In anticipation of the day in 754 when Zacharias' successor, Pope Stephen II, would make the journey to Frankland in person to consecrate his accession officially, Pippin had himself crowned and anointed by Saint Boniface of Fulda—the most distinguished of the Benedictine monks who had come to Frankland from Northumbria.[46] Then, to express his thanks, *King* Pippin brought a forcible halt to the Lombard encroachment and conferred upon the pope the so-called "Donation of Pippin"—a deed to a score of cities and fortresses filched from the old Byzantine Exarchate of Ravenna.

Thus, did the Carolingian dynasty supplant the Merovingian. But if the mayors had gained a throne, the papacy had gained much more. Not only was she confirmed in her sovereignty over central Italy—obtaining territories over which she would exercise dominion for the next thousand years—but she also established her prerogative in legitimizing the rule of kings.[47] Moreover, she had reinforced a very desirable alliance with Frankland in her dubious quest to achieve a universal City of God in Europe under the aegis of Catholicism. This latter pretension—the dream of universal dominion—would tempt the papacy into concocting a pair of forgeries in support of its claims. The first—dating to the latter half of the 8th century—was the "Donation of Constantine," whereby the Roman emperor, Constantine the Great, on relocating his capital to Constantinople in the 4th century AD, allegedly conferred upon the papacy not only spiritual dominion over the Church, but temporal dominion over the West.[48] The second, the "Pseudo-Isidorean Decretals," produced at Rheims around AD 850, maintained that laymen could not sit in judgment over clerics accused of crimes, but must defer to Church courts—an act that effectively absolved clergymen from state authority.[49] Add to this, the pope's prerogative in anointing (and thus legitimizing the power of) kings and emperors, and the papacy bade fair to establish itself as the "high priest, censor, judge, and divine monarch of Christendom."[50] Nor was this aspiration entirely bereft of noble sentiment. "For more than a thousand years," says Wells, "this idea of the unity of Christendom, of Christendom as a sort of vast Amphictyony, whose members even in wartime were restrained from many extremities by the idea of a common brotherhood and a common loyalty to the Church, dominated Europe. The history of Europe from the fifth century onward to the fifteenth is very largely the history of the failure of this great idea of a divine world government to realize itself in practice."[51]

The Reign of Charlemagne and the Establishment of the Frankish Empire

In 768, Pippin died and was succeeded by his two sons, Charles and Carloman, amongst whom the kingdom was, of course, divided. Charles was immediately confronted by a

Merovingian[52] revolt in the Aquitaine (on the Atlantic Coast, south of Neustria), which Carloman would not help him to subdue. The latter's recalcitrance might have spawned a civil war between the brothers had Carloman not died in 771, leaving Charles free to claim all Frankland for himself.[53] Thus began the remarkable reign of "Charles the Great" or "Charlemagne."

If Clovis had been the first to unite the Franks under a single king, Charlemagne was the first to aspire to a confederation of all Europe.[54] By perceiving the extraordinary unifying potential of Christianity (particularly when it is presented to prospective converts at the point of a sword), he very nearly realized this bold ambition. At his accession, Frankland was encompassed by contentious German tribes: Saxons to the northeast, Bavarians to the east, and Lombards in Italy. (Spain, of course, was held by the Moors.) Charlemagne eventually went to war with all of them. In 772, he invaded Saxony after the pagans killed a number of proselytizing missionaries and pillaged Frankish churches in the borderlands. Reaching the Weser River, the Franks burnt or cut down the Irminsul—an enormous tree trunk revered by the Saxons as the pillar upon which the heavens rested.[55] But if they thought this had settled the matter, they were sorely mistaken. While the disunited Saxons could not muster anything like the army of the Franks, they managed to keep their tormentors off balance for another thirty-three years by relying on guerrilla tactics and ambushes. Frankish garrisons had either to withdraw or face a steady stream of casualties—the worst of it coming in 782 with the massacre of a sizeable Frankish force at Suntel Mountain.

Irate over this defeat, Charlemagne had 4500 Saxon nobles beheaded in a single day, and meted out further retribution in a savage three-year war. But these actions served only to unite the pagans in their obstinacy. Exhausted, Charlemagne finally agreed to withdraw his forces from Saxony if Prince Widukind, his Saxon arch-nemesis, would agree to be baptized (785).[56] The proposal was accepted, but peace was only transiently achieved. In 804, Charlemagne invaded Saxony again, and this time he decided to quash Saxon resistance permanently by deporting and dispersing most of the population.[57]

In the interim, war had occurred with each of the other German tribes. In 774, Charlemagne crossed the Alps to attack the Lombards who were again chastising the papacy. Confronted by an impassable palisade in the Alps, Charlemagne lost his nerve and contemplated withdrawal. His veterans, however, scaled the surrounding heights and outflanked the fortification.[58] Most of Lombardy now submitted without resistance, while the Lombard king fled to the walled city of Pavia where the Franks placed him under siege. Trusting his soldiers to mop up, the impulsive Charlemagne paid an unannounced visit to Rome. At first, Pope Hadrian took alarm; but on being reassured that Charles had come to pay homage to the city's shrines in the fashion of a devout Catholic rather than to pillage, the pontiff assumed a less timid demeanor—even convincing his pious guest to sign a document reaffirming the Donation of Pippin prior to his departure.

When Pavia fell after a nine-month siege, Charlemagne proclaimed himself king of the Lombards—a usurpation that provoked an immediate rebellion of the Lombard nobility. Charlemagne, however, was not to be trifled with. The revolt was crushed making him undisputed master of northern Italy and unofficial overlord of the Papal States.

The next barrier to be breached was the Pyrenees. In 778, Charles crossed the range in an effort to extend his hegemony into Spain. On reaching the Ebro, however, he realized that Spain's Christians were no less hostile than her Muslims. Thus, when Widukind staged another of his ubiquitous uprisings in Saxony, Charles was forced to withdraw.⁵⁹ This proved no easy matter. While negotiating the pass at Roncesvalles (the Valley of Thorns), the Frankish rearguard was ambushed by Basque mountaineers. The exact details are unknown, but the episode cannot have been any great improvement on Custer's experience at the Little Big Horn. When his baggage train failed to arrive in camp, Charles marched back with his main force to find the entire detachment killed—crushed under rockslides or cut down in scattered pockets after grim hand-to-hand combat.⁶⁰ The defeat was subsequently celebrated in the epic medieval poem, *The Song of Roland*, which glorifies the commander of the fallen detachment, and replaces the Christian Basques with an army of Muslims. Although Charlemagne never returned to Spain in person,⁶¹ his generals eventually carved out a piece of territory beyond the Pyrenees—the so-called Spanish (or Gothic) March—which reestablished a Frankish presence on the Ebro.

Elsewhere, the vassal state of Bavaria was cowed into submission, and then treacherously annexed in violation of Frankish assurances (787). Frankish troops also marched against the Hun-like Avars (795), breaking into their ringed fortresses to appropriate not just their land but a vast treasure comprising "the rapine of two hundred and fifty years."⁶² Overall, Charles' campaigns were stunningly successful. The only real trouble spot was in the north, where Frankland's coast fell prey to the Norse raiders of Scandinavia, whose seafaring acumen rendered them immune to reprisal from the Franks who hadn't the first inkling about naval warfare. Nunneries and monasteries were particularly hard hit in these raids since they were rich and incapable of defense.⁶³ In Charlemagne's last years, a fleet was constructed, but to no avail.⁶⁴

Otherwise, the bulk of Europe had been fashioned into something resembling a single state for the first time since the fall of Rome. It was a realm fit for an emperor, and thanks to the intervention of Pope Leo III it would soon have one. Leo had succeeded Charlemagne's old friend, Pope Hadrian, in 795, only to be greeted by a coup aimed at restoring the Roman Republic.⁶⁵ Branded a corrupt adulterer, Leo was seized during a procession by bungling captors who attempted without success to extirpate his eyes and tongue with a knife.⁶⁶ Rescued by

Charlemagne, illustration of mask reliquary at Aachen Cathedral (© Depositphotos.com/Igor Golovniov).

the Duke of Spoleto, he obtained sanctuary in Frankland. The Franks took him back to Rome under military escort, and Charlemagne arrived to orchestrate his formal restoration the following year. To repay this kindness, Leo approached Charlemagne while the latter knelt in worship at Saint Peter's on Christmas Day, 800, and placed a crown on his head. Einhard, the king's Lilliputian contemporary biographer, tells us that Charlemagne was appalled to have the onerous burden of empire thrust upon him when already he was king of the Franks and Lombards.[67] This did not, however, prevent him from accepting the honor. Indeed, he sought to make it official by soliciting recognition from a real empire—namely, that of the Byzantines.

Relations with Byzantium had not always been amicable, and Charlemagne's zealous Catholicism did little to warm things up. It was no problem that he had forcibly converted the Saxons or suppressed a Spanish heresy known as "Adoptionism" (which rudely surmised that Jesus had been adopted by God as opposed to possessing an actual biological relationship).[68] But when Pope Hadrian ratified the Council of Nicaea ending Byzantium's Iconoclast Controversy (787), Charlemagne had tried to impose a royal veto. He submitted a list of eighty-five defects in the Byzantine position, and when Hadrian minimized these objections, Charlemagne pressed ahead—summarizing his case in the so-called *Caroline Books*, which provoked official condemnation of the Nicaean decrees at the Council of Frankfurt.[69]

Further friction with Byzantium was engendered by Charlemagne's discussions at court with the eminent Northumbrian monk, Alcuin. These talks led to the king's famous "*filioque*" thesis, which asserted that the procession of the Holy Ghost was from the Father "and from" the Son, rather than from the Father "through" the Son as the Byzantines were sometimes fond of saying. Charlemagne's version was officially adopted into the Latin litany in the 11th century, whereupon it became the professed cause of the Schism of 1054 between the Greek and Roman Churches—each side contending that it was one thing to say "and from," but that to say "through" was an entirely different matter. Only four centuries later, with Constantinople on the verge of extinction, did the two sides realize that there had actually been no significant difference; but by then it was too late to effect a profitable reconciliation.

Just the same, now that Charlemagne was an emperor, he sorely needed Byzantium's blessing, and as it happened, he was in a good position to barter for it. For reigning in Constantinople at that date was not an emperor, but the usurping empress, Irene, who hardly commanded the loyalty of her own flock. Such circumstances gave Charlemagne an inspired idea. He would marry Irene so that each might confirm the other's position (802).[70] The monumental union would have reunited the Eastern and Western Empires. Sadly, instead of receiving an answer, Charlemagne was apprised that Irene had been overthrown before she could give the matter proper consideration. Worse still, her former treasurer, Nicephorus I, succeeded her, and absolutely refused to recognize Charlemagne's imperial title. In an effort to coerce the new Byzantine ruler, Charlemagne opened relations with the latter's archenemy—the Abbasid ruler, Harun al-Raschid. Harun played along, presenting Charles with an extraordinary clock, a pet elephant named Abul Abbas and the key to the Holy Sepulcher (signifying that he, and not the Byzantine emperor, was the rightful protector of the Christian holy places).[71] Still, Nicephorus steadfastly refused recognition. Only in 812, after Byzantium had suffered a devastating defeat at the hands of the Bulgars, did Charlemagne obtain a hesitating recognition—and even then he had to surrender all claim to Venetia and Dalmatia to get it.

Charlemagne was at last an emperor, but had he truly founded an empire? Efforts were, indeed, made to weld the realm into a unified state. Frankish kings had traditionally traveled from place to place without a fixed residence. To promote stability, Charlemagne abandoned this custom, establishing a centrally located capital at Aachen (Aix-la-Chapelle), where an imposing palace and basilica were built.[72] Einhard, who had not yet begun work on the emperor's biography, was then serving as a sort of public works commissioner, and oversaw the construction of these buildings, as well as the laudable wooden bridge over the Rhine at Mainz (which, unfortunately, burned down just prior to the emperor's death).[73] Less successful was a venture to bridge the Rhine and Danube Rivers with a canal—an engineering feat that was not actually accomplished until the 19th century.[74]

Myriad peoples had been absorbed into the realm—faster, indeed, than they could be assimilated. Thus, a lenient attitude was adopted with regard to local customs. But a body of royal decrees, known as "capitularies," had to be followed by everyone. Imperial overseers, known as *missi dominici* or "lord's ambassadors," toured the countryside to provide rudimentary centralization of authority, and to see that the capitularies were enforced. If the now dilapidated Roman roads and poor communications prevented constant supervision, it was hoped that the imperial agents could at least raise anxiety over impending visits, remedy a few injustices, and report findings back to the emperor.

Ultimately, however, it was neither Charlemagne's capitularies nor his *missi dominici* that united the Carolingian Europe. Rather it was his insistence that all his subjects accept Roman Catholicism. In our own day, Western nations practice separation of church and state, but such was not the case in the empire of Charlemagne. Those he conquered were frequently given a choice between conversion and the sword. The emperor's favorite book was Augustine's *City of God*, and he considered himself the pope's mentor in the quest to realize a universal godly city on Earth.[75] In a capitulary of 789, he complained that a lack of reliable religious manuals was impeding Christianity's progress.[76] In hopes of remedying this situation, he insisted that the monastic schools adopt a standardized curriculum. He was himself an avid student, even learning the necessary calculations "to investigate the motions of the heavenly bodies most curiously, with an intelligent scrutiny."[77] Though fluent in Latin and passable in Greek, Einhard tells us that the king could not write. Still, a milestone in penmanship was achieved during his reign with the development of "Carolingian miniscule," a stylized non-cursive script, which greatly enhanced the legibility of works copied in monasteries while reducing corruption and loss of information.[78]

Despite these achievements, Frankland was only barely ruled by its ruler. Nor did it long survive his decease. Rome endured for nearly five hundred years after the death of Augustus. By contrast, the Carolingian Empire fell to pieces a mere generation after Charlemagne's demise, and then hobbled into oblivion over the ensuing century.

Yet by spreading what remained of Greco-Roman-Christian culture into Germany, Charlemagne had actually upstaged the Romans.[79] For the first time, says Bemont, "barbarism ... was thrust back beyond the Elbe."[80] Seen in this light, the longevity of the Carolingian Empire is of minor import. Indeed, it would have broken apart sooner if the emperor had had more than one surviving son. But his scheming eldest child, Pippin the Hunchback (who had commanded the Frankish forces in the storming of the ringed fortress of the Avars[81]) had long since been disinherited—ending his days in a monastery after attempting to usurp his father's throne. Of four other sons produced by Hildegard (Charlemagne's favorite bride), Lothar died at birth, while Charles Jr., and another Pippin were carried away by plague. Even the beloved elephant, Abul Abbas, expired before the emperor. Thus, when Charlemagne succumbed, probably to pneumonia after overexerting himself at hunting (January 28, 814), the entire empire was handed over in one piece to his least competent son, Louis—known variably to history as Louis the Pious or Louis the Debonair.

In retrospect, the former diminutive is more apropos. Louis had been crowned by his father, without the intercession of the pope—a direct challenge to papal control over the coronation of kings and emperors. But Louis threw away this advantage by inviting the pope to legitimize his reign in a repeat ceremony after Charlemagne's death. He then purged the court of Charlemagne's concubines and raucous German advisors. Little surprise that the banished favorites became a nucleus of opposition to the new emperor—and they were not alone in their dissatisfaction. On learning that his domains were to be handed over to Lothar (Louis' eldest son and heir-apparent), the emperor's nephew, Bernard, staged a rebellion in Italy. He was defeated and condemned to blinding. But the punishment was inflicted so ineptly that it killed him, whereupon a rueful Louis garnered further contempt with a display of public penance unsuited to his station.

The emperor already had three sons, but a second marriage, to a domineering beauty named Judith, led to the birth of a fourth. At Judith's bidding, Louis attempted to change his will and leave the bulk of the kingdom to his new son, Charles. Rather than be dispossessed, the elder sons took up arms, and challenged their father at Colmar on the Field of Lies (833). No battle was fought. The emperor's army deserted to his rebellious sons, and he himself was imprisoned.

This might have settled matters, but the victorious brats soon became engaged in a bitter rivalry, thus allowing their father to regain power (834). The rest of the reign was marked by unrest. Indeed, when the emperor succumbed to illness in 840, he was again at war with one of his defiant sons—Louis the German. The emperor's official will divided the empire between his eldest son, Lothar, and his youngest son, Charles (the son of Judith—also known as Charles the Bald). Having never relinquished his desire to receive the empire in one piece, Lothar immediately attempted to usurp the domains of his younger stepbrother. Charles countered by entering into league with his other stepbrother—i.e., the disinherited Louis the German. Their forces clashed at Fontenoy (841), where the carnage—40,000 dead in all—was sufficient to end Frankland's reign as Europe's preeminent military power.[82]

Despite the casualty count, the battle achieved no decisive result. Although Lothar had been worsted, he was able to raise new levies amongst the Saxons and Danes. Charles and Louis responded with the Oaths of Strassbourg by which they swore to remain allied (842). Geographically, the war was one of both sides against the middle—with Louis' followers hailing from the Germanic part of the Empire and Charles' inhabiting what had once been Gaul. Indeed, for the soldiery to understand what had been agreed, each prince had to recite the oath in the other's language—Charles in an early Germanic tongue, and Louis in *romance*, the precursor of French.

The overmatched Lothar understood both languages, but couldn't win a battle in either of them. Consequently, he put his signature to the Treaty of Verdun (843)—an agreement that was to shape the course of European history for a millennium. The document awarded the territories that had once comprised Roman Gaul to Charles. There, the blending of Latin and Germanic influences was destined to produce a new people: the French. East of the Rhine, however, there had been little Latin influence, and this territory—left to Louis the German—remained distinctly Teutonic, thus laying the foundation for modern Germany. Between these partitions lay the domain of Lothar, including Italy, Switzerland, Burgundy, Alsace, Lorraine, Belgium and Holland: a thin, indefensible strip extending for a thousand miles down the center of Europe, and destined to be a perpetual Franco-German battleground.[83] As one historian sums it up: "The antagonism of nationalities was a consequence of the treaty of Verdun; not, as has been said, the treaty a consequence of the antagonism of nationalities. By establishing between countries purely German and countries purely French an intermediate state, made up of territories in which the two languages and peoples were mixed, France and Germany were forcibly awakened to a consciousness of themselves."[84] (Put more succinctly by Thatcher and Schwill: "The history of Germany and of France as separate nations begins with 843."[85])

The Barbarian Revival and the Carolingian Decline

With Frankland on the road to fracture and decline, barbarians suddenly appeared on her shores. The Norsemen (i.e., Northmen) of Denmark, Norway and Sweden, whom Charlemagne had not had sufficient means to Christianize, were experiencing a rise in population which the limited supply of arable Scandinavian land could not sustain.[86] The result was wholesale emigration. From Norway, the population expanded westward into Scotland, Ireland, Iceland, Greenland and even North America. Swedish Norsemen descended into Eastern Europe and established themselves as princes of Kievan Russia.[87] Not even Constantinople was safe. From Russia, the Norsemen twice traversed the Black Sea to assault the Byzantine capital.

The Danes targeted their expansion against England and the Frankish kingdoms. For a time, they contented themselves with coastal raids, but soon they adapted their navigational expertise to the broad river networks of Europe, and began pillaging towns well inland. Killed amidst these raids was the era's chief chronicler, the soldier-monk, Nithard, a bastard grandson of Charlemagne, whose skull wound was still evident when his corpse was disinterred and reburied during the 11th century.[88] In 845, a raiding army approached Paris, and executed more than one hundred Frankish hostages outside the walls.[89] An alarmed Charles the Bald handed over a load of silver weighing 7000 pounds to purchase their withdrawal. Soon thereafter, he abandoned all pretense of centralized rule, and issued the Edict of Mersen (847), advising his free subjects to turn to their local lords for protection.[90] The germinal seed of feudalism was thus sown. In France it had been concluded that the safety of the individual could only be assured through an alliance with people of greater influence. A pyramid of power rapidly developed in each locale. The most powerful person, whether a great landowner or ecclesiastic, gained the allegiance of a group of lesser persons by granting them "fiefs" in the form of land or some other sought-after commodity in return for loyalty and military service. The new companions of the leader would then gain similar loyalties below themselves—for example, by hiring tenants to till the soil.[91] Though often termed the feudal "system," the institution varied markedly from one locale to the next.[92]

It was, in the words of G. B. Adams, "confusion roughly organized"[93]—"as chaotic and irregular (say Thatcher and Schwill) as the period in which it arose."[94] As the Viking raids progressed, isolated manors had no choice but to become self-sufficient, and commerce virtually died out as a means of bringing distant communities together. Nor was there circulating written literature. In fine, cultural exchange all but ceased as the once-unified realm of Charlemagne became a dominion of localism.

The Carolingians, meanwhile, were dying off as quickly as their disintegrating patrimony. Lothar died in 855, bequeathing Italy and the imperial crown to Louis II (his eldest son), Provence to Charles (his youngest son), and the rest (i.e., the territory lying between East and West Frankland) to Lothar Jr. (his middle son). When the younger Lothar died in 869, his uncles, Charles the Bald and Louis the German, appropriated his kingdom for themselves—agreeing to its division by the Treaty of Mersen (870).[95] On the heels of this usurpation, Charles the Bald led his cavalrymen to a notable victory over the Norsemen in West Frankland (873). Two years later, on Christmas Day, 875, he obtained the imperial crown. But he died in 877, and his son and successor, Louis the Stammerer, survived him by just two years. The Stammerer's son, Louis III, also met an early death: After gaining his own signal triumph over the Norsemen, he rode headlong into a gate portal while pursuing a favorite concubine. He died of his injuries several days later (882).[96]

Although Charles the Simple, a boy of five, was next in line for the West Frankish throne, the French nobles opted instead for the adult ruler of East Frankland, Charles the Fat, the son and heir of Louis the German. Frankland was thus reunited, but her new ruler proved inept. In 885, the Norsemen descended upon Paris with an armada large enough to encompass a six-mile stretch of the Seine. Although Charles the Fat possessed a large army, he did nothing to succor the beleaguered city—leaving its defense to Count "Eudes"—or "Odo"—the son of a renowned barbarian-fighter named Robert the Strong. Odo persevered against the odds and Charles was deposed for his negligence—Odo being elected in his place (February 888). The Robertian or "Capetian" House thus temporarily supplanted the Carolingian dynasty—a substitution that would become permanent a century later.

Unfortunately for the new ruler, the defense of Paris was a difficult act to follow. Odo's subsequent efforts against the Norsemen were more bloody than successful, and the nobles eventually abandoned him in favor of Charles the Simple, the very prince they had rebuffed at the accession of Charles the Fat. Hoping to purchase peace, the new king granted a portion of northern France to the powerful Norse chieftain, Rollo (911). Rollo accepted baptism as part of this arrangement, but refused a command to kiss Charles' foot as a token of his subservience, saying: "Never will I bend the knee before the knees of any, and I will kiss the foot of none." When the Frankish courtiers insisted, Rollo "ordered one of his warriors to kiss the king's foot. The Northman, remaining bolt upright, took hold of the king's foot, raised it to his mouth, and so made the king fall backward, which caused great bursts of laughter and much disturbance amongst the throng." Charles took the prank in stride, returning "well-satisfied ... to his domains, [while] Rollo departed ... for the town of Rouen" (i.e., the chief city of his new domain).[97]

The agreement at last put paid to the Norse depredations. They ceased their piracy, and behaved, as best they could, like civilized Catholics. In time, the term "Norsemen" was corrupted to "Normans," and Rollo's duchy came to be called "Normandy." But the affair did not go over well with the Franks. In 922, they ousted Charles and handed the throne to Duke Robert, brother of the long-deceased Odo. The following year Robert and Charles met in battle at Soissons. Robert was killed, but Charles lost the battle and was cast into prison, where he eventually died. The crown, meanwhile, fell to Rudolf, the son-in-law of the slain Robert. Once more, the Carolingians had been nudged out, but when Rudolf died childless in 936, they gave it one final fling—capturing and holding the throne until 987, when their last claimant, Louis V, died without heir.

With the support of the Church and the nobility, the Capetians now put forth a new candidate—Hugh Capet, whose accession marks the beginning of a lasting dynasty. The Capetians—the family name actually dates to Hugh, who was called "Capet" because he attired himself in an abbot's cape[98]—would reign in France for the next 340 years, although their authority was markedly hampered for much of that period by the realm's now-entrenched feudalism. Indeed, the first handful of Capetian rulers held less land than many of their vassals, and did well just to hold the crown on their heads.

Otto the Great and the Birth of the Holy Roman Empire

Germany likewise wriggled free of the Carolingians during the 10th century. During the reign of Charles the Fat, Charles the Simple had taken sanctuary with the ruler's illegitimate and rebellious nephew, Arnulf. When Charles the Fat was overthrown, Arnulf seized the throne of East Frankland and led his minions to a crushing victory over the Danes on the River Dyle (891).[99] His victory was so decisive that the barbarian threat to East Frankland ought to have ended then and there. Unfortunately, the Vikings were not the only marauders in the neighborhood. Looming on the Eastern Frontier was an army of Hungarian Magyars. Just before AD 900, they crossed into East Frankland, subjecting the Germans and Italians in their path to horrid atrocities. Entire villages were laid waste—the men being exterminated, and the women taken as war brides. Rumor accused the Magyars of being wild men who drank the blood and devoured the hearts of their victims, and their Finnic speech—as alarming as it was alien—made the most outrageous claims appear true.[100] Swarming into Bavaria, the frenzied horse archers exterminated the Bavarian nobility in a single battle (July 6, 907).[101] Unable to resist them in the field, the Germans sought sanctuary within walled towns.

Defeat was followed by anarchy, and all was made worse by the fact that Arnulf's successor in East Frankland was a boy of six, named Louis the Child. The dukes of Saxony, Swabia, Franconia and Bavaria—the four major duchies of which Germany was composed—promptly arrogated power to themselves at the expense of the crown, and when Louis the Child died without issue at the age of eighteen (911), the enfeebled Carolingian House ceased to reign in Germany.

The powerful dukes now elected one of their own—Duke Conrad of Franconia—to serve as king. Conrad promptly attempted to assert his authority over those who had elected him, but with so little success that at his death (918) his brother and heir chose not to claim the throne.[102] Consequently, the dukes held a new election and bestowed the crown on Henry of Saxony—also called "the Fowler" since he was out hawking when told of his elevation.[103] Henry declined to have his enthronement consecrated by the church, choosing instead to rule on the basis of his election alone as a "feudal" king. Unlike Conrad, he was determined to govern in collaboration with the dukes—leaving them independent within their own duchies in return for their fealty and military allegiance.[104]

The Magyars, meanwhile, continued their marauding, and as Henry had no means of combatting them in the field, he purchased an end to their aggressions with the payment of tribute (924). A respite of nine years was gained thereby, during which time Henry placed one-ninth of his soldiery in the Saxon towns, preparing fortifications and assembling grain stores to create a place of refuge for the locals in time of invasion. At the same time, he drilled his infantry in the art of horsemanship and the use of the lance.[105] The new tactics were tried out upon the Slavs, from whom Henry seized Brandenburg and Prague.[106]

Henry "the Fowler," engraved by C. Deucker, 1859 (© Depositphotos.com/Georgios Kollidas).

By 933, his preparations were complete. Instead of the annual tribute payment, he sent the Magyars a dead dog, signaling that the time had come to fight.[107] "My companions," cried Henry as the hostile armies confronted each other near Merseberg, "maintain your ranks, receive on your bucklers the first arrows of the Pagans, and prevent their second discharge by the equal and rapid career of your lances."[108] So well did his lancers carry out these instructions, that the panicked Hungarians dropped their accouterments and galloped away in flight.[109] A year later, Henry beat the Danes and seized Schleswig.

Henry died three years after his victory over the Magyars, but the "Saxon" dynasty he founded continued under his son, Otto I (also known as Otto the Great, ruled AD 936–973). As his first acts, Otto had the church anoint him king and announced that Aachen, the capital of Charlemagne, would serve as the royal seat.[110] Having thus intimated that he would not rule like his father as a feudal king, he imposed his authority on the fractious duchies—replacing the Franconian and Bavarian dukes with his own relatives. Next, he subdued the Slavs and Czechs on his eastern frontier, establishing an archbishopric at Magdeburg to Christianize them.

Amidst these varied preoccupations, Otto failed to notice the rapid resurgence of the Hungarians, who capitalized on his inattentiveness to make astonishing forays across the breadth of Germany and into France.[111] In 955, the Hungarians surprised Otto in Bavaria at Lechfeld, near Augsburg—crossing the River Lech to seize his baggage train from behind. The Saxons found themselves surrounded on broken ground, but a fierce charge by Otto's valorous son-in-law, Duke Conrad the Red, drove the Magyars back.[112] Thrown into disorder, the reeling Hungarians found that their surprise foray across the Lech had left them without an escape route. Trapped with the river at their back, says Gibbon, "their past cruelties excluded them from the hope of mercy. Three captive princes were hanged at Ratisbon, the multitude of prisoners was slain or mutilated, and the fugitives who presumed to appear in the face of their country were condemned to everlasting poverty and disgrace."[113] Although Conrad was mortally wounded (he was struck in the throat by an arrow after unfastening his cuirass to catch his breath[114]), Otto's victory was decisive.

With the frontier secure, Otto turned his attention to Italy. The Mediterranean had not escaped the era of invasion. Once a "Roman lake," the sea had been overrun by Arab corsairs. Sicily was seized in turn by the Omayyads of Spain and the fanatical Shiites of Egypt. The latter raided the coast of Italy, throwing the southern half of the peninsula into chaos.

Things were little better in northern Italy, where rival claimants had reduced the Lombard kingdom to chaos, nor in the center, where Rome itself had become a hotbed of factionalism. Elected by the city's unruly nobles, the popes were now hardly more than pawns. By the early-10th century, their authority had fallen into the manipulative hands of Theodora and Marozia, a Machiavellian mother and daughter who had accrued vast influence by way of the bedroom. In the papal annals, their ascendancy is revered as the "Rule of Harlots."

Theodora was the wife of a patrician serving at the Lateran (the precursor of the Vatican), but in her spare time, she lavished her attentions on Pope John X, who owed his position to her patronage.[115] Marozia, however, was not nearly so fond of Pope John, and on eclipsing her mother, she had him suffocated (928).[116] "A rare genealogy"[117] now ascended St. Peter's throne. Over the next one and a quarter centuries, Marozia's illegitimate son, her grandson, two great grandsons, and one great-great grandson would wear the papal miter.[118] Of this ludicrous troupe, it was the second, John XII, who most studiously "renounced the dress and decencies of his profession."[119] Says Gibbon of this ignoble pontiff, "We read with some surprise that the worthy grandson of Marozia lived in public adultery with the matrons of Rome; that the Lateran palace was turned into a school for prostitution; and that his rapes of virgins and widows had deterred the female pilgrims from visiting the tomb of St. Peter, lest, in the devout act, they should be violated by his successor."[120]

By 962, the authority of this unworthy prelate was near collapse. Desperate for succor, he turned to the Saxon king, Otto I, now Europe's supreme monarch, offering to proclaim him emperor in return for material support. Otto already had some experience in Italian politics. Years before, he had brought an army into the peninsula on the very chivalrous pretext of rescuing a captive princess whom he subsequently married. (Not out of love, it should be noted. The girl held a claim to the Lombard throne, which, by their nuptials, passed to Otto.) Anxious, now, to secure his position in Italy, Otto cheerfully obeyed the papal summons, stopping off en route to appropriate the iron crown of the Lombards.

When he reached St. Peter's, a grateful Pope John fulfilled his promise. On February 2, 962, he crowned the Saxon king as Europe's first "Holy Roman" Emperor. Pope John might, however, have been less hasty; for no sooner was the crown atop Otto's head, than the papal miter was removed from his own. Otto had insisted that the pontiff abandon his profligacy. The latter refused, and schemed to find himself another emperor. Otto, therefore, placed him on trial for his immorality, and deposed him.[121] Here was a stunning precedent. Under the Carolingians, the papacy had established itself as the sanctifier of royal authority. Now Otto had seized the prerogative in making and unmaking popes. When duty called Otto back to Germany, John managed to reinstate himself, but within the year he was dead—murdered by the husband of one of his mistresses.[122] He was twenty-seven years old.

Henry IV vs. Hildebrand: The Investiture Controversy

By the time Otto died in 973, the Church had become the leading instrument of his authority. He alone chose candidates for the German bishoprics, and with the bishops in his pocket he was able to solidify his hegemony over Germany's tribal dukes.[123] Likewise, the campaign of 962 had delivered much of northern and central Italy into the Ottonian orbit, leaving only southern Italy outside the pale. To redress this last imbalance, Otto II (Otto's son and successor; ruled, 973-983) invaded the south in 982. But the expedition ended in disaster. At Stilo, the Saracens annihilated the emperor's army—the emperor himself swimming to the safety of a nearby ship. (Finding that the vessel was Byzantine, he dove back into the water and swam on.)[124] A year later, he succumbed to disease at the tender age of 28, leaving a three-year-old boy—Otto III (ruled, 983-1002)—as heir to the throne.

This latest in the succession of Ottos matured into an ardent admirer of Charlemagne—so much so, that in AD 1000, he opened the great emperor's crypt to gaze upon his remains, and did not close it again until he had stolen a ring from the corpse's finger, which he wore until his dying day.[125] Little wonder, then, that the overriding dream of his life was to reestablish a true Western Roman Empire as his hero had almost done. Toward this end, he elevated Gerbert of Aurillac (i.e., Pope Sylvester II) to St. Peter's chair (999). Gerbert, a former Archbishop of Rheims, was an accomplished mathematician who introduced the abacus to Europe and promoted the adoption of Arabic numerals after learning of them from contacts with the Spanish Omayyads.[126] Together, pope and emperor aspired to bring an end to the prevailing factionalism in Rome—Otto because he wanted to establish the city as the capital of his new Roman Empire, Gerbert because he wished to restore the temporal power of the papacy as laid out in the centuries-old Donation of Pippin. Despite these inharmonious ambitions, the pair managed to subdue the city's fractious nobility[127]—including Crescentius (the most vexing of their opponents) whom they beheaded. Unfortunately, Otto presumed to take Crescentius' widow as his mistress, and she, feigning supplication, poisoned the twenty-two year old emperor to foil his Roman designs (1002).[128] With the emperor dead, imperial authority disintegrated, and Otto's retainers had to keep their swords drawn to escape the peninsula with his corpse.[129] Gerbert died the following year.

Two decades after Otto's abortive effort to resurrect Rome, the "Saxon" dynasty founded by Henry the Fowler died out and was superseded by the "Salian" (1024). The Church, too, underwent a metamorphosis. For more than a century, she had been attempting to reform herself from within. As early as AD 910, a new monastic order based in the French town of Cluny had dedicated itself to the restoration of religious sanctity. Soon, other monasteries embraced the cause, until, by the end of the 11th century, Pope Gregory VII

(1073–1085, formerly the archdeacon Hildebrand) felt the time ripe to institute the so-called "Cluniac Reforms."[130] Determined to prevent a recurrence of the "Rule of Harlots," the reformers forced upon the Church the oath of celibacy that remains in force to this day. (The more cynical among us might associate the celibacy vow—and its corollary prohibition on marriage and begetting a family—with the Church's concern that a prelate controlling Church property might bequeath the land to a secular son, thereby annulling the Church's title.[131]) The reformers likewise forbade "simony" (i.e., the selling of Church offices). But the main impact of the Cluniac Reforms was political, for it was on their account that the "Investiture Controversy" arose.

With the demise of the Ottonians, the Roman nobility resumed its prerogative in electing popes—a situation that degenerated, in 1046, into complete anarchy, with three popes simultaneously claiming Saint Peter's chair, and a fourth (chosen by the emperor to supersede them all) apparently murdered.[132] To avert further mayhem, papal electioneering was transferred to the College of Cardinals (1059). What remained at issue, however, was the appointment of Europe's bishops. In the renewed milieu of piety, the pope held that these were his agents, and that Europe's spiritual unity depended upon their allegiance to him. But matters were not so simple. Most European bishops possessed extensive ecclesiastical estates, given to them as fiefs by the temporal lords or kings who had hitherto enjoyed the privilege of nominating them to their posts. Indeed, pliant tools in the bishoprics had been a cornerstone of royal authority since the reign of Otto I. Were popes to assume a monopoly on ordaining these clerics, and were the latter, in consequence, to transfer their temporal loyalties to the Holy See, the lay rulers of Europe stood to lose control over more than a quarter of their domains—a usurpation they were not likely to take lying down.[133]

The battle lines were thus drawn for the Investiture Controversy—a medieval power struggle of enormous temporal import. The crisis was reached during the reign of King Henry IV who ascended the throne of Germany at age six (1056). The German nobility attempted to increase their own privileges at the expense of this child, and it was not until 1075, with a victory on the Unstrutt, that Henry was able to put them in their place. His victory was immediately undercut, however, by word from Rome that the right of investiture (i.e., the ceremony in which bishops were officially invested with their powers) would henceforth be reserved to the Church. Henry blatantly refused to comply with a measure that would deprive him of a key pillar of support. In answer to Gregory's decree, he sent a letter opening with the salutation: "Henry, King not by usurpation but by holy ordination of God, to Hildebrand, now no Pope but false monk."[134] Unacquainted with this particular brand of cordiality, the "false monk" decided to issue a writ of excommunication—probably before he was done reading Henry's letter.

If Henry had failed to anticipate this predictable response, his mutinous vassals did not hesitate to exploit it. Forming a league against their wounded king, they declared that his throne would be forfeit if he could not convince Gregory to lift his ban within the year. Henry made clear his willingness to repent, but the pope announced that he would not amend his decision until he had discussed the matter with the German nobles, whereupon he set out from Rome to confer with them.[135] Henry well understood that if his nobles put the right deal on the table, the pope would hang him out to dry. In the end, only his knowledge of Church protocol saved him. Knowing that the pope could not withhold his pardon from a willing penitent, Henry intercepted Gregory at Canossa before the latter had had an opportunity to reach Germany, and stood barefoot outside his quarters dressed in rags until the reluctant pontiff agreed to rescind the excommunication (January 1077).

Pope Gregory had won the battle but he had lost the war. Free from the papal ban, Henry garnered enough support to fend off the nobility (who tried twice to supplant him with rival claimants) and to renew the struggle over investiture. A second excommunication (1080) was unavailing. Betrayed once, the nobility would no longer do the pope's bidding. Henry marched on Rome and placed Gregory under siege until the latter's Norman "ally," Robert Guiscard, drove him off. Unfortunately, once Henry was gone, Guiscard's troops sacked the city they had come to save, and Pope Gregory was forced to flee the now hostile populace. He died at Salerno, lamenting his exile to the last (1085).

It has been argued that Pope Gregory was driven to embark upon the Investiture Controversy out of the highest motives. The guiding aspiration of his life, we are told, was the establishment of the *civitas Dei*—"City of God" on Earth—led in righteousness by the Church and its infallible agent, the pope.[136] Toward this end, he sought to disentangle his clergy from worldly pursuits. The decree of 1059, deputing the election of popes to the College of Cardinals, accomplished as much for the papacy by making election to the papal office independent of the empire and the Roman mob. The investiture struggle, along with the outlawry of simony and of clerical marriage, helped sever similar base ties between secularism and the lesser clergy.[137]

In sum, Gregory believed "that the only way to rule the world was by means of a clergy that had renounced the world."[138] His dying words in Salerno are said to have been, "I have loved justice and hated iniquity, therefore I die in exile."[139] But if his goals were righteous, the reader will nonetheless detect a strain of hypocrisy and ambition in a pontiff who allowed himself to be proclaimed pope by popular acclamation at Rome without deference to the College of Cardinals' new electoral prerogatives (which he himself had helped frame while still an archdeacon), or who relied on a collection of forgeries—some old (i.e., the Donation of Constantine and the Pseudo-Isidorean Decretals), some new—to support his professed authority to veto contrary Church council rulings, issue infallible decrees and excommunicate malevolent lay rulers.[140]

As for his part, Henry IV continued to fight the investiture struggle until his death in 1106, pitting his own notion of centralized imperial authority against the Church's dream of a universal City of God on Earth. By 1122, however, the opposing sides were so exhausted that they finally agreed to a compromise—the so-called Concordat of Worms—whereby the new Emperor, Henry V, restored certain properties appropriated from the Church, and deferred to the Pope in the selection and ceremonial investiture of bishops. In return, Pope Calixtus II conceded that, as landowners, the bishops stood to influence worldly affairs, and that the emperor ought thus to attend the investiture ceremony in order to endow the nominee with the temporal authority incumbent upon his office, and to receive, in return, the nominee's oath of fealty in all non-spiritual matters.

1066

It has now been nearly 1,000 years since England was last successfully invaded—an oddity of sorts given the number of times she was invaded in the 1,000 years before that.

In the 1st century AD, the Romans gave the population a good thrashing, and then set up a civilized province of trading towns and centrally heated country villas that the citizenry rather liked.[141] For two centuries, the province's tranquility was preserved by Hadrian's Wall, but during the 360s AD, the barrier was breached by the Scottish Picts who laid waste the country villas and sent the populace scurrying into walled towns for safety. There was no security for a generation, until Stilicho, the famed Roman general, arrived to repair the ramparts (AD 399).[142]

A decade after this, however, the entire Roman garrison had to be withdrawn for continental service against the rampaging Goths and Vandals (AD 409). The Picts again ravaged Britain, and the latter's pained entreaties for Roman assistance went unanswered. With few alternatives, the Britons invited the pagan Angles, Saxons and Jutes to cross to the island from Germany. The Germans halted the Picts, but finding the Britons ripe for plunder, they proceeded to conquer the island for themselves. According to Bede: "Public as well as private structures were overturned; the priests were everywhere slain before the alters; the prelates and people ... were destroyed with fire and sword; nor was there any to bury those who had been thus cruelly slaughtered. Some of the miserable remainder, being taken in the mountains, were butchered in heaps. Others, spent with hunger, came forth and submitted themselves to the enemy for food, being destined to undergo perpetual servitude, if they were not killed even upon the spot."[143]

The progress of the Anglo-Saxons was temporarily halted at Badon Hill (AD 500), where the Britons won a stunning victory that the chronicler Nennius attributes to a living, breathing Artorius, or Arthur.[144] Ultimately, however, the German trespassers emerged victorious, and Britain was transformed into Angle-land or "England."[145]

It took another invasion of sorts—this one carried out by Gregory the Great's Benedictine monks—to convert the new pagan rulers to Roman Catholicism. But even in this pious labor, the sword played its part. In 655, King Oswy—a Celtic Christian who had recently reunited the fragmented lands north of the River Humber into a single "Northumbria"—routed the powerful pagan army of Mercia on the banks of the River Winwaed. By the time Oswy eschewed the Celtic creed (with its devil-may-care attitude toward calculating the date of Easter) in favor of Roman Catholicism at the Synod of Whitby (664), Northumbria had become the dominant power, and Catholicism the dominant religion, on the island. Alas, only one of these developments was to be of lasting import. For, hardly had the Whitby decision brought England into the orbit of Western European Christendom, when Oswy's successor, Egfrid, was ambushed in an ill-fated attempt to subdue the Picts (685). With him perished the flower of the Northumbrian army, and thereafter, England existed as a confusion of small kingdoms—the most powerful being the very Mercia that King Oswy had subdued in 655.

Located south of Northumbria, in the center of England, Mercia spread her dominion over the entire southeast, including Kent. Offa, her last great king, added a portion of Wales to the realm—cementing the new boundary with a dyke of imposing length. He also minted his own coins—including a gold *dinar* cast from an Arabic die, whose ornamental Arabic lettering, indecipherable at the time, proclaimed Allah to be God and Mohammed his messenger. (The papacy unwittingly accepted some of these coins when Offa paid his annual tribute to Rome.)[146]

At Offa's death (796), Charlemagne—who had never got on well with the Mercians—

championed the claim of Egbert, the king of rival Wessex, who had lived in exile at the Frankish court for thirteen years. With Charlemagne's help, Egbert returned to England (802) and began a career of conquest that, by 828, made him master of the island.

Unfortunately, by this time, the Danes had begun to arrive. They were first sighted in Dorset, where a customs collector mistook them for salesmen and insisted that they pay the usual tariff (787).[147] The Danes hewed him to bits and embarked on a career of conquest. By 850, they had plundered London twice. In 865, they ransacked Kent, in 866, East Anglia, in 867, Northumbria, and, in 868, mighty Mercia.[148] In 870, they captured King Edmund of East Anglia, tied him to a tree, shot him full of arrows and threw his head into a shrubbery.[149] Having subdued all local resistance, they turned south to chastise the Saxons. But here they encountered their first worthy opponent—the Saxon king of Wessex, Alfred the Great (ruled AD 871–899).

The rivals came to grips at Ashdown, where Alfred—then but a prince—seized the initiative and led a victorious uphill charge while his pious brother, King Ethelred, attended morning prayers. The next battle was a defeat in which King Ethlered incurred mortal wounds (871). Alfred succeeded him, but was defeated in his turn at Wilton a month later. There followed four years of uneasy truce, and three years of desultory fighting. Then came disaster. During the Twelfth Night celebration of 878, Alfred's army was taken by surprise at Chippenham and put to rout. For four months, the king hid in the thickets with a handful of followers. But in April, he reassembled his forces, and defeated the Danes at Edington— a victory so decisive that Guthrum, the Danish chieftain, accepted baptism.

A staunch advocate of learning, Alfred sought to reverse the slide into ignorance that had afflicted the island since the end of the Northumbrian Renaissance. He established a court school modeled on that of Charlemagne, issued his own law code and became facile enough at Latin to translate Bede's *Ecclesiastical History*, Boethius' *Consolations of Philosophy* and Pope Gregory's *Pastoral Care* by his own hand.[150] He might also have learned from his studies the phalanx tactics of ancient warfare—for, while the battle of Ashdown (871) had been won by a furious charge, Alfred is said to have held the Danes at bay for an extended period with a rampart of shields in defeating them at Edington seven years later.[151]

In 886, Alfred drove the Danes out of London. He then negotiated a treaty that (i) recognized a Danish sphere of influence—the so-called "Danelaw"—in northeastern England, and (ii) set equal value on the lives of Danes and Englishmen (hitherto, the Danes had felt themselves superior). The treaty held firm for six years. But in 892, Danish pirates sparked a four-year war after crossing over from the continent in two separate fleets. The war ended in 896, when Alfred sealed off the Thames to maroon the invaders after they strayed too far inland along its course. In the same year, Alfred commissioned the construction of a coastguard of "long-ships" to prevent further Norse landings. Within the year, the new fleet cornered a Danish squadron off the Isle of Wight.[152] Most of the Danes got away, and not a few of the long-ships ran aground due to poor seamanship, but a pair of enemy vessels were captured, and their crews were sent to the gibbet.[153]

Although Alfred died in 899, his worthy successors brought the Danes to heel on the battlefields of Tettenhall (910) and Brunanburh (937). By the mid–10th century, the realm was unified and at peace. Sadly, in 979, the throne fell to Ethelred the Unready, a weakling who had somehow insinuated his way into the otherwise remarkable gene pool of Alfred the Great. At almost the same hour, the mainland Danes decided to make another excursion to the island. Ethelred levied a tax, called the "danegeld," in an effort to buy them off. The Danes took the money but continued their depredations, while their fellows in Denmark, hearing of the payout, continued to invade in droves. In retaliation, Ethelred ordered the indiscriminate slaughter of his own indigenous Danish population (1002). It is not exactly clear what he hoped to accomplish by this peculiar policy. What is clear is that it backfired. The Danish king's sister was among the dead, and, to avenge her, the Danes redoubled their attacks. More territory slipped from Ethelred's grasp, and in the end, the king had to flee with his Norman wife to Normandy (1013). He returned three years later only to drop dead, whereupon Canute the Great of Denmark usurped the English throne.

For a time, Canute's rule was hindered by the heroics of Ethelred's son, Edmund Ironside. But Edmund died mysteriously after a defeat at Asses Hill, and for the next two decades, Canute reigned with impunity. During this interlude, he inherited Denmark's throne, and conquered Norway's—thus putting himself in the remarkable position of ruling three kingdoms at once. Sad to say, his heirs could not sustain this impressive empire—in part because Norway immediately rebelled,[154] and in part because within seven years, all of his heirs were dead.

The stage was thus set for the return of the Wessex line of English kings. When the last Danish heir died (1042), Ethelred's son, Edward the Confessor, returned from exile in Normandy to reclaim the throne of his forefathers. His pious reign encompassed twenty-four years of ceaseless prayer, during which time it apparently did not occur to him to carry out the labor of producing an heir. In the momentous year of 1066, he died without issue, leaving the succession to be contested amongst three pretenders: Harold of England who, under Edward, had occupied an office akin to Mayor of the Palace; Harald Hardrada (i.e., "the Ruthless"[155]) of Norway, a bloodthirsty veteran of the Byzantine and Russian armies who had been enticed into the fray by Harold of England's dispossessed and deranged brother, Tostig[156]; and William "the Bastard"[157] of Normandy (the illegitimate progeny of the previous Norman duke, Robert "the Devil," and a tanner's daughter named Arletta) who believed he held the strongest claim of all since Edward the Confessor had allegedly willed the country to him. (This is said to have occurred when William visited England in 1051.)

King Alfred the Great of Wessex, 19th century engraving (© Depositphotos.com/Georgios Kollidas).

And the plot gets thicker still. For, in 1064, Harold of England had managed to wreck his ship near the coast of Normandy. Apprehended by one of William's vassals, he had been thrown in prison. William promptly freed him. The two became fast friends—even serving together on a minor military campaign wherein Harold helped drag several Normans from a pool of quicksand.[158] Before departing, Harold (allegedly) forswore his claim to the throne in favor of his rescuer—perhaps in gratitude for his salvation, or, more likely, to secure his freedom from an amicable imprisonment at William's hands.

Despite William's claims, Harold was something of a local favorite. Not only was he a longtime resident of Wessex, but he had been designated as the rightful successor by the English *witan* (i.e., council of wise men)—whose job it was to arbitrate in cases of an empty throne. Push, of course, was not long in coming to shove. Harald of Norway landed in northeastern England with the treasonous Tostig in tow, burnt Scarborough, beat the Northumbrians at Fulford, and proceeded to march on York. While waiting at Stamford Bridge to receive the city's surrender, however, Harald and Tostig were surprised to behold the approach of a cloud of dust and a "forest of lances." It was the army of England, from which a party of knights galloped forth, one asking:

> "'Where is Earl Tostig, son of Godwin?' 'He is here!' cried Tostig. 'Your brother salutes you,' rejoined the Saxon; 'he offers you peace, friendship and your former honors.' 'This is a sensible offer,' said Tostig; 'and ... what does he offer to my noble ally, King Harald?' 'Seven feet of English soil,' haughtily replied the warrior, contemplating the Norwegian's huge person; 'a little more, perhaps, for he is taller than most men.' 'Then,' cried Tostig 'my brother, King Harold, may prepare for the fray.'
>
> "The Saxons retired slowly. Tostig was still looking fixedly at his antagonist. 'Who is the warrior with such a proud tongue?' asked Hadrada. 'King Harold, son of Godwin,' said Tostig. 'Why did you not tell me so?' cried Hadrada; 'he would not have lived to boast of having defeated us.'"[159]

Battle was joined forthwith—Harold of England obtaining a victory of such proportions that the invading army, which had come to the England in three hundred ships, required but twenty-four to sail home.[160] Both Harald Hardrada and Tostig were killed—the former being felled by an arrow in the neck. (Since they had not expected a fight that morning, neither man had bothered to don his protective chain mail.)[161]

Harold of England had won a great victory. Alas, he had no time to celebrate it. For hardly was his sword sheathed before he was apprised of a second invasion. Hastening southwards, he collided with William of Normandy at Hastings. The date was October 14, 1066.

In the new contest, Harold occupied the better ground—the ridge of Senlac Hill. He also possessed a superior body of infantry in his housecarls, whom he positioned in the center of his line with militia on either flank. In total, he commanded about 8000 men. William had no more, but he did possess archers and cavalry (which Harold lacked).[162] To begin the festivities, the Normans staged a frontal assault, only to be chased back down the ridge by Harold's militia. Rumor announced that William had been killed, but he soon resurfaced at the head of a second, more fearsome assault. Although this one produced a heated exchange with the housecarls, it, too, was thrown back.

Frontal assaults having gotten him nowhere, William resorted to a trick. He ordered his cavalry forward against the militia on Harold's left, and, after a short scuffle, had them

Panel from the Bayeux Tapestry depicting a scene from the Battle of Hastings, Bayeux, Normandy, France (© Depositphotos.com/Joris Van Ostaeyen).

withdraw again in mock disorder. The undisciplined militia took the bait, and pursued the cavalry down the ridge. Once they had been lured onto the marshy plain below, however, the Norman cavalry wheeled about, and put them to slaughter. This done, William ordered his archers to fire a high volley at the housecarls. According to one chronicler, so heavily did the arrows rain down, that those on the receiving end cowered beneath their shields with their eyes squeezed shut.[163] Before they could recover, William's horsemen had galloped back up the hill and fallen upon them. Harold, still fighting, was struck in the eye by a descending arrow, and then hewn in pieces by the swarming foe. It was more than the housecarls could bear. They quit the field in panic, leaving the kingdom to the Normans.

Since the countryside was soon knotted with castles garrisoned by the overbearing and brutish Normans who laid everything waste and put down all resistance by the sword, it is generally agreed that 1066 was not one of England's better years. As master of the realm, William, now surnamed "the Conqueror," taxed his new subjects down to the last cow—keeping a record of everyone's slightest possession for just this purpose in his so-called *Domesday Book*. All landholders—or at least those who had not had their lands filched outright (as all too many did)[164]—were forced to swear allegiance to William, as were England's bishops, who were invested in their offices not by the pope (controversies on the continent notwithstanding), but by their king.

The First Crusade: Europe Becomes Offensive

To balance William's conquest of England, the rest of the Normans conquered southern Italy. In 1016, a shipwreck deposited a group of Normans on the Italian shore near Salerno. They had been on their voyage home after a pilgrimage to the Holy Land, but

Salerno's inhabitants prevailed upon them to remain and drive off the bands of Saracen raiders who had become the bane of the port. On completing this godly task, the pilgrims returned to France with fond remembrances of the blissful anarchy they had witnessed in southern Italy. Their glowing descriptions could not but serve as a temptation to their daring Norman brothers back home, and within a few decades every brigand in the valley of the Seine was marching south with visions of pillage and plunder.[165] Led by popular nobles such as Robert Guiscard (i.e., Robert "the Cunning"[166]), whom we met in the last section, these enthusiastic marauders staked a claim to almost everything south of Rome. The papacy, however, had its own claim upon this region, and in 1053, Pope Leo IX raised an army to defend his interests. Guiscard defeated and captured the pontiff at Civitate—making up for the impiety by swearing fealty to the Holy See. As part of this transaction, a number of revenue-rich Italian properties belonging to the Byzantine emperor were trodden underfoot by the Normans and handed over to Pope Leo. Constantinople's patriarch promptly demanded their restitution to the emperor. The papacy refused to comply, with the result that the two sides excommunicated one another—thus inaugurating the schism between the Roman and Greek Churches that exists down to our own day (1054).

Relations between the papacy and the Normans, however, could not have been better. In 1059, Robert Guiscard received the pope's blessing for his continuing usurpations in southern Italy (1059). Indeed, for good measure, the papacy presented Robert with the island of Sicily—a somewhat peculiar gift, given that the Saracens ruled Sicily and the Holy See had no authority there. Not one to be deterred by technicalities, Guiscard dispatched an army to the island under the command of his brother, Roger.

The cordiality between East and West was by no means enhanced by these carryings on, and matters only degenerated when Guiscard betook himself to conquer the Byzantine Empire. As we related in Section I, the Norman won a notable victory at Durazzo (1081), but before he could capitalize on it, Pope Gregory VII summoned him back to Rome to save the city from Henry IV of Germany (who had been bribed to attack Rome by the Byzantines).

Just when hostilities seemed certain to escalate, however, the death of Guiscard and events in the Holy Land conspired to soften the bitterness of the East-West rivalry. The Abbasid Sunnites had long ruled the Holy Land from Baghdad, but, in the 11th century, the rival Fatimid Shiites of Egypt seized the district along with much of Syria. At the same hour, an army of fanatical Turkish converts to Islam—the Seljuks—stormed into Baghdad from the east. Unable to resist the tide, the Abbasid Caliph came up with the very good idea of bestowing the title "sultan" upon the Seljuk leader, while deputing him to prosecute the war against the Fatimids.

En route to the Holy Land the Seljuks inflicted a disastrous defeat on the Byzantines at Manzikert (1071). Shortly afterwards, they conquered the greater part of Asia Minor—and so matters stood for a generation. But by AD 1095, the Byzantine emperor, Alexius I Comnenus, was contemplating the reconquest of Asia Minor,[167] and in pursuit of this scheme, he sent ambassadors to Piacenza, where Pope Urban II had convened a general church council. The Byzantine ambassadors were instructed to seek the pope's assistance in raising a moderate-sized army of Western mercenaries. Arguing that it would be better "to repel the barbarians on the confines of Asia, rather than to expect them in the heart of Europe," the envoys obtained a ready hearing.[168] Urban, however, decided to expand upon

Alexius' program; for he saw in the Byzantine petition a chance to rid Europe of the barbarians who already resided there—i.e., the continent's fractious knights and nobles whose incessant brawls and skirmishes in the name of chivalry had put the "feud" into "feudalism." Decades earlier, the church had attempted to put a brake on private warfare by enacting the "Truce of God" (~1050), which forbade such antics from sundown each Wednesday to sunrise each Monday.[169] But the effect had been modest at best, and Urban now perceived an alternative remedy. Rumors were already current at this time of Seljuk atrocities against Christian pilgrims to the Holy Land. Hence, on convening a second council—at Clermont—in the autumn of 1095, Urban could cite reports "of an accursed ... race wholly alienated from God," who had left the holy places "irreverently polluted with the filth of the unclean." Upon this pretext, he invoked a "Holy War" to rescue Christ's Sepulcher from the infidels. Lamenting that Christians should kill one another when they ought to be killing the unbeliever, he declared, "Let hatred therefore depart from among you, let your quarrels end, let wars cease, and let ... controversies slumber. Enter upon the road to the Holy Sepulcher; wrest that land from the wicked race and subject it to yourselves." His plea seized the imagination of the assembly, moving the multitude of listeners to cry in unison: "It is the will of God!"[170]

For a fleeting moment, the papacy had become the beacon of a unified Christendom. News of the "crusade" spread like wildfire. While Urban animated the nobility, a peculiar figure named Peter the Hermit, who sported a beard that fell to his waist,[171] and who smelled very much like the donkey upon which he rode,[172] inflamed the common folk. Soon, there was no need for preaching at all, for the people scarcely spoke except to exhort one another.[173] The response, says William of Malmsbury, surpassed all expectation: "The Welshman left his hunting; the Scotch his fellowship with vermin; the Dane his drinking party; the Norwegian his raw fish."[174] Nor had Pope Urban hurt recruitment by offering a "plenary indulgence" or "full remission of sin" to those who took the cross. "At the voice of their pastor," says Gibbon "the robber, the incendiary, the homicide, arose by thousands to redeem their souls by repeating on the infidels the same deeds which they had exercised against their Christian brethren."[175] It was a fine way for Europe to be rid of such ne'er-do-wells, but their exodus did not augur well for Asia.

An unruly throng carried out the initial campaign. In anticipation of the coming debacle against the Muslims, the cast of this so-called People's Crusade (1096) tested their mettle against lesser infidels. Thus, the unsuspecting Jews of Speyer, Worms, Mainz, Cologne, Prague and Ratisbon became the object of merciless, unprovoked pogroms which the civic leaders and clergy were powerless to stop (though many risked their lives in the attempt).[176] Barred from participation in the guilds, many medieval Jews had become successful moneylenders, and the debtors of Germany happily served as guides for crusaders seeking the nearest Jewish Quarter.[177] Peter the Hermit played no role in these pogroms. The group he led did not molest the Jews. The chief perpetrator was the German Count Emico of Leningen, who had no affiliation with Peter, though two of Peter's associates, Gottschalk and Fulcher, were behind the attacks in Ratisbon and Prague.

The wholesale slaughter of defenseless Jews proved such a confidence-builder that on experiencing the unfamiliar babbling of the Hungarian Magyars a bit further down the road, Count Emico's crusaders did not hesitate to issue their battle cry anew.[178] But peculiar language or no, the Hungarians were already Catholic. They had renounced shamanism under duress during the reign of their saint-king, Stephen I, on New Year's Day 1001. Truth be told, the conversion had not gone well. Indeed, when Stephen finally died in 1038, the Hungarians stuffed his chief minister into a barrel and lobbed him into the Danube to make clear their continuing dissatisfaction. But by 1095, Catholics they definitely were, and they took vehement issue with this new attempt to convert them forcibly to a religion that they already practiced. They fought back, and in the ensuing donnybrook Emico's legions were annihilated.

On the heels of this debacle, Peter the Hermit arrived in Hungary with his own throng of Christian warriors. Relations were at first cordial, but a crusader's attempt to purchase a pair of shoes led to a slight quibble which soon degenerated into open warfare, in which the crusaders exacted some forty casualties for every one of their own.[179] They could not, however, sustain this level of success. On reaching Nish, they were routed by the Bulgars who seized Peter's war chest—a setback that reduced the bearded holy man to tears.[180] The survivors trod on to Constantinople.

Stained glass window depicting Crusaders, Cathedral of Tours, France (© Depositphotos.com/Joris Van Ostaeyen).

Emperor Alexius had not envisioned an uncontrollable rabble when he first applied for mercenary support from the West. He had gone to bed a statesman seeking a modest military alliance and had awoken (in the phrasing of *Encyclopædia Britannica*) "a magician, who has uttered a charm to summon a ministering spirit, and is surrounded on the instant by a legion of demons."[181] He knew not how to cope with this cruel metamorphosis. When Peter's riffraff army showed up, the emperor ordered them to remain outside the capital ramparts. His instructions were ignored. The ragamuffins swarmed into the suburbs—accosting women, burning houses and plundering everything at hand.[182] To avert further mayhem, Alexius rounded up his guests and ferried them across the Bosphorus with the helpful advice that they should await the arrival of the professional crusading armies already en route from Europe. Peter the Hermit seconded this recommendation, but the enthusiasm of his minions was now beyond restraint. They made a beeline for the closest Turkish stronghold—Nicaea—where they finally distinguished themselves in their first encounter with the true infidel by seizing and eating the children of some curious "Turks" who happened to be standing about. (In all likelihood, these "Turks" were actually Christians living under Turkish rule.)[183]

This encounter was to be the height of their achievement. A lust for booty now caused the throng to disperse, allowing the Turks to strike back at them piecemeal. One party was intercepted by a Turkish force and pursued into a nearby castle, where they surrendered after a period of starvation. Two weeks later, the rest were lured into an ambush in a narrow gorge. Most were killed, but a few were brought back to Constantinople in an amphibious rescue operation dispatched by Emperor Alexius.[184] The Turks piled the corpses left behind into a grisly pyramid. (Later on, the bones were employed as building materials for a crusader fortification.[185]) So ended the "People's Crusade."

A few months later, the professional crusaders—the knights and nobles of Europe—finally made their appearance. After swearing fealty to the emperor (albeit reluctantly) and pledging themselves to hand over any former imperial territories that fell into their hands, they obtained passage to the Asiatic shore and placed Nicaea under siege. But the investment was inadequate. The Turks supplied themselves via Lake Ascania, which abuts the city on the west, and an attempt to undermine the walls came to naught. The crusaders sought to demoralize the defenders by decapitating every Turk they could lay their hands on and slinging the heads over the ramparts.[186] The Turks responded in kind—hoisting up the bodies of fallen crusaders with grappling hooks and using them as missiles for their own catapults.[187] When, however, a squadron of Byzantine vessels appeared on Lake Ascania, and when a column of Franks marched into view, bearing the heads of the defenders' hoped-for reinforcements atop their lances, the city finally capitulated—the Byzantines contriving to get their own forces admitted to the stronghold first, rather than trust the crusaders to abide by their oath to relinquish the prize to the emperor (June 19, 1097).

After a triumph in the open field at Dorylaeum, the holy warriors set course for Antioch, which was only reached after a deadly march beneath a blazing sun. As at Nicaea, severed heads were displayed atop pikes and then catapulted back into the city, but the crusaders lacked the means for a proper siege, and, when they ran out of food, the whole affair took a disturbing turn.[188] Half-starved, King Tafur, leader of a depraved crusader faction known as the "Ribalds," sought counsel from Peter the Hermit. To be sure, there was no food in sight, but the region positively abounded in Turkish corpses. Peter suggested cooking them with salt, and this recipe proved so satisfactory, that once the supply of corpses on the field had been exhausted, the Ribalds exhumed more bodies from a nearby cemetery and ate them, too. Antioch's Turkish defenders watched all this in disbelief. But Bohemond and Robert Curthose (the sons, respectively of Robert Guiscard and William the Conqueror) found it all highly amusing, and obliged Tafur with a bottle of wine when he confessed to them, amidst much guffawing, that so much food had made him thirsty.[189]

Scenes such as these caused Antioch to lose heart. A traitor eventually opened the gates to Bohemond, and the entire Turkish garrison was put to the sword. But by this time, there were no provisions *inside* the city either. Nor was this the worst of it. Hardly had the crusaders bolted the town gate, before a Turkish relief force arrived to place them under siege. Clutching at straws, a priest named Peter Bartholomew, unearthed the pointed end of a lance from beneath the altar of Antioch's Church of Saint Peter, claiming that it was the very weapon with which Jesus had been stabbed at the crucifixion.[190] The miraculous discovery spurred the famished Crusaders to attempt a madcap sortie. By now hunger had put them into a pleasing state of delirium, and as they attacked, they experienced a mass hallucination of Christian saints descending from Heaven to swell their ranks.

Incredibly, the Turks broke and ran. Even better, they abandoned their supply train. Unfortunately, the issue ended less happily for Peter Bartholomew. As commanding general, Bohemond was aghast that the plaudits owed to his leadership were being attributed instead to divine intervention.[191] He questioned the authenticity of Bartholomew's lance, and when his doubts were seconded, the unfortunate man was forced to defend his claim by undergoing the "ordeal by fire." With the whole multitude of crusaders anxiously looking on, Bartholomew "came forth and kneeled down ... to recommend him[self] unto god; [and] when he had made his prayer he took the spear and entered into the fire, and passed through it, and ... when the people saw this ... they ran for[th] to kiss him."[192] Having survived the ordeal, Bartholomew was literally mobbed by appreciative crusaders who would certainly have proffered official recognition to his lance, had he only refrained from dying of his burns shortly afterwards.

Renewing their march, the crusaders came at last to their main objective: Jerusalem. Far from being at the mercy of the hated Turk, the city had been retaken by Egypt's Fatimid Shiites the previous year. At the crusaders' approach, the Fatimid governor cast out the city's many Christians, lest they league with the enemy. The Jews, to their misfortune, were allowed to remain. An initial attack by the crusading host was repulsed for want of ladders and siege engines. But when ships from Genoa and England put in at Jaffa with supplies, this want was made good. A priestly vision instructed the Christian warriors to fast for three days and walk barefoot around the city's perimeter in supplication to God. This they did despite being taunted for it by the city's defenders. Then completing work on their ladders and siege engines, they moved to the attack, breaching the north wall with a siege tower manned by Duke Godfrey of Bouillon and his crossbowmen (July 14, 1099).[193]

The crusaders now stormed into the city and embarked on a massacre. Panicked Muslims sought sanctuary in a structure mistaken by the attackers for the "Temple of Solomon." (Apparently, the al-Aqsa Mosque.[194] There had been no Temple since the Romans destroyed it in AD 70). "And if you desire to know what was done with the enemy who were found there," Godfrey of Bouillon later boasted to the pope, "know that in Solomon's Porch and in his temple our men rode in the blood of the Saracens up to the knees of their horses."[195] The knights, says William of Tyre, "went together through the streets with their swords in their hands and slew and smote right down men, women and children, sparing none.... They slew so many in the streets that there were heaps of dead bodies.... It was [a] great pity for to see, if it had not [been] the enemies of our lord Jesus Christ."[196] A few hapless infidels sought refuge on the "Temple" roof. Christian arrows brought most of them down, while the survivors were simply hurled to their death after the crusaders climbed up. It was afterwards rumored that some of the Arab victims had swallowed gold coins in hopes of preserving them. The crusaders immediately set about disemboweling individual corpses, until someone had the much better idea of burning them all in a heap and sifting for coins in the ashes.[197] The Jews had taken refuge in Jerusalem's main synagogue, which the crusaders promptly burnt to a cinder.

The territories conquered by the crusaders were organized into four "Latin" kingdoms. From north to south along the coast were the County of Edessa, the Principality of Antioch, the County of Tripoli and the Kingdom of Jerusalem. The policies of these states were immediately unproductive. As an initial measure, the crusaders relieved the patriarch of Jerusalem of his duties, and replaced him with a Catholic prelate. This set the Latins at odds with Byzantium at a time when they would have done better to cooperate. Bohemond flouted his oath to Alexius entirely. Defeated and captured by the Turks, he purchased his own freedom and escaped to Europe, hiding from his ubiquitous enemies—Turkish and Byzantine—by sealing himself in a coffin with a putrefying rooster to mimic the odor of death.[198] Once arrived in Italy, he obtained papal backing for another crusade. He chose instead to attack Byzantium, but was defeated in his effort to repeat his father's success at Durazzo (1107). He died four years later.

Amidst ever-mounting Turkish pressure, the Latin states attempted to consolidate their position. But despite the establishment of two militant monastic orders—the Knights Templar, founded in 1119, for the dual purpose of fighting the Turks and defending the pilgrimage routes, and the Knights Hospitaller, organized in 1130, to fight the infidel and care for the sick and wounded—they were torn asunder by petty internecine squabbling that foretold their ultimate ruin. The end would have come sooner, but Islam was likewise rent by internal struggle, including infiltration by hashish-smoking Shiite fanatics from Persia—the *hashishin* (pronounced "assassin" by the Christians, thus adding a new word to the lexicon)—whose *modus operandi* was to surprise and murder their unwary Sunnite opponents.[199]

The Crisis of the Church and the Emergence of the European Monarchies (1066–1272)

Peter the Hermit returned safely to France, and founded a monastery, which he filled with relics from the First Crusade. The papacy basked in the apparent success of the Holy War—but she had, in fact, sown the seeds of her own downfall. Amidst the religious fervor surrounding her crusade certain shortcomings within the Church could no longer escape notice. To some, the Holy See seemed more interested in accumulating wealth and tending to secular affairs than in fulfilling her spiritual duties. Moreover, she had ceased to be the sole symbol of European unity—a niche she had monopolized since the time of the Norse invasions. The north Mediterranean coastline was now largely in Christian hands, and for the first time, Venetian and Genoese traders established permanent commercial outposts in the East. The popularity of their imports had a two-fold negative impact on the papacy: In the first place, the Eastern trade gave Europe its first taste of consumerism. The populace began to clamor for manufactured goods, which had formerly been produced and consumed within the isolated market of the feudal manor. By 1300, surplus handicrafts were being displayed at large fairs attended by customers from all over Europe.[200] Thus, trade came to rival religion in its ability to bring Europeans together. Secondly, as commerce increased, town populations began to grow; and while a village of 300 souls might willingly pay for the protection of a feudal lord in the time of the Norse invasions, a town of 20,000 could fend for itself, and resented such impositions in an era of ready commerce. The result was an urban emancipation movement wherein scores of towns obtained their political freedom—often simply by purchasing it, but, when necessary, by insurrection.[201] In time, these "independent" towns became a natural support base for their national monarchs as both struggled to escape the confining clutches of feudalism and the Church.

As a final challenge, the crusades opened new horizons for the West by bringing it into contact with the learning of the East. After the Christian conquest of Toledo in Spain (1076), Arabic translations of the Greek classics began to percolate back to the West. Among these works were Aristotle's treatises on logic, embellished with thought-provoking Arabic commentary, and free of the myriad errors found in extant Western monkish versions.[202] Increasingly, the well-educated segments of European society found intellectual stimulation in these treatises, and with this stimulation, new reasons to question the dogma of the Church.

Hence, by the end of the 12th century, the Church and papacy were under siege from myriad directions—and whilst they struggled, the kingdoms of Europe began to emerge from the mist of the Dark Ages to present yet another challenge.

The 12th Century: Louis VI and Louis VII of France; Henry II of England

At the time of the First Crusade, only England could boast a strong national monarchy—that established by William the Conqueror in 1066. In contrast, France was a patchwork of unruly dukedoms—some of which belonged to England's Norman king who still controlled Normandy and other parts of the French mainland. The French monarchy, therefore, became embroiled in a centuries-long struggle to increase its authority at the expense of the nobility (and of England). When the House of Capet unseated the French Carolingians for good in 987, Hugh Capet controlled no more than his own estates, which were a good deal smaller than those of his leading nobles. The dynasty did not at first prosper. Robert II (ruled, 996–1031) was a good enough fellow to be remembered in history as "the Pious," but his aggrandizement to the royal estates was quite modest, while his successor, Henry I (ruled, 1031–1060), was defeated twice in attempts to conquer Normandy. Henry's son, Philip I (ruled 1060–1108), could scarcely open the gates of Paris without fear of being carted into captivity by one of his unruly nobles.[203]

It was not until the reign of Louis VI (ruled, 1108–1137) that things began to improve. Louis cultivated new bases of support by championing the clergy and townspeople against the excesses of the baronage (or petty nobility), whose outlawry against defenseless Frenchmen earned them renown as history's first "robber barons."[204] By middle age Louis was rightly called "the Fat" since he had grown too obese to mount a horse, but as a youth, he had cut a fine figure: Clad in a brass helmet shaped like the thin end of an egg,[205] "he stormed the strongest tower as if it were the hut of a peasant, and ... piously destroyed the impious."[206] When his vassal, Count Charles of Flanders, was assassinated, Louis had one of the killers fed to the crows, and another given over alive to a ravenous dog. At Auvergne, he paraded the captured knights of a renegade count before the walls—each holding aloft the hand that had been severed from his other arm.[207] But the great coup of the reign occurred when the Duke of Aquitaine was compelled to swear fealty, and to give his daughter, Eleanor, in marriage to Louis' son (i.e., the future Louis VII). The consummation of this marriage held forth the promise of adding the extensive duchy of Aquitaine to the territory of the French king—an acquisition that would effectively double the royal domains.

In the event, the opportunity was missed. Louis VII succeeded to the throne in 1137 fully intending to continue his father's policy of aggrandizement. In 1142, however, a military foray against the town of Vitry took a calamitous turn. The village was taken easily enough from its irksome feudal lord, but when its thirteen hundred inhabitants sought refuge in a church, Louis' hotheaded soldiers burned them all alive.[208] Desperate to regain his status as a God-fearing Christian, the penitent monarch enlisted in the Second Crusade.

Preached by Saint Bernard, the Second Crusade was the West's response to the Muslim recapture of Edessa, which fell amidst scenes of stumbling panic in 1144. Louis departed in 1147, bringing his queen, Eleanor of Aquitaine. From start to finish, the crusade was a catastrophe. To set the tone, Conrad III, the Holy Roman Emperor, decided to take on the entire Muslim army before the French could come to his support. At Dorylaeum, Conrad's troops suffered annihilation. Louis, upon his arrival, took a different route, reaching Attalia on the coast of Asia Minor, where he sought to arrange sea transport to Antioch. But either because he could not meet the ticket price for his men or because there were not enough ships to transport them all, he simply abandoned them to the approaching Muslims (who massacred them), and purchased fares for his immediate party.[209] In the denouement, the crusaders did manage to place Damascus under siege. Just when they seemed to be making headway, however, folly or treason convinced the leaders to move their base from its original position, in a well-watered orchard, to a barren plain where there was no water at all. The new camp was unpromising in the extreme, and the arrival of Turkish reinforcements soon made it patently untenable. Conceding defeat, the crusaders returned to their homes (1148).[210]

While Louis was fighting the Turks, his wife Eleanor remained in her bedroom, where she is alleged to have made the only worthy conquests of the entire Second Crusade. In 1152, Louis had their marriage annulled on this account. But if he thought he was consigning Eleanor to oblivion, he was soon disabused. Within two months, his passionate former queen wed Henry Plantagenet of England. Two years after that, Henry inherited the English throne, as Henry II (ruled, 1154–1189), and Eleanor rose to the rank of queen for the second time in two marriages.

Her new husband was a great-grandson of William the Conqueror, but his road to the throne had been a peculiar one, and his accession marked the inauguration of a new dynasty in England. The odyssey began when William the Conqueror's son, William II (ruled, 1087–1100) had an arrow fired directly into his head in what was officially termed a "hunting accident." Afterwards, the throne was contested between the Conqueror's younger sons, Henry and Robert "Curthose" (whom we met fetching a bottle of wine for Tafur the cannibal during the First Crusade). Based upon age, the latter had the better claim, but in 1106, Henry crossed over to Normandy and routed Robert's Normans at Tenchebrai. Afterwards, Henry I ruled for thirty-five years (1100–1135), gaining renown as the "Lion of Justice" for establishing the supremacy of the "King's Law" in England, and for correcting the inequities fostered by his predecessors. He had hoped to leave the throne to his sole legitimate son, William, but this boy died when his ship—piloted by drunken buffoons[211]—was splintered on the rocks while crossing the English Channel from Normandy. The succession was thus contested between Henry's only other legitimate child (a daughter named Matilda, whom Henry betrothed to Geoffrey Plantagenet, Duke of Anjou) and his nephew, Stephen of Blois. The English baronage unanimously chose the latter—preferring a son of a daughter of William the Conqueror, to a daughter of a son.

Although Stephen "reigned" for nineteen years (1135–1154), chaos ruled. The nobles who had supported his accession ignored his decrees while engaging in a mad scramble to increase their own wealth and influence. We read, in this sad era, of hot-tempered Englishmen being "hanged up by the feet and smoked ... with foul smoke," and of "knotted strings [being tightened] about men's heads ... till they entered the brain."[212] Stephen laid plans to bequeath this mayhem to his son, Eustace, but the latter did not survive long enough to gain the inheritance. The ball, therefore, passed back into Matilda's court, for her marriage with Geoffrey Plantagenet had, in 1133, produced a son: namely, the selfsame Henry who grew up to marry Eleanor of Aquitaine. Faced with the prospect of civil war, King Stephen agreed to make Henry his heir. As a result, when Stephen died (1154), the "Norman" dynasty gave way to the "Plantagenet."

Louis VII's annulled marriage had thus dealt a double blow to the

King Henry II of England, engraving published by Thomas Kelly, London, 1830 (© Depositphotos.com/ Georgios Kollidas).

French monarchy; for not only was the Aquitaine lost to France—it was delivered to England! By adding the province to his already extensive holdings in France (i.e., Normandy, Anjou, Maine and Touraine), Henry became master of considerably more French territory than the French king. The sole consolation for Louis was in knowing that Eleanor's second marriage was no less stormy than her first. The overbearing (and faithless) Henry eventually confined the meddlesome woman to her castle where she remained in captivity for sixteen consecutive years.[213]

Marital discord notwithstanding, the English monarchy soared to new heights under Henry's leadership. His policies were paid for by taxes obtained from tradesmen and nobles alike. Fealty to the king had been required of the latter since the time of William the Conqueror. Under Henry the crown commuted this to a cash payment. The revenues thus collected were audited in the presence of the king, whose ministers employed a checkerboard tablecloth as a rudimentary abacus (hence the name "exchequer" for the English revenue office). Perhaps Henry's greatest achievement came in the realm of judicial reform. While the continent imported the Justinian Code from Constantinople and studied it at Bologna's new law school, Henry developed a separate legal system for England known as Common Law—so-named because it provided the kingdom with a uniform or "common" law code.[214] By purchasing a royal "writ," a litigant could avoid the parochialism of the local law courts, and have his case heard before the King's Bench under precedent-based standardized laws.[215] Better still, the royal courts offered trials by jury—although the "jurors" would be called "witnesses" today, since they had knowledge of the case and were required to give testimony under oath. (Verdicts, alas, were still determined by ordeal.)

Its shortcomings notwithstanding, Henry's code was popular, and royal authority was greatly enhanced by it. Only the clergy remained outside the pale. By tradition, their transgressions were separately governed under the "Canon Law" of the Church. Much irked by a system which allowed "criminous clerks" to elude his jurisdiction (and his court fees), Henry tried to impose a compromise known as the Constitutions of Clarendon (1164), whereby the Church retained the authority to conduct her own trials, but the royal courts determined punishment for those who were convicted. Should a case pit a clergyman against a layman, the crown would decide whose court had jurisdiction.[216] The offer seemed generous enough to its author, but it was opposed tooth and nail by his former chief minister, Thomas Becket, who was now archbishop of Canterbury. When Becket proved recalcitrant, Henry cried out to his courtiers: "What! Among all these cowards whom I have fed, is there none who will rid me of this miserable priest?"[217] Four of the king's knights dutifully confronted Becket at the altar and hacked him to pieces (1170). The reckless act left Henry in danger of excommunication. To avert the threat, he had to abandon the Clarendon confrontation.

Left to his own devices, Henry would have made good this domestic setback with a triumphant foreign policy. He danced circles around his French counterpart, Louis VII, and would have fared just as well against Louis' successor Philip "Augustus."[218] Sadly, Eleanor bore Henry a litter of impatient brats, and once she had been confined to her castle, Eleanor enlisted two of this brood, and her ex-husband, Louis VII, in an effort to undermine Henry's authority. Henry thwarted her (1174), but his remaining years witnessed repeated attempts by his sons to oust him from his throne and by the French to chase him from the continent. He died embittered—by some accounts delirious or insane[219]—after learning in his last days, at Chinon, that his youngest and favorite son, John, had been plotting against him along with the others.

The Dawn of the 13th Century: Richard the Lion-Hearted and John Lackland of England; Philip II Augustus of France; Frederick Barbarossa, Henry VI and Otto IV of Germany

The realm now passed to Henry's third son, Richard the Lion-Hearted (ruled, 1189–1199)—the older siblings having died in rebellion. Inheritor of his father's bravado as well as his kingdom, Richard felt nowhere more at home than on the field of battle. He therefore viewed the Third Crusade, which had been proclaimed just prior to his accession, as a godsend. The new war was sparked by a Latin raid on a Muslim caravan escorting the sister of Saladin—then the dominant figure in the Islamic world. Saladin demanded retribution, and when he did not receive it, he declared a "*jihad*" or holy war. At Hattin, near Lake Tiberias,[220] he routed a Latin army—seizing the True Cross, which the zealous Christians had carried into battle, and beheading over one hundred captured Templars and Hospitallers.[221] While the reeling Latins sought refuge within the peninsular port of Tyre, Saladin captured Jerusalem (September 1187). The papacy responded with a call to arms.

The crusade to reclaim Jerusalem attracted the most formidable figures in European politics. From Germany came Frederick "Barbarossa" (i.e., "Red Beard") leader of the House of Hohenstaufen and king of Germany since 1152. For thirty-four years, he had also held the office of Holy Roman Emperor—having been crowned by Pope Hadrian IV after assisting in the capture and execution of Arnold of Brescia, a social revolutionary who had established a short-lived republic in Rome (1155). However, from that time onward, Barbarossa had been at odds with the papacy owing to his persistent efforts to conquer northern Italy. In six campaigns, the emperor managed a brutal sack of Milan and the temporary occupation of Rome. But, in 1167, malaria drove his army from the peninsula, and when he tried to return a decade later, Pope Alexander III's "Lombard League" routed him decisively.

The disastrous Italian wars distracted Barbarossa from his troubles at home, where the aristocratic Welf party—the powerful opponents of centralized monarchy in Germany—used his absence to further their own designs. By 1190, however, the emperor had recouped his losses. The Welf leader, Henry the Lion, was disgraced in a conflict with the bishop of Halberstadt,[222] while the pope was wholly outmaneuvered by a dynastic marriage between Barbarossa's son, Henry (later Henry VI of Germany, ruled 1190–1197), and the Sicilian princess, Constance, heiress to the prosperous and brilliantly administered kingdom of the Two Sicilies, which had been founded in 1130 by Robert Guiscard's nephew, Roger the Great. Having labored so long to exclude the emperor from northern Italy, the papacy must have been vexed mightily to see him "conquer" the south through marriage.

But now, Barbarossa was off to lead the new crusade; and making tracks to the Holy Land with him were England's Richard the Lion-Hearted, and France's Philip Augustus (ruled 1180–1223), the one time nemesis of Richard's father, Henry II. It is a rare occasion, indeed, when three monarchs can agree to act in concert—and this was not one of those occasions. Setting off without waiting for the others, Frederick suffered fearful losses traversing hostile Asia Minor, and then drowned crossing the River Seleph in the face of a stiff current. Richard and Philip at least managed to reach Acre alive. But one modest town could not accommodate two inflated egos, and after bickering to the point of exhaustion, Philip packed up and returned to France, where he sought to repatriate Richard's Angevin lands by force.[223]

Richard was too much in his element to rush back after him. Even before Philip's departure, the English king had taken Muslim-held Acre by storm. Confronted thrice by Saladin's forces, Richard came away with three victories—at Arsuf, Ascalon and Jaffa. When Saladin dithered in the payment of a ransom, Richard brutally executed 2700 Muslim captives in full view of the enemy camp. His triumphs made him the hobgoblin of Saracen children, and won him his famous moniker "Lion-Heart."[224] But they did not deliver Jerusalem into his hands—which was unfortunate, since its recovery had been the whole point of the crusade. Already the campaign had cost him heavily in men, and even if he took the Holy City, his officers reluctantly told him, it was too exposed to be made proof against counterattack. Thus, with Jerusalem's spires visible on the horizon, Richard gave up—riding away with his face covered rather than gaze again at the prize he could not obtain.[225]

Nor was fate through with him. En route home, his ship sank in the Adriatic, and when he tried to continue the journey by land, he was apprehended and imprisoned—first by Leopold of Austria, whom he had insulted during the crusade, and then by the new Holy Roman Emperor, Henry VI, who begrudged him his alliance with the Welf leader, Henry the Lion, and sorely needed the ransom money the king could command.

But Richard could not be detained permanently. He eventually returned to inflict an embarrassing defeat on Philip Augustus near Freteval, where the French king retreated so hastily that he had to abandon his ledgers, seal and baggage train to the victor (1194).[226] On regaining the lands that Philip had seized from him, Richard invaded the domains of an unruly vassal with whom he had a score to settle. He was in the process of meting out the level of death and destruction to which his victims had grown accustomed, when an arrow fired from the besieged lord's castle struck him in the shoulder. Despite his violent career, Richard found it incredible that anyone would actually fire an arrow at him. As he lay dying with a festering, gangrenous wound, he asked to see his killer, of whom he inquired: "Wretch! What had I done to you that you should have attempted my life?" The archer offered the reasonable enough explanation that: "You have put my father and brother to death, and wanted to hang me."[227] To prove his magnanimity, Richard informed his prisoner that he was to be pardoned. The prisoner scornfully declined this offer. Life did not interest him. He craved only the death of the king. Turning a deaf ear to these insolent remarks, Richard insisted, and the archer was set free—only to be apprehended and burned alive once the king was dead.[228]

Owing to his wars in France and the Holy Land, Richard spent but six months in England during a reign of ten years, which probably explains why he is so fondly remembered there. At his death, the throne fell to the youngest and weakest of the sons of Henry II: John "Lackland" (so-named because all his father's lands had already been willed to his older siblings by the time he was born). John (ruled, 1199–1216) had been the ally of Philip Augustus against his brother, Richard, and had sought to sustain this alliance, even after Richard's death, by swearing fealty to the French king. But the great object of Philip Augustus' reign was to break Angevin (i.e., English) power on the continent, for the French monarchy could not hope to improve its station until this was done. Thus, when John married a woman already promised to one of Philip's vassals, Philip took the side of the latter, and declared John a felon for refusing to answer a summons regarding the matter. Since John had sworn fealty to Philip, his failure to appear meant that his French lands were forfeit.[229] Accordingly, Philip invaded Normandy with the support of John's estranged young nephew, Arthur of Brittany—the heir of Anjou, Maine and Touraine (1203). John soon captured Arthur and his leading knights, but he squandered the advantage by having Arthur murdered—for the crime provoked Anjou, Maine, Touraine and Brittany to declare for Philip Augustus, who promptly hurled the English out of Normandy as well. Thus, with the exception of distant Aquitaine, the continental power of the English monarchy had been shattered (1206).

John immediately began canvassing for allies to help him regain his lost domains. The papacy seemed a likely source of support, since the reigning pontiff, Innocent III (pope, 1198–1216), had once excommunicated Philip Augustus for divorcing the lovely Danish princess, Ingeborg, without church sanction. (By one account, Philip discovered, on their wedding night, that she had bad breath.[230]) But, since that time, events had intervened to restore Philip Augustus to favor.

At issue was the French county of Toulouse. Free, as yet, from royal authority, Toulouse had gotten itself into the bad graces of the Church by adopting the so-called "Albigensian," or "Cathar," heresy. In the view of the Albigensians, the material world was the domicile of sin, where the individual soul was fated to reincarnate repeatedly until it achieved "perfection." Then, having rejected all earthly vice, it would live out a final life of self-denial and piety on Earth before obtaining entry into heaven.[231] In 1207, Raymond VI, Count of Toulouse, was excommunicated for adhering to the heresy. In retaliation, a papal legate was murdered. At this, Pope Innocent declared a crusade against the Albigensians.

While Philip Augustus did not personally take part in this crusade, he gained points by giving his blessing to the papal cause—not the least because he stood to obtain Toulouse by doing so. In the same interlude, England's bungling King John not only failed to obtain papal support against Philip, but got himself excommunicated. He had attempted to fill the vacant archbishopric of Canterbury with a pliant tool. The cathedral monks countered with their own nominee. At length, Pope Innocent intervened, deposed the pretenders of both parties, and appointed Stephen Langton to the office (1207). But John refused to comply with this ruling, even when the pope excommunicated him and placed his country under interdict. Only when Philip Augustus (at Innocent's bidding) raised an army with which to depose John from his throne did the English king finally relent (1213).

As war was therefore averted between France and England, Philip decided to employ his newly raised levies against another of his unruly counts: namely, Count Ferrand of Flanders. Ferrand sought to preserve himself by allying with King John. Soon, their little coalition attracted a third adherent in John's nephew, Otto IV, the Welf emperor of Germany.

Otto had come to the throne by a roundabout route. The previous emperor—Barbarossa's son, Henry VI—had died prematurely at Messina while organizing an abortive expedition to conquer Constantinople. At the time (1197), the legitimate heir (i.e., Henry's son, Frederick—of whom we shall presently hear more) was still a toddler. Control of the state was therefore hotly contested between Philip of Swabia (the deceased emperor's brother) and the aforementioned Welf candidate, Otto. Pope Innocent saw in this struggle an opportunity to escape the imperial vise. By deposing the Hohenstaufen, and enthroning the Welfs, he could remove southern Italy from the imperial orbit. The Two Sicilies might remain in the hostile hands of the Hohenstaufen, but German imperial authority would now rest with the friendly Welfs.[232]

It was an inspired plan, save only that it required a miracle to bring it to fruition. Despite a decade-long civil war replete with men being cast alive into kettles of boiling water,[233] Philip of Swabia simply commanded too much support to be overthrown. But just when Pope Innocent decided to give in and sanction his accession, the Swabian was assassinated, and the German crown was handed de facto to Otto (1208). Innocent returned, therefore, to his original plan of crowning Otto emperor (1209), while administering the Two Sicilies himself until Henry VI's young son, Frederick, reached majority.

It seemed that the pope had gotten his miracle, but now things came unraveled; for once in possession of the imperial crown, Otto reneged on all his former promises to the Church, and assumed a hostile posture. Left in the lurch, Innocent turned for succor to his one reliable ally—Philip Augustus of France. Otto countered this appeal by joining King John of England in the latter's quest to regain his lost Angevin lands.

The battle lines were now drawn. In 1214, John invaded Philip's domains from his base in the Aquitaine, laying siege to La Roche-au-Moine, while Otto advanced from the east, supported by the count of Flanders. Philip routed John's forces first, and then wheeled about to engage Otto's Germans and their Flemish allies near Bouvines Bridge (July 1214). In the midst of this bloody encounter, Philip attempted a personal charge against Otto, only to topple from his mount and disappear in a sea of German light-armed troops. Amazingly, his armor preserved him long enough for his knights to hack their way to his rescue. Afterwards, his troops turned the tide. Pressed on both flanks, the imperialists took to their heels. Otto's horse was wounded in the eye, and the emperor himself was nearly throttled by a French knight. Before many witnesses, he ran from the field screaming.[234] The reverse cost him his throne.

John Lackland, meanwhile, returned to England to find his own throne in jeopardy. His barons would not rally to the architect of so many disasters, and the king's roll call tallied but seven knights beneath his banner.[235] Hoping to benefit from John's predicament, the barons confronted him at Runnymede, and forced him to put his seal to the famed *Magna Carta* (1215). (They would have forced him to sign it had he not been illiterate.[236]) This document restored feudal privileges to the English baronage and gave a modicum of leverage to the merchant class. It constituted a monumental restriction on arbitrary rule—and what is more, the barons had it in writing. Unfortunately, the pope (who had accepted John's vassalage in 1213) rewarded their impudence by excommunicating the lot of them. Seeing their cause all but lost, the rebel barons offered the throne to Louis of France, the son of Philip Augustus, and grandson, by marriage, of Henry II of England. Louis' army reversed the scales. Driven from his throne, John lost the crown jewels in a bog and dropped dead of dysentery (1216).[237] But with his demise, the notion of a Frenchman on the English throne lost its appeal, and after an interregnum lasting nine days the crown was delivered to the rightful claimant: John's malleable nine-year-old son, Henry III. Louis of France fought on with the support of those barons who had gone too far to turn back, but after a defeat at Lincoln, their cause was lost.

The Mid–13th Century: Saint Louis of France; Henry III of England; Frederick II and the Imperial Interregnum

The turbulent intrigues of the early 13th century had worked to the advantage of one man. Philip Augustus had broken the Angevin stranglehold on France, captured Artois from Flanders, and destroyed the prestige of the Holy Roman Empire. At his death in 1223, he was succeeded by his son, Louis of France (now Louis VIII), whose three-year reign witnessed the successful completion of the Albigensian Crusade. From its humble beginnings at Béziers, where 7000 defenseless Cathars—men, women and children—were massacred in the Church of the Madelaine (1209), this sordid caricature of a crusade was nothing more than a thinly-veiled effort to divest Languedoc of her wealth and autonomy. After Béziers, the "crusaders" captured the Cathar stronghold of Minerve—forcing its submission by smashing the sheltered stairwell leading to the town water source with a giant catapult. One hundred and forty recalcitrant Cathars were burnt at the stake.[238] Another 400 were burnt at Lavaur, where the local Catholic nobles were hanged for good measure.[239] Across Languedoc, Albigensians were dragged to death by horses or thrown into pits and pelted with rocks.[240]

Presiding over these atrocities was the French nobleman, Simon de Montfort, who included in his program the despoliation of Languedoc's Catholic aristocracy. This put him at odds with King Peter II of Aragon, who was liege lord to some of the victims. Famous for his own crusading victory over the Moors of Spain, King Peter marched to Languedoc

Section II: City of God

at the head of 40,000 men to confront de Montfort's army of 4000. Sadly, Peter was surprised by a sudden charge, and got his throat slit open in full view of his troops who promptly fled the field (1212).[241]

For the next six years, de Montfort and his "crusaders" ran amok through Languedoc, until a stone fired from a catapult by the women of Toulouse struck the commander square on the helmet, breaking open his head, and scattering brains, eyes, and teeth in every direction.[242] That was the end of de Montfort, but not of the struggle, which persisted until the French monarchy crushed all resistance, and the papacy unloosed the newly formed Inquisition on the surviving heretics.

This grim victory extended French monarchical supremacy to the Mediterranean coast, and made France the dominant power in Europe. But Louis VIII did not live to enjoy the spoils. His untimely death in 1226 delivered the throne to his eleven-year-old son Louis IX (known to history as Saint Louis, ruled 1226–1270). The French nobility promptly rebelled against the boy-king, hoping thus to regain their former ascendancy. But the people of Paris thwarted this endeavor by arming themselves with makeshift weapons and escorting the royal family into the capital with shouts of, "Long live the king!"[243] Over the course of several years, the ringleaders of the rebellion were defeated and exiled to the Holy Land, but the fighting continued under the tutelage of England's King Henry III, who hoped to capitalize on the mayhem to regain the Angevin inheritance. Only when Henry's army was defeated at Taillebourg in 1242 did the feudal war finally end.

Soon afterwards, a mysterious illness left King Louis so debilitated that one of his two nurses took him for dead and had to be restrained by the other from drawing a sheet over his head. The altercation roused Louis from his stupor, and finding that he had recovered the power of speech he bade the nurses fetch him a cross, saying that he would thank God for his miraculous recovery by launching a crusade to retake Jerusalem.[244] In 1248, he set out for Egypt with an armada of 1800 ships—enough, according to his contemporary biogra-

Saint Louis (Louis IX of France) in royal costume. Reproduction of a glass window in Saint-Louis de Poissy church. Published by *Magasin Pittoresque*, Paris, 1844 (© Depositphotos.com/Antonio Abrignani).

pher, Jean de Joinville, that "it seemed as if the whole sea, as far as the sight could reach, was covered with ... sails."[245] The fleet put in at Damietta to the harrowing din of enemy horns and tymbals; but once ashore the crusaders kept the Saracen cavalry at bay with a wall of shields and lance points.[246] Sadly, the decision was then taken to march on Cairo without first securing Alexandria as a base of operations.[247] The Muslim attitude toward this advance proved most vexing. A bounty was placed on crusader heads, and until Louis finally developed an efficient sentry system the sultan's minions stole into the Christian camp on a nightly basis to decapitate one or two of his slumbering holy warriors.[248] An attempt to bridge a tributary of the Nile was deftly countered by the Mohammedans who simply widened the river from the opposite bank faster than Louis' engineers could construct their causeway. The king's workmen came under fire from Saracen catapults, and the towers erected to protect them were incinerated by Greek Fire so that the causeway had to be abandoned altogether.

The setback was only temporary. The discovery of a ford allowed the crusaders to gain the opposite bank further downstream. They promptly stormed the town of Mansourah only to be thrown into disorder by the locals who pelted them from the rooftops with wooden beams and other heavy objects (February 8, 1250). A counterchange was then unleashed upon them by the Mamelukes—Egypt's fear-inspiring slave warriors—and by the time the crusaders managed to extricate themselves, they had lost nearly three hundred mounted knights.[249] Further bloodletting outside the town, resulted in panic on both sides. The Saracens abandoned their tents and sent carrier pigeons to Cairo to sound the alarm of defeat.[250] Some fled down the Cairo road, and on this account, Joinville counts the engagement a tactical victory. But clearly it was a strategic defeat. Scores of crusaders drowned in the Nile and the ruinous casualties precluded any thought of pressing on.

Louis and his knights remained where they were to await a supply convoy—the arrival of which was imminently expected. While they waited, the bloated corpses of their comrades, drowned in the fighting, rose to the Nile surface and floated lazily past them. The grisly scene is described by Joinville: "At the end of eight or ten days, the bodies of those who had been slain ... floated down the river until they came to the small bridge [near us] ... and the arch was so low that it ... prevented the bodies passing underneath. The river was covered with them from bank to bank so that the water could not be seen a good stone's throw from the bridge upward." The crusaders sought for their friends among the dead, but the swollen bodies were unidentifiable.[251]

On the heels of this demoralizing episode, starvation and dysentery rendered the military situation untenable. The supply convoy never arrived. The Saracens had seized it en route. Belatedly apprehending the hopelessness of the situation, the king gave the order to withdraw on April 5th, but by then it was too late. The Saracens fell upon them, slaughtering sick and wounded crusaders on the riverbank before they could board the departing galleys. Those lucky enough to cast off were soon overtaken. The Saracens cut them to pieces and pitched their bodies into the Nile. A day later, the retreating army was overwhelmed near Fariskour, and the king himself was taken prisoner. Hundreds of captured crusaders were beheaded on the spot for refusing to renounce Christianity. Only a handful were ransomed.[252]

To celebrate their victory, the Mamelukes, who formerly had been the slaves the Egyptian sultan, cut out their sultan's heart, and seized all Egypt for themselves. (They would hold the province until the 19th century.) Louis and the remnant of his army were liberated in return for the surrender of Damietta and a large cash indemnity. They proceeded to Syria in the forlorn hope of continuing the crusade from there, before finally returning to France in 1254.

Convinced that his failure had been brought about by insufficient piety, the king dressed plainly upon his return to France, fed the poor by his own hand, provided for the sick and the aged, founded hospitals and established charitable asylums—one for the blind, and another to rescue pauper women who had fallen into prostitution. He had always been a devout Catholic, attending mass twice a day, praying long into the night and receiving communion six times annually. At Lent he would give up wine (which he always watered down to avoid drunkenness) and drink only beer—wincing at every sip since he could not stand the taste. He never swore and made certain not to laugh on Fridays.[253] And he had his chaplain scourge him from time to time so that he could be a better man—a secret that was revealed only at death when the marks were discovered on his back.[254] It was for traits such as these that Louis would be canonized as a saint just twenty-seven years after his death. But he also had the taint of religious bigotry. During his reign the Inquisition took hold in France.[255] Heretics were cruelly persecuted—many being sent to the stake. Blasphemers were branded on the lips.[256] Although Louis treated Jewish converts with favor, he persecuted those who remained faithful to their religion, requiring them to identify themselves by affixing a yellow badge to their clothing, confiscating a proportion of their wealth and arbitrarily cancelling a third of all debts owed to them.[257] When he threatened to bar them from moneylending altogether on a charge of usury, however, the barons of France stopped him, saying that the country's peasants and merchants would perish without Jewish loans and that, besides, the interest rates charged by Christian moneylenders were worse.[258]

In temporal matters, Louis made the king's coinage the standard of the realm at a time when 80 non-standardized local mints were operating, and established the *parlement* in Paris to serve as a court of appeal for those who felt cheated by rulings in the local feudal courts. He judged many cases himself with scrupulous fairness.[259] These acts went far to enhance the royal power at baronial expense—a major step forward for the French monarchy.

The English monarchy, in contrast, had taken a major step backwards. Louis' contemporary, Henry III of England (ruled 1216–1272), had squandered England's wealth in reckless foreign adventures—finally breaking the bank in a failed bid to wrest Sicily from its Hohenstaufen rulers. Taxed to the limit to pay for this scheme, the English barons rebelled and formed what came to be called the "Mad Parliament" (1258), which forced the king to adhere to the *Provisions of Oxford*—a document stipulating (i) the expulsion of Henry's unpopular foreign advisors, (ii) at least three meetings of parliament annually and (iii) transfer of authority from the crown to a committee of fifteen nobles. Henry had no choice but to acquiesce. Once in charge, however, the ruling nobles could agree on nothing, and in the consequent chaos Henry laid plans to reassert his authority.

His opportunity came in 1259, when he signed the Treaty of Paris with Saint Louis. Although the French king might have demanded almost any terms from his beleaguered counterpart, he went against the advice of his councilors and ceded the duchy of Guienne (comprised of Gascony and the westernmost remnants of the Aquitaine) to Henry, ruling that Philip Augustus had seized it from the English unfairly.[260] In return, Henry officially withdrew his claims to the remainder of the lost Angevin inheritance. The enhancement of prestige that accrued to Henry by the acquisition of Guienne convinced the English monarch that he might now throw off the *Provisions of Oxford*. The nobles resisted the attempt, and the resulting civil war so exhausted the rival parties that in January 1264 king and parliament agreed to defer to the adjudication of Saint Louis, whose reputation for probity recommended him as an arbiter.

If the parliamentarians thought they were in for a fair hearing, they had misjudged their man. The *Provisions of Oxford* had already been condemned by the papacy (1262), which should have made Louis' decision predictable from the start. The French king declared the *Provisions* null and void, and granted Henry all his former privileges except those specifically prohibited by the *Magna Carta*.[261] The barons could not abide such a blow. Under the *Provisions*, governing authority lay in their hands; a reversion to the *Magna Carta* would return authority to the king.[262]

The issue could only be settled by force of arms. Led by the transplanted Frenchmen, Simon de Montfort, Earl of Leicester (son of the Albigensian crusader and brother-in-law of the king), the barons met Henry's army at Lewes. At the outset, their center fell back in rout, but their wings, composed of mailed cavalry, fell upon the flanks of the advancing royalists, defeated them heavily and captured the king himself.[263] In captivity, Henry was reduced to a mere puppet, while ruling authority was vested in a new council and parliament—the latter including, for the first time, burgesses and yeomen in addition to nobles and clerics. The parliamentarian victory seemed complete, but de Montfort now overstepped himself. With the support of the middle class parliamentarians, he elbowed his fellow barons aside, and pushed through his own decrees. At this, the barons flocked to the banner of the king's son (the future Edward I), who was willing to guarantee the privileges they stood to lose under de Montfort.[264] The baronial defection was decisive. In August 1265, de Montfort was killed in battle at Evesham. His limbs were hewn off to serve as grisly icons in the towns that had supported him.[265] Henceforth, King Henry reigned with the support of the privilege-seeking barons.

By this time, however, the idea of parliament was so entrenched that the assembly could not be abolished. Its mission was not yet well defined—indeed the next king (Edward I) would only consult it when he needed revenue grants. But its very survival threw a wrench into the workings of arbitrary government, and on this account England would never be the same.

Compared with the British and French kings, the Holy Roman Emperor had just experienced a renaissance in arbitrary rule—not in Germany, mind you, but in Sicily. Following the battlefield defeat of Otto IV, the German crown fell to Frederick II Hohenstaufen, who crossed into Germany to assert his claim. The young prince obtained papal support by agreeing to keep the kingdoms of Sicily and Germany separate, and by promising to embark on a crusade once his throne was secure. He was crowned at Aachen—Charlemagne's old capital—in 1215. But after procuring a power base amongst the Cistercian monks and Teutonic Knights as a counterpoise to the nobility, Frederick left Germany, and journeyed to Sicily (1220)—explaining to an alarmed Pope Honorius III that he intended to embark from there for Damietta to give succor to the struggling crusaders of the Fifth Crusade. In truth, he had no such intention; for he was determined to wield even more authority than his grandfather, Barbarossa, and had no thought of departing for the Holy Land until he had accomplished his aim.

In the end, his achievements were astonishing, and Frederick came to be called *Stupor Mundi*, "the Wonder of the World." He created what many regard to be the first state on the modern model—convening a parliament before either Britain or France had done so (1225).[266] To supply his government with knowledgeable and devoted civil servants, he established the University of Naples. Likewise, he reorganized the Sicilian economy, substituting import-export tariffs for the outdated internal tolls levied locally by the nobility. (The latter had only stymied trade without any noticeable benefit to the crown, while the former created a continuing source of revenue.)[267] When war forced a currency shortage, the emperor prevented an interruption of commerce by issuing stamped leather coins, backed by a personal pledge of redemption.[268]

Frederick was a patron of the arts. He promoted agriculture—combatting a plague of caterpillars by making farmers apprehend and turn in a fixed number of the creatures on a daily basis.[269] He codified Sicilian law and was a benefactor of the medical school at Salerno. He spoke six languages, traveled with a personal zoo of rare animals, wrote the best book ever on falconry,[270] conducted scientific experiments, retained Leonardo Fibonacci to teach him mathematics, bathed with scandalous frequency (once a week)[271] and tolerated Muslims and Jews.

On the other hand, he tied political enemies up into bags with poisonous snakes and hurled them into the Mediterranean,[272] forced Jews to wear long beards or to sew yellow patches onto their shirts lest they be mistaken for Christians,[273] and forbade marriage to foreigners (though he himself married one or two), arguing—rather ominously for a German—that such unions imperiled racial purity.[274] One of his scientific inquiries was said to have involved sealing a man in a barrel, which was opened at death to prove that souls do not ascend to heaven (no soul was found in the sealed barrel—just a corpse).[275] When Saint Francis of Assisi paid him a visit at Bari, Frederick whisked a beautiful prostitute into the holy man's bedchamber as a practical joke, and then observed through a hole in the wall as the embarrassed monk labored (successfully) to keep her at bay.[276] He ignored each of his three wives in succession, while attending to his harem of dancing girls—a gift from the sultan of Egypt.[277] He persecuted heretics, but was so at odds with the papacy that the Church branded him the "Antichrist." And worst of all, he did everything in Sicily, in direct violation of his promises to the Holy See, sacrificing the last hope for a unified medieval Germany to the mirage of becoming a truly "Roman" emperor. His royal domains in Germany were bartered to the nobility in return for money and support in his quest to subdue Italy, where he created the most authoritarian regime of the period. Says Burckhardt, he transformed "the [Sicilian] people into a multitude destitute of will and of the means of resistance"—accomplishing the feat with a police force composed of Saracens "who were deaf to the cry of misery and careless of the ban of the Church."[278] The policy not only produced a damaging drift toward decentralization in Germany, but precipitated a war between the emperor and the papacy that proved the undoing of both.

The conflict began when Frederick failed to keep his promise to assist in the disastrous Fifth Crusade. To avert an immediate rupture, the emperor assured the pope that he would arrange a crusade of his own. But the offer was a ruse. Frederick ordered his German knights to assemble for the proposed expedition in hostile northern Italy. Predictably, the Lombards blocked the Alpine passes. (After their wars with Frederick's grandfather, Barbarossa, they were not about to allow a large German force to assemble in their midst.) Frederick protested loudly, if insincerely, that the northern cities were jeopardizing his crusade, and suggested to Pope Honorius that they should be placed under the papal ban for so irreligious an action.[279]

But Honorius wasn't born the previous day. He knew that if he followed this advice, Frederick would invade northern Italy on the pretext of supporting the papacy. The prospect of Lombardy falling into the emperor's hands, leaving the Papal States flanked by imperial territory north and south, was more than Honorius could bear. All thought of a crusade was abandoned while the pope attempted to negotiate a settlement between the hostile parties. In 1226, however, Honorius died, and his successor, Pope Gregory IX, absolutely insisted that Frederick cease his shenanigans and embark for the Holy Land. After delaying as long as he could, the emperor finally set sail for Syria in September 1227, only to return within days, pleading illness after pestilence broke out in his fleet. Gregory excommunicated him on the spot.

Thus prodded, Frederick got back on his ship and set out for real in September 1228, even though, as an excommunicate, he was no longer authorized to do so. It was the oddest crusade yet. Once arrived in the East, Frederick used his fluent Arabic to conclude negotiations he had been pursuing all along with the Egyptian sultan, Al-Kamil, against whom he was supposed to be fighting. Without engaging the infidels in a single major battle, Frederick arranged the Treaty of Jaffa (1229), whereby he secured Jerusalem, the important port of Sidon, and a corridor of territory connecting these prizes to the Christian stronghold of Acre.

This may have been Frederick's notion of a crusade, but it wasn't Pope Gregory's. The leader of a Holy War wasn't supposed to negotiate, he was supposed to fight.[280] Indeed, in this case, he was supposed to lose, or at least get bogged down in a war long and costly enough to preclude further machinations in Lombardy. Gregory not only refused to rescind Frederick's excommunication, he annulled his transactions, and placed Jerusalem under interdict. This last did not sit well with the local populace, and when Frederick finally boarded his ship to leave the Holy Land, they pelted him with refuse.[281] On his return, the emperor only managed to get the bans lifted by confirming papal prerogatives in Sicily in a pretended act of supplication (1230). As usual, the ploy was devoid of sincerity. Within a year Frederick promulgated the *Constitution of Melfi* (1231), divesting the Sicilian clergy and great nobles of their temporal authority. Henceforth, all worldly affairs were to be administered by civil servants educated at the University of Naples.

Frederick's position in Sicily was stronger than ever. By 1235, he was ready to renew his designs upon Lombardy. To forestall him, the Lombards schemed with Frederick's neglected son, Henry, to foment an uprising in Germany. Frederick nipped this rebellion in the bud, and placed his wayward son in perpetual imprisonment.[282] Then, to repay the Lombards for their "calumny," he invaded northern Italy. At Cortenuova (November 1237), his German knights and Saracen horsemen won a victory so decisive, that Frederick's dream of a Roman empire based in Italy seemed within his grasp. In celebration, the emperor staged an old-fashioned "triumph" at Cremona, marching at the head of his troops and zoo animals, with the conquered Lombards straggling behind.[283] Delirious with success, he demanded the unconditional surrender of Milan, the strongest of the Lombard cities. The Milanese refused, saying, "We fear your cruelty, for we know it by experience; we had rather die under our shields by sword or spear than by treachery, starvation and fire."[284]

On receiving this reply, the emperor laid siege to the rebellious city of Brescia. But the Brescians broke his investment with the help of a captured imperial engineer. The unexpected check incited all northern Italy to rise in revolt against the emperor. Pope Gregory advanced the rebel cause by securing the alliance of Venice and Genoa, and by excommunicating Frederick for a second time (March 1239). Forthwith, Frederick turned his legions about and marched on the Papal States. Gregory summoned a church council to take further action against him, but Frederick seized the ships bearing the invited prelates, and no less than one hundred leading churchmen found their way into the imperial dungeons. Still, Frederick was unable to force his way into Rome, and when Pope Gregory died (1241), the impasse took a new twist. Already, Frederick had resorted to the aforementioned issuance of leather coinage to meet the rising cost of the war, and the College of Cardinals rightly calculated that he would not press the siege of Rome in such straits if the possibility existed that an amicable successor might be elected to Saint Peter's chair. As a result, the cardinals delayed the election for two years, before finally selecting Innocent IV. Wholly ill disposed to Frederick, Innocent convened the Council of Lyons (1245), to discuss what measures should be taken against him. Although Jerusalem had fallen again to the Saracens, the council ignored the Holy City's plight in favor of a crusade against Frederick.

Though Europe's monarchs had no stomach for Holy War against one of their own, the council's sentence prompted a general uprising across the Italian peninsula. Frederick took the offensive—besieging Parma from a newly built fortification dubbed "Vittoria" (i.e., Victory). But in February 1248, while he was out hawking, his camp was overrun with loss of his crown, seals, treasure, and—most insufferable of all—his dancing girls. In Parma, a dwarf was seen roaming the streets with the imperial diadem on his head.[285]

Frederick never recovered from the blow. He died in 1250 with his Roman dream unrealized—willing the empire to his son, Conrad IV, whom Pope Innocent also excommunicated. With the latter's premature death in 1254, Hohenstaufen rule in Germany came to an end. For more than a decade afterwards, however, the family pressed its claims in Sicily. In 1258, after scattering a papal army sent to oppose him, Frederick's bastard son, Manfred, seized the Sicilian throne. From there, he marched on Lombardy to pursue the dream, shared with his father, of dominating all Italy. Intent on ousting him, the papacy offered the Sicilian crown first to a son of England's Henry III, who was unable to make headway, and then to Charles of Anjou, the brother of Saint Louis, who promptly brought a French army into Italy.

Manfred, whose addiction to pleasure and reliance on Saracen soldiers had gained him the epithet, "Sultan of Lucera," was slow to realize the magnitude of the Angevin threat.[286] He had been scheming at the conquest of Constantinople and busying himself with the hunt when the sudden French advance roused him from his reveries. Defeated at Benevento (1266), he eschewed a chance for safety in flight, and galloped into the mêlée to meet a soldier's death. His nephew, Conradin—the last of Frederick's line—now took up the Hohenstaufen mantle. Shrewd and zealous beyond his fifteen years, the "lion cub" received a triumphant welcome in Rome.[287] But at Tagliacozzo (1268), a near victory was converted into rout by a well-timed ambush of the pretender's entourage.[288] Captured in flight, Conradin was hauled off to hostile Naples, and decapitated in the public square.

Sicily belonged to the victor, Charles of Anjou, who ruled as an odious, if efficient, occupier prior to seeing his own pretensions at Mediterranean empire foiled by the Sicilian

Vespers.[289] The Holy Roman Empire, meanwhile, had fallen to shambles. The once proud monarchy had become so decentralized under Frederick II, that when the throne fell vacant in 1254, the nobility tried to get by with no emperor at all. A costly nineteen-year interregnum ensued, wherein an English and Spanish pretender vied haplessly for the crown, until the nobility, fearing a lapse into total chaos, finally identified a candidate to their liking. Unassuming at his accession, Rudolph of Hapsburg[290] fathered a dynasty that would hold the imperial title with few interruptions until the office ceased to exist in 1806. But his election did not yield instant stability. Rudolph and his immediate successors cared less about centralized imperial authority than they did about adding to their own family estates.[291]

Thus, by the time Saint Louis died at the gates of Tunis in the abortive Eighth Crusade (1270), the power of the German empire had been woefully compromised. England's monarchy, too, had been profoundly shaken due to her confrontations with Philip Augustus, the papacy and her own nobility. Of the three major European powers, France had clearly proved ascendant over her sister monarchies. Only one other power could claim as many victories: the papacy. Papal power had been on the rise since the time of the Cluniac reforms. The investiture controversy had ended in a significant—if compromise—victory for the Holy See, and the initial call to the crusades had for a time rallied the continent behind the pope.

The accession of Innocent III marked the papacy's high water mark. Trained as a jurist, Innocent used his knowledge of the law to retain those prerogatives the papacy already enjoyed and to expand them in every direction at the expense of Europe's temporal rulers. The papal ban, wielded to such effect against Henry IV during the 11th century, was re-invoked under Innocent against Philip Augustus of France, John Lackland of England and Otto IV of Germany—each of whom was brought to heel by its bitter sting.

Never had the papacy won so many battles in its bid to establish a City of God under a papal monarchy—and never had it so clearly lost the spiritual war in which it was nominally engaged. "Earnest Christian pilgrims ... at Rome," say Thatcher and Schwill, "were shocked to hear nothing about spiritual matters, but to find the mouths of all the clergy incessantly filled with talk about temporal affairs."[292] The papal ban had been employed so frequently that subsequent rulers—such as Frederick II—practically ignored it, while the crusading spirit had degenerated with each passing call to arms. The Fourth Crusade, which occurred under Innocent's watch, had been little more than a Venetian business venture. Its chief result—the ruinous sack of Constantinople (1204)—had forever crippled Byzantium's capacity to shield the West against the Islamic advance.[293] Eight years later, the Italian traders did themselves one better. A mass delusion had seized the children of France. Thousands flocked to the Mediterranean coastline believing that the sea would part to allow them to cross to the Holy Land. While they awaited this miracle, the traders rounded them up and sold them to Muslim slave traffickers. This was the dreadful "Children's Crusade" of 1212. It was Frederick II—not Pope Innocent—who apprehended the responsible entrepreneurs and had them hanged.[294] It was Innocent again who invoked the brutal Albigensian Crusade.

In making crusades and excommunications a petty business, the church had sacrificed her moral standing. She pursued a temporal prize when spiritual struggles were her proper sphere.[295] Her reputation had been sullied, and by the dawn of the 14th century she was poised to enter upon a new era of disrepute.

The Dawn of the 14th Century: Edward I of England and Philip IV of France

The papacy's latest problem stemmed from a dispute with the monarchs of England and France. The death of England's feeble King Henry III in 1272 delivered the throne to Edward I (ruled, 1272–1307), who was as strong as his father had been weak. To avert the chaos of the previous reign, the king made an exhaustive study of royal and baronial powers. His *Quo Warranto* statute (1290) closed all baronial courts that could not prove their legitimacy on the basis of a royal charter. On the other hand, he confirmed the baronial privileges outlined in the *Magna Carta*, and convened the so-called "Model Parliament" (1295), to which he summoned knights and townsmen as well as lay and ecclesiastical lords.[296] The motive behind these "noble" gestures, not surprisingly, was the need for money.[297] Edward's aggressive foreign policy demanded an enormous cash outlay. By swallowing his pride and asking parliament to approve the necessary grants—in effect, surrendering to that body the prerogative in ratifying royal tax levies—he was able to secure the necessary funds.

Edward was now free to pursue his policy of aggression. In the west, he exterminated enough Welshmen to bring the fair province of Wales into his domain (1283).[298] A similar strategy was tried against the Scots, whose weakling king, John Balliol, had been appointed by Edward himself after the legitimate ruler managed to break his neck by cantering off a mountainside in the pitch of night.[299] Appointed or no, Balliol chose to resist Edward's encroachments. He forged an alliance with France, with whom Edward was at war, and sent raiding parties across the border. A number of English villages were burned. Edward retaliated with the sack of Berwick—the inhabitants being put to a merciless slaughter until the sight of a woman being hewn apart as she was giving birth prompted an order to desist.[300] There followed, at Spottsmuir, a pitched battle in which the Scots were routed.

But William Wallace (better known to the modern reader as "Braveheart") now seized the mantle of Scottish resistance, and in a series of deadly guerrilla raids spread panic through Edward's northern garrisons. In September 1297, the

King Edward I of England, 19th century engraving (© Depositphotos.com/Georgios Kollidas).

English attempted to draw Wallace into open battle at Stirling Bridge on the River Forth. About half the English cavalry had crossed over, when Wallace, observing from a nearby height, gave the signal to his confederate, John "Pin" Wright (who was suspended in a basket beneath the bridge), to remove the structure's support pin.[301] The bridge promptly collapsed, pitching riders and their mounts into the depths, while those already on the far bank were attacked in flank and massacred to a man.[302]

A second clash ensued at Falkirk, nine months later. This time, however, King Edward himself commanded the English forces. To oppose him, Wallace arrayed his men behind a marsh, which greatly hampered the English attack. Moreover, he formed his heavy infantry into four circular hedgehogs, or "*schiltrons*," with pikes dug into the ground facing outward as proof against a cavalry charge.[303] It is generally agreed that these dispositions were exemplary. Unfortunately, Wallace had entrusted his cavalry to the vacillating Scottish nobility, who spurred their horses in flight rather than fend off an English flanking maneuver. Although the English still could not penetrate the Scottish hedgehogs, they *were* able to make mincemeat of the archers stationed between them. There was nothing now to prevent Edward's bowmen from coming to close range, whence they released a deadly barrage of arrows into the *schiltrons*, wreaking enough death and destruction to allow the cavalry to break in and hack the patriotic Scots to pieces (July 1298).[304] Wallace remained at large until 1305, before being captured and horribly executed in a public spectacle.

The Scottish debacle entailed significantly more expenditure than had been earmarked for it—particularly when one considers that Edward was also waging a costly war with France in order to maintain his hold on the Aquitaine (consisting at this date of Guienne and Gascony). Strapped for cash, Edward decided that the English clergy must start paying taxes. Coincidentally, the French king, Philip IV (ruled, 1285–1314), had reached the same fiscal conclusion in France at almost the same moment. Known as "Philip the Fair" (for his handsomeness rather than for his character, which, as one historian assures us, "was far less attractive than his face"[305]), Philip was the benefactor of the French merchant class—promoting their trade and recruiting them as advisors of state. It did not escape him that a strong, revenue-producing middle class would serve as a useful counterweight to the French nobility in the drive to centralize royal authority. To buttress his position, Philip established the Estates General, the first parliament ever convened in France—making sure, as Edward had done in England, that it contained numerous merchant commoners on whom he could rely for support.

But in the end, Philip found that he required rather more money than he was able to extract by these means. Like Edward, therefore, he resorted to taxing the clergy without papal consent. Complaints of royal abuse poured into Rome from the clerics of both nations. Outraged, Boniface VIII (pope, 1294–1305) issued a papal bull, entitled *Clericis Laicos*, threatening the dueling monarchs with excommunication if the taxation continued (1296). He was forced to back down, however, when Philip outlawed the exportation of currency from France, thus interrupting the flow of funds from French bishoprics to the Holy See.[306]

The issue remained unresolved until 1300, when pilgrims flocking to Rome for the centennial festivities offered so many donations that two attendants literally had to rake the money into the papal treasury.[307] In celebration of this windfall, Boniface issued a new bull, *Unam Sanctum*, declaring that good relations with the pope were essential to salvation.

Plans were laid to excommunicate Philip, but the French king was forewarned, and obtained permission from the Estates General to launch his own preemptive strike. Guillaime de Nogaret, Philip's chief minister (and sometimes henchman), whose father had been condemned as a heretic in the Albigensian Crusade, gathered a force of 1600 men and accosted the octogenarian Boniface in his bedroom at Anagni, where the pontiff lay clutching a cross as his sole instrument of defense.[308] Before the intruders could drag their quarry back to France, however, the villagers of Anagni intervened to set him free. Sadly, the shock of this episode proved fatal. Boniface died within weeks, to be succeeded briefly by Benedict XI, and then by Clement V (Pope, 1305–1314), a man cast from much more malleable material. Indeed, Clement never set foot in Rome. Instead, he moved the papal residence to the French town of Avignon (1309) that he might better serve Philip.

Papal prestige thus sank to its lowest ebb, and that of the empire was not far behind. Germany's magnates had been well pleased, at first, to find a ruler who was too busy aggrandizing his own properties to interfere in their affairs. But when Rudolph of Hapsburg added chunks of Europe the size of Austria and Styria to his own estates, they thought better of yielding the crown to his son, Albert, and chose instead to bestow it on the weaker House of Nassau, and its pretender, Adolph I (ruled, 1291–1298). Adolph's popularity soon waned, leading him into a fatal war with the Hapsburgs, which delivered the empire to Albert after all. But Albert's much-anticipated reign was not a success, and, in 1308, a spiteful nephew arranged his assassination.

Temporarily disinherited—the family would not regain the imperial title until 1437—the Hapsburgs sought to muscle in on the bustling commerce of the St. Gothard Pass in present-day Switzerland.[309] At Morgarten (1315), however, the Swiss—who were in the process of making their "forest" cantons independent of the empire—dealt them a mortal blow. In a narrow defile, with a lake to one side and steeply rising terrain on the other, the Swiss swooped down upon the Hapsburg cavalry with their terrifying halberds—eight-foot battle-axes, which could cut through armor as though it were butter. With no room to maneuver, the surprised Austrian cavalry attempted flight. Finding their route blocked by their own infantry, they simply stampeded over them, crushing them underfoot or knocking them into the lake, while the Swiss halberdiers chased after them to finish the slaughter.[310]

The imperial diadem, meanwhile, passed from one ruling house to the next.[311] After Albert, the royal prerogative was enjoyed by Henry VII of the House of Luxemburg (ruled, 1308–1313) who died of malaria while attempting to unite Italy under imperial rule. Henry's successor, Louis the Bavarian (1313–1347), obtained the throne in a contested election and spent the first nine years of his reign in civil war with a rival claimant. Immediately thereafter, he entered upon an unceasing quarrel with the papacy, which reached a crescendo when Pope John XXII declared him excommunicate. Offended at this move by a pope based in Avignon serving the whim of the French king, Germany's great magnates did something that they had never done before—they rallied behind their own emperor.[312] In a meeting at Rense they declared that imperial elections were a German affair and that the papacy had no authority in the matter (1338).[313] This was a great victory for Louis, but he promptly forfeited the advantage by scheming at the annexation of the Tyrol, the procurement of which would have made him too powerful for comfort. Consequently, the magnates abandoned him again and elected a rival claimant—Bohemia's King Charles. Charles was defeated in an attempt to wrench the Tyrol from Louis' grasp, but when Louis died unexpectedly on a hunting expedition, Charles assumed the imperial mantle as Charles IV (ruled, 1347–1378).

The new ruler took it upon himself to put an end to the chaos that had reigned in Germany since the fall of the Hohenstaufen. It was evident to him that without a formalized legal proceeding for filling a vacant or contested imperial throne, the nation (such as it was) would continue to be riven by conflict and civil war as it had been for a century.[314] Hence, in 1356, he promulgated the *Golden Bull*, which bestowed upon seven "electors" the perpetual right to elect a new emperor whenever the throne fell vacant. In four of these principalities—Bohemia, Brandenburg, Saxony and the Palatinate—the electors were secular rulers whose office was hereditary. In the other three—Mainz, Cologne and Trier—the post was held by an archbishop. All seven were given the right to impose taxes and coin money, and their holdings were declared immune to imperial tinkering.

It has been said that the *Golden Bull* "confessed and legalized the independence of the Electors and the powerlessness of the crown."[315] A century later, the Emperor Maximilian would lament that while Charles might be considered a true father to Bohemia (where, as king, he did many fine things), the empire could only view him as a stepfather.[316] Having held the imperial office for nine years at the time of the bull's issuance, however, Charles had enough experience to know that the monarchy was too feeble an instrument to keep the peace in Germany and that any attempt to make it stronger would lead to civil war. He believed he had found the answer in federalism—a league of seven great magnates with a vested interest in maintaining order under the nominal leadership of an emperor chosen by themselves. (Nor was it a disadvantage that in his capacity as Bohemian king he was one of the exalted seven.)[317] As no part in the imperial electoral or coronation process was conceded to the papacy, the bull represented a triumph of German nationalism over papal internationalism. Still the blow to central authority was unmistakable.

The waning of papal and imperial influence in Europe left England and France as the continent's leading powers, and as each desired preeminence over the other, the two nations found immediate occasion to quarrel. Edward I held the Aquitaine in fief from Philip the Fair, and their overlapping jurisdiction in local matters kept them ceaselessly at odds. Moreover, they sanctioned piracy of each other's shipping with both parties committing acts of shocking barbarity. One side or the other—history is not sure which—amputated the hands and feet of an entire enemy crew and set them adrift to die. Captured seamen were hung from mastheads and left to decompose. In time, such actions provoked a full-scale naval engagement off the coast of Brittany in which Edward came off the better (1293).[318] Philip had his revenge on land—ousting Edward from the Aquitaine (1297). But during the ensuing five-years' truce, the French king attempted to commandeer the rich commerce of Flanders, with the unhappy result that an army of French mounted knights perished in the mud at Courtrai at the point of Flemish pikes (1302).[319] The disaster—an early indication that the age of equestrian chivalry was ending[320]—forced Philip to make peace with England by reinstating Edward in his fief. There ensued a second mêlée in Flanders—this one at Mons-en-Pevele, where Philip personally led his troops to victory.[321] But the triumph was in no way decisive. The Flemish war dragged on, and to pay for it, Philip resorted to the most malicious expedients. More than once, he debased the coinage; and, when the bounty from this cheat of his own people fell short of expectation, he had recourse to anti-Semitism—driving the Jews (some of whom were his creditors) from the kingdom, and confiscating their assets (1306). (Edward I had cast them out of England with equal callousness in 1290.)

Perhaps the strangest of all his measures, however, was the mass arrest of the Knights Templar (1307). Founded in the early days of the crusades, the Templars had amassed a tremendous fortune by absorbing the composite wealth of their initiates,[322] collecting tithes and charitable donations, and by acting as bankers. But now the crusades were over. Acre, the last Christian stronghold in Syria, had fallen to the Saracens in 1291. To be sure, the Templars had defended the town to the end—many of them being crushed in the rubble when undermining caused their fortress to collapse.[323] But Acre had succumbed just the same, and now, the knightly order was unemployed.

Being immensely rich and having no reason to exist was a bad combination in the cash-strapped France of Philip the Fair. The king's first move was to seek personal membership in the order—his pretext being a desire for solace following the death of his wife (1305).[324] But suspecting the king of scheming at their riches, the Templars respectfully declined his illustrious application. The sequel was their mass arrest on fabricated charges of heresy and wantonness—the indictments being "proved" by subjecting the holy men to unspeakable tortures until some of them "confessed." When the pope subsequently interceded on the Templars' behalf and forced a trial lasting years, a number of defendants retracted their confessions. But Philip put an end to these shenanigans by burning a few dozen retractors at the stake, thereby inducing the rest to retract their retractions. The order was duly abolished—the Master Templar and a few others being burnt alive to make things official—whereat a portion of their funds were appropriated by the crown despite papal insistence that all said moneys be turned over to the Knights Hospitaller.

Meanwhile, across the English Channel, Robert the Bruce, a Scottish nobleman, had declared himself king of Scotland after murdering his powerful rival, John, the Red Comyn, who had contrived to betray him to Edward I. Harried into hiding, the Bruce thought, for a time, of capitulation. But, on seeing a spider spin its web with dogged persistence, he declared that a king of Scotland would not be outdone by a bug. At Loudon Hill (1307), he confounded the English knights with a series of hidden trenches that disrupted their attack and left them sitting ducks for his spearmen. Edward I, now old and sickly, vowed to crush his unruly neighbor once and for all. But he died on the march to the Scottish frontier, leaving the crown to his wastrel son, Edward II (ruled 1307–1327), whose principal talent in life lay in being dominated—willingly or unwillingly—by one universally detested chief councilor after another.

There followed several years of lightning raids and guerrilla sorties by the Scots, before England's new king finally met the Bruce in open battle at Bannockburn (1314). As usual, the mailed English knights could make no headway against the tightly massed Scottish *schiltrons*, so Edward attempted to repeat the tactic used by his father at Falkirk by bringing forth his archers. At Bannockburn, however, the Scottish cavalry were in patriotic hands. They cut the archers to pieces in a rapid charge, while the Bruce's spearman pressed the English, front and flank, pitching them by the dozen into a nearby gorge.[325] At this, the English broke and ran with Edward in the lead, and though the war continued through the end of the 1320s, the Bruce's stunning victory effectively secured Scotland's independence for the next four centuries.

When not courting disaster on the field of battle, Edward II spent his reign watching his hated favorites follow one another to the executioner's block. The first, Piers Gaveston was beheaded at the insistence of the disgruntled nobility. Hugh Dispenser, who came after him, was killed in a particularly alarming way. Accused of carrying on a homosexual relationship with the king, his genitals were hacked off and burnt before his eyes. Then, since he was a "false traitor of heart," his heart was torn—still beating—from his chest and burnt, too.[326] Ultimately, Edward himself was overthrown and murdered by his wife's lover, Roger Mortimer, who contrived an ingenious means of sodomizing the king to death with a hot iron poker. Not a single incriminating mark could be found on the body, but the surrounding countryside had evidence enough of foul play listening to their dying king's hideous screams.[327]

The Hundred Years' War Begins: Sluys, Crécy and Calais (1340–1347)

Less than a year after these events, Charles IV, king of France (ruled, 1322–1328), died without an identifiable male heir—the first time a Capetian monarch had done such a thing since the dynasty began 341 years earlier. Philip of Valois, a nephew of Philip the Fair, claimed the vacant throne, but England's Queen Isabelle immediately objected that, as a daughter of Philip the Fair, she and her issue held a stronger claim. Her son, England's King Edward III (ruled, 1327–1377), for whom she was serving as regent, was duly put forward as a rival pretender[328]; but it was ruled that the throne could not pass through the female line even to a male heir.[329] Hence, the contest went to Philip (now Philip VI) to whom Edward subsequently did homage for his possessions in France (namely, Guienne and Pontheiu).

Alas, the crown of France was not the sole object of contention between the two kings. The Scots had won their independence under Robert the Bruce in 1328, but as they refused to restore the lands of those Scottish nobles who had supported England in the war (as required by treaty), the latter rebelled and sought succor from King Edward. At Halidon Hill (1333), Edward won a decisive victory over the patriotic Scots who promptly appealed to Philip for assistance in their cause. Philip gladly obliged them in hopes of keeping Edward too bogged down in Scotland to cause trouble on the continent.[330]

At about the same time, Edward received at his court the French outlaw, Robert of Artois, who had lost his familial lands (in Artois) to the rival claim of his aunt and niece. Robert brought suit. But as an unfavorable judgment was expected, he sought to strengthen his case by employing forged documents and (most probably) by poisoning his aunt and niece, who died under circumstances as mysterious as they were opportune. Indicted as a sorcerer[331]—which was a serious charge in those days—Robert fled to England, after which he reminded King Edward of his claim upon the French throne at every opportunity. Philip, for his part, threatened to confiscate the lands of anyone who assisted the outlaw—a hint to the English king that his lands in France might thus be declared forfeit.[332]

There was also some difficulty in Flanders, where, in 1328, the commercial faction had risen up against the rule of Philip's feudal subject, Count Louis, only to be decisively beaten by a French army at Cassel. Cruel retribution was taken against the Flemish rebels, which only served to create more ill will against Count Louis and the French king. Because the whole of Flemish commerce consisted of cloth making, which in turn was completely dependent on a continuing supply of English wool, England could not turn a blind eye to these events. Indeed, as Philip had seen fit to meddle in Scotland, Edward saw no reason why he should not do the same in Flanders. English bribes confirmed the Flemish commercial party in its opposition to the French crown.[333] In retaliation, Philip ordered the arrest of every Englishman in Flanders (1336). Determined to be no less bold, Edward shut off the supply of wool, causing a simultaneous crisis for the merchants of England and Flanders, who in consequence clamored in unison for war with France.[334]

As a clash of arms was now inevitable, Edward renewed his claim upon the French throne—not the least because of the arguments of his Flemish ally, Jacob van Artevelde, who noted that under feudal law the Flemish people must fight for their "king" (as Edward would have been had he been king of France).[335] In retaliation, France raided the English coastline, torching Portsmouth and Southampton (1338). Philip then collected a massive naval force at Sluys with the intention of crossing the English Channel for a full-scale invasion (1340).[336] Before the fleet could embark, however, a makeshift armada led by King Edward surprised it in its moorings, and achieved a victory so decisive that the French were virtually expelled from the Channel (an item of news that had to be broken to King Philip by his court jester after all other officials demurred).[337]

Surprisingly enough, the engagement at Sluys had been decided by archery—a skill in which the English, armed with the longbow, held a decided advantage. Adopted during the reign of Edward I, who had endured its devastating effect in the Welsh war before employing it to his own profit at Falkirk, the longbow was accurate to a distance of 200 yards, could slice through armor at sixty, and could be fired ten times a minute as compared to four or less times for the French archer's crossbow.[338] To make sure that men were available to use the new weapon, the crown declared participation in any sport other than archery to be a capital crime.[339] Its tactical employment was brought to perfection in Edward III's victory over the Scots at Halidon Hill. Thereafter, it was customary for English knights to fight on foot, presenting an impenetrable wall of spears to the enemy, while companies of archers, positioned between these phalanxes and on the flanks, exhausted the onrushing foe with deadly volleys of missile fire.[340]

After Sluys, the English Channel was open, but a lack of money prevented Edward from capitalizing on the fact. Not until 1346 did the English land an expeditionary force on the Norman coast. Once arrived, however, it marched unopposed down the valley of the Seine, burning, raping and plundering everything in its path. With the flames visible on the horizon from the walls of Paris,[341] Philip assembled the knighthood of France and came out to meet the invaders at Crécy. The hour was late, and the French had long been on the march when the rival armies came within view of each other. Consequently, King Philip decided to delay battle until the morrow in order to rest his tired troops. Unfortunately, those in the rear of his army were unaware of his order to halt and pressed ahead. The vanguard thus had no choice but to continue moving forward until it came within range of the English longbowmen.

"As soon as the foremost rank saw [the English]," says Froissart, "they fell back at once, in great disorder, which alarmed those in the rear, who thought they had been fighting."[342] To avert disaster, King Philip ordered his Genoese crossbowmen to engage the English archers. But the Genoese—who only consented to advance after lodging an emphatic complaint about their day's march—proved no match for their adversaries. Indeed, they had hardly unloosed a single volley of bolts before a shower of arrows from the longbows convinced them to cast down their weapons and flee. Watching them run helter-skelter toward their own lines, King Philip cried out in disgust: "Kill me those scoundrels; for they stop up our road!"[343]

Most inauspiciously, the French knights did as they were told, and as they hacked and hewed their own Genoese auxiliaries to pieces, the English fired a hail of arrows into the confused mass. There was now no question of averting battle. Disentangling themselves from the Genoese, the French knights pressed on until they reached the English men-at-arms, who repulsed them in hand-to-hand combat. The king's son, Edward, Prince of Wales—known popularly as the "Black Prince"—"won his spurs" in this exchange. Meanwhile, Welsh knifemen roamed the field finishing off the enemy wounded, until the French casualty list became insupportable. Philip's ally, the aged and blind Bohemian King John of Luxembourg (the father of Emperor Charles IV, author of the *Golden Bull*), was slain along with his retinue after being guided into the fight. King Philip himself was wounded, and his nobles insisted on his departure from the field. (He took refuge at Amiens).

For England, it was an unprecedented victory. In order to exploit the advantage, however, Edward required a Channel port to serve as a base of operations. Accordingly, he besieged Calais. The city held out for nearly a year (1346–1347), subsisting in the end on a diet composed mostly of rodents.[344] Towards the end, King Philip attempted to relieve the city—capturing a tower held by thirty-two English archers on nearby Sangate Hill. But the effort was costly in men, and Philip could get no closer since the English had blocked all the approaches to Calais save a narrow bridge on which the French would have been sitting ducks. Relying on a sense of fair play, Philip sent the following message by envoy to the English King: "Sir, the king of France informs you ... that he is come to the hill of Sangate, in order to give you battle, but he cannot find any means of approaching you: he

The hand-cranked crossbow was no match for the longbow at Crécy (© Depositphotos.com/Patrick Guénette).

Illustration of the Battle of Crécy showing English longbows against French crossbows, from the *Chronicles* of Jean Froissart, currently housed at the Bibliothèque Nationale de France (Wikimedia Commons). (http://commons.wikimedia.org/wiki/File%3ABattle_of_crecy_froissart.jpg)

therefore wishes you would assemble your council ... and fix upon a spot where a general combat may take place."[345] Edward declined this chivalrous challenge, and Calais, without hope of relief, succumbed to the English siege. But now, events in a different port, far away on the Black Sea, intruded upon England's string of successes.

A Brief Interlude: The Black Death (1348–1349)

In 1344, Janibeg, Khan of the Mongol "Kipchak" Empire, intervened in a conflict between Christians and Muslims at the Black Sea port of Kaffa. The Christians were Genoese traders whose outpost at Kaffa had been established as part and parcel of the increasing commerce stimulated by the crusades. Janibeg sided with the Muslims. He besieged Kaffa for two years, when suddenly a mysterious illness broke out amongst his troops (1346). The Genoese, peering over their walls, must have rejoiced at their enemy's discomfiture. But their celebration was cut short when Janibeg decided to catapult his dead over the battlements and into the heart of the city. The alarmed citizens deposited the unclean carcasses into the Black Sea, but as the corpse barrage continued, signs of the strange and horrible affliction appeared amongst the Genoese themselves. Those yet to be stricken abandoned Kaffa in horror, and set sail for Genoa.[346]

In early October 1347, the first ships to arrive in Europe bearing the plague touched home at the Sicilian port of Messina. The Genoese passengers were visibly ill, and their illness, the bubonic plague or "Black Death," spread through Europe like a brushfire. As the English eyewitness, Henry Knighton, reports: "Memory could not recall so universal and terrible a mortality since the time of Vortigern ... in whose reign ... the living did not suffice to bury the dead."[347]

So quickly did the disease kill that ships at sea had no time to put in before the entire crew perished.[348] One of these floating tombs navigated aimlessly to the shore of Norway, thus delivering the pestilence to Scandinavia.[349] People went to sleep in perfect health and were already corpses at sunrise; physicians dropped dead next to their patients,[350] and lawsuits had to be dismissed because no litigant was alive to testify.[351] Tittering at the misery of their English neighbors, the Scots raised an army for invasion, but the merry band of warriors succumbed to the malady before they could cross the border.[352]

As the death toll mounted, the fabric of European society came unglued. Some gave themselves over entirely to licentiousness, including a group of monks at Auwa, who looted the coffers of their monastery in order to finance their excesses.[353] Fields went unplowed. Farm animals were left to fend for themselves. Nor was this solely the result of the drop in population, for those who survived saw no reason to tend to their duties with the apocalypse upon them. "[T]his sore affliction entered so deep into the minds of men and women," writes Giovanni Boccaccio in the introduction to his masterpiece, *The Decameron*, "that, in the horror thereof, brother was forsaken by brother, nephew by uncle, brother by sister, and, oftentimes husband by wife; nay, what is more, and scarcely to be believed, fathers and mothers were found to abandon their own children untended, unvisited, to their fate, as if they had been strangers."[354] Similarly, a chronicler from Siena reports that "one brother fled the other; the wife abandoned the husband ... and I, Agnolo di Tura, called Grasso, buried five of my sons in one trench with my own hands; and many others did the like. And also there were some that were so badly covered up that the dogs dragged them out, and ate [the] bodies.... No bells tolled, and no one wept at any misfortune that befell, for almost every person expected death ... and many men believed and said: 'This is the end of the world.'"[355]

The disease ran its course in one of three ways. Pneumonic plague, a febrile illness spread by respiratory droplet, caused the patient to cough foul-smelling blood, and brought death in three days. Bubonic plague, spread by the rat flea, produced swellings known as "buboes"—first in the groin and armpit, then spreading elsewhere—which turned black and putrefied with malodorous pus. Typically, the victim had had quite enough of this version by the fifth day. Finally (and worst), there was a septicemic form, also spread by the rat flea, wherein the causative bacterium, *Yersinia pestis*, overwhelmed the bloodstream and killed within 24 hours.[356] In all, a third of Western Europe perished, as did a third of Islam. Asia, whence the plague arose, was no less ravaged. Physicians had little to offer beyond advising those not yet afflicted to flee for their lives. No remedies were developed. Quarantine—so named because Italian ports placed incoming ships in isolation for forty days (i.e., "*quaranta giorni*")—was the only medical innovation.[357] Milan's quarantines were timeless: The houses of victims were walled over by government decree, and the death rate was a paltry fifteen percent.[358]

There were not enough doctors or priests to attend the dying, and, in some cases, those who *were* available hesitated to perform their offices. In England, laymen were invited to confess to one another. Pope Clement VI consecrated the Rhone River since so many corpses had been deposited there, and seeing that this was not enough, he proclaimed all who died of the plague to be forgiven their sins.[359] Clement was urged to stay in his quarters by his surgeon Guy de Chauliac, who kept two fires perpetually lit to protect him.[360] Though scared out of his wits, the surgeon ventured out to treat the ill, left a written description of the various forms of the disease, and then fell sick of it himself.[361] Miraculously, he survived. Alfonso XI, king of Castile, was not so lucky. He became the sole European monarch to die of the disease when he refused to let an outbreak among the Muslims dissuade him from attacking Gibraltar in 1350.[362]

The general opinion on the origin of the disease fell into two categories. Enlightened men argued that the malady resulted from "bad air" produced by a misalignment of the planets, while less-learned folk held to the equally defensible hypothesis that it was owed to the wrath of God. This latter belief gave spawn to the flagellants—wandering troupes of ascetics who publicly flogged themselves in terrible ways, apparently in the belief that the Plague God could be appeased by an adequate show of penance. At first, even the pope seemed to think they were on to something, but the flagellants proved too excessive in their zeal. A prevailing bigotry held that the Jews had caused the epidemic by poisoning well water. In Basle, hundreds of Jews were burned to death after being herded into a wooden building—the scene being

A "Dance of Death" motif in art reflected the medieval obsession with the universality of death in the aftermath of the Bubonic Plague. In this 1895 engraving based on a Hans Holbein work of 1549, a peddler fails to convince Death that he is due in the market with his wares (© Depositphotos.com/Patrick Guénette).

repeated in Freiberg, Speyer and scores of other towns.[363] At Strassbourg, the town council was overthrown by the mob for attempting to protect the city's two thousand Jews—the latter being conducted forthwith to the Jewish cemetery, where they were crowded onto a great wooden scaffold and incinerated. Only those who accepted baptism were spared, and many of these were burnt later.[364]

As they traveled from town to town, the flagellants waged their own anti–Semitic terror campaign. In Frankfurt, the unsuspecting Jews were torn in pieces after the zealots incited the populace against them. To his everlasting credit, Pope Clement publicly proclaimed the Jews innocent,[365] but the flagellants persisted in their excesses. Unwilling to abide such conduct, Clement outlawed their public displays and allowed the lay authorities to curb their activities by force (1349).[366]

Although the disease was poised to descend again on the unhappy continent both in the near future and for centuries to come, the initial havoc ceased around 1350. Certain that its ravages would be regarded with skepticism by coming generations, Francesco Petrarch, wrote to his brother, saying: "Oh, happy people of the future, who have not known these miseries and perchance will class our testimony with the fables."[367] Yet the plague had left an indelible imprint: The Church, which had been unable to attenuate the malady's ravages, would soon be attacked by the likes of Wycliffe and Hus; while the kings of France and England, would scarcely find the manpower to resume their conflict.

The Hundred Years War Resumes: From Poitiers to Limoges (1356–1372)

King Philip successfully evaded the plague, only to die of unrelated causes in 1350. His son, John II, succeeded him. Vexed by a rash of English provocations, the new king obtained funds from the Estates General to resume the Hundred Years' War, and with these monies, he financed a truly marvelous defeat at Poitiers (1356).

In point of fact, the English had preferred not to fight, but the fleet-footed French overtook them with a river at their backs and refused to take their preferences into account.[368] Vastly outnumbered, England's Black Prince arrayed his 8000 troops on a wooded slope, and worked desperately to entrench them. The timely arrival of two Cardinal-legates gave him an extra day to do so, for their forlorn attempt to negotiate a truce served only to delay the French attack until the following morning.

Refusing a recommendation that he surround the English and starve them out, King John divided his army into three ranks of infantry and a vanguard of cavalry. This latter unit, comprising the elite of John's officer corps, was given the task of scattering the English archers. But to reach the English position, they had to charge four-abreast along a narrow passage flanked on either side by hedges and marshes. And whilst they did so, the archers unloosed upon them such a devastating barrage from their longbows "that the French did not know which way to turn ... to avoid their arrows."[369] Of the three hundred nobles who set out, scarcely any escaped death, wounding or capture. Thus, when John's first infantry rank stumbled over their mangled bodies to attack the English center, they had no veteran commander to lead them. After a stiff exchange, they withdrew in panic, prompting the second rank to flee behind them without even engaging.[370]

Seemingly unfazed by these setbacks, King John led his third rank forward against the English, whose archers, having exhausted their ammunition, were now scurrying about the battlefield in a feverish attempt to recover what arrows they could from the corpses of their victims.[371] As the English were still vastly outnumbered, Prince Edward's advisors recommended the speedy capture of King John as the likeliest way to victory. Accordingly, Edward ordered the bulk of his force forward against John's division, while a party of archers and men-at-arms struck simultaneously at the enemy flank. According to the French chronicler, Geoffrey Le Baker, King John fought admirably—proving himself worthy of the Valois name by lopping off heads and limbs and knocking out teeth. On that day, he displayed a certain facility at disembowelment, and—depending on what exactly is meant by the word "detruncate"—there is reason to suspect that he cleaved some of his adversaries in half cross-wise. Unfortunately, his bodyguards were being cut down in equal numbers, and as these stumbled away, absent limbs or tripping over their own intestines,[372] the king's division finally wavered and broke, leaving King John with a handful of retainers, who "were so intermixed with their enemies, that at times there were five men attacking one gentleman."[373]

Still, King John fought on—sustaining two facial wounds after his helmet was jostled from his head.[374] At his side, his fourteen-year-old son, Philip, sought to warn him: "Father, ware right! Father, ware left!"[375] But now, the English men-at-arms surrounded him, shouting, "Surrender yourself, surrender yourself, or you are a dead man!"[376] Seeing no one of suitable rank to accept his surrender, John inquired as to the whereabouts of the Black Prince. A voice replied: "Sire, he is not here; but surrender yourself to me, and I will lead you to him." King John removed his right-hand glove and handed it to the man who had spoken.[377] As he did so, says Froissart, "there was much crowding and pushing about, for every one was eager to cry out: 'I have taken him!'"[378]

With the king in enemy hands, a regency was established in France under John's eldest son, Charles, who promptly convoked the Estates General. Far from granting him money to continue the war, however, the Estates staged a revolution—seizing the dies for casting coins, and chasing King John's corrupt former ministers into hiding (1357). A "Grand Ordinance" was passed granting extensive governmental powers to the Estates, and when Charles attempted to defy the measure, Etienne Marcel, the parliamentary leader, burst in on him in his rooms, and murdered his chief councilors with such brutality that the regent was bespattered with their blood.[379]

Simultaneous with these events, the countryside fell prey to its own brand of violence. It was hard enough on the peasantry to have to bear the pillaging of enemy troops in times of war, but with the fighting temporarily on hold, roving bands of their own unemployed French soldiers—the dreaded "Free Companies"—roamed hither and yon, plundering them with equal facility. Left to fend for themselves by the cowardly nobility (who likewise oppressed them), the peasants took up arms and assumed the offensive: "These wicked [peasants]," says Froissart, "plundered and burnt all the houses they came to, murdered every gentleman, and violated every lady and damsel they could find.... Among other infamous acts, they murdered a knight, and having fastened him to a spit, roasted him before the eyes of his wife and his children, and, after ten or twelve had violated her, they forced her to eat some of her husband's flesh, and then knocked her brains out.... When they were asked for what reason they acted so wickedly; they replied they knew not, but they did so because they saw others do it; and they thought that by this means they should destroy all the nobles and gentlemen in the world."[380]

Known as the *Jacquerie* after the jacket, or "*jacque*," they wore,[381] the peasants pillaged their way to the outskirts of Meux, where they encountered a company of mounted knights formed up in battle order. The knights cut down 7000 of them at a blow, and then embarked on a campaign of extermination in which an estimated 20,000 peasants lost their lives. When, subsequent to this, an army of knights converged on Paris, the revolution came apart. Abandoned by his following, Etienne Marcel made a run for it, only to have his head cleaved open with an axe.[382] French parliamentarianism would not recover from the blow for another four centuries.

English parliamentarianism, on the other hand, was doing just fine. Indeed, parliament had now established itself as the final arbiter of all royal tax petitions. This might have caused friction in normal times, but the plundered riches flowing in from France created a great willingness on the part of parliament to approve the king's levies. Far from being viewed as an imposition, the revenues were looked upon as a business investment that, so far, had produced an excellent return.[383] It was, therefore, with some consternation that parliament's savvy investors received news of the Treaty of Bretigny (1360), which "ended" the war. As late as 1359, Edward III had been as happy as parliament to continue the war, but when he attempted a new invasion at the end of that year, he found that between his own former ravages and those of the *Jacquerie* there was no longer any land suitable for plundering. Consequently, he could not feed his troops, and as the French would not consent to meet him in the open field, he saw no choice but to cut his losses and confirm the aforementioned treaty.[384] By its terms, England gained absolute sovereignty (i.e., without feudal obligations) over the Aquitaine, Calais and Ponthieu, as well as a large war indemnity. In return, Edward III relinquished his claim to the French throne, and King John was released, leaving behind two sons as hostages until the war indemnity was paid. When one of his sons subsequently escaped, John chivalrously returned to a comfortable captivity in England, where, to the considerable sadness of his hosts, he died in 1364.

The French regent, Charles, was now officially crowned king as Charles V. Surrounding himself with able ministers and excellent soldiers, including a Breton officer named Bertrand du Guesclin who was given overall command of the French army with the title Constable of France, Charles restored order to the realm. By 1369, he felt secure enough to repudiate the humiliating Treaty of Bretigny. On the pretext of complaints made in Aquitaine about the severity of English rule, Charles ordered the Black Prince to come to Paris to acquit himself as though he were still a feudal subject. Naturally enough, the Black Prince refused. The result was war. This time, however, the English could make no headway. Constable du Guesclin (a man so ugly that it was celebrated in poem[385]) would not be lured into a pitched battle, but hovered in the periphery to harass the English whenever the passage of time forced them to retreat.[386] In utter frustration, the Black Prince sacked the town of Limoges, which had recently defected to the French cause (1370). Having breached the walls by undermining, the English rushed in and murdered 3000 of the inhabitants without regard to age or sex, or to guilt or innocence. No mercy was shown even to women and children who begged the prince for their lives on bended knee.[387]

This disgraceful conquest was to be the last for the Black Prince, who had to be borne into the city on a litter due to a mysterious illness that swelled his body and afflicted him with fever and diarrhea.[388] After returning to England, he made one last serious attempt at invasion, but a contrary wind prevented his landing (1372). He died of his illness in 1376, and was followed to the grave a year later by his father, Edward III. The succession thus fell to the Black Prince's ten-year-old son, Richard II (ruled 1377–1399). Although France was unable to capitalize on England's leadership crisis, the tide of the war had already turned. Indeed, at his death in 1380, Charles V—known ever after as Charles the Wise—could boast that he had driven the English completely off the mainland except for a few coastal strongholds.

A Lengthier Interlude: Domestic Turmoil in England and France (1380–1415)

For the next three decades, neither side was able to mount a decisive campaign. Following on the heels of her succession crisis, England was thrown into chaos by the Peasants' Revolt of 1381. Similar in some respects to the revolt of the *Jacquerie* in France, the rebellion stemmed from a labor shortage following the Black Death. For a time, the surviving English peasants were in a position to sell their skills to the highest bidder. Unfortunately, the drop in population had simultaneously decreased the demand for agricultural produce, thus driving down prices. As a result, manorial lords found themselves paying more to get their lands tilled, while selling their produce for less. To avoid operating at a loss, they prevailed upon parliament to pass the Statute of Laborers (1351) and other measures, which tied peasants to their estates and forced them to work for unreasonably low wages.[389]

By 1381, the misery attendant upon these laws had been compounded by increasing tax levies for the foundering war effort. Driven to the brink, the peasants rebelled. Giving voice to their grievances was the Lollard preacher John Ball—"a crazy priest in the county of Kent" by Froissart's estimation—whose sermons gave early echo both to communism and to egalitarianism: "My good friends, things cannot go well in England ... until everything shall be in common; when there shall neither be vassal nor lord, and all distinctions leveled; when the lords shall be no more masters than ourselves. Are we not all descended from the same parents, Adam and Eve? And what can they show, or what reasons give, why they should be more masters than ourselves except, perhaps, in making us labor and work for them?"[390] Froissart calls his brand of logic "absurd," but Ball's listeners walked away saying to each other, "John Ball preaches such and such things, and he speaks truth."[391]

Rallying behind the soldier of fortune, Wat Tyler—a "tiler of houses, a bad man, and a great enemy to the nobility"[392]—sixty thousand peasants marched on London to demand justice from King Richard. Gaining access to the locked city by threatening to burn it down if they were barred,[393] the marchers made their way to the Tower of London, where they demanded an audience with the King and an accounting of all government expenditures from his chancellor, saying that if the latter "did not render such an account as was agreeable to them, it would be the worse for him."[394] To prove they meant business, they struck off the heads of several prominent Londoners—among them, the unfortunate chancellor, who was never given a chance to render his accounts. The sight of heads being paraded through the city atop pikes convinced King Richard to announce that he would meet the throng outside London and assent to their demands. Already, he had agreed to abolish serfdom and revoke the unfair labor laws of the 1350s, but when he ventured outside the city the following day, Tyler demanded that he also confiscate Church estates and eliminate class privilege. The king agreed except in the case of royalty.[395] Far from finding this satisfactory, Tyler grew angry and spoke to the king with great effrontery. Shocked at this breach of protocol, the Lord Mayor of London cried: "Truly, does it become a stinking rascal as thou art to use such speech in the presence of the king, thy natural lord?" Then drawing his sword, he "struck Tyler such a blow on the head as felled him to his horse's feet," whereupon "one of the King's squires ... leaped from his horse, and drawing a ... sword ... thrust it into [Tyler's] belly, and thus killed him."[396]

Tyler's demise, coupled with the capture and execution of the preachers John Ball and Jack Straw put paid to the revolution. The concessions made by the king were formally revoked by parliament.[397] But the uprising was just the beginning of King Richard's difficulties. The Black Death had disrupted the very fabric of feudal society. Not content with the advantages given them by the aforementioned Statute of Laborers, many great barons had fundamentally altered their relationship with the peasantry. Rather than distributing fiefs in exchange for fealty or service as they had formerly done, they began leasing their lands in exchange for regular cash payments.[398] The change was not without ramifications. Financial risk was now to be borne by the individual peasant, who had to till the soil and sell his produce as best he could, while the lord's rental income was virtually guaranteed. Indeed, to the great detriment of Richard II, the new status quo provided hefty bankrolls to England's power hungry barons—chief among them, Thomas, duke of Gloucester, the king's ambitious uncle, who established himself as a menace to the crown by using his wealth to hire a mercenary army.[399]

With an empty treasury and an extravagant court, King Richard was intent on making peace with France. But Uncle Gloucester thought otherwise, and those who had profited from the war lent him exuberant support. In 1388, Gloucester's mercenaries put a royal army to flight at Radcot Bridge, leaving the duke in a position to dictate policy to the king. Packed with his supporters, parliament ordered the execution of the king's ministers, thus winning for itself the historical epithet, the "Merciless Parliament."

Although King Richard declared his majority the following year (1389), he made no effort to avenge himself for nearly a decade. In 1397, however, rumors reached his ear that Gloucester planned to depose and imprison him for pursuing peace with France. He, therefore, decided to act: Gloucester was apprehended and strangled with a towel, while his chief followers were made to suffer exile or death.[400] Richard, however, carried his retributions too far, and when he showed no signs of desisting from his reign of terror, the barons began to fear for their collective wellbeing. Indeed, it was rumored that the king would spurn them utterly, and cast his lot with the common masses.[401]

In this milieu, the unexpected exile and disinheritance of Henry Bolingbroke, the powerful Duke of Lancaster, proved the last straw. Every man of property felt a threat to his interests, and, to a man, the baronage raised the standard of rebellion (1399).[402] Richard's position quickly became untenable. Returning to England after quelling a rebellion in Ireland, he encamped for the night with his army of 6,000 men. On awaking at dawn, he found that the entire lot had abandoned him.[403] The charge of conspiring with the masses was false. There was, in fact, no class upon which he could rely. When he surrendered at Flint, even his trusty greyhound, Math, deserted him and took up position next to Bolingbroke.[404]

He abdicated on a promise of safety, but died mysteriously in prison soon thereafter—his crown being bestowed upon Bolingbroke who, as Henry IV, introduced the House of Lancaster to the English throne.

The situation was no less chaotic in France. When Charles the Wise died in 1380, the throne fell to his twelve-year-old son, Charles the Mad (ruled 1380–1422), who after a promising beginning to his reign,[405] lapsed into intermittent psychosis, the first manifestation of which occurred on a hot afternoon in August 1392. The king—who had been suffering from headaches and fevers for months—was on the march with his army, when, startled by an unexpected noise, he suddenly wheeled upon his retinue, raised his sword and cried, "Advance!" By some accounts, the madman cut down four of his retainers before he could be disarmed.[406] And though he soon became lucid again, the recurring conviction that his body was composed of glass, and that his lurking enemies would break him in pieces,[407] incapacitated him, and made him easy fodder for the machinations of his ambitious relatives. Chief among these were his brother, Louis of Orleans, and his uncle, Philip the Bold of Burgundy, the youngest son of King John II. (We met the latter on the field of Poitiers, bidding his father, "Father, ware right! Father, ware left!"). Philip took the early lead in this power struggle, largely owing to a fortuitous marriage, which delivered the rich county of Flanders into his possession. Upon his death in 1404, his son, John "the Fearless" (so-called because he had fought without fear alongside the crusaders at Nicopolis in 1396),[408] succeeded to his possessions. Three years after that, John decided to end France's factional quarrels by having Louis of Orleans assassinated. But far from producing peace, it gained for John the undying enmity of the victim's two young sons. As these boys were as yet too young to lead their party, their supporters identified a capable figurehead in Count Bernard of Armagnac (hence the name "Armagnacs," which history has bestowed upon this faction). Based mainly in southern and western France, the Armagnacs clamored for war against England, hoping thus to drive the English from their remaining strongholds in the nearby Duchy of Guienne. By 1411, however, John the Fearless and his Burgundian party controlled the king. More important, they ruled over Flanders, which made them desirous of peace with England, lest a blow be dealt to the lucrative Anglo-Flemish commerce in wool.[409]

Agincourt

While France endured these vicissitudes, Henry IV (Bolingbroke) was too busy dodging assassination plots and quelling revolts by the Scots, the Welsh and his own nobility to think of renewing the continental war. Bolingbroke had not, in fact, been rightful heir to the throne he had ascended (a distinction enjoyed by his nine-year-old cousin, the earl of March). At his death, his son and successor, Henry V (ruled 1413–1422), had no better claim to the throne than he. This new Henry, however, thought that he might render the illegitimate dynasty popular if he could win a great victory over the French and return to England laden with spoils of war. Barring this, by enlisting them to fight, he might at least keep the restless English baronage too busy for conspiracy.[410] He therefore reanimated the defunct English claim to the French throne,[411] granted amnesty to those who had conspired against his father, and laid plans to resume the contest with France while the French were still divided (1414). In September 1415, he landed near Harfluer on the inlet of the Seine with an invasion force 10,000-strong. But he sustained so many casualties in the capture of this port that he had to abandon his plans for a march on Paris and make for the safe haven of Calais before winter set in.

On reaching Agincourt, he found his path blocked by the French. As usual, the latter held a vast numerical advantage—their numbers variably estimated at anywhere between twenty-five and fifty thousand armored knights, as opposed to one thousand English men-at-arms and six thousand archers (many of whom were afflicted by starvation and dysentery.)[412]

On October 25, 1415, the English arrayed themselves in a good defensive position on a plowed, rain-drenched field, bordered by dense woods on either side. Doubting their prospects, many of Henry's men had spent the preceding hours availing themselves of confession and writing their wills,[413] but their king now addressed them, "exhorting and begging them to do well," and reminding them that their forebears "had gained many splendid victories over the French, and caused them marvelous discomfiture."[414]

It soon became apparent, however, that the French did not intend to attack Henry's army in its current position. Thus, to avert a prolonged standoff in which his ill-supplied troops would only grow hungrier, the English king advanced his force within range of the longbows and ordered his archers to fire volleys at the reticent enemy. The ruse worked. Chafing at Henry's boldness, the French knights vied with one another for the chance to retaliate. So heavy was their armor, however, that their horses plunged hoof-deep into the mud at each step. Nor was this the lone impediment to their advance. They were hampered by a constant barrage of arrows, and on drawing closer, they encountered sharpened wooden stakes fixed in the ground facing outward, so as to put the unlucky or inobservant French mount at risk of impalement.[415] In attempting to negotiate this last barrier, the French were subjected to a woeful hail of fire from the longbows, this time at point-blank range.

Knights toppled from their horses and could not lift themselves out of the mud. And now, into the ruinous milieu, came the first wave of heavily armored French infantry, advancing with heads bowed, since the English arrows "fell so heavily that no one durst uncover or look up."[416] Hearing the sound of hoof beats, however, a few must have peaked just in time to see the riderless horses of their fallen comrades careening towards them in their effort to escape the missile fire. The infantry were sent sprawling atop those already mired in the mud, and there was much asphyxiation amongst those at the bottom.[417] Against the odds, a few French knights emerged from this obstacle course to give battle to the English men-at-arms. One even managed to smash an ornament on King Henry's helmet before being killed. Ultimately, however, the French first wave was put to flight, and in their retreat they managed to sow disorder in the second wave, which was attempting to come to their support.

As the French attack lost momentum, Henry ordered his archers to throw down their bows and attack the knights who were stuck in the mud. Being more agile, since they were not weighed down by armor, the archers knocked over those knights who were still standing, and thrust daggers through their helmet visors, or beat them to death with "hatchets, mallets, axes, falcon-beaks" and other sundry weapons.[418]

A virtual sea of corpses now lay before the English line. But the third wave of French infantry was still in the field, and what is more, Henry's baggage train—located to the

Depiction of the Battle of Agincourt (in which the longbow again played a decisive part), from Enguerrand de Monstrelet, *Chronique de France*, early 15th century (Wikimedia Commons). (http://commons.wikimedia.org/wiki/File:Schlacht_von_Azincourt.jpg)

English rear, where the French prisoners were being kept—suddenly came under attack. It was only a raid by local peasants in search of booty; but Henry thought himself surrounded, and ordered the massacre of his prisoners lest they capitalize on the changed circumstances to rejoin the fray. His men hesitated—not out of conscience mind you, but because they stood to lose out on the hefty ransom the prisoners would have fetched. But Henry was adamant, and the order was carried out. If nothing else, the slaughter dampened the fighting spirit of the French third wave. On beholding the fate of their captive brothers, they began to desert the field. (Nor was the ransom entirely lost—for at battle's end, the English "found some good prisoners still alive" underneath the ones they had killed.)[419]

Thus, Henry had his victory—in the view of many historians, the most stunning in English history—and with it an open passage to Calais. From there, he set sail for England to raise reinforcements, before returning, in 1417, to pursue the brilliant, if grisly, siege campaign that was to make him master of all Normandy within two years.

This alarming string of success frightened even John the Fearless, who believed that unless his Burgundians and the rival Armagnacs ended their quarrels and united, the entire country would fall to Henry. A peace parley was duly arranged with the French king's eldest son, the "Dauphin" Charles, at Montereau (1419). But just when all was settled and John knelt in homage, a refractory Armagnac cleaved his head open with a battle-axe. The blow, apparently as surprising to the dauphin as it was to the victim, forfeited the chance of reconciliation. Bent on revenge, John's son, Philip the Good, rallied the Burgundians and defected outright to the English.

The new arrangement left the Armagnacs and the dauphin in a ticklish position. Charles the Mad was now completely incapacitated, and his wife, Queen Isabeau—who did not much like their son, the dauphin,[420] by whose faction she had formerly been imprisoned[421]—was fully prepared to make peace on disastrous terms. In May 1420, she invited King Henry to meet her at Troyes, where she made the surprising disclosure that the dauphin, was actually a bastard—the product of her own infidelities. She then contrived to have her husband, Mad Charles, pen his name to the treasonous Treaty of Troyes, whereby their daughter, Catherine, was betrothed to King Henry who thus became heir to the French throne.

Buttressed by his Burgundian alliance and treaty with Queen Isabeau, King Henry thwarted the hapless Armagnacs in their bid to occupy Paris, and then drove them from the vicinity in a whirlwind campaign. Unfortunately, he contracted dysentery in the process, and in August 1422, he died at Vincennes. Less than two months later, his father-in-law, Charles the Mad, also died. But this did not leave the Dauphin Charles as sole claimant to the throne. For, prior to King Henry's death, his French wife, Catherine, had borne him a son—Henry VI—who was duly crowned King of England *and* France with Burgundian support. The Armagnacs, of course, protested that their puppet, the dauphin, was the lawful ruler.

With three armies roaming the countryside, France lapsed into a state of chaos so dire that even farm animals perceived the danger. Says one chronicler: "If any kind of cultivation was still carried on ... it could only be done close to cities, towns, or castles, no farther away than the watch could be seen, stationed on a high lookout, whence he could observe the robbers as they approached. He would then give the alarm by means of a bell.... This happened so frequently in many places that so soon as the oxen and plow animals were loosed, having heard the signal ... they would, taught by long experience, rush to a place of safety in a state of terror. Even the pigs and sheep did the same."[422]

At Verneuil (1424), the English and Burgundians thrashed the Armagnacs so decisively that the latter had to retire behind the Loire. And even there their position was undermined by the dauphin's alleged illegitimacy. Indeed, the feeble young pretender seemed more mayor of Bourges (where he held his court) than king of France.[423]

The Maid of Lorraine

By 1428, the Armagnacs were at their last gasp. Orleans, the gateway to southern France, was under siege. The bulk of the city lay on the northern bank of the Loire, protected by high walls. A pair of towers, known as the Tourelles, guarded the bridge leading southwards to the suburbs on the opposite bank of the river. The English focused their attack on the latter, and captured the Tourelles in October 1428. But just when it appeared that the Armagnac cause could not possibly be sustained, that rare occurrence—the miracle—intervened to shift the scales. Joan of Arc, a seventeen-year-old peasant girl from the Armagnac town of Domrémy, claimed that the dauphin's legitimacy had been proclaimed to her by saintly voices, which likewise commanded her to rouse the country against the English. Known afterwards as the maid of Lorraine, young Joan appeared at the dauphin's court at Chinon in 1429—identifying him immediately even though an imposter had been put forward in an effort to confound her. She whispered a private message to the dauphin—what she said remains obscure to this day—and though he was more or less convinced that she was a witch,[424] he placed her in command of his army. An uncompromising general, Joan dismissed the doubts of her skeptical officers, and led her troops forthwith to an assault on the English at Orleans. In an attempt to regain the Tourelles, she received an arrow wound in the chest. The English, who were terrified of her, thought her dead, but after being carried from the field, she "sat up and drew the arrow out with her own hands."[425] The Tourelles were retaken, and the English had to abandon the siege (May 1429). Never again would they be so close to winning the war.

In June, Joan routed a combined Anglo-Burgundian force at Patay, and in July, she escorted the dauphin to Rheims, where he was officially crowned king as Charles VII. But this was the apogee of the maid's success. In September, she was wounded in the thigh in a failed effort to take Paris, and, in May 1430, the Burgundians captured her at Compiègne. Forsaken by the king whose throne she had saved, she jumped from a high tower in a forlorn attempt to escape. Surviving almost unscathed, she was recaptured and ransomed to the English, who kept her in shackles, subjecting her to insults and rough treatment while trying her on charges of witchcraft, heresy, apostasy and idolatry—"crimes," say Thatcher and Schwill, "which only the Middle Ages could invent."[426] A year after her capture, she was burned alive at Rouen (May 1431). (It is reported that the English soldiery were in such a rush to see her dead that they cried to her confessor: "How now! priest, are you going to make us dine here? Away with her!"[427] By the time the spectacle was over, however, most of her tormentors were weeping.[428] One distraught English official cried out: "We are all lost; We have burned a saint."[429])

We have now come to the denouement of the war. Despite Joan's demise, the Burgundians soon penned their signatures to the Treaty of Arras (1435), whereby they defected to the French king and dashed England's hopes for victory. In April of the following year, Paris was liberated from its English garrison, and though England fought on, she was losing ground and finding it increasingly difficult to pay for the war.

Not so France. The chief threat to her interests in the late 1430s was not English arms, but bands of her own Armagnac soldiers who roamed the countryside plundering friend and foe alike. Known as "the flayers," says one historian "the horrible tortures which they inflicted in order to compel the hapless peasants to disclose their savings are among the most revolting incidents of a period in which horrors are the rule rather than the exception."[430] What was needed was a disciplined standing army maintained by regular pay, and under the circumstances, the Estates-General was more than happy to approve the necessary tax levies. The Ordinance of 1439 supplied Charles VII with 1.8 million *livres* annually for the purpose, and forbade the raising of armed forces without a royal license and a captain chosen by the king.[431] By 1448, the reorganization was complete. A standing army of cavalry armed with the lance, infantry armed with the bow, artillery and engineers stood ready to serve the king, and by 1451, it had driven the English from Guienne and Normandy, leaving Calais as the sole remnant of England's once extensive continental empire. At Castillon, in 1453—the self-same year that Byzantium succumbed to Ottoman artillery[432]—a last English effort to win back Guienne was repulsed by French cannon. After more than 100 years of conflict, the war came to an end. Plagued by division for centuries, France, by virtue of her victory, would escape the Middle Ages as a geographically unified state.[433]

The Fault Line of Religious Unity

The artillery barrage at Castillon did more than end the Hundred Years War. It shattered the very foundations of feudalism. Neither the archer's longbow, nor the knight's armor, nor even the feudal lord's castle could withstand the destructive power of cannonry. The whole medieval edifice was left to dangle by a thread—and this, too, was about to be severed.

The papacy had made a bad showing during the Hundred Years War. Until 1377, Christ's vicars had remained in Avignon serving the interests of France. But in that year, Pope Gregory XI mustered sufficient nerve to return to Rome and take up residence at the Vatican (the new palace of the Holy See) where he soon died. The French-dominated College of Cardinals was all for returning to Avignon, but the people of Rome surrounded their convocation, shouting: "Listen to us, my lords cardinals: allow us to elect a pope: you are too long about it. Choose a Roman, for we will not have one of any other country."[434] Convinced of their sincerity, the cowed cardinals chose a hundred-year-old Roman cleric who promptly died of the excitement. Scarcely amused, the populace cried: "Make quite sure, our lord cardinals, you give us a Roman pope, and one that lasts this time. If not, we'll come and make your heads redder than your hats."[435] Within twenty-four hours, the cardinals put forward the Archbishop of Bari, who took the name Pope Urban VI.

News of the election was received with transports of joy in the ancient capital. Some months later, however, the happy citizenry was aghast to learn that the cardinals had reconvened outside of Rome for a new election, claiming (truthfully enough) that their initial choice had been made under duress. The result was the Great Schism (1378–1417),

Joan of Arc depicted at the coronation of Charles VII; 1854 oil on canvas painting by Jean Auguste Dominique Ingres currently housed at the Louvre (Wikimedia Commons). (http://commons.wikimedia.org/wiki/File%3AIngres_coronation_charles_vii.jpg)

wherein one pope, Urban VI, sat at the Vatican with the support of England, Italy and the Holy Roman Empire, while another, the so-called "anti-pope," Clement VII, ruled from Avignon with the backing of France, Scotland, Spain and the College of Cardinals.

It was said in jest that the schism was a great boon for the faithful, for if a penitent was refused remission of sins by the usual pope he could now obtain a second opinion from his rival.[436] But the matter was a serious one. Within the Church, a "conciliar" movement took form, which held that a "general council" representing the whole Church could exercise supremacy over an obnoxious pope in order to prevent abuse of the papal office. In 1409, just such a council was convened at Pisa with the object of ending the schism. By this date, Urban VI and Clement VII were dead. Gregory XII now held the Vatican, and Benedict XIII, Avignon. The council declared them both deposed, electing Alexander V to replace them, but as the council possessed no means of enforcing its decision, the number of popes merely increased to three.[437]

From the outset, the Great Schism had been deeply troubling to the laity. The unsavory situation convinced the Oxford theologian, John Wycliffe (1320–1384), to defy a papal pronouncement, and translate the Bible into English. His intention was to enable common laymen to ignore the schismatic priesthood, and seek truth directly from Scripture. In England, his followers came to be called "Lollards," or "mumblers," since they prayed in muffled voices.[438] Charged with heresy, Wycliffe obtained sanctuary from a powerful patron—the English baron, John of Gaunt. His message, meanwhile, found a worthy champion on the continent in Jan Hus of Bohemia. Hus, unfortunately, had no protectors. In 1415, the Church invited him to defend his beliefs at the Council of Constance in southwest Germany. Far from honoring an imperial guarantee of safe conduct, however, the council denounced the Bohemian as soon as he arrived, and then burnt him at the stake. (Although Wycliffe had now been dead for three decades, the council thought it prudent to have his remains disinterred and burnt as well.)

Thinking the issue resolved, the council proceeded to depose all three reigning popes as a prelude to ending the schism. But now it encountered a new snag, for its membership was divided on the question of whether to elect a new pope immediately or to institute desired reforms first so that, once chosen, the pope would be bound by them. A compromise was reached whereby the papal election took precedence, but with a guarantee that two further general councils

Bohemian Priest Jan Hus, engraved by Hans Holbein (© Depositphotos.com/Georgios Kollidas).

would be summoned within the next seven years and at least one every ten years after that. On the basis of this agreement, Cardinal Oddo Colonna was duly elected under the name of Pope Martin V.[439]

No sooner had Martin assumed the papal miter, however, than he reneged on the agreed upon conciliar guarantees and leveled a charge of heresy at those who believed that general councils might overrule the pope (1417).[440] The battle lines were thus drawn between those who held that Church councils were supreme and those who insisted upon papal supremacy. But for the time being, the battle could not be fought, for a heresy of greater import had meanwhile been smoldering in Bohemia. Enraged by the disgraceful treatment of Jan Hus, their spiritual leader, the Bohemians staged a general rebellion in 1419. To deal with the uprising, Pope Martin proclaimed a crusade to extirpate the "Hussite" heresy (1420). Lured by the prospect of booty, the chivalry of Europe marched confidently into Bohemia, only to discover that the Hussites' military tactics were no less alarming than their religious beliefs. When the armies came to grips, the one-eyed Bohemian commander, Jan Zizka, employed his baggage train as a mobile fortress—forming the wagons into a protective laager from which his men could fire their infernal hand guns and cannon to the utter devastation of the armored crusaders.[441]

In all, Pope Martin V dispatched five crusading armies to Bohemia, and although Zizka succumbed to plague in 1424 with the deathbed request that his skin be used to make a war drum,[442] the Hussite success continued. In the fifth and final crusade (1431), the enthusiastic singing of the approaching Hussites was enough to put an army of 130,000 crusaders to flight before the combatants ever came in sight of one another.[443] Indeed, the ultimate failure of the Hussite movement was owed not to any action of the papal crusaders, but to civil war between the radical Hussite commoners and their more moderate aristocratic counterparts.

The radicals (also known as the "Taborites" from the city where they held their assemblies) had decided that it would be best if all goods were held in common so that men might live in perfect brotherhood. The Hussite nobility would have found scruple enough with this proposal, but when certain Taborite voices called for women to be held in common along with the goods, the nobility opted out of the project entirely and sought reconciliation with the Church.[444] Once this purpose was achieved at the Council of Basle, the Taborite radicals and their Priest-Captain, Prokop the Bald (the architect of many of their prior victories), were put to rout at Lipany (1434).[445]

Having won its battle against heresy for now, the Church proceeded to demonstrate that it had learnt nothing. In 1439, a fresh schism erupted between the reigning pope, Eugenius IV, and the "conciliarists"—i.e., those clerics who held that Church councils could overrule papal decrees in periods of abuse. At Basle, the conciliarists elevated a new anti-pope, Felix V, but the employment of this tired expedient merely dealt a blow to the conciliarist cause. Pope Eugenius, meanwhile, managed to *increase* his own prestige by convening the Council of Ferrara (1438–39) where the desperate Byzantine Emperor, John VIII Palaeologus, consented to adopt Roman Catholicism in return for Western assistance against the relentless Ottomans. In another era, this agreement—ending the four-hundred-year old schism between the Greek Orthodox and Roman Catholic churches—might have produced momentous consequences. But the hour was late and Byzantium could not be saved. Nevertheless, the contest between the papacy and the conciliarists had ended in a papal victory.

Consequently, Catholicism escaped the Middle Ages with its spiritual hegemony intact—but only narrowly. The Church had manifestly failed in its mission to usher mankind toward an earthly City of God and had exposed its own worldly susceptibilities in the attempt. The seed of its overthrow had been sown by the teachings of Wycliffe and Hus who pointed to Scripture, rather than to the clergy, as the font of truth—an idea that would provoke a revolution of irresistible force, sweeping away forever the dream of a Europe united under Catholicism.

The story of that revolution—and its own failure to sustain a mission of Godly virtue—is the topic of the next section.

Societal Achievements

It is a fact worth noting that ancient Rome never developed a system of universal education or a means of disseminating important political and scientific information. The body politic therefore never developed a unified notion of civics. H. G. Wells counts this as a major factor in that civilization's failure to sustain a system of republican self-governance—the office of emperor ultimately becoming necessary to maintain even a façade of unity amidst the expansion and civil wars of the late republic.[446]

But the collapse of the Western Roman Empire 500 years later threatened a calamity of far greater magnitude—the extinction of all Western learning. Realizing that the rise of barbarism had placed knowledge and education on the verge of oblivion, a few notable figures labored to keep the flame of enlightenment alive. Following the sack of Rome by Alaric the Visigoth in AD 410, the learned jurist and proconsul Martianus Capella of Carthage compiled an encyclopedia of Roman knowledge concentrating on the seven liberal arts. Entitled *De Nuptiis Philologiae et Mercurii* it was divided into a basic *trivium* composed of grammar, rhetoric and logic, and a more advanced *quadrivium* consisting of music, geometry, arithmetic and astronomy. The last of these is something of an historical curiosity, for Capella seems to have understood that Mercury and Venus orbited the Sun, and certain passages from his work on astronomy may have influenced Copernicus' heliocentric theory of the solar system a millennium later.[447]

During the reign of Theodoric the Ostrogoth (AD 493–526), the court official Boethius (AD 480–524), translated Aristotle's works on logic into Latin. He intended to translate more, and it was a great blow to medieval learning that his paranoid master had him executed before he could do so.[448] Boethius' contemporary, and fellow court official, Cassiodorus (AD 490–585), had better luck—surviving into old age. Wholly devoted to the preservation of classical knowledge, Cassiodorus hoped to found a Christian academy at Rome[449]—a scheme that was ruined by Justinian's reconquest of Italy. Forced to pursue his goal by a different avenue, Cassiodorus entered a Benedictine monastery and started a tradition, soon to catch on throughout Europe, whereby monks devoted a portion of their day's work to the copying of important classical and religious manuscripts. The system was not a perfect one. As often as not, the monkish scribes tasked with making copies worked from the error-ridden reproductions of their monastic brothers, which they compounded with their own mistakes, while the original works lay hopelessly buried in ill-organized monastic libraries.[450]

The efforts of Capella, Boethius and Cassiodorus did something to fan the dimly glowing embers of knowledge in a world lapsing into intellectual darkness, but overall the tendency was towards decline. By Charlemagne's time, the Latin language and script themselves had become debased—a process that Charlemagne and his education minister, Alcuin, did something to curb by standardizing script with the creation of Carolingian minuscule and by establishing "public" schools in the monasteries which were open to students who were not inclined to become monks.[451] The monasteries thus became the main centers of basic education during the Middle Ages—the curriculum being composed primarily of Capella's aforementioned *trivium* and *quadrivium*.

The monastic approach tended to rely on rote learning, which had the effect, intended or not, of stifling innovation. But things became rather more interesting during the 11th century when a heated philosophic controversy arose between the adherents of "realism" and "nominalism." The "realists" held that the universe possesses ideal "universals" that constituted the only "real" truth. According to their viewpoint, which was considered orthodox at the time, the universe possessed (as an example) an ideal universal horse, which they argued was the horse that people meant when they invoked the word "horse."[452] This ideal horse, to realists, was the only real horse, while the individual horses one might encounter in day-to-day life were but imperfect horse-like facsimiles. The nominalists held the opposing "radical" opinion that the word "horse" is nothing but a name, and that the only true horses are those seen in day-to-day life. The latter view had dangerous implications for the Church—for if one were to take the nominalist view that the only real popes were the imperfect fellows that followed one another into the Lateran or Vatican, it could not be long before someone asked whether an ideal "infallible" pope (in the realist sense) had ever existed. The whole dogma of the Church might then be called into question.[453]

The ill effects of the nominalist challenge to Church thought were compounded by the appearance in the West at the same time of Latin translations of Arabic commentary on the works of Aristotle. The most important of these was the commentary of Averroës of Cordoba, and though it has been derided in modern times as "a Latin translation of a Hebrew translation of commentary made upon an Arabic translation of a Syriac translation of a Greek text," its appearance had the inconvenient side effect of enhancing the nominalist school's heretical queries of Church dogma; for the Church had engraved its interpretation of Aristotle's teachings in stone, and the Arabic commentaries offered alternative (though not necessarily more accurate) understandings.[454]

The radical party's leading light at this time was the popular Paris teacher Peter Abelard. Born in Brittany in 1079, Abelard was adept enough at Aristotelian logic by his third decade to outdebate his professor, William of Champeaux, and to establish himself as the most renowned teacher in France. His career was transiently interrupted by a clandestine love affair with the beautiful and brilliant Heloise—a girl less than half his age, whom he impregnated out of wedlock. The two were secretly married, but the girl's vengeful uncle brought their amorous intrigues to a halt by having the scholar castrated by hired cutthroats. Taking solace in his studies, Abelard published *Sic et Non* ("Yes and No"), in which he used Aristotelian logic to demonstrate the contradictory nature of the saintly quotes traditionally used by the Church to settle doctrinal disputes (1120). The treatise made a good case for adopting reason, rather than blind obedience to quotes, as a basis for determining religious truth.[455] Abelard was ordered to defend his position before the Council of Sens in 1141, but was never given a chance to speak. Saint Bernard, head of the Cistercian monastic order, shouted him down, arguing that reason raises no question that cannot be answered by sufficient faith.[456] Abelard soon died of despair (1142), whereupon he was dealt a posthumous blow by one of his former students—Peter Lombard—who refuted the tenets of *Sic et Non* in a work entitled *Sentences*, which "proved" that the authoritative quotes of the Catholic saints *did* convey a consistent message. In truth, the book was as much a victory for Abelard as it was for the Church, for Lombard had used Aristotelian logic to get his point across, thus reinforcing the idea that reason ought to be the measure of religious truth.[457]

Besieged not just by the new logic but also by growing discontent over perceived corruption and worldliness among the clergy, the papacy struck back—sanctioning the foundation of two new monastic orders: The Franciscans, or Grey Friars (founded by Saint Francis of Assisi (1182–1226), who set a commendable example of austerity while spreading the message that reason was immaterial to religion),[458] and the Dominicans, or Black Friars (founded by Saint Dominic (1170–1221), who were so intent on bringing heretics to justice, that their detractors secretly referred to them with the pun, "*Domini canes*," or "God's watchdogs").[459] Like the Franciscans, the Dominicans preached austerity, but they held a very different view of the new logic. Indeed, in a feverish effort to reconcile Arabic and Greek learning with the Christian faith, they became Europe's leading teachers. Born of their industry was the movement known as "scholasticism"—an unlikely marriage of reason and theology which culminated in the publication of the famous twenty-two-volume encyclopedia, *Summa Theologica*, by Saint Thomas Aquinas (1225–1274), which catalogued (to the last atom) the varied ways in which reason "supported" the position of the Church. Aquinas' thinking is revered to this day, but as a group, the "schoolmen"—as the proponents of scholasticism were called—were unable to hold the fort against the intellectual explosion of the Renaissance. In the end, they were undone by their own erudition and increasingly incomprehensible arguments. As Erasmus later complained: "They hedge themselves about with such an array of magisterial definitions, conclusions, corollaries, propositions explicate and implicate, and do so abound in subterfuges, that chains forged by Vulcan himself could not hold them ... so readily do they think up and rattle out new and prodigious terms and expressions."[460]

Before we leave the topic of education, we should mention that Peter Abelard did something more for the field than champion the use of reason. He was also the exemplar of the popular teacher who greatly increased the desire of students across Europe to pursue higher education. In Abelard's time and after, students gathered from around Europe to study under popular teachers in various cities. Their presence tended to be an economic boon for the host community, but something of a social nightmare. The students were masters of indiscipline, starting brawls with the city dwellers that required police intervention. In one famous brawl in Paris, the police killed five students, and the student body threatened to withdraw to another location. The result was the founding of the University of Paris on the basis of special privileges granted by the king to keep the students in the French capital (AD 1200).[461]

Derived from the Latin "universitas," the term "university," as employed in that era, merely implied an association—in this case between teachers and students. It did not entail today's notion of a fixed campus.[462] As guilds were the order of the day, the association between teachers and students took this form, with the teachers positioned as masters and the students as apprentices.[463] The topics of study were organized into four "faculties"—medicine, law, theology and the arts. Learning was focused on unquestioning memorization of venerable ancient authorities. The Justinian Code and Digests were imported from Constantinople and studied at the great law school in Bologna. (Thus did Roman law begin to supplant German tribal law.[464]) At the medical school in Salerno, students followed the dictums of Galen and Hippocrates and learned also the teachings of Avicenna (the Arab "prince of physicians.") In science and logic, Aristotle remained the chief authority. Although his "inductive" method of enquiry (wherein conclusions were reached on the basis of observation) might have laid the foundation of experimental science, Aristotle thoroughly underrated its importance in favor of his "deductive" method (whereby conclusions were derived from logical argument). Hence, his medieval disciples hadn't the slightest inkling of the importance of experiment.[465] The deductive methodology, says the eleventh edition of the *Encyclopædia Britannica*, was "thoroughly well suited to the requirements of an age in which the ideal of human thought was not discovery but order, and in which knowledge was regarded as a set of established propositions...."[466]

Although the verdict of history has changed during the past half-century, the medieval mindset formerly led to the period's dismissal as a "Dark Age" bereft of accomplishment. To Gibbon, the era encompassed "the triumph of barbarism and religion,"[467] and it would not be wrong to note that many of the innovations that *did* occur during the Middle Ages had their roots outside Europe. The introduction of the abacus—so crucial to the resurgence of European commerce—was an import from the Muslim world. Gerbert of Aurillac, who introduced it to the West prior to becoming Pope Sylvester II, was also acquainted with Hindu-Arabic numerals, and the importance of their subsequent introduction to Western mathematics can scarcely be overemphasized. (To provide some perspective, modern authors have beckoned their readers to attempt multiplication or division with Roman numerals[468] or any computation whatever with Egyptian hieroglyphs.[469])

Gunpowder traces its origins to distant China where it had been used in fireworks since AD 1000. The advancing Muslims were the first to adapt it to warfare. In the century after Crécy (AD 1346), Europeans would bring it to prominence on the battlefield, and, as Charles van Doren notes, the West has relied on technology over numbers ever since.[470] Paper was another Chinese import. The Muslims learned how to manufacture it from the Chinese after the Sino-Muslim imbroglio at Samarkand (AD 751). Following the Black Death in Europe six centuries later, the clothing of the dead was put to use in the mass-production of rag paper, so that by the time the printing press came along (a derivation of a Korean invention), there was an abundant supply available.[471]

Gunpowder and the printing press were medieval innovations of literally world shattering significance. Ironically, the world they shattered was the medieval one itself—gunpowder by overcoming the defensive capacity of the knight's armor and of the castle wall, the printing press (that elusive invention that might have done something to preserve the old Roman republic had it come 1,500 years earlier) by precipitating an explosion of knowledge that released Europe from the fetters of medieval dogma.

But even if Europe's turbulent middle age featured more than its share of backward thinking, it was hardly an era frozen in time or wholly reliant on outside innovation. In fact, by the end of the period one finds evidence of some surprisingly modern thought. During the 13th century, for example, several Italian city-states took the revolutionary step of abolishing slavery.[472] In 1328, Marsiglio of Padua penned a treatise entitled *The Defender of Peace*, in which he argued that "the power of making laws should belong to the whole body of citizens, for there is no lawgiver among men superior to the people themselves ... the people know their own interests best and will not legislate against their own interests.... Perhaps a king is the best head for the state, but the monarch should be elected and not hold his office hereditarily, and should be deposed if he exceed his powers."[473] Hence, if the notion of popular sovereignty originated in ancient Greece, its modern roots, like those of egalitarianism and communism, can be traced to the more progressive minds of the Middle Ages.

Likewise, the era produced at least one champion of the experimental method. More advocate than practitioner,[474] the 13th century English monk, Roger Bacon of Oxford (1214–1292), wrote prophetically of its unbounded potential: "Instruments for navigation can be made that will do away with the necessity of rowers, so that great vessels, both in rivers and on the sea, shall be borne about with only a single man to guide them and with greater speed than if they were full of men. And carriages can be constructed to move without animals to draw them, and with incredible velocity. Machines for flying can be made in which ... skillfully contrived wings are made to strike the air in the manner of a flying bird."[475] Such foresight is astounding for a 13th century monk.[476] Bacon is renowned for experimenting with gunpowder decades before military men got hold of it.[477] He knew something of optics and foresaw the invention of telescopes and eyeglasses. (The latter, in fact, are thought to have been invented in the form of reading glasses about five years prior to his death.[478]) He compiled his "great work" or *Opus Maius* in hopes of recruiting Pope Clement as a patron of science. Unfortunately, Clement died within a year of its completion, and bereft of his powerful ally, Bacon was persecuted by the many English monks whose outlook he had criticized.[479]

Alchemy, that much derided pseudoscience seeking to turn base metals into gold (on the flawed assumption that gold was the only pure metal and all other metals were merely gold tainted with imperfections) also did something to advance the experimental method since experiment comprised its very foundation. Introduced to Europe from the Arab world in the 12th century, it ultimately laid the foundation of modern chemistry and pharmacology.[480]

Architecture—particularly that employed in the construction of churches—was another field of high accomplishment in the Middle Ages. Two great forms dominated the scene. The Romanesque churches of Italy featured windows and doors topped by rounded arches. The main hall was rectangular, and was intersected toward the rear by another rectangular hall, set perpendicularly, so that the floor plan formed a crucifix. An attempt was made to export this style to the north during the 11th century, but northern climes were less sunny, and the windows did not provide enough light—their size being limited by the structural forces placed on the walls by the rounded window arches. Thus, a second form—the Gothic—came into being. The vaulted ceiling in these cathedrals no longer reposed on the walls, but on a series of internal support columns and external flying buttresses. Moreover, the window arches tapered upward to a point or vertex—an innovation that so reduced strain on the walls that massive windows could be incorporated. Indeed, in many cathedrals, the sections of wall between the support columns appear to be composed mostly of glass.[481]

The other great architectural accomplishment of the Middle Ages came in the realm of castle building. Before the advent of gunpowder, these structures were all but impregnable, involving such defenses as a moat (which could only be crossed by draining or filling it if the drawbridge was up), an iron gate—or portcullis—guarding the entry, crenelated walls from which archers could fire their missiles and then step aside to take cover, and the thick-walled round tower—or "keep"—where a final stand could be made if the walls were breached (although some castles also had concentric inner walls to which the defenders could withdraw before resorting to the tower).[482] Personal defense, in the form of body armor, was comprised mostly of chainmail and helmet until the 14th century, when plate armor came fully into vogue (barely in advance of gunpowder).[483]

In agricultural science, the Middle Ages witnessed advances that are aptly described as groundbreaking. During the first half of the medieval period, the spread of the heavy plow along with improvements in harnessing, first of oxen and later of horses, allowed for the conversion of vast tracks of forestland into farmland.[484] Animals employed in teams improved the efficiency and capability of the plow but complicated the issue of turning about. Consequently, much farmland was plowed in long strips to keep turning to a minimum. Left behind was upturned soil in a ridge and furrow pattern—the ridges tending to stay drier in extremely moist seasons and the furrow tending to retain moisture in times of drought thereby increasing the chances of a reasonable crop yield.[485] The productivity of cultivated land was increased dramatically by the adoption of the three-field system—one third of the land being employed to grow a winter crop, one third a spring crop and the last third to lie fallow for the grazing of cattle who restored the soil's fertility with their manure. The role of the three fields would rotate annually, so within a three year period a given plot would have grown a winter crop, a spring crop and spent a year fallow. By the 12th century, the improved yield made Europeans the best-fed people history had known.[486]

The development of machinery was hampered by the guilds, sometimes because the craftsmen did not want their livelihoods threatened, but just as often because of quality control concerns. (In many cases, machines produced an inferior product). However, the guildsmen did not seem to miss the grinding of grains by hand and made no protest against the spread of water and windmills to supply the power for such tedious work. Cistercian monasteries were laid out on a plan that brought water in at one end to power a mill for grinding corn and crushing olive seeds, before running off to service the kitchen, washroom and latrine, and finally emptying into a sewer.[487] The water powered blast furnace allowed for a vast increase in the production of iron, lowering its cost and increasing its availability for various applications. Other technological achievements of the Middle Ages include the mechanical clock (the invention of which has been described by Gies and Gies as "one of the most elegant solutions ever devised to a problem in mechanical engineering"[488]), the spinning wheel for the making of thread, the magnetic compass, cobblestone pavement and four-wheeled wagons with pivoting front wheels to reduce the turning radius. In military affairs, the counterweight trebuchet and the medieval crossbow were markedly superior to their prototypes from the ancient world.

Much of what we know about the medieval period is owed to its chroniclers. Among the best were Einhard, who wrote a biography of Charlemagne, Joinville and the other chroniclers of the crusades; Gabrielle De Mussis, Agnolo di Tura and Giovanni Boccaccio who lived and recorded the terrors of the Black Death; and, of course, the incomparable John Froissart, chronicler of the Hundred Years' War. In literature, we find the ideal of the

Norse hero in Beowulf and that of the Christian hero in the Song of Roland, but the religious spirit of the period is perhaps best reflected in Dante's *Inferno*, a descriptive tour of heaven and hell which contains the first flickering of Renaissance humanism.

By 1453, Europe had advanced far beyond the Dark Ages, when the Church was the only tying bond between the insulated communities of a provincial continent. The commerce that had aided the rise of kings had also promoted the exchange of ideas, and shattered the barriers that separated the isolated feudal manors of the Christian universe. Now, with the introduction of the printing press, the means was available to disseminate knowledge on an unprecedented scale. Moreover, the works of classical antiquity had at last resurfaced—some unearthed in Italy, others brought to Europe from fallen Constantinople.

If, in spite of all this, Gibbon is justified in saying that "barbarism and religion" waxed triumphant for a millennium, let us now move forward to see them overthrown.

Section III

City of Man

The Renaissance, Reformation and Thirty Years' War

The War of the Roses

The year 1453 was a splendid year for cannonry. On the Bosphorus, the awful engine breached the walls of Constantinople and Byzantium fell to the Turks. Less than two months later, John Talbot, Earl of Shrewsbury, attempted to rally England's flagging fortunes in the Hundred Years' War with an attack at Castillon in France. Having taken personal part in the great English victory at Agincourt thirty-eight years earlier,[1] Talbot seems to have hoped that the English longbow might again work its magic. Unfortunately, his French opponents in the new contest awaited him with field artillery in fortified earthworks. Talbot's force was annihilated, and Talbot himself killed (although the fatal blow was delivered by axe, not by projectile).[2] The battle marked the end of the Hundred Years' War, and established once and for all that France was not a fiefdom of the English crown.[3]

For most countries, a century and more of perpetual warfare would have been entirely sufficient, but the situation was otherwise in England. Unable to defeat the French, the English turned on one another—embarking on a thirty-year civil war in which the rival houses of York and Lancaster vied for the crown. Known as the Wars of the Roses, the struggle had its roots in the prolific fecundity of the great fourteenth century monarch Edward III (ruled 1327–1377).

The family tree is sometimes helpful to historians in matters of royal succession, but in Edward's case the researcher is apt to become more confused.[4] To accommodate the king's increase, the straight lines and ninety-degree branch-points of the traditional family tree must give way to curves, which swing back on themselves in parabolic fashion so that the numerous children of one wing of the family do not rush headlong into those of the next. Worse still, the same people suddenly appear more than once at remote and unexpected regions of the tree. This is bad enough in that it is confusing, but it becomes even more unpalatable when one discovers the horrible reason for these double entries (a point to which we will return presently).

Edward III, the victor of Sluys and Crécy fathered thirteen children. Ten survived to adulthood, five of them sons.[5] The eldest of these, Edward the Black Prince, died a year before the king. Thus, when the king himself died (1377), he was succeeded by his grandson, Richard II (i.e., the Black Prince's son). When this heirless grandchild was in turn overthrown for alleged tyranny, the line of the Black Prince came to an end. Strictly speaking, the succession should now have fallen to the family of Lionel, the second son of Edward III. Instead, Lionel's family was passed over, and the crown was bestowed upon Henry Bolingbroke (i.e., Henry IV), a descendant of John of Gaunt, the third of Edward's sons and patriarch of the House of Lancaster (1399).[6]

At first, hardly anyone complained about the disorderly succession. There was to be sure, a revolt in Wales under Owen Glendower, and another in the north under the Percies, but these weren't clearly driven by any principle. And any dissent beyond this was silenced by the great victory of Bolingbroke's son, Henry V, at Agincourt. After eighty years of war, it appeared as if England might swallow France whole. Indeed, in 1431, Henry VI, the third Lancastrian to reach the throne, was crowned king of France in accordance with the Treaty of Troyes. But the French considered this coronation a farce, since the question of illegitimacy that had once plagued their own rightful claimant, Charles VII, had already been dispelled, and (more importantly) because Henry had been crowned king of France by the English, not by themselves.[7] Thus, to England's great misfortune, the war continued, resulting in a series of disastrous defeats that threatened the nation with bankruptcy.

King Edward III of England, 18th century engraving by G. Vertue (© Depositphotos.com/Georgios Kollidas).

Only now—after three reigns, spanning five decades—was the House of Lancaster finally censured for holding the English throne in violation of the strict line of succession. But their opponents, who insisted that Richard of York was the legitimate claimant, appeared to have got it all wrong. A close look at the chaotic family tree reveals that the House of York was actually descended from the *fourth* son of Edward III, and thus held an even weaker claim to the throne than the Lancasters. But appearances can be deceiving, and Richard's heritage was a good deal more convoluted than the Lancasters wanted to admit. For while it is true that York's father, Richard of

Cambridge, was a son of the *fourth* son of Edward III, the wise fellow had married a great granddaughter of Edward's *second* son. York was born out of this union, and was thus descended from *both* the *second* and *fourth* sons of Edward III. His genes, it could be argued, had stolen a march, and fallen upon the rear of the House of Lancaster, which had sat by idly while the Yorkists bettered themselves through matrimony.[8]

It is hoped that in this confusion of names and houses, it has not been lost on the alert reader that Richard of York was the offspring of two people who were already related prior to marriage (this being the hideous explanation behind the double entries in the family tree). But York's was a different era, and despite what movies like *Deliverance* have taught our own generation about what can happen when, for example, cousins marry, no such anxieties were held by 15th century Englishmen. Indeed, no one cared in the slightest. By the 1450s, in fact, Richard of York had achieved great celebrity. Loyal to the point of chivalry, he had risked life and treasure in a noble effort to achieve victory in the Hundred Years' War. But rather than support him, England's malleable King Henry VI gave free rein to a pair of corrupt councilors—the Dukes of Suffolk and Somerset, who managed to enrich themselves while bankrupting the exchequer and losing ever greater chunks of France. For a time, the wicked dukes deflected blame for the foundering war effort on the blameless York, but as the disasters accelerated after the latter's recall their conspiracy was not a success.

Suffolk was first to fall. He was impeached and then murdered while en route to a continental exile (1450). Somerset might have remained in power, but news of the decisive defeat at Castillon precipitated the first of Henry VI's psychotic breaks. He seems to have been catatonic, for he could neither walk nor speak, and paid no heed to his surroundings.[9] The opposition capitalized on his incapacity to oust the greedy Somerset, and install Richard of York as regent with the title "Lord Protector" (1453).

York proved a competent and economical ruler, and all was well in the kingdom until Christmas Day 1454, when, just as suddenly as he had gone insane, King Henry regained his lucidity. The able York was dismissed. Worse still, the hated Somerset was reinstated. It was enough to provoke a Yorkist revolt. The king and his retinue were waylaid at St. Albans, where Somerset was cleaved to bits with an axe (1455). Richard was again named Lord Protector, but the king would have none of it, and with the assistance of his overbearing wife, Queen Margaret (of Anjou), he managed to oust Richard a second time. Another battle ensued wherein the Yorkists were victorious, but in the sequel, they were outmaneuvered at Ludford Bridge (1459), and rather than fight against heavy odds, York and his chief adherents fled into exile.

With victory in her grasp, Queen Margaret convinced the after-named "Parliament of Devils" to issue a bill of attainder, disinheriting and outlawing the entire Yorkist party (1459). Driven by self-preservation, the latter reassembled their army and won a stunning victory at Northampton (1460)—a success so intoxicating that York proclaimed himself king in Henry's stead. Even his most devoted followers wavered at this bold step, however, so he renounced his claim in return for being reinstated yet again as Lord Protector. But he also insisted on being named heir-apparent to the throne in lieu of King Henry's son.

Rather than suffer such terms, Queen Margaret organized a new army on behalf of her husband and son. Lured from his castle near Wakefield, Richard was defeated and slain (1460). His severed head—contemptuously adorned with a paper crown—was impaled atop the town gates of York.[10]

York's death did nothing to end the war. Indeed, all that had been accomplished thus far in the seesaw struggle was to establish a precedent of pursuing vanquished survivors from the field of battle so as to slaughter them in cold blood—a quaint tradition that was repeated after every major engagement for the duration of the war.

Seeing no end in sight, the Yorkists decided that they needed a king of their own after all, and rallied behind Richard's eldest surviving son, Edward, Earl of March. The new pretender promptly won a crucial victory at Towton (1461) amidst a great slaying of Lancastrian nobles. Indeed, so many of the defeated party drowned in an adjacent stream that those following on their heels were able to use their bodies as a makeshift bridge.[11] Edward was now truly king—becoming, as Edward IV, the first of the House of York to be so recognized. His success, however, was largely owed to his talented chief minister, the Earl of Warwick, who now sought to make of the young king a pliable tool. Edward resisted, and the military struggle gave way to a political one—the headstrong statesmen vying for ascendancy in a remarkable duel of marriages.

The opening engagements of this matrimonial war were intimately entangled with affairs in France. In the 1460s, the French monarchy was still at odds with the same duchy of Burgundy that had acted so treasonously during the Hundred Years' War. When renegade French nobles formed the rebellious League of the Public Weal and fought the French army to a draw at Montlhéry with Burgundian assistance (1465), Warwick took the side of the French King, Louis XI (ruled 1461–1483)—a wily diplomat whose well-directed bribes weaved such a web of intrigue in European affairs that he came to be called the "Spider King."

Hoping to prevent King Louis from succoring Queen Margaret (who was, after all, a daughter of France), Warwick arranged a marriage between young King Edward and a French princess. But just as these negotiations were being finalized, Edward confessed that he had, in fact, already secretly married Elizabeth Woodville, who hailed from an English family of humble status and Lancastrian leanings (1464). Utterly aghast, Warwick made a flustered attempt to smooth things over with the insulted Louis XI, but even as he did so Edward delivered a second blow by betrothing his sister, Margaret, to the French king's sworn enemy, Charles the Rash, Duke of Burgundy (1468).

Clearly, Edward had established the early lead in the marriage war, but he had taken no account of Warwick's two marriageable daughters, Isobel and Anne. Warwick espoused the former to Edward IV's shifty brother, George, Duke of Clarence, with a general notion of placing Clarence on the throne (1469). Civil war was the predictable result. Warwick defeated one of Edward's lieutenants at Edgecote, but Edward riposted with a smashing victory at Losecoat Field (1470), where Warwick's troops threw off their jackets so as to flee with greater celerity.[12] (Warwick and Clarence escaped to France).

The more Warwick came to know Clarence, the less he came to trust him. Consequently, he played his final card—bestowing the hand of his second daughter upon (dare it be uttered) Edward, Prince of Wales, the son of the very Henry VI whom Warwick had helped to depose a decade earlier. Returning unexpectedly from France at the head of a large Lancastrian force, the treasonous Warwick seized the reigns of government from the unready King Edward who fled by ship to the Netherlands. Forthwith, Warwick restored the crown to his new in-law, the sometimes insane (and always impressionable) Lancastrian, Henry VI (September 1470).

But Warwick's victory was fleeting, for the deposed King Edward had an important new in-law of his own in the aforementioned Charles the Rash of Burgundy. With financial support from this prince, King Edward returned to England, gained control of London where the populace came out in throngs to greet him, and captured Henry VI. Then, bearing the hapless Henry with him, he confronted the turncoat, Warwick, at Barnet in a grisly three-hour struggle on a field so thickly shrouded in fog that some of Warwick's men accidentally engaged each other instead of the enemy (1471).[13] The Lancastrians were disastrously routed—Warwick, himself, being cut down in attempted flight after being cornered in a thicket.

Far from losing hope, the Lancastrians rallied to the banner of dead Warwick's son-in-law, Edward, Prince of Wales. But the prince was defeated by the army of Edward IV at Tewksbury (1471), where a whole new harvest of Lancastrian nobles (including Prince Edward) was put to the sword—the majority falling at a point in the field known as Bloody Meadow.[14] Shortly thereafter, the long-deposed Henry VI was put to death in the Tower of London at King Edward's command.

Apart from the minor matter of having to execute his own brother—the incorrigible duke of Clarence, who was dunked in a wine cask until he was dead (1478)—Edward's reign proceeded with quiet success after the victories of 1471. Indeed, the king felt secure enough to ally himself outright with Charles the Rash of Burgundy in hopes of resuming the Hundred Years' War. But when, in accordance with this alliance, the English landed an army at Calais, the Burgundian ruler failed to keep the rendezvous. Moreover, the weather proved too rainy for a major campaign.

The English army was thus stranded in the mud on the French coast—a predicament that was only narrowly retrieved by the quick-witted Louis XI. Sensitive to the invaders' plight, the French king invited the whole English army to dine alongside his own troops at Amiens. While the opposing soldiery ate, drank, fraternized and cavorted with prostitutes,[15] Edward and Louis agreed to the Treaty of Picquigny (1475), whereby Edward obtained a large annual tribute, and the Hundred Years' War—which had seen no action since Castillon (1453)—was officially declared *fini*. The only loser in these negotiations was Charles the Rash. Had he joined his forces with those of Edward as promised, he might have broken the power of France, and achieved his dream of erecting an independent "middle kingdom" in the center of Europe.[16] But now, having alienated England, he had to pursue his goal alone. And since he has intruded into our story, we will briefly examine his subsequent career.

In addition to his own duchy of Burgundy, Charles the Rash controlled the Franche Comté to the east, and the geographically separate Low Countries (Holland and Belgium) to the north. To unite these disparate territories, Charles needed to wrest from France the intervening provinces of Alsace and Lorraine. But the former province abutted northern Switzerland, and in attempting to usurp it (without English help now that he had betrayed Edward), Charles fell into conflict with the Swiss who, not coincidentally, had been generously bribed by Louis XI to keep the duke occupied.[17]

As usual, the French king's money was well spent. He was only too familiar with the fighting capabilities of the Swiss. While still dauphin of France, he had attacked them at St. Jacob-en-Birs (1444). With regards to manpower, the odds were fifteen to one in his favor,[18] but he suffered so many casualties in the ensuing "victory" that he vowed never to cross swords with the Swiss confederates again. In contrast, Charles the Rash was entirely delusional when it came to Switzerland's military prowess. The Swiss "backfield-in-motion" tactics had been the bane of superior Hapsburg armies at Morgarten (1315) and Sempach (1386). They had even routed Charles' Burgundian forefathers at Laupen (1339). But Charles was no student of history, and he moved against them without the slightest hesitation. At Grandson (1476), he ordered his center to withdraw, in a bold attempt to lure the Swiss forward into a Cannae-like double envelopment. Unfortunately, the foreign mercenaries manning his flanks had no idea what he was doing. Taking his purposeful retirement for flight, they turned tail and ran just as the Swiss were being reinforced by newly arrived troops. The outcome was a disastrous defeat.[19]

Not to be deterred, Charles attacked the Swiss again at Morat. This time his initial dispositions ensured catastrophe before the first sword had been unsheathed. A less rash man might have cut his losses. But in 1477, Charles engaged the Swiss for a third time at Nancy. It was to be his final effort. His army was outflanked and annihilated, while he himself received a halberd blow "which clove his skull in two."[20] His naked corpse was found two days after the battle, face down in a frozen pond.[21] Since he had no male heirs, it appeared that his nemesis, Louis XI, would repatriate his once great duchy. Indeed, the French king's troops seized Dijon, the Burgundian capital. But the duke's daughter, Mary of Burgundy, put an end to the Spider King's encroachments by marrying Maxmilian, the son and heir of the Holy Roman Emperor. With imperial support, the Burgundians defeated a French army at Guinegate (1479), thus securing the Low Countries for Mary and Maxmilian. Louis had to content himself with the conquest of Burgundy proper and Franche-Comté—and the latter was only temporarily held. In 1493, Louis' successor ceded it to the Hapsburgs.[22]

The Burgundian tragedy stood in stark contrast to the commercial boom being enjoyed in England, whose new treaty with France was now being touted by certain pundits as "the Merchants' Treaty."[23] Wealthy and unencumbered, King Edward was finally at leisure to attend to his favorite pastimes: drunkenness, gluttony and debauchery. Any two of these vices he might have survived. The triad killed him. He expired at forty in April 1483, bequeathing his kingdom to his son, the Prince of Wales (yet another Edward). But since the prince was only twelve, the king's loyal brother, Richard of Gloucester, was named Lord Protector and empowered to act as regent. Hitherto, Richard had given unwavering support to Edward IV, serving him well at the battles of Barnet and Tewksbury, before being made overlord of northern England (a hotbed of political strife that he administered with stunning success). He was in this northern district when the king died, but it was not distance that prevented him from attending the royal funeral. Rather it was the failure of the Woodvilles (Edward's wife's family) to let him know of his brother's demise. They had been too busy raiding the royal treasury and promoting their own interests at Richard's expense.[24]

When Richard was finally notified, he marched on London with his supporters, ostensibly to take up his position as Lord Protector. Very quickly, however, he seems to have conceived other ideas. At his command, a handful of Woodville partisans were summarily executed. The crowning of the Prince of Wales was cancelled—the prince and his younger brother, Richard, Duke of York, being imprisoned in the Tower. Lord Hastings, who refused to forsake the princes' cause, was dragged from a meeting of Richard's supporters and executed without trial. Next came the extraordinary revelation (quite possibly true[25]) that the princes were actually illegitimate byproducts of a bigamous marriage and that Uncle Richard, being next in line, was the rightful claimant. Feigning protest, he was crowned Richard III on July 6, 1483.

Shakespeare's play about the new king errs in portraying Richard as a hunchback with a shriveled arm. He possessed neither deformity.[26] Likewise, it incorrectly blames him for a series of crimes he did not commit. Unfortunately for Richard (presuming he hoped to be remembered favorably), it is extremely difficult to exonerate him for the one crime that really matters—namely, the execution of the princes in the Tower of London.[27] His coronation provoked a rebellion in the southwest in favor of the imprisoned Prince of Wales. But even as the uprising was being organized, rumor announced that the princes had met their doom.[28] Legend has it that the boys were smothered with their bedding and buried beneath a staircase in the Tower—and a pair of skeletons was, in fact, found there two centuries later. If we subscribe to the writings of Sir Clements R. Markham,[29] we may doubt whether Richard had anything to do with these grisly goings-on. The damnable problem is that there is no record of the princes being heard from after 1483, and since Richard remained in power for two years beyond that date, most historians are hesitant to pin the responsibility on anyone else.[30]

King Richard III of England, engraving published by Thomas Kelly, London, 1830 (© Depositphotos.com/Georgios Kollidas).

Richard's overthrow, however, seems not to have occurred in response to events in the Tower, but rather because, after quelling the southern uprising, he enlisted cronies from his old stomping grounds in the north to lord it over the defeated rebels.[31] The clannish southerners responded to this intrusion by searching (rather diligently) for an alternative claimant to the throne. The Lancastrian pretenders had all been killed off, save one: the exiled Earl of Richmond, Henry Tudor—"the only imp now left of King Henry VI's blood."[32]

Young Henry was the grandson of Owen Tudor who had married the widow of Henry V. In normal circumstances, being the grandson of the remarried widow of a former Lancastrian king would not have imparted a particularly strong claim to the throne.[33] But a claimant was needed, and it was decided that Henry would simply have to do. Without giving King Richard a chance to make good, a not insignificant cadre of nobles sailed to Brittany and enlisted in the service of the exiled pretender.

After landing safely in Wales in August 1485, Henry and his party of adventurers confronted Richard at Ambien Hill on Bosworth Field, where the king had deployed a hastily organized army. Richard had but one loyal ally, the Duke of Norfolk, whom he placed in charge of his vanguard. Richard, himself, led the second line. Behind him was a large force under the Earl of Northumberland, whose loyalty, however, was open to question. Two prominent nobles—Lord Thomas Stanley and his brother, Sir William Stanley—arrived with their armed adherents, but rather than commit to one side or the other, each waited on the flanks of the field, ready to join whichever side appeared to be winning.

Henry Tudor entrusted his vanguard to the Earl of Oxford who immediately engaged Norfolk. After a great deal of axe swinging, Norfolk was cut down, prompting King Richard to advance into the scrum with the second line. The doubtful Northumberland, however, did not, or perhaps could not, come to his support. (Some have suggested that the narrowness of the terrain may have impeded him.[34]) In any event, once it became apparent that Northumberland would remain a spectator, Richard staked everything on a personal sortie against Henry Tudor. He killed Henry's standard-bearer and knocked down a rather imposing knight, but the pretender was just out of reach.[35]

Far from offering his kingdom for a horse at this point, Richard seems actually to have declined the offer of a mount—even after it became clear that the Stanleys had now intervened against him.[36] Though his army was routed, the king fought grimly on, protesting the whole while that he had been betrayed, until at length his enemies encompassed him on all sides and smote him.[37] Stripped of his armor—"naught being left about him so much as would cover his privy member"[38]—his corpse was abused and callously interred at Leicester. The news of his demise was said to have been received with much sorrow in the city of York, which had supported him to the end.[39]

Richard III was the last of the Plantagenet line. To be sure, an army of disgruntled Yorkists had a final go of it at Stoke, where they rallied to the banner of a ten-year-old boy named Lambert Simnel, who was falsely said to be the son of the Duke of Clarence (1487). But they were defeated, and, for better or worse, England was home to a new dynasty—the "Tudor"—behind whom the houses of York and Lancaster finally united for the first time in three decades.

So many nobles had succumbed throughout the years of slaughter that Henry Tudor (now Henry VII, ruled 1485–1509) had the advantage of initiating his reign when there was scarcely anyone left to oppose him. To prevent future rebellions, Henry established the so-called "Court of Star Chamber," which answered only to the king, and efficiently disposed of troublemakers after secretive trials.[40] Lambert Simnel got off easily—his bid for the kingdom ending with an embarrassing sentence to work in the royal kitchen.[41] But Perkin Warbeck, masquerading as one of the dead princes of the Tower, was sent to the gallows for his repeated efforts to seize the throne.

In effect, Henry VII ruled absolutely, yet he made a show of seeking the consent of parliament for his actions—a concession he could well afford since he had packed that assembly with newly ennobled supporters. Parliament, in turn, could support him without cost since he had filled the treasury with the riches of suppressed nobles, and squared the balance by collecting "benevolences" which he claimed from the well-dressed because they clearly had money to spare, and from the shabbily dressed because of all the money they had saved on clothes.[42] At his death, the royal coffers were full.

In foreign affairs, Henry secured the support of the Spanish monarchs, Ferdinand and Isabella, by betrothing his son, Arthur, to their daughter, Catherine. (Later, when Arthur met an untimely death, another son—the future Henry VIII—became Catherine's husband in his stead. This marriage, as we shall presently see, would lead to England's break with the Catholic Church.) Hence, at his death in 1509, the Tudor dynasty was secure on the throne.

Italy Prior to the Italian Wars

During the period of the Hundred Years' War, Italian sovereignty was shared out amongst five competitors: Naples, the Papal States, Florence, Milan and Venice. The southernmost, Naples, had been ruled first by Normans, and then by the Hohenstaufen, Angevins and Aragonese, before finally becoming independent even of Aragon.[43] At the close of the 15th century, a nobility of transplanted Spaniards still clung to power, but its authority was fragile and fading.

In central Italy, the Papal States, extending across the breadth of the peninsula from the Tiber to the Po, were hardly better off. By now, they were "Papal" in name only. The "Babylonian Captivity" at Avignon (1308–1377) and the "Great Schism" (1378–1417) had undermined the Holy See, allowing much of her dominion to be usurped by the petty aristocracy. In 1347, Rome itself was lost, as Cola di Rienzo, a utopian orator and self-proclaimed "Tribune of the People," attempted to restore the Roman Republic. Rienzo neutralized the fractious nobles with a citizen militia, provided for the city's paupers, orphans and widows, and rendered the streets safe with a justice code worthy of Hammurabi. (Had it not been for the clemency of the aggrieved party, an eye would literally have been exchanged for an eye on one occasion, while on another, Rienzo had the murderer of one of his couriers buried alive beneath the victim's corpse.[44]) An army of mercenaries, sent by the local nobility to unseat him, was repulsed, and Rienzo ruled justly, if self-righteously, until the papacy used its leverage to bring about his downfall (December 1347). Six years later, the papacy reinstated him in a bid to counter the resurgent influence of the Roman nobility. But when Rienzo raised taxes, he roused the city's ire. An angry mob promptly killed him in the street leaving the irascible aristocracy free to impede papal rule for another century.

Just as fragmented, but far more prosperous, were the republican city-states of northern Italy, which had dominated Mediterranean commerce since the crusades. By combining their resources, the cities had resisted encroachment by the Hohenstaufen in the 12th and 13th centuries, but cooperation was hardly the norm. In 1298, Genoa defeated Venice in a sea battle famous for the capture (by the Genoese) of Marco Polo.[45] Venice quickly rebounded to become the district's ascendant city-state only to encounter rivalry from Florence and Milan. For the next two centuries, the entire region fell prey to internecine warfare, fought by mercenary armies under the direction of professional officers known as *condottieri*.

Even within cities there was factional strife, pitting the Ghibellines, who supported the old secular and imperial interests of the defunct Hohenstaufen, against the Guelphs, who favored papal ascendancy. Violent street brawls between these parties threw the tiny republics into chaos, from which there was no escape save the tyranny of an influential family or condottiere.[46] But once in power, these absolutist mini–Caesars were adept at making enemies, and not a few succumbed to dagger blows—most frequently in church, since this was the only place the little tyrants ever let down their guard.[47] For a time, the powerful Visconti family ruled Milan. After them came the Sforzas, whose court boasted Leonardo da Vinci.

Most famous of all, however, were the Medici of Florence. Machiavellian in their diplomacy, they were nonetheless ardent patrons of the arts. Sculpture, painting and architecture adorned their city and trumpeted their fame. Cosimo Medici—the dynasty's founder—attained such popularity during a thirty-year tenure (1434–1464), that when he died the whole of Florence marched in his funeral procession.[48] Democracy was absent from the family's program, but their people scarcely cared, for their collective imagination was captivated by the Medici's unending parade of pageantry.

Well, not quite unending. In 1494, France invaded Italy and the city experienced disaster. Unable to resist the French juggernaut, the Medici accepted a humiliating treaty. Rather than comply, the populace rebelled and handed power to the monk, Girolamo Savonarola, an ascetic revolutionary who preached that Florence's fame in the arts was nothing but a decorative facade concealing a nucleus of tyranny and ungodliness. For four years, the city lived by Savonarola's Rule. But ultimately his pious example—not to mention his failed economic policy—tried the people's patience. The end came in 1498, by which time Savonarola had been excommunicated for charging the church with corruption. Since he would not desist from his diatribes, the papacy laid a threat of interdict upon the city. For the inhabitants, this was the final straw. With their livelihoods at stake—for the interdict would have cut off commerce with the outside—someone suggested that Savonarola undergo the ordeal by fire. Savonarola declined, but one of his prominent supporters offered to undergo the ordeal in his stead. On the appointed day, rain and a protracted debate over what Savonarola's second might carry into the flame led to postponement. Robbed of their day's entertainment, the mob rioted. Bereft of supporters, Savonarola was arrested. The mob abused him as he was taken to prison where he confessed to heresy under torture. On May 23, 1498, he was hanged and burned with two supporters—the ashes being cast into the Arno.[49]

Four years later, Florence came to be ruled by the republican, Piero Soderini, whose chief advisor was a little-known political theorist named Niccolò Machiavelli. Sadly, by this time (1502), the economy that had fueled the art and murder of the Italian Renaissance was wallowing in recession. Control of Mediterranean trade had long been the cornerstone of northern Italy's influence, but in 1463, the indomitable Mehmet II, the conqueror of Constantinople, instigated a sixteen-year naval war that handed mastery of the eastern half of the sea to the Ottomans. By 1480, Mehmet had captured the port of Otranto on the Italian mainland, and had he not died unexpectedly a year later, all Italy might have succumbed.[50]

Yet the threat was not as dire as it seemed. At Constantinople, the Venetian Quarter remained open for business, and Venetian ships were likewise welcome at Beirut and Alexandria. Indeed, matters could not be otherwise since Venice was Turkey's business partner in the lucrative spice trade.[51] What finally toppled Italy from her perch and made her ripe for invasion was not the Ottoman onslaught, but competition from an expanding commercial universe.

It all began when Portuguese adventurers, sponsored by Portugal's Prince Henry the Navigator (1394–1460) and King John II (ruled 1481–1495), sailed southward to Africa's Gold Coast to wrest control of the African gold trade from its previous stewards—the

Muslims. The wealth therefrom helped finance the long coastline crawl of their compatriot, Bartholomew Diaz, who rounded the Cape of Good Hope in the midst of a violent tempest in 1488. (He was oblivious to what he had done until the storm cleared.[52]) A decade later, Vasco da Gama used the same route to travel all the way to India (1498), forever fracturing the Turko-Venetian spice monopoly.[53]

In the meantime, a Genoese navigator named Christopher Columbus obtained funding from the Spanish court to seek a *westerly* route to India. As a result, he made his accidental discovery of the New World, thus providing Spain with an unprecedented source of gold and silver.[54] Hence, while Italian commerce began to contract during the "Age of Discovery," that of Europe as a whole expanded beyond all parallel.

Nor did the repercussions stop with the overthrow of Italian commercial supremacy, for the influx of precious metals also promoted an economic revolution, wherein the guild-based economies of the Middle Ages began to wane in favor of a fledgling capitalism.[55] As the financially independent master craftsman gradually gave ground to the financially dependent laborer,[56] Europe's entrepreneurial middle class flourished. This, in turn, enhanced the power base of Europe's national monarchs who had long relied on the commercial classes for support. Consequently, the kings of Spain, France and England were able to consolidate their authority as never before. Feudal lords simply did not have the financial wherewithal to compete in an era of cannon and musketry. Nor could their castle walls sustain an artillery bombardment.[57] Whereas, formerly, a strong castle might withstand a siege for months or years, it now required luck to survive a week.[58] Consequently, Europe's kings were becoming less like feudal lords, and more like national rulers.[59] It was a race toward centralization, and over the next two centuries, Italy and Germany would pay the price for not keeping pace. Indeed, their disunity would make them the battlefields of Europe.

The Italian Wars Commence

In 1483, Louis XI, France's Spider King, died. His son and successor, the less subtle Charles VIII (ruled 1483–1498), was but fourteen in that year, and ruled for a time under the guidance of his elder sister, Anne. The latter—"the least foolish woman in France" in their father's misogynistic estimation—arranged a dynastic marriage between Charles and the heiress of Brittany (the last French duchy to remain independent of the crown). But the hand of the prospective bride had already been promised to the Hapsburg emperor, Maximilian, who retaliated by invading Franche Comté (so recently obtained from Burgundy). England's Henry VII likewise sought to forestall a marriage that would deliver Brittany to the French crown, while Spain stole away with disputed Roussillon. Had Anne remained in power, she would have devised suitable ripostes to these acts of defiance, but the events themselves encompassed a number of years (1488–1492) during which time Charles VIII had begun to rule in his own right.[60]

Rather than meet the threats gathering on his borders, King Charles dreamt of conquering Italy—an endeavor that would transform France from nation into empire. To lend a sense of legitimacy to this intended aggression, he invoked the long defunct Angevin claim to the kingdom of Naples, over which Charles of Anjou had ruled so unsuccessfully two hundred years earlier. Naples, of course, lies at the base of the Italian peninsula, and to reach it Charles would have to traverse the provinces in between. It would therefore behoove him to purchase the neutrality of his European rivals, which he did by relinquishing his claim to the territories they had stolen from him.[61] This accomplished, he gathered his army and marched southward into Italy.

Florence stood in the way, but rather than oppose him, Piero de' Medici met Charles at Sarzana and surrendered Pisa and three other Tuscan cities to France in the name of peace. Apprised of this craven surrender, the Florentine citizenry ran riot, chasing Piero out of the city and handing power to Savonarola. (Nor would they accept Piero back when Charles occupied Florence and demanded his reinstatement—the issue being settled instead by the payment of a fine that helped to hasten Charles on his way.)[62]

Next in the field of obstacles were the Papal States, where Charles came to grips with Pope Alexander VI (the former Rodrigo Borgia). History has accused this not-very-devout pontiff of everything from poisoning to incest. Much of it—though perhaps not enough—has been proven untrue. But one thing is clear: Alexander was bent on making the papacy dominant again—at least in the Papal States—and he was remarkably adept in pursuing his goal. His task began in Rome, where prior to his ascendancy, state salaries went unpaid, and brigandage was so rampant that on one occasion the ambassadors of the Holy Roman Emperor were forced to surrender everything but their shirts to highway robbers on the outskirts of the city.[63] After just two years in office, however, Alexander had balanced the papacy's ledgers,[64] cast the quarrelsome Guelphs and Ghibellines from the capital[65]—many of them directly into the Tiber as corpses—and converted Hadrian's Mausoleum into a papal fortress-refuge known as Castle Santangelo. The castle was connected to the Vatican by a covered passageway which was completed just in time—for it was to the castle that Alexander repaired when Charles VIII appeared at the gates of Rome, chivalrously assuring the prostitutes of the city that no harm would come to them.[66]

Unable to oppose him directly, Alexander allowed Charles to proceed toward Naples. But once the king was gone, the enterprising pope turned the tables by forming an alliance with Venice, Milan, Spain and Germany on the pretext of fighting the Turks. Known as the Holy League, the little coalition wasted no time in pursuing its real object, which was to threaten Charles' supply lines.[67] Hence, scarcely had Charles gotten himself crowned king of Naples, before he was compelled to withdraw. (A downright shame, really, since given a chance to rule he cannot have proved worse than his Neapolitan predecessor, King Ferrante I, who had a quaint habit of mummifying his murdered political rivals and placing them on display in his private museum.[68])

In the event, it proved much harder to get out of Italy than to run roughshod over it. Marching northwards, Charles collided with a superior Italian force at Fornovo (1495), and was only saved by a rainstorm that caused great inconvenience to the opposing artillery and cavalry. In the ensuing fracas, Charles' pikemen overwhelmed the Italian knights—many of whom were left to wallow in the mud until a party of hatchet-wielding French auxiliaries "broke up their head-pieces, and ... knocked out their brains."[69]

The battle was won, but the war was lost. The French scurried back to France, and in Rome, Alexander was hailed as a hero for driving them out. Moreover, Charles VIII died in 1498, and relations with his successor, Louis XII, were much more cordial. Louis needed an annulment of his first marriage so that he could marry his predecessor's widowed queen.

(As the reader may recall, the latter was the heiress of Brittany, which Louis very much wanted to keep.[70]) Alexander obligingly provided the annulment, and Louis reciprocated by betrothing Princess Charlotte of Navarre to Alexander's son, Cesare Borgia, who became a French duke as part of the bargain. So cozy did the web of relations become that, when Louis launched a new invasion of Italy in 1499, young Cesare marched with the French.

The pretext for the war was the discovery of a hitherto ignored branch of the Visconti family tree, which placed King Louis in line to rule Milan. Louis indignantly branded the Sforzas (who had succeeded the Visconti in 1450) as usurpers, and led forth his legions to reclaim his lost patrimony.[71] On October 6, 1499, his army occupied Milan.

Simultaneously, Pope Alexander's son, Cesare, was gaining control of the Papal States with French support. Having commissioned Leonardo da Vinci as his engineer, Cesar laid siege to the castles of one unruly noble after another. Where force did not prevail, deceitful diplomacy usually did the trick, and by 1502, the Papal States were once more subservient to the Holy See.

Duke Cesare handled temporal matters, and Durant feels that he did a top-notch job.[72] But other historians are less sympathetic. Indeed, Cesare's reputation is scarcely better than his father's—and scarcely less deserved. History has absolved him of the murder of his elder brother, Giovanni, (who is said to have rivaled him for the incestuous attentions of their lovely sister, Lucrezia[73]). Likewise, there is no definite proof of his involvement in an unsuccessful attempt to kill Lucrezia's beloved second husband, Alfonso, the duke of Bisceglia. Alfonso himself, it should be noted, was sufficiently convinced of Cesare's complicity to fire an arrow at him from the window next to his convalescence bed. And when he was throttled to death for doing so, there was no doubt whatever that Cesare had issued the order for it. Moreover, it does say *something* about a man if he has need (as Cesare did) to keep both a professional strangler and a professional poisoner on retainer.[74]

Alas for the Borgias, murder and military success did not translate into longevity. At a small outdoor gathering held on August 5, 1503, in the sweltering heat of Rome, they were stricken with malaria (although Burckhardt, who doesn't much like either of them, insists that they accidentally poisoned themselves with a meal intended for a cardinal whose estates they wished to usurp).[75] In either event, Alexander did not survive. His corpse is said to have been hideously bloated in the summer heat—the strength of six (snickering) laborers being needed to press it into its coffin.[76]

The next Pope (Pius III) reigned but one month, and was succeeded by Giuliano della Rovere, who took the name Julius II. Burckhardt calls him the "saviour of the Papacy."[77] Certainly, he put a halt to the simony (i.e., the selling of Church offices) and nepotism practiced by his Borgian predecessor. Machiavelli censures Cesare Borgia for allowing Julius' election when he might have contrived to prevent it. Both men were intent on dominating the Papal States (particularly the hotly contested Romagna district to the northeast)— Cesare for himself (perhaps as prelude to the conquest of the greater part of Italy), Pope Julius because they belonged by right to the papacy.[78] For a time there was a basis for cooperation against Venice, which had its own designs on the Papal States, but the rival pretensions of the two headstrong men could not help but come to the fore, with the result that Cesare spent most of the period between 1503 and 1506 in prison. At length, Cesare's estranged wife contrived his escape, and in March 1507, he died at war, fighting in the service of his wife's brother, the king of Navarre.[79]

A Brief History of Spain to 1469

The demise of the Borgias had a sharply negative impact on French fortunes in Italy. After taking Milan, Louis XII had tried his hand at the old Angevin claim in southern Italy by agreeing to a partition of the Neapolitan kingdom with King Ferdinand of Spain (1500). But when it came to diplomacy and intrigue, Louis was entirely overmatched by the wit of Ferdinand and the emergent strength of Spain, and to better understand this, we must bring ourselves up to speed on Spanish history.

In ancient times, Spain was ruled first by Carthage and then by Rome. At the time of Rome's fall, the Visigothic tribe, which had done its part to bring about that empire's demise, resided in Gaul. But a defeat at Poitiers at the hands of King Clovis and the Merovingian Franks forced the Visigoths to remove their capital to Toledo in Spain, where over the course of nearly two centuries twenty-five Gothic kings ruled without distinction.[80] Plagued by incessant familial rivalry, fifteen of this total were either assassinated or overthrown. Last to rule was Roderic, whose usurpation of the throne roused the fear or enmity of Count Julian, the commander of the crossings from Africa. In a bid to depose the new king, Julian enlisted the support of North Africa's Muslims, and in the phrasing of Gibbon, "his rash invitation ... produced the calamities of eight hundred years."[81] In AD 711, Julian helped ferry an army of 5,000 Muslims into Spain under the Berber commander, Tariq, whose name remains immortalized at his landing site—Gibraltar (i.e., "Gebel al-Tariq," or Rock of Tariq). King Roderic came to meet Tariq with an overwhelming force, but Julian, whose treachery was as yet unknown, defected from the Christians with his troops in mid-battle throwing the Christian army into a panic.[82] Roderic drowned in attempted flight and in the course of seven years, the Muslims obtained control of all Spain excepting the northernmost regions, which came to comprise the Christian kingdoms of Leon, Navarre and Aragon.

For three centuries, the Mohammedans held sway, obtaining the acquiescence of the native populace by granting religious freedom in return for tribute payment. But in the roster of reigning emirs or caliphs, only a few showed themselves capable of consolidated rule. The Omayyad prince, Abd al-Rahman I (ruled 758–790), escaped the slaughter of his kinsmen in Damascus during the Abbasid revolution to secure control of Spain with an army recruited among the blacks of Africa. Spain thus became an independent emirate (later renamed the "caliphate" of Cordova).[83] His namesake, Abd al-Rahman III ("the Great" ruled, 912–961) is remembered for restoring order after fifty years of lawlessness had rendered the roads—even between major cities—entirely unsafe.[84] But by the end of the 10th century, the caliphate had seen its last capable ruler—al-Mansur (ruled, 981–1002), who led the final Moorish advance into the Christian regions, pillaging as far as Santiago de Compostela, home to the shrine of St. James (997).

At al-Mansur's death the caliphate of Cordova disintegrated into a mass of petty kingdoms, thereby setting the stage for a Christian revival in the peninsula.[85] Ferdinand I of Castile (ruled, 1035–1065) gave this revival its first impetus by bringing the rival Christian province of Leon under his sway. Sadly, at his death, the newly united patrimony was divided between his sons, Sancho and Alfonso VI, who promptly declared a winner-take-all war on one another rather than profit jointly by an attack on the disunited Muslims. Abetted by Rodrigo Diaz de Vivar—the famed "El Cid" of Spanish lore—Sancho got the upper hand in this conflict, inducing Alfonso to seek temporary refuge in the Muslim city of Toledo.

But in 1072, Sancho was murdered under obscure circumstances, and Alfonso (ruled, 1065–1109) obtained the entire domain. At this, the Christians ceased fighting each other, and directed their energies against the "Moors" (as the Muslims—who had, after all, crossed into Spain from North African "Morocco"—were known).

The fact that conquered territory became the spoil of the conquerors fueled the zeal of the Christian advance, and to secure their winnings, the Christian rulers provided for the establishment of chartered towns in the borderlands whose inhabitants enjoyed liberal rights and liberties in return for participating in the defense of the realm. The Christian nobility, whose estates were aggrandized with every conquest, were relieved of taxation in return for serving in the cavalry, and later (in the 12th century) the monastic military orders of the crusades—including the Knights Templar and the Knights of St. John—were induced to join the struggle through generous land grants.[86]

In 1085, the Christians achieved their most stunning coup to date by capturing Toledo (King Alfonso's former refuge in central Spain). Moors and Christians inhabited this city in roughly equal numbers, and the conquering Castilian king showed his awareness of the situation by extending liberal treatment to the entire populace. On this account, he came to be known as "The Emperor of the Two Religions."[87]

The fall of Toledo compelled the Moors to seek a means of arresting the Christian onslaught. Eventually they appealed to a fanatical North African Islamic sect known as the Almoravids. Led by a certain Yusuf, the Almoravids defeated Alfonso at Badajoz in 1086—a victory that brought the Christian advance to a temporary halt. The Almoravids, however, were not courteous guests. They imposed their will on the indigenous Moors by force, and the discontent that ensued prevented the Muslims from capitalizing on their victory over the Christians.

The impasse was breached by the arrival in Spain of the Almohads—a sect even more fanatical than the Almoravids. These intrepid warriors seized the caliphate and made ready to encroach upon the Christian regions. Opposed to them, however, was a crusading coalition forged by Castile's Alfonso VIII (ruled, 1158–1214). To secure the allegiance of Leon (which was again separate from Castile), Alfonso had betrothed his daughter to the epileptic Leonian king, Alfonso "the Slobberer." The adherence of Navarre and Aragon was likewise obtained, and the remaining ranks were filled out by the monastic military orders. At Las Navas de Tolosa, the Christian force utterly routed the Almohads (1212), after which an unbroken series of Christian triumphs—including the capture of Cordova (1236) and Seville (1248) hurled the Moors back on their last stronghold: Granada.[88] From this outpost, they would fend off the Christians for nearly 250 years—an accomplishment that Henry Hallam attributes to "the superior means of resistance which the Moors found in retreating. Their population, spread originally over the whole of Spain was now condensed, and ... no further compressible, in a single province."[89]

Further explanation for the Moors' staying power may be found in the character of the era's Christian kings. The dramatic recession of the Moorish tide had left in its wake a patchwork of Christian states. Leon and Castile were united for good on the death of Alfonso the Slobberer (1230). Navarre, Aragon and Portugal remained separate (though the last did not render her independence secure until 1385, when English archers and superior tactics helped her defeat the Castilians at Aljubarotta). Bad rulers can be identified as easily in one as in another of these small kingdoms, but Castile was most powerful, so we'll seek our examples there. We may begin with Alfonso X (ruled, 1252–1284), who, in Hallam's view, "might justly acquire the surname of Wise for his general proficiency in learning, and especially in astronomical science; if these attainments deserved praise in a king, who was incapable of preserving his subjects in their duty."[90] Alfonso wasted his reign in a forlorn bid to win the Holy Roman crown before engaging in war with his own son, Sancho IV, who disputed the father's choice of a successor. Sancho (ruled, 1284–1296) emerged from this contest with the throne, but spent his reign in intrigue, murder and rivalry with the nobility.

Despite these foibles, Castile loomed as Iberia's predominant state. What was lacking was a capable ruler, and in Alfonso XI (ruled, 1312–1350), Castile thought it had finally gotten one. Alas, in the prime of life this monarch immortalized himself in the medieval annals by succumbing to the Black Death—the only European king ever to do so. (He contracted the illness on refusing to abandon the siege of Moorish Gibraltar in 1350 despite an outbreak there.)

Alfonso's successor and sole legitimate heir, was Pedro the Cruel (ruled, 1350–1369). But the father had also spawned a litter of illegitimate pretenders, whose existence precipitated a sort of Spanish "War of the Roses" in which the hapless Pedro was cast in the role of Richard III. For good reason, Pedro had two of this vexatious brood beaten to death. Less easily excused, however, is the murder of his wife, Blanche de Bourbon, whose sole apparent crime was that she presented an impediment, however slight, to the king's ability to attend to his mistress, Maria de Padilla. (According to Durant, Pedro's courtiers were so enthralled by the latter's beauty that they joyously imbibed her bathwater.[91]) Pedro showed a softer side to his Jewish subjects. While the rest of Europe committed atrocities against the Jews who stood falsely accused of poisoning well water to perpetrate the Black Death, Pedro argued that, "being numerically a feeble people, [the Jews] required special protection."[92] Several Jews served him faithfully at court in gratitude for his benevolence.

In the meantime, Henry of Trastamara, the eldest of Pedro's illegitimate half-brothers, attempted six times to seize Pedro's crown. Pedro defeated him in the first five—most decisively at Najera (1367), where he received crucial assistance from England's Black Prince. Says Froissart of this encounter, "This was a marvelous dangerous battle," ... in which "many a man [was] slain and sore hurt."[93] Henry's men "had slings, from which they threw stones with such force as to break helmets and skull caps ... [but] the English archers, according to their custom, shot sharply with their bows, to the great annoyance and death of the Spaniards."[94]

In the aftermath of this contest, Pedro unwisely neglected to pay the Black Prince for services rendered, and when a pestilence broke out among the latter's soldiers, the prince took them back to France to await further service in the Hundred Years' War.[95] Hence, when Henry gave usurpation a sixth try at Montiel (1369), Pedro's luck finally ran out. After a defeat in the field, he was lured from the battlements under false pretenses, only to receive a fatal dagger blow at the hands of his brother while the latter's henchmen held him still.[96] Henry now assumed the throne as Henry II (ruled, 1369–1379).

The house of Trastamara produced such off-color figures as Henry III, "the Sufferer" (ruled 1390–1406), who sounds like a sad case (although he appears to have been a capable prince), and Henry IV, "the Impotent" (ruled 1454–1474), who must have ruled at a time when people were very mean. The reprehensible nickname by which history remembers him might not even have been merited given that his wife bore him a daughter named Juana. But his detractors assure us that the girl's real father was a courtier named Beltran de la Cueva. Indeed, Juana is known to history as Juana la Beltraneja, and her claim to the throne was cast aside on the basis of her doubtful lineage. As a result, Henry's famous half-sister, Isabella, became his heir.

Ferdinand and Isabella

In 1469, five years before she succeeded to the throne, Isabella married Ferdinand, heir to the throne of neighboring Aragon. The marriage promised to unite the two largest kingdoms in Spain and to enhance greatly the power of the monarchy. No surprise, then, that the Castilian nobility, enjoying relative freedom in a disunited peninsula, strongly opposed the union. One grandee even catapulted a stone at Ferdinand's coach as the young prince traveled to the wedding.[97] Nor was the aristocracy's concern unwarranted. Ferdinand and Isabella excluded the nobility from the council of state, ignored the *cortes* (i.e., the Castilian parliament) for a period of fourteen years, and attempted to consolidate all authority in the crown. Fanatical religious intolerance was their most potent weapon. Catholicism was forced upon the Spanish people, not only because the royal couple were devout, but also because religion was a ready-made tool for centralizing authority.[98] The Spanish Inquisition, introduced in 1478 to persecute converted Jews who had supposedly lapsed in their adherence to Catholicism, ultimately assumed the burden of rooting out "heresy" wherever it raised its head. Even the papacy found the Inquisitors' handiwork shocking. Informants were allowed to make accusations without having to reveal their identities to the accused. Condemned heretics forfeited their estates to the crown (a brazen conflict of interest) and were then burned at the stake in a public spectacle designed to silence those who opposed the royal power. (Recantation at the stake was rewarded with death by strangulation before the pyre was set alight.[99])

The year 1492 was the monarchy's watershed year. In October, Columbus discovered America. But other momentous events had already transpired—including the long delayed conquest of Moorish Granada by Christian crusaders after a ten-year siege. There seems to have been some confusion at the end of this war; for the Moors, with whom Ferdinand and Isabella had been fighting were offered lenient terms (later to be reneged upon), while the Jews, who had helped to finance the royal army,[100] were suddenly told that they must convert to Catholicism or leave the realm. Over 100,000 Jews promptly fled, leaving their assets to be appropriated by the bigots who had cast them out.

In the long run, the crown's insistence on religious unity was a sublime blunder—costing the state many of its most productive citizens. But to Ferdinand and Isabella it seemed a stunning success. By the dawn of the new century, the joint rulers were ready to play power politics on an international scale—something that Spain, hitherto, had not possessed the capacity to do.

And this at last brings us back to the partition of Naples agreed to by King Ferdinand and Louis XII of France after the latter's occupation of Milan. Of this compact (the so-called Treaty of Granada, 1500), Machiavelli would write, "The French have little skill in matters of State, for whereas before, Louis was sole umpire in Italy, he now entertained a partner, and whereas Louis might have made the king of Naples his pensioner, he turned him out and put the Spaniard in his place, who turned out Louis himself."[101]

In accordance with the terms of their treaty, the pair cooperated in the subjugation of Naples only to declare war on one another over the division line. In the early going, Louis had more troops in the field and obtained the upper hand. For a time, the Spanish troops and their Italian allies were confined to the citadel of Barletta, where they endured the catcalls of the French army, which took up position outside the walls. But when the French declared that the Italians were not masculine enough to defend their own country, the latter called a halt to the war and sent thirteen champions into the field to settle the matter against thirteen men chosen by the French. The Italians swept the contest, carrying thirteen battered French knights into captivity. Spain's "Great Captain," Gonzalo de Córdoba, promptly ransomed the Frenchmen and returned them to their own lines, but the spirit of his men was now so buoyed that he could move to the attack.[102]

A decade earlier, this same Gonzalo de Córdoba had relied on cavalry for the conquest of Granada, but in his Italian campaigns infantry played the decisive role. By 1503, the Spanish foot had been reorganized into formations called *coronelias*, the forerunners of the *tercio* phalanxes that would be the bane of Europe for the rest of the century.[103] The *coronelias*—featuring pikemen dressed in the light armor of conquistadors, and "arquebusiers" (musketeers armed with an early and cumbersome form of musket)—so devastated the French at Cerignola and Garigliano (both fought in 1503) that in the aftermath of the latter battle the fleeing French could not even defend themselves against the local peasantry. Many had the very clothes stolen off their backs. Desperate to escape the cold—for it was the dead of winter—the fugitive Frenchmen piled into the dunghills around Rome. The next day, the Roman populace beheld their naked corpses—hundreds of them—frozen and submerged to the neck in excrement.[104] Hence, owing to a needless treaty (proposed, it should be noted, by Ferdinand[105]), the whole of Naples was lost to Louis.

The fall of the Borgias and the defeat of the French threw Italy into chaos. Hoping to capitalize on the general confusion, Venice bolted the Holy League and attacked the Papal States, seizing Faenza, Rimini and Ravenna. Pope Julius II answered this aggression by forging a new coalition—the League of Cambrai—boasting such powerful signatories as the kings of France and Spain (whose recent differences had been smoothed over), and the Holy Roman Emperor, Maximilian, who held a vague claim to the Venetian-controlled city of Padua (1508).[106]

Too old to lead charges into the breach himself, Julius was nonetheless a fighting pope, who rode at the head of his marching columns and directed strategy within range of the enemy's artillery.[107] In the present conflict, however, the decisive clash was fought without him. At Agnedello (1509), the French-dominated League forces smashed the Venetians, and in the wake of the victory, Julius placed Venice under interdict until she surrendered the cities she had usurped (1510).[108]

The victory, however, had been more French than papal, and Pope Julius had now to contend with the resurgent aspirations of France, whose armies were again roaming to-and-fro in northern Italy. To be rid of them, Julius organized a new Holy League (1511), to which incredibly enough, Venice was a willing signatory. Ferdinand of Spain signed on, too, and when Louis XII complained that the Spanish king had now deceived him twice, the latter retorted: "He lies, the *drunkard*; I have deceived him more than ten times."[109] In the end, Julius' alliance also encompassed Swiss mercenaries, the Holy Roman Emperor and England's Henry VIII.[110] Yet when the rival armies clashed at Ravenna on Easter Sunday,

1512, the French, ably led by King Louis' nephew, Gaston de Foix, came away with a smashing victory.

Were it not for fate, the victory might have cemented the French hold on northern Italy,[111] but de Foix was killed in the fighting and without his leadership, the armies of France were soon everywhere in retreat. Swiss forces drove them out of Milan; King Ferdinand occupied "Spanish" Navarre (i.e., the portion of that kingdom located south of the Pyrenees); and Henry VIII sortied into France to defeat them on their own turf at Guinegate (1513) in what was afterwards called the "Battle of the Spurs" since the defeated French showed more spirit spurring their horses in flight than they had during the actual fighting.

The French collapse marked the end of an era. In 1513, Pope Julius died. A year later, Louis XII, now a widower, married a sixteen-year-old girl, "and to please [her], changed his whole manner of life." Where formerly, he was in bed by six, he now stayed up until midnight, and after two months of this gallant exertion, "he fell ill of a disease which defied all human remedies, and ... rendered up his soul to God."[112]

With the extinction of its main participants, the first phase of the Italian Wars drew to a close, leaving France with little more to show for her extensive labors in Italy than an outbreak of syphilis.[113] Indeed, the only victors to emerge from the chaotic succession of alliances and counter-alliances were Spain's double-dealing King Ferdinand, who regained control of Naples, and the Medici, who were restored to power in Florence after Spanish troops chased that city's pro–French Soderini regime into exile.

But the outcome of most consequence in these early Italian Wars was hardly even perceived by the combatants. For in thwarting the designs of France, the less powerful states of Europe were forced to combine, and, in doing so, they inadvertently stumbled upon the "balance of power" principle. Henceforth, it was taken as a maxim of international relations that the hegemony of any one state would threaten the independence of the others, and that it was necessary, in such circumstances, for the lesser states to unite to preserve their liberties.[114] It is their role in the development of this principle that makes the early Italian Wars significant in the history of Europe.

The Reformation and Charles V

Europe had discovered the balance of power principle in the nick of time; for with French power broken, the continent found itself face-to-face with an even greater menace: the Hapsburgs. Indeed, the imperial electors had scarcely handed the throne back to them (1438), before the Hapsburgs began biting off whole chunks of Europe. Their conquests were obtained not through war, but through marriage. To be sure, there were some setbacks: Frederick III (1440–1493) let Hungary and Bohemia slip from his grasp. But this same ruler scored a masterful coup by espousing his son and successor, Maximilian I (ruled 1493–1519), to Mary of Burgundy, the heiress of Charles the Rash (1477). The union brought the Low Countries and, later, the Franche Comté into the Hapsburg fold, though Burgundy itself was conceded to France.

Given his own chance to rule, Maximilian proved himself an even better matchmaker than his father. In 1496, he arranged the wedding of his son, Philip the Handsome, to Juana the Mad, daughter of Spain's Ferdinand and Isabella. Although this betrothal may not sound particularly promising, it paid off beyond all expectation when the gods smote anyone and everyone standing between Juana and the Spanish succession. Among those carried away, was Juana's husband, Philip, which was something of a relief to King Ferdinand who had never intended to leave newly united Spain to the Hapsburgs.

Juana, to put it mildly, did not share her father's sense of consolation. Driven mad by the loss of her faithless, good-for-nothing husband, she refused, for an extended period, to let Philip's coffin out of her sight. Periodically, she raised the lid and embraced the corpse.[115] Finally, her advisors prevailed upon her to bury the unfortunate fellow—which she mercifully did—but she then refused to bathe, preferring to stare at the gravesite from her palace window for forty-nine consecutive years until death took her, too.[116]

Needless to say, no one asked this woman to rule Spain. But this meant that her son must rule—and he, as a grandson of Emperor Maximilian, was a Hapsburg of the selfsame genus and species that so discomfited King Ferdinand. Born to Philip the Handsome and Juana the Mad in 1500, Prince Charles was crowned king of the Netherlands at Philip's death in 1506, and awaited only the death of King Ferdinand to inherit the entire Spanish empire. When this came to pass in 1516, it was enough to upset most everyone. But things were about to get even worse, since Emperor Maximilian (also near death), was laboring to add the imperial throne and its territories to his grandson's patrimony.

In the end, Maximilian achieved his goal. But it wasn't the power of his persona or his eloquence at debate that secured the Holy Roman Empire for Charles against such formidable rivals as Francis I of France and Henry VIII of England. Nor was it marriage (which was a good guess for those of you who have been paying attention). Rather it was the strategic dispersal of bribes. The Hapsburg's, you see, had the backing of the Fuggers—a family of bankers who were so liberal with their donations that the electors quite forgot the money they had already pocketed from Francis I, and voted en bloc for Charles. (Nor did it hurt that a pro–Hapsburg army was encamped on the outskirts of Frankfurt, where the election took place).[117]

In October 1520, Charles was crowned "King of Rome" at Aachen. His countenance was something less than awe-inspiring. The best reassurance that could be offered to Pope Leo X (1513–1521) by Cardinal Girolamo Aleander was that the young emperor seemed to be significantly more intelligent than he looked.[118] As J. H. Elliott

Charles V, Holy Roman Emperor and King of Spain, 19th century engraving (© Depositphotos.com/ Georgios Kollidas).

notes, Charles' oversized Hapsburg jaw caused his mouth to hang open, giving him the appearance of an imbecile. Even worse, he did not know a word of Spanish.[119] In later years, he learnt it along with French and Italian; but left to his own devices, he preferred not to speak at all.[120] (Occasionally, he uttered a few words in German to his horse.[121]) He was notoriously indecisive, but if events conspired to force a decision from him, he tended to be bull-headed in its pursuit.[122]

While his visage was not impressive, Charles' territories certainly were. The domains of the new titan virtually encircled France. Having never fully recovered from its wars with the Hohenstaufen, the papacy was alarmed to find Naples again in the hands of a German emperor.[123] It seemed that the medieval plan for a worldwide City of God had gone terribly awry to produce a worldwide City of Hapsburg.

Still, Charles had cause for dismay. Despite the fact that he was their common prince, the various states nominally under his control played by their own rules, granting different measures of authority to the crown with one hand, while imposing varying degrees of restraint with the other.[124] There were diplomatic problems, too. Even before Charles became emperor, Francis I of France (ruled 1515–1547) invaded northern Italy in an effort to forestall the impending Hapsburg encirclement. After a dangerous crossing through an obscure Alpine pass, Francis' vanguard surprised and captured a papal cavalry force at Villafranca. Francis himself, meanwhile, descended from the Alps with the rest of his army by another route. Threatened in flank by this maneuver, the district's defenders—a group of Swiss mercenaries who had been hired by Milan's Sforza family—made a tactical retreat. The French offered them a bribe to withdraw completely, but just when they were on the point of accepting it, a fanatical Swiss cardinal changed their minds with a sermon so inspiring that they attacked the instant he was finished.[125] The result was a bloody, two-day clash at Marignano (1515).

On the first day of this encounter, the French were driven back by the Swiss phalanxes. Francis, charging wildly, had a pike driven through his helmet.[126] But by sundown, the French had rallied somewhat, and on the following day, their field artillery gave the Swiss what one chronicler describes as "a very warm reception indeed."[127] Still, the Swiss pressed on, and the French left flank might have crumbled had Francis' Venetian allies not arrived to turn the tide. The Swiss now very definitely fell back. Some attempted a last stand in a headquarters building seized from the French. Their pursuers burnt the edifice down with the defenders in it.[128] By noon, the remainder of the Swiss army was in flight. According to an eyewitness, the maimed fugitives streaming from the field conjured an image from Dante's Ninth Circle of Hell.[129] Milan was defenseless, but before occupying the city (to which the Hapsburgs held a rival claim), Francis had himself knighted by one of his grandees.

Intent on regaining everything that had been lost by his predecessor, Francis went on the offensive again soon after the election of Charles to the imperial throne. In 1521, his forces attempted to seize Spanish Navarre. At the time, Charles was preoccupied with Spain's so-called *Comunero* Revolt. Instigated by the realm's disgruntled townsfolk, who resented Charles' habit of extorting taxes from Spain for his far-off imperial designs,[130] this months-long rebellion seemed destined to end in social revolution. Assisted by this distraction, Francis' lieutenant, Andre de Foix, overran Spanish Navarre and made a foray into Castile. But in April 1521, the *Comuneros*, weakened by squabbling and ineffectual leadership,[131] were routed at Villalar, and afterwards de Foix was beaten and captured at Logroño.[132] (Spanish Navarre reverted to Spain.)

Such challenges were trifling, however, in comparison with a firestorm that was now brewing in Germany. The new problem, bizarrely enough, was precipitated by an architectural project in Rome. In the brief interlude between Louis XII's abandonment of the Italian Wars and Francis I's resumption of them, Pope Leo X decided to complete Rome's new and beautiful St. Peter's Cathedral. To defray the costs of this lavish enterprise, he dispatched salesmen throughout Europe to sell "indulgences" (i.e., papal dispensations offering salvation to anyone who could afford the purchase price). Among the sellers of these remarkable certificates, was a certain Dominican friar named Johann Tetzel, who assured prospective penitents that their cash would not only absolve them of previous sins, but that "any sins you may commit hereafter shall all be blotted out" as well.[133] In other words, if the sinner acted now, he could purchase remission of past *and future* sins at one low price. Nor was it too late to absolve dead loved ones. Tetzel bade pious men who had no personal need of dispensation to consider a less fortunate friend or relative who might yet be in purgatory "suffering in those awful flames"—for the purchase of an indulgence would "cause that soul to be immediately released from purgatory, and to be borne on angel-wings to heaven."[134]

Tetzel's persuasive salesmanship produced a steady stream of revenue, but given time for reflection, a number of his customers entertained doubts about the validity of their purchases. To calm their anxiety, they brought their certificates to the attention of the professor of theology at the University of Wittenburg—a certain Augustinian monk named Martin Luther.[135] Luther was taken aback. His own life experience had taught him that ritual contrition for past sins could not, of itself, ensure salvation. "If ever a monk had got to heaven by monkery," he testified, "I should have been he, for all that a monk could do, I did."[136] The realization drove him first to despair and then to an intensive study of Scripture and the writings of the early Church fathers, which in turn convinced him that one could attain salvation only through one's own individual faith in God—not from the sacraments and good works suggested by the Church (for these were worthless if unaccompanied by an inward reformation of the heart), and certainly not from some bogus indulgence. What need was there for piety or remorse if the slate could be wiped clean by a financial transaction? God's love was not open to purchase, nor could man, as a sinner, claim to be worthy of it on the basis of outward piety.[137] The only recourse was to faith. If the individual sinner was sincere in this, God, in His infinite compassion, might have mercy on his soul.

This was a most intriguing argument—objectionable only in that it was heresy, since it removed the necessity of having the Church as a mediator between man and God.[138] But having contemplated the matter at some length (while seated, by his own admission, on a chamber pot in the monastic lavatory[139]), Luther refused to confirm the indulgences. Tetzel publicly rebuked him for this brazenness. Luther answered with his famous "Ninety-five Theses," which he affixed to the church door at Wittenberg on October 31, 1517. In this extraordinary document, Luther argued that the pope might have power to release a penitent from his penance, but he could not, by an indulgence, expunge his sins. Indeed, the very notion of selling indulgences was inherently flawed. "It is certain that, when the money rattles in the chest, avarice and gain may be increased, but the effect of the intercession of the Church depends on the will of God alone." ... "It is a very difficult thing, even for the most learned theologians, to exalt at the same time, in the eyes of the people, the ample effect of pardons and the necessity of true contrition. True contrition seeks and loves punishment, while the ampleness of pardons relaxes it and causes men to hate it...."[140]

By March 1518, the theses had been translated from Latin into German, gaining undesired celebrity for Luther, who soon found himself proclaiming publicly that neither popes nor Church councils were infallible, and that legitimate authority in religious matters therefore lay in Scripture alone (June-July 1519).[141] Luther's heresy was now clear for all to see, and when he expounded upon his views in a series of written dissertations, Pope Leo issued a papal bull giving him sixty days to recant (June 1520). Luther defiantly burned the bull in public. His excommunication was thereby sealed, but his doctrine was more popular than ever. Indeed, when the Holy See ordered the burning of Lutheran books, Luther's supporters in Mainz substituted Catholic ones, and chuckled as the unwitting papal authorities burned these instead.[142]

Charles V, who had called together the imperial diet (i.e., parliament) at Worms in hopes of consolidating his authority as emperor, found attention so riveted on Luther that he reluctantly offered the monk safe passage to defend his doctrines (April 1521). Despite the fate of Hus a century earlier, Luther agreed to appear. When his contention that the individual could glean truth directly from Scripture without priestly guidance was denounced as a reawakening of the heresies of Hus and Wycliffe,[143] Luther refused to recant, telling the assembly: "Let me be refuted and convinced by the testimony of the Scriptures, or by the clearest arguments; otherwise I can not and will not recant; for it is neither safe nor expedient to act against conscience. Here I take my stand. I can do no otherwise, so help me God, Amen."[144]

There was no chance that such reasoning would sway the emperor. Luther had not just threatened Christian unity—he had also inconvenienced Charles' financial mentors. Half of all proceeds from papal indulgences were to have been handed over to the powerful Fuggers to repay a tremendous debt owed by the Archbishop of Mainz. Luther's challenge to Tetzel (who traveled with a Fugger accountant) had slowed sales dramatically.[145] Little wonder that Charles issued this stinging rebuttal in the "Edict of Worms": "A single monk, led astray by private judgment, has set himself against the faith held by all Christians for a thousand years and more, and impudently concludes that all Christians up till now have erred"[146] ... "Accordingly, in view of ... the fact that Martin Luther still persists obstinately and perversely in maintaining his heretical opinions ... we have declared and made known that

Martin Luther, theologian and leading figure of the Protestant Reformation, engraved 1859, Nordheim, Germany (© Depositphotos.com/Georgios Kollidas).

the said Martin Luther shall hereafter be held and esteemed by each and all of us as a limb cut off from the Church of God, an obstinate schismatic and manifest heretic."[147]

The safe conduct granted Luther three weeks to flee before imperial police would be given orders to arrest him. Luther's powerful benefactor Frederick the Wise, elector of Saxony, got to him first—melodramatically "kidnapping" the monk in order to give him sanctuary. Under the elector's protection, Luther translated the New Testament into German so that his growing throng of followers could read it. His biblical prose would lay the foundation for modern German literature.[148]

Charles, meanwhile, returned to Spain, took an Iberian queen (Isabella of Portugal), and healed his conflict with the Spanish Cortes. To the delight of his Castilian subjects, he prepared for a prolonged stay in the recently troubled kingdom. (Hitherto, he had been an absentee tax collector.) While away from Germany, he appointed his brother, Ferdinand, to be imperial regent. Even better, he arranged for Ferdinand to marry the daughter of the king of Bohemia—a move that paved the way for the return of Bohemia and Hungary to the Hapsburg fold. In 1522, Charles even managed to hurl Francis I out of Milan.

Despite these achievements, all was not well. At home in Germany, the Lutheran storm was gathering momentum—but now, sincere religious fervor increasingly gave way to self-interest as men learned to turn the new doctrine to their own advantage. During the so-called Knight's War (1522–23), for example, Germany's lesser aristocracy used Lutheran doctrine as a pretext for seizing Church properties. With the wealth thus obtained, they hoped to buttress themselves against the ceaseless encroachments made on their rights and privileges by the empire's great princes. In retaliation, the princes pooled their resources to form the Swabian League, and utterly defeated the knights with a professional Hapsburg army.

In 1524, however, the downtrodden peasantry of the Black Forest staged a far more ominous rebellion aimed at liquidating the aristocracy altogether. From the peasants' vantage point, the era's religious abuses were as nothing compared to its social abuses. At Memmingen, they issued a document entitled "The Twelve Articles" demanding an end to the repression that had reduced them to servitude. When this was followed by the traditional riots and atrocities incumbent upon a popular uprising, Luther himself denounced their cause, advising the nobility that "whosoever can, should smite, strangle, and stab, secretly or publicly, and should remember that there is nothing more poisonous, pernicious, and devilish than a rebellious man."[149] As the hapless peasants were no better organized than an unruly mob, the forces of the Swabian League slaughtered them by the thousand. In May 1525, their leading figure, Thomas Münzer, an anarchist who so clothed his arguments in gospel as to be taken as a prophet, was captured and executed.[150]

The religious disturbances in Germany provided the French king, Francis I, with a new opportunity to intervene in Italy. In 1524, his troops again occupied Milan, now ravaged by plague, and placed Pavia under siege. Charles, however, had obtained a promise of troops from the Diet of Worms and was determined that their deployment should determine "whether he should become a very poor Emperor, or Francis a sorry King."[151] Accordingly, imperial forces came to Pavia's assistance in January 1525. They found the French encamped in the city's walled-off park of Mirabello, and sought to surprise them by toppling the park wall. The endeavor proved far too noisy, however, and after creating a breach, the imperialist forces were unhappy to perceive through the rubble a patently unsurprised French army marshaled for battle with artillery at the ready.[152] A vicious cannonade thundered into the imperial arquebusiers, scattering heads and limbs in every direction.[153] Believing the battle won, Francis ordered a general advance. But in moving forward, he blocked the line of fire of his own guns and exposed his flank to a body of imperial pikemen who staged a ferocious attack while the rest of the imperialists reformed their lines. Caught in the maelstrom, his horse killed beneath him, his army being cut to shreds, Francis continued the fight until he was overpowered and taken prisoner—the fact that he had been recognized being a matter of luck as those around him were mercilessly butchered.[154]

Francis purchased his release on the most humiliating terms. By the Treaty of Madrid, he ceded the coveted duchy of Burgundy to the emperor, and renounced the Angevin claim on Italy. Once at liberty, however, he disavowed the agreement, and formed the League of Cognac with Florence, Venice and the papacy—all of whom perceived the balance of power shifting ominously toward Charles V. Even the Turks were approached for assistance—the Ottomans and the French being natural allies, since their respective expansive designs placed both nations at odds with the Hapsburgs.[155]

In answer to these machinations, imperialist forces struck at the league's most vulnerable link: Rome. Arriving with their pay in arrears, and rendered leaderless by the death of their commander at the outset of the assault, the undisciplined imperialists went berserk—sacking the city like so many Vandals,[156] while the indecisive Pope Clement VII (the second of two Medici popes—the first having been Leo X) took refuge in Castle Santangelo (1527). By month's end, 2,000 Italian corpses had been deposited in the Tiber, and an even greater number adorned the streets in varying states of decomposition.[157]

Francis riposted by dispatching an army to Italy, which retook Pavia, and advanced on Naples. But in the ensuing siege of that city, the army was first ravaged by plague, and then routed in attempted flight.[158] When the rest of the League armies were beaten at Landriano (1529), the king had little choice but to sign the Peace of Cambrai—also called The Ladies' Peace, since Francis' mother and Charles' aunt were the chief negotiators. By its terms, Francis renounced French claims to Milan and Naples, obtaining in return an annulment of his prior cession of Burgundy to the emperor. With this treaty the "Italian phase" of the Hapsburg-Valois wars came to an end.

The Reformation Takes Wing

Charles V might well celebrate his new-won ascendancy in Italy. But in Germany, things were otherwise; for, in addition to the continuing religious turmoil, the empire now had to contend with an attack by the Ottoman Turks.

The trouble had begun when a group of haughty Hungarian nobles severed the nose and ears of a Turkish diplomat. In retaliation, Suleiman (Solomon) "the Magnificent," the Turkish sultan (ruled, 1520–1566) seized the Hungarian stronghold of Belgrade (1521).[159] Egged on by the French, who were seeking aid from any quarter after Pavia, Suleiman dispatched an army of 100,000 men to conquer all of Hungary. Standing in their way were 25,000 Hungarians, led by the twenty-year-old Hungarian king, Louis II Jagiellon. When the rival armies met at Mohács (1526), the Hungarians compounded their numerical disadvantage with an imprudent cavalry charge. Suleiman's artillery all but exterminated them.

Wounded in the head, King Louis fled pell-mell into a bog where he fell beneath his horse and died of suffocation. Afterwards, the Turks fashioned a pyramid for their sultan out of 1,000 Hungarian heads.[160]

Under most circumstances, this would have been regarded as a setback. But Charles V's brother, Ferdinand, the regent of Germany, was also brother-in-law to the dead (and heirless) Hungarian monarch. As a result, he became de facto heir to Louis' throne, which encompassed not just Hungary but Bohemia. The Bohemians welcomed Ferdinand with open arms, but the Hungarians, cowed by the rampaging Ottoman army, opted instead for the Turkish puppet, John Zápolya. Ferdinand seized part of Hungary from Zápolya in 1527, but this angered the Turks, who promptly advanced to the very gates of Vienna (1529), which they would have taken by siege had their supply lines not been inadequate. After posturing before the walls of the great Austrian city for two weeks, their provisions ran out forcing their withdrawal.

Nonetheless, the Turkish problem had fixed the attention of Ferdinand, leaving him powerless to halt the spread of Lutheranism in Germany. Despite the defeat of the knights and the peasants, the new religion continued to grow, numbering among its adherents several great princes and not a few members of the formerly reliable Swabian League.[161] A perfunctory imperial decree issued at the Diet of Speyer (1529) sought to tilt the balance back toward Catholicism by restricting Lutheran freedom of worship. Unwilling to comply, the Lutherans responded with a declaration of protest (for which they were derided as "Protestants").[162]

In far away Spain, Emperor Charles could no longer ignore the crisis. Returning to Germany for the first time in seven years, he convened the Diet of Augsburg (1530) hoping to resolve the religious conflict so that a unified front could be presented to the Turks. The Lutherans obliged him with a conciliatory document—the so-called Confession of Augsburg. But the Catholics responded with their own manuscript—the Confutation—which, being not conciliatory at all, precluded a negotiated settlement. In exasperation, Charles imposed his own lopsided solution on the parties. The Lutherans were to return to the Catholic fold within six months or prepare for war. All ecclesiastical real estate seized by the Lutherans was to be restored to the Church.

Alas, the resources available to Charles for enforcing this decree were not proportionate to his boldness in issuing it. Knowing as much, the Protestants organized the League of Schmalkalden to consolidate their opposition to him (1531). Hence, the result of Charles' unilateral diktat was an impasse cleaving the empire into two armed camps. In the ensuing sixteen years, the two sides found but few occasions to cooperate—the most notable example occurring in 1534, when a radical religious sect, the Anabaptists, seized the reins of government in the city of Münster. Asserting their emphatic belief that worldly associations compromised religious integrity, the Anabaptists preached complete separation of church and state and nonparticipation in secular affairs.[163] Only the intensely pious were accepted into their congregations, and adult rebaptism was required of all (baptism of newborns being held to be meaningless since it was involuntary). Led by elected ministers, Anabaptist congregations used scriptural precepts to guide their daily lives. Believing the second coming of Christ to be imminent, the fanatical congregation of Münster proclaimed a communistic "New Jerusalem" (1534). They harried unbelievers from the city, and enforced doctrinal conformity with a reign of terror. They provided a haven for runaway nuns, and as the men of the city were now outnumbered, they legalized polygamy to provide the erstwhile religious ladies with husbands.[164]

Even a Lutheran and a Catholic could agree that this last measure was blasphemy. After an extended siege, Münster's Anabaptists were betrayed by one of their own parishioners, allowing a combined Lutheran-Catholic force to storm an undefended stretch of the town wall (1535). Having obtained a pledge of safety, the last defenders laid down their weapons, only to be perfidiously butchered.[165] For the next three centuries, the rotting corpses of their ringleaders were left on display in cages suspended from Münster's church steeple.[166]

No sooner was this godly extermination complete, sad to say, before the Lutherans and Catholics were again at loggerheads. Within the empire, neither side could get the upper hand. Further afield, however, Protestantism was clearly on the march. In Scandinavia, Sweden found the creed useful in securing its independence. Tied to Denmark and Norway since 1397, when Norway's indefatigable Queen Margaret fused the three states into one with the Union of Kalmar, Sweden opted for separation at the dawn of the 16th century. The Danes attempted to thwart this aspiration by condemning 82 Swedish patriots to death by drowning or decapitation—an event that became known as the "Stockholm Massacre" (1520).[167] But this atrocity only stoked the flames of Swedish nationalism. Gustavus Vasa, a scion of Sweden's ancient ruling house, had escaped the massacre by masquerading as a worker in the Swedish copper mines. Raising an army of miners and peasants, he defeated the Danes in 1523 and declared Sweden independent with himself as king. Because the Church had backed the Danes, he appropriated its lucrative properties to finance his new government (1527) and converted the state to Lutheranism.[168]

Six years later, the throne of Norway and Denmark itself devolved upon the Lutheran prince, Christian III (much to the discomfiture of Emperor Charles who had meddled in the succession in favor of a Catholic candidate). During this same interval, Switzerland conjured its own brand of Protestantism under the tutelage of Ulrich Zwingli of Zurich (1484–1531). Although Zwingli agreed with Luther's notion that faith was the key to salvation, he held differing views on the sacraments. While Luther believed that the wafer and wine of the Lord's Supper literally contained the body and blood of Jesus, for example, Zwingli considered them merely symbolic. The two squared off in public debate over this issue at the Colloquy of Marburg (1529), but neither could sway the other to his views and their movements remained separate. Returning to Switzerland, Zwingli delved into the political realm, seeking to create a more democratic system of representation than had existed hitherto. His efforts alarmed the state's strongly Catholic forest cantons, which stood to lose their disproportionate leverage in the Swiss diet.[169] When Zwingli persisted, it came to war. At the battle of Kappel (1531), Zwingli, bearing the banner of his army, was killed on the field—his corpse being grossly mistreated afterwards by the fanatical Catholics.[170]

In the decade after Zwingli's death, a new and more severe form of Protestantism was to take hold in the Swiss city of Geneva. In 1534, John Calvin (1509–1564), a Frenchman from Picardy, had summarized his own version of Protestantism in a tome entitled *Institutes of the Christian Religion*, which preached the omnipotence of God, the authority of Scripture, and the predestination of men's souls. Exiled from France for his opinions, he was making his way to Strassbourg when the people of Geneva (where he had intended to remain but one night) convinced him to alter his plans and lead their city's Reformation (1536).[171]

The goal of the Genevans was political. The city was an independent republic, but its overbearing neighbors, Catholic Savoy and Protestant Bern, posed an ever-present threat to its autonomy. Rent by internal discord, the city fathers believed that a new creed might finally allow Geneva to present a united front and retain its independence.

They would have done well to entertain other options. To this point, the residents of Geneva had been as fun loving an assemblage of libertines and fornicators as were to be found in any city. Indeed, so rampant was prostitution in Geneva that the city's prostitutes had nominated their own "Brothel Queen" to reign over the red-light district.[172] But Calvin quickly put an end to all that by mandating piety in all things. Horrified that he actually wanted them to live in accordance with the tenets of the *Institutes*, they sent him away, but in 1541, they called him back for the same political motives just described and allowed him to enact his program.[173] By the mid-1550s, his vaunted "church government" or "theocracy" was firmly in place, and Calvin himself was dictator of his own little City of God.[174] His twenty-three-year stewardship proved uncompromising in the extreme. Catholicism was outlawed, attendance at Sunday sermons was made compulsory, women's hairstyles were regulated, and parishioners caught dancing or singing bawdy songs were put in jail for three days.[175] The city's inhabitants were spied upon—often through their own glass windows since curtains were forbidden.[176] Witchcraft and blasphemy were punished with execution (in one case a child was decapitated for striking a parent[177]), lesser crimes with exile or the lash. The slightest indiscretion might land one before the "consistory," a body of clerics and town elders empowered to pass judgment in morality cases. Such vigilance seems hard to justify for men who believed that an individual's salvation or damnation was predetermined by God; but the reality in Geneva was that man's fate was determined by a far harsher judge: the great and powerful Calvin.

Though he himself had once been chased from France for his beliefs, Calvin demonstrated a notable lack of compassion towards other religious fugitives. The Spaniard Michael Servetus, for example, had evaded the footfalls of his Catholic pursuers for the better part of two decades after authoring his heretical treatise, *De Trinitatus erroribus*, in which he abandoned the idea of the Father, the Son and the Holy Ghost for a Unitarian creed that might have lowered the barriers between Judaism, Islam and Christianity.[178] His flight took him first to Paris, where, under an assumed name, he studied medicine in the same classroom with Andreas Vesalius. Incredibly, he was accomplished enough in this second career to discover that blood circulates through the lungs in passing from one side of the heart to the other. (It was another century before Harvey realized that blood circulates through the entire body.)[179] But Servetus never let his attention stray long from religion, and in 1553 a second heretical work, the *Restitution of Christianity*, got him arrested in Vienne, France, after Calvin (whose doctrines Servetus had also impugned) spitefully exposed him as the author. Servetus escaped, but made the fatal blunder of stopping in Geneva on his way to safe haven in Naples. Caught attending one of Calvin's sermons incognito, he was condemned as a heretic, and sent to a hideous death at the stake.[180]

Calvin's was the most unforgiving of the Reformation creeds—a despotic Protestantism led by a one-man inquisition. Yet Calvinism did not cling to the awful rigidity of its originator, and it swiftly amassed an international popularity far exceeding that of Lutheranism. It spawned the Huguenots in France, the Presbyterians in Scotland and the Puritans in England. Some signed on believing that to be a Calvinist was to be among God's elect—an assurance that Calvin himself would never have conceded to anyone with the possible exception of himself. The doctrine was a rallying point for those militantly opposed to Catholicism in Scotland, and held particular appeal for Europe's new and growing entrepreneurial class since, after Calvin's death, prosperous believers came to regard their wealth as evidence that God had elected them for salvation.

In comparison with Geneva's Reformation, England's stands out as comic relief. Henry VIII (ruled 1509–1547) had once been a happy enough Catholic to pen the *Assertio Septem Sacramentum* (*The Defense of the Seven Sacraments*, 1521) in response to the writings of Luther. Pope Leo X was so satisfied with this treatise, that he dubbed Henry "*Defender of the Faith.*" At the time of the *Assertio's* publication, Henry had already been king for twelve years—enough time to exhaust the brimming treasury bequeathed to him by his frugal father. He passed his afternoons at hunting, falconry and tennis, leaving the drudgery of government work to his chancellor, Cardinal Thomas Wolsey, a worldly cleric bent on obtaining the papal chair for himself and a formidable station in the game of European power politics for his king.

Protestant theologian John Calvin. Illustration from *Journal Universel*, **Paris, 1859 (© Depositphotos.com/ Antonio Abrignani).**

Both enterprises came to naught. Wolsey's diplomacy caused England to shift to-and-fro between the camps of Francis I and Charles V, spending inordinate sums of money without ever garnering a substantial gain for England. The most extravagant example of this maneuvering occurred in June 1520 with a two-week peace celebration held by Henry and Francis at Val d'Or in France. The entire aristocracy of both nations attended the outdoor extravaganza, which was so lavishly decorated with gold cloth and satin as to be called the "Field of the Cloth of Gold." The monarchs got on famously. At one point, Henry surprised Francis with a playful wrestling hold only to be thrown on his back. At another, the kings took turns pretending to be one another's groomsmen.[181] Yet within the year, Wolsey would break the peace, and realign the English crown with the imperial interests of Charles V.

Through it all, Henry stayed focused on what was really important: his games. While hawking in 1525, the urge struck him to pole vault over a ditch. Under so much weight, the pole snapped like a twig, delivering the king head and shoulders deep into a pool of mud—exactly upside down, feet kicking impatiently in the air. He was only narrowly saved from drowning by an alert courtier.[182] And the omens were no better in his home life. His rapturous love for his first wife, Catherine of Aragon, was strained by her failure to provide him with a male heir. After six pregnancies, she had produced but one living child—a daughter, Mary. As Catherine was now forty and barren, Henry abandoned her—seeking an annulment from Pope Clement VII, on the grounds that she had formerly been married to his brother, Arthur, ostensibly making their union incestuous.

In nine out of ten cases, this would have been pretext enough for an annulment. Unfortunately, in this case—known to history as the king's "Great Matter"—the queen was a daughter of Ferdinand and Isabella, which made her the aunt of Emperor Charles. Charles accordingly placed immense pressure on Pope Clement to deny Henry's petition. Caught in the middle, Clement dillydallied, and his dillydallying spelt the end of Cardinal Wolsey. Henry dismissed his minister in a rage for failing to obtain the pope's consent, and would have beheaded him had the threat alone not caused the hapless cardinal to die of fright (1530).

The chancellorship was now thrust upon the famed humanist, Sir Thomas More, despite the fact that More didn't want the post, and didn't sympathize with the king's marital intentions. Henry turned, therefore, to another member of the Royal Council, Thomas Cromwell, with whom he hatched the most remarkable scheme of his entire reign. If Rome would not grant him an annulment, the king would annul his ties with Rome. Thomas Cranmer, a royal hireling (and hitherto a low-ranking churchman), was suddenly invested as Archbishop of Canterbury, and, from this lofty pedestal, authorized the king's annulment. (And not a moment too soon, since Henry had already impregnated Ann Boleyn, whom he had taken secretly as a second wife). In an even bolder step, parliament passed the "Act of Supremacy," proclaiming Henry "Supreme Head" of the new "Anglican Church"—i.e., the Church of England (1534). By this Act, the so-called "Reformation Parliament" severed all bonds with the papacy.

The new chancellor, Thomas More, had formerly rebuked Luther for having entangled himself in the bowels of Satan with his heresy, and he reacted no better to Henry's notion of Church reform.[183] In 1532, when it first became clear that the king planned to usurp ecclesiastical authority, More resigned the chancellorship in a huff. Despite pleas from family and friends, the "man for all seasons" went to the block rather than violate his principles by complying with the "Henrician Reformation" (1535). For a time, his severed head adorned London Bridge.

While he had the headsman's attention, Henry scrounged about for any surviving members of the deposed Plantagenet line, and ordered their execution lest they serve as a rallying point for intractable Catholics. The saddest victim of this purge was surely the sixty-eight-year-old Lady Margaret, daughter of the Duke of Clarence, who hid from her guards, and had to be dragged squealing to the chopping block (1541).[184] The king's religious policy provoked uprisings in Lincolnshire and Yorkshire, but these were put down with a mixture of false promises and timely executions, while the "Dissolution of the Monasteries" (1536) secured the support of the rich, who purchased monastic properties from Henry as quickly as he could confiscate them from the defenseless monks. (The policy was a disaster for the poor who subsisted largely on monastic charity.[185]) The "Ten Articles" of 1536 and the "Six

Articles" of 1539 laid down the tenets of the new Anglicanism. Apart from having the English king as its "pope," the Church of England could scarcely be distinguished from that of Rome. It was the king's "Middle Way"—Catholicism was retained in all its essentials lest the faithful grow anxious; but that "foreign meddler," the pope, was stripped of his powers to collect revenues in England or to influence English affairs. It all seemed perfectly reasonable—except, of course, to those who weren't in the middle. Loyal Catholics and proponents of a true Reformation were alike subject to arrest and possibly execution for giving too loud a voice to their conscience. (On one occasion, perfect symmetry was achieved as three Protestants were burnt and three Catholics sent to the block, all on the same day in July 1540.[186])

On the bright side, Henry was now free to annul his marriages as he pleased. In all, he took six wives, two of whom (Ann Boleyn and Catherine Howard) had their heads lopped off in order to make room for the others. The king was deadly serious about his brides. When his union with Ann of Cleves proved disagreeable (1540),[187] he had Thomas Cromwell beheaded for having arranged it. He finally did produce a male heir—the feeble Edward VI—but the lad would survive him by just six years (scarcely enough to warrant the trouble of a Reformation).

The Counter-Reformation and the Peace of Augsburg

As the Protestant tide washed over England and northern Europe, the Catholic Church commenced its own reform movement: the so-called Counter-Reformation. Begun under Pope Paul III in the 1530s, it gathered momentum at the Council of Trent (held intermittently between 1545 and 1563). Doctrinal issues were clarified during these proceedings, and steps were taken to weed out corruption. But no attempt was made to placate Protestantism. Indeed, a new monastic order—the Society of Jesus or "Jesuits"—was dispatched to win back Protestant lands (which it did with notable success in many regions).

The Jesuits had been founded, and were still led, by Ignatius Loyola, a former soldier who experienced a religious awakening after sustaining a cannonball wound at the battle of Pamplona during the Hapsburg-Valois Wars (1521). He received the Last Sacraments,[188] but survived—not just the wound, but the three brutish operations it took to set his leg properly—and as his deformity precluded further military service, he resolved to place his military talents at the disposal of Jesus.[189]

Loyola condoned neither Luther's idea that faith alone could bring salvation, nor Calvin's scheme of predestination. To be sure, faith was important, but so were the choices of men. Loyola's *Spiritual Exercises*, published in 1548, urged men to identify their own sins on a daily basis—abolishing such behavior of their own free will in order to follow in God's path. His organization performed extensive missionary work, organized relief for the poor, tended to the sick and established some of the best schools in Europe. Emerging from Italy and Spain, where Catholicism had retained its predominance, the Jesuits ultimately won Poland, Hungary, and several south German principalities (Bavaria among them) back to the Catholic fold.[190] Protestantism retreated into northern Germany, Scandinavia, the Netherlands and England. In southern Europe—where a papal bull had established the Inquisition to root out heresy with powers to detain, confiscate wealth and impose the death penalty (1542)[191]—the new religion could only be practiced clandestinely.

But in 1542, the Jesuit efforts had barely begun, and Charles V was left to fight the good fight almost alone. As if war with France and Turkey (1536–1537) was not enough, he was on bad terms with England and Denmark, and had his hands full at home with the Lutherans. Seeing no alternative he attempted, yet again, to effect a settlement with the latter. In April 1541, a diet was convened at Regensburg for this purpose, but after a promising beginning, the talks broke down—largely owing to secular fears among the electors and princes that reconciliation would leave Charles in too powerful a position.[192]

For the next six years (1540–1546), the domestic cease-fire tottered on a tightrope while Charles attended to foreign affairs. In 1541, the Turks had renewed their drive into Hungary, defeating Charles' brother Ferdinand at Buda. Charles struck back with an amphibious assault on Algiers, but his fleet foundered in a storm, leaving Turkish pirates free to roam the Mediterranean.[193] Adding insult to injury, Francis I (who declared war on Charles in 1542 in a final bid to gain Milan) allowed the Turkish fleet to winter at Toulon alongside the French (1542–43).[194]

Diplomacy, however, now brought Henry VIII into the fray on the imperial side; and while Henry seized Boulogne, Charles captured Saint-Dizier, thus threatening Paris. Beneath the weight of this two-pronged invasion, Francis I put pen to the Peace of Crépy. Although the terms weren't carried out, the fighting stopped, thus removing the French thorn from Charles' paw (1544).[195] Cut adrift by Charles, Henry VIII sued for peace with Francis a month later, having bankrupted the English treasury in a quixotic campaign to reverse the verdict of the Hundred Years' War.[196]

Ignatius Loyola, founder of the Jesuits and leading figure of the Counter-Reformation, 19th century engraving (© Depositphotos.com/Georgios Kollidas).

With his foreign difficulties solved, Charles V implored Pope Paul III to convene the aforementioned Council of Trent to readdress the religious stalemate (1545). Inadequately represented, however, the Protestants refused to participate. To make matters worse, Frederick of the Palatinate converted to Lutheranism in January 1546, thus giving the Protestants a majority in the imperial electoral college. Faced with the prospect of a Lutheran supplanting the Hapsburgs when it came time to elect the next emperor, Charles resolved on war.[197] At Mühlberg (April 1547), his army—outnumbered but buoyed by his presence—routed the forces of the Schmalkaldic League at a cost of but fifty men.[198]

At last, the emperor's prospects seemed bright. Armed resistance within Germany had been crushed, the Turks were sidetracked in a Persian campaign, and Charles' formidable rivals, Francis I of France and Henry VIII of England, had both died that very year (1547). But to achieve his victory at Mühlberg, the emperor had had to rely in part on sympathetic Protestant princes who were willing to let politics take precedence over religion. He could hardly impose a hostile settlement on those Lutherans who had just supported him, even if he had possessed the financial and political wherewithal to do so (which he did not).[199] Thus, at the Diet of Augsburg (1548), he stopped short of outlawing Lutheranism—merely promulgating the so-called "Augsburg Interim," which obliged the Lutherans to conform more closely to Catholic protocol until a permanent solution to the religious impasse could be reached.

The attempt to render this solution was undertaken at a new session of the Council of Trent, which the Lutherans agreed to attend (1552). Sadly, the agendas of the attendees were entirely incompatible—the Lutherans seeking to establish once and for all that Scripture alone was the ultimate authority in religious matters and that Church councils could overrule the pope, Charles seeking to forge an agreement that would make the reunited Church a tool of his own imperial designs, and the papacy seeking to preserve its threatened prerogatives.[200]

Charles left the failed council believing that he still held the better cards, but his fortunes were now to take a decided turn for the worse. His most talented military commander, the Lutheran prince, Maurice of Saxony, felt ill rewarded for the service he had rendered to the emperor in the recent war. Intent now on restoring his good name among his fellow Lutherans, he defected to the anti-imperialists and marched against the emperor at the head of a Protestant army (1552). Caught unawares at Innsbruck where he was wintering without any troops, the gout-ridden emperor hobbled into his litter, and was borne away on a nocturnal flight through the Alps. Despite wind and rain strong enough to drench the fleeing party's torches and leave them stumbling in the dark, the emperor ultimately reached safe haven[201]—in part because Maurice had no desire to capture him. (As he explained to those who felt otherwise, "I have no cage big enough to hold such a bird."[202])

Seizing upon Charles' embarrassment, the new French king, Henry II, usurped the bishoprics of Metz, Toul and Verdun on the border of Lorraine. Charles rallied his forces in an attempt to get them back, but was repulsed. On the day after Christmas, 1552, he conceded defeat. Retreating from Metz in a snowstorm, his broken army suffered calamity. With victory over Protestantism as distant as ever, the battle-worn emperor was finally willing to compromise. The result was the Peace of Augsburg (1555), whereby each of Germany's three hundred princelings was empowered to determine the religion of his own subjects— though the choice was strictly limited to Catholicism or Lutheranism (Calvinism and Anabaptism being absolutely excluded). This formula, the *"cuius regio, eius religio"* ("whose realm, his religion"), gave final acceptance to the existence of Lutheranism, thus conceding once and for all that there would be no worldwide City of God under Catholicism as the successor to fallen Rome.

Nor would there be a worldwide City of Hapsburg. At the end of his reign, Charles V became increasingly withdrawn. Rather than attend to the affairs of state, he spent hours with his collection of clocks—never satisfied until he had caused them to tick synchronously.²⁰³ Thoroughly exhausted by the strain of ruling his empire, he abdicated in 1556, and retired to a convent in Estramadura, where he spent his last years making puppets and other trifles.²⁰⁴ After a dress rehearsal in which he listened to his own funeral oration while reclining in a coffin, he passed on to his reward on September 21, 1558.

For nearly four decades, he had been overwrought by foreign and civil war, but owing to a pact signed with his brother in 1531, his successor would not have to bear such burdens. The agreement obliged Charles to divide his inheritance, which he reluctantly did—leaving his German provinces and the imperial throne to his brother, Ferdinand, and everything else to his son, and preferred heir, Philip II (ruled, 1556–1598).

The Women Who Would Be Queen

In 1553, Edward VI of England—the son and heir of Henry VIII—died of pneumonia at the age of fifteen. The rightful heiress to the English throne was Edward's half-sister, Mary Tudor, who, as a daughter of Catherine of Aragon (Henry VIII's first wife), had the Catholic zeal of Spain in her very blood. In hopes of keeping the realm Protestant, a court cabal had secured a will from the dying Edward excluding Mary from the succession on the basis of her supposed illegitimacy as the offspring of a marriage that had been annulled. On the authority of this document, they attempted to deliver the throne to Edward's unwilling Protestant cousin, Lady Jane Grey. The farce cost the unfortunate sixteen-year-old girl her head, and after a delay of scarcely ten days, Mary assumed her rightful place as queen.

Precocious enough as a child to inspire pride in her father, Henry VIII, Mary became an object of Henry's wrath once he decided to seek an annulment from her mother. From age eleven to twenty she was separated from her mother, not even being permitted visitation rights when Catherine lay dying (1536). To avert further cruelty on the part of her father, Mary was compelled to sign a document recognizing him as rightful head of the English church and confirming her own "illegitimacy." Thereafter father and daughter were nominally reconciled.²⁰⁵

It is an accident of history that has left Mary's reputation sullied as a cruel tyrant. She keenly felt the stigma of the document that her father had forced her to sign. During the reign of her half-brother, Edward, she refused to practice the Anglican religion, instead hearing Mass privately in her chapel in violation of the law of the land. For Mary, restoration of the Catholic religion in England was not simply a matter of religious principle. It was a means of erasing the charge of illegitimacy that still hovered over her. The Church had never sanctioned the annulment of her parents' marriage. Hence, its restoration would render the accusation of illegitimacy null and void.²⁰⁶ For this reason, the restoration of Catholicism was the chief object of her heart's desire, and in this aspiration she was not without support, for under Edward VI, English Protestantism had become too radical for the popular taste.

For her own part, Mary was inclined toward moderation—pardoning many of those who had supported Lady Jane Grey in the first days of her reign and giving assurances to those who had obtained lands seized from the Church under Henry and Edward. Unfortunately, the reconciliation with Rome required reinstitution of the realm's heresy laws, and unless these were enforced, Mary's Counter-Reformation would risk exposure as a charade.[207] The result of this quandary was that during the course of her five-year reign, some three hundred leading Protestants were burnt at the stake—in some cases, a sack of gunpowder being added to the pyre to quicken the proceedings.[208] Among the victims was Henry VIII's pliant Anglican Archbishop, Thomas Cranmer, who had recanted his heresies under duress only to disavow the decision afterwards. (At the stake he is reported to have pressed his writing hand into the flames so that it might burn first for having signed the recantation.)[209]

The brutal anti–Protestant campaign won for Mary the sobriquet by which history still remembers her: "Bloody Mary." Nor was it the sole cause of discontent with her reign. In 1554, Mary married Philip II of Spain, whose succession to the Spanish throne in 1556 made her queen of two nations simultaneously. The honor was a dubious one, for it provoked widespread fear in England that English wealth would be put at Philip's disposal for the furtherance of Spanish designs in Europe. The concern became manifest when the marriage embroiled England in the costly war with France that Philip had inherited from his father. In symbolic terms the outcome could not have been worse, for participation in this imbroglio resulted in the loss of Calais, England's lone remaining possession from the heyday of the Hundred Years' War. While France celebrated, anti–Spanish sentiment in England attained new heights. A boiling point might have been reached, but in 1558, Mary died prematurely of an abdominal tumor (grotesquely mistaken for pregnancy) thereby severing the bond with Spain.

She was succeeded by her very un–Catholic half-sister, Elizabeth I (ruled 1558–1603)—the fruit of Henry VIII's short union with Anne Boleyn—who, hitherto, had had to employ all her wits to avoid being cast as a heretic into one of Mary's bonfires. Bankrupt, Philip attempted to maintain the English alliance by proposing marriage to the new queen, but unlike Mary, Elizabeth was far too cunning to become a pawn of Spanish interests. Bereft of options, Philip signed the Treaty of Câteau-Cambrésis (1559) with France's equally bankrupt Henry II (ruled 1547–1559). By its terms, France retained possession of Calais and the bishoprics of Metz, Toul and Verdun (seized from Charles V), but was excluded from Italy—the battleground over which Valois and Hapsburg had now fought a sixty-five year duel.

To consummate the agreement, King Henry betrothed his daughter to King Philip. There followed an elaborate wedding ceremony that included a jousting tournament in which Henry lustily took part. Over his first two opponents, he prevailed with ease. Unfortunately, his third rival, Gabriel, Comte de Mongonmery, shattered his lance on the king's shield—a splinter from the jagged stump finding the slit in Henry's visor, transfixing his eye, and lodging in his brain.[210] Ambroise Paré, the French court physician and father of modern surgery, removed what he could of the debris, but when the king showed no signs of recovery, the other great physician of the age, Andreas Vesalius, was summoned from Belgium to impart his expertise. The heads of a few decapitated criminals were brought forth to be skewered with Mongonmery's broken weapon. Vesalius and Paré dissected the remains to determine the feasibility of an operation. Either from this, or from a different test performed by Vesalius, they concluded that the king's wound was mortal.[211] Henry succumbed on the eleventh day of his suffering, and was succeeded by his adolescent son, Francis II.

Though only fifteen years old, Francis II was already married to Scotland's Catholic queen, Mary Stuart. Besides being possessed of the crowns of both Scotland and France, Mary was next in line, after Queen Elizabeth, for the English throne. To further this claim, she denounced Elizabeth as illegitimate, citing Pope Clement VII's refusal to sanction the 1532 marriage between Elizabeth's parents (Henry VIII and Anne Boleyn). Mary's policy, if successful, would have united England, Scotland and France under one crown—a goal that was strongly supported by the war party in France, which hoped to use the resulting power combination to offset the Hapsburg menace.[212] Scarcely had Mary put forward her claim, however, when her husband died of an ear abscess (1560). No longer queen of France—the throne having passed to her brother-in-law—Mary prepared to return to Scotland.

In the same year, however, the Scots had overthrown the regency of her mother, Mary of Guise (whose French origins and influence were despised), and had embraced Calvinist Presbyterianism as preached by John Knox—a master of fire-and-brimstone rhetoric who had spent some time in Geneva where he seems to have proved himself more Calvinist than Calvin. A bill establishing Presbyterianism and outlawing Catholicism and the celebration of Mass passed the Scottish parliament in August 1560. Upon her return the following year, Mary refused to ratify the act, but did promise not to interfere with the new religion and to hear Mass only privately in her chapel. Calvinists of Knox's ilk were not appeased. When Mary attempted to hear Mass at Stirling, a hostile mob brutalized the priests before they could reach her.[213]

Popular despite her failure to reach a religious compromise with the uncompromising Knox, Mary chose a singularly unpopular second husband in Henry, Lord Darnley (1565). The union produced a son (the future James I of England), but was fraught with discord as the ambitious Darnley, who had expected to co-reign with the queen, found himself excluded from power. Angry that Mary's court favorite—the Italian musician David Rizzio—had more say in policy than he (and suspecting the two of having an affair), Darnley gave his blessing to an attempted coup in which Rizzio was stabbed more than fifty times and the queen taken captive by a cadre of disaffected nobles (1566).[214] Before the night was over, however, Mary convinced Darnley to reconsider. They escaped together to Dunbar and then to Edinburgh escorted by a loyal cavalry force. Afterwards, Darnley contracted smallpox, and though Mary dutifully acted as his nurse, rumor accused her of complicity when he was found strangled in a field outside their temporary dwelling at Kirk o' Field (on the outskirts of Edinburgh), with the dwelling itself blown to smithereens by gunpowder while Mary was conveniently away.[215]

Darnley had been a widely detested mediocrity, particularly after the murder of Rizzio, when "he became the scorn of all parties alike, and few men dared or cared to be seen in his company."[216] Given the number of his enemies, Mary might well have escaped suspicion in his death. Indeed, public opinion initially accused Lord Bothwell (who had led the cavalry force that had escorted Mary and Darnley from Dunbar to Edinburgh after Rizzio's murder).

Far from ordering Bothwell's arrest, however, Mary married him—after scarcely three months as a widow and after helping to secure his divorce from his first wife. Seeing this as proof of her guilt, Scotland rebelled almost to a man. At Carberry Hill (June 15, 1567), Mary and Bothwell were abandoned by their troops in the face of a better-trained rebel force. Agreeing to surrender if Bothwell were allowed to escape (he died later in a Danish prison), Mary was conducted back to Edinburgh where the mob denounced her in loud tones as a "murderess" and a "whore." Five days later, her accusers produced a small silver casket containing eight love letters purportedly written by Mary to Bothwell and proving her complicity in Darnley's murder. The authenticity of these so-called "Casket Letters" is debated to this day, but they were sufficient in the eyes of the Scottish parliament to force her abdication. She was imprisoned in Lochleven Castle. Her supporters liberated her within the year, but were defeated in battle at Langside, and Mary had to seek sanctuary in the unwelcoming arms of her cousin. Elizabeth I of England, the very queen she had formerly sought to dethrone.[217] Despite a papal bull excommunicating her for doing so (1570), Elizabeth proceeded to keep Mary under house arrest for the better part of two decades. There she became the focus of various Catholic plots against Elizabeth's crown—the last of which would end in her beheading.

The French Wars of Religion to 1572

In France, too, the 1560s were a time of religious tumult. While the Hapsburg-Valois Wars had bankrupted the French monarchy, many nobles had prospered by it, and found the treaty of Câteau-Cambrésis and the consequent outbreak of peace a bitter pill to swallow. Francis, Duke of Guise, who had obtained great popularity by capturing Calais from England in the late war, and whose family had profited greatly from the rivalry with Spain, rose to the position of Minister of War only to find that France could no longer afford to fight.[218] The duke likewise championed Catholicism against Protestantism, and in this struggle he had a powerful ally in his brother, Charles, whose cleverness in diplomacy matched the duke's brashness in war. Charles was cardinal of Lorraine, and his high rank in the Catholic Church—which commanded 40 percent of French wealth—afforded him a grand income with which to support the causes of Catholicism and the war party. Moreover, as brothers of Mary of Guise, the duke and cardinal were uncles of Mary, Queen of Scots, who was at this time (1558–1560) still the wife of Francis II and thus queen of France. Through her, the Guises were able to exert undue influence upon the adolescent king, with the duke serving in the aforementioned post of Minister of War and the cardinal becoming the king's chief civil councilor.[219]

In both the religious and the political sphere, the chief adversary of the Guises' program was French Calvinism. At its genesis, this religion had been confined to secret nocturnal meetings. In the city of Tours, the Calvinists had gathered by night at the gate of King Hugo whence they derived their name, "Huguenots" (originally a term of derision.)[220] But by 1559, the religion had become the fastest growing creed in France, and was now openly practiced. Attempting to nip matters in the bud, the Guises used their influence to have eighteen "heretics" burned at the stake during the latter half of 1559. In retaliation, a cadre of irate Protestant nobles conspired to oust them from power (March 1560). But the plot was exposed, and the perpetrators were brutally executed—some being tied in sacks and thrown into the Loire.[221]

Still, the Protestant voice could not be silenced. The popular Huguenot leaders, Louis, Prince of Condé (a direct descendent of the famed Saint Louis), and Gaspard Coligny,

Admiral of France, both urged religious coexistence, and this sentiment found a powerful adherent in the Queen Mother, Catherine de Medici—the widow of Henry II.[222] Upon the death of Francis II in December 1560—which delivered a significant blow to the influence of the Guises—Catherine had become regent of France for her underage son, Charles IX (a nerveless ten-year-old imp who still slept in her bedroom[223]). Rather than see the realm rent in twain, she steered a middle course, assisted by her harem of beautiful concubines—the so-called *escadron volant* or "flying squadron"—whose methods of persuasion tended to soften all opposition. By the Edict of January (1562), a limited toleration was granted to the Huguenots. But as their numbers swelled, they demanded more concessions. Violence broke out anew. In March of 1562, the duke of Guise was struck in the face by a rock after hearing Mass at Vassy. His soldiers, who were already outside the church exchanging insults with a congregation of Huguenots, retaliated with a massacre, killing between twenty and forty Protestants, and maiming a hundred others.[224]

Within a month, the crisis had given sprout to open civil war (April 1562). In return for 6000 fighting men, the Huguenots ceded Le Havre to Elizabeth I of England—promising to exchange it for Calais in the event of victory. But the Protestant army was defeated at Dreux before it could link up with the English, and to cut their losses, the Huguenots accepted the Edict of Amboise (March 1563), reaffirming the old status quo of limited toleration. (In the meantime, Elizabeth's forces were driven from Le Havre.)

The new truce was an uneasy one. At the outset, a nineteen-year-old Huguenot assassinated the duke of Guise, and the authorities thought it reasonable to punish the youth by allowing a quartet of horses to tear him limb from limb.[225] Hatreds continued to simmer, and by 1567, open warfare had resumed—the Huguenots placing Paris under siege until March 1568, when an indecisive bloodletting at St.-Denis forced them to withdraw. There was another truce, and then more war, and now the outrages multiplied. A throng of Huguenots entered a Catholic monastery, and compelled the monks to lynch one another. The Catholics were no better. They burnt a Huguenot prison with the inmates still inside, and, at Auxerre, they tore a hundred hapless Huguenots apart and flung their remains into a sewer.[226] After surrendering on the battlefield at Jarnac, the Prince of Condé was shot dead with a pistol (March 1569).[227] Only when Condé's compatriot, Admiral Coligny, threatened a second march on Paris, did the slaughter finally cease.

By the conciliatory Treaty of St.-Germain, Charles IX granted the Huguenots freedom of worship throughout France (Paris excluded), as well as temporary autonomy in four cities—most notably the port of La Rochelle. Catherine de Medici sought to buttress this agreement by arranging the marriage of her daughter, Margot, to Henry, the Protestant king of Lower Navarre (i.e., the independent portion of Navarre, north of the Pyrenees). Admiral Coligny was summoned to manage the proceedings, but the popular Protestant leader used his position instead to canvass in favor of war with Spain, believing that the nation's rival religious factions would unite for this popular common purpose. The impressionable King Charles was won over by Coligny's reasoning until the Queen Mother suddenly intervened. Unwilling to tolerate a rival influence over her son, Catherine conspired with the Guises to have Coligny murdered. As fate would have it, however, the admiral knelt to tie his shoe just as the assassin fired his arquebus.[228] He escaped, therefore, with nothing worse than a wounded arm and an untied shoelace.

News of the attempted assassination provoked a frenzy among Coligny's Huguenot followers, thousands of whom had flocked to Paris for the wedding. To forestall a general uprising, the Queen Mother simply expanded her recipe for murder. She informed her spineless son that all the Huguenot leaders assembled in Paris, including Coligny, were to be exterminated that very night. A flabbergasted King Charles balked, but he hadn't the courage to defy his mother. Within hours, he had rendered his infamous decision to do more than his mother demanded. "By God's death," he cried in agitation, "since you think proper to kill the admiral I consent; but all the Huguenots in Paris as well, in order that there remain not one to reproach me afterwards!"[229]

Thus began the St. Bartholomew's Day Massacre. At 3:00 a.m. on August 24, an army of soldiers burst into Coligny's residence. Hearing them approach, the admiral bade his retinue to save themselves, saying: "I have no further need of human succor.... For me it is enough that God is here, to whose goodness I commend my soul, which is so soon to issue from my body."[230] Hardly had his attendants made their escape, when the murderous throng barged in. "Art thou the Admiral?" cried one. "I am," answered Coligny, "and thou, young man, shouldst respect my gray hairs."[231] At this, the murderers struck him with a halberd, and thrust him through seven times. The corpse, or still breathing body,[232] was then cast from an upper story window to the courtyard below, where the new duke of Guise brutally gave it a kick in the face, declaring: "We have happily begun. Let us now go for [the] others."[233]

Moments later, the bells tolled at the Palace of Justice as the prearranged signal for indiscriminate slaughter. Huguenot men, women and children were rounded up and mercilessly butchered—the city gates being locked shut lest any get away. Henry, the new Prince of Condé, and Henry of Navarre were saved by the intervention of the Queen Mother. Ambroise Paré, who had been tending to Coligny after the initial assassination attempt was ushered to safety by the king.[234] Some took advantage of the mayhem to carry out their own personal vendettas, irrespective of religion.[235] All told, as many as 10,000 murders were perpetrated—3,000 in Paris, the rest in the surrounding countryside. On hearing of it, Pope Gregory XIII held a celebratory Mass in Rome, and set to work on a commemorative medal, while Philip II of Spain listened to a report of the incident and laughed for the first and only time in his adult life.[236]

Coligny's head was embalmed and sent to the Vatican—although it apparently never arrived—while a troupe of rude children laid hold of his body and dragged it through the Paris streets. On viewing the putrefying corpse several days later, King Charles callously remarked that: "The smell of a dead enemy is very sweet."[237] But in truth, he never forgave himself. He died of tuberculosis a year and a half later with nightmares of the murders haunting him until the end.[238] Nor had anything been gained. Religious war broke out anew in October 1572.

The Turkish War

Of all the European nations to suffer domestic religious turmoil in the 1560s, Spain suffered least. Within her borders the ever-present Spanish Inquisition kept heresy to a minimum. The meager few who could not restrain themselves from Protestant sentiments, or who lapsed from their forced conversions back into Judaism or Islam, were readily disposed of by auto da fé, a public ceremony—more popular in the Spain of that era than the bull fight[239]—in which heretics were burnt at the stake.

Blessed with domestic tranquility, Philip II felt free to pursue holy war beyond the borders of Christendom. Four decades earlier, the Ottoman ruler, Suleiman the Magnificent, had expelled the Knights of St. John from the island of Rhodes. Unable to reverse the damage, Philip's father, Charles V had provided the Knights with a new refuge on Malta. In the 1560s, however, Suleiman attempted to oust them even from this haven. It was no easy task. The island had been fortified with modern star-shaped forts, replete with pointed bastions capable of firing outward or of giving flank support to its neighbors. The Turks thus came under fire no matter which portion of the perimeter they attempted to attack.[240] To be sure, one fort was pulverized by Turkish artillery; but the Birgu bastion held out, and when Philip II sent reinforcements, the Turks withdrew in a huff (1565).[241]

At home in Spain, the Turkish threat engendered new doubts about the loyalty of the nation's "Moriscos"—Muslim converts to Christianity—and of the sincerity of their conversions. Accordingly, edicts of the most bigoted sort were passed outlawing their traditional music and forcing them to marry in public so that proper Christian ritual could be confirmed. Subjected to such hostile scrutiny, the Moriscos of Granada rebelled. They were put down with great ferocity, their communities were broken up and they were forced to disperse through the rest of Spain where they could not act in concert (1568–1570).[242]

In the meantime, the Turks had advanced anew in the Mediterranean to capture Cyprus—flaying the garrison commander alive and forwarding his straw-stuffed skin to Constantinople where it was employed as an ornament in the slave emporium.[243] The alarm was now such that Spain, the papacy and Venice leagued together in perpetual alliance to protect the Mediterranean from the infidel. In 1571, a combined fleet of Spanish, Venetian and papal vessels fell upon the Turkish navy at Lepanto off the coast of Greece. Their ensued one of the most remarkable sea battles in history—the last great clash of rowed galleys, involving no less than five hundred vessels with some 160,000 men aboard (half of them rowers).[244] Despite the alliance that had brought it into being, the Christian fleet was anything but unified. Indeed, its Spanish and Venetian confederates hated one another. But the fleet's charismatic commander, Don Juan of Austria—the illegitimate half-brother of Philip II—forced them to work in concert by interspersing their ships.[245] The Turks opened the encounter with a bid to envelop the confederate flanks. Owing to the closeness of the shore, however, the attempt was thwarted. Consequently, the battle was decided at the center of the rival lines. There, Don Juan's flagship engaged its Turkish counterpart, and, despite a torrent of missile fire, boarded it in force. Wounded in the forehead by a musket shot, the Turkish admiral, Ali Pasha, spent his final moments bargaining ineffectually for his life.[246] The Christians struck off his head, and paraded it atop a pike in full view of the enemy.[247] The sight precipitated a panic among the Ottoman fleet, five sixths of which was either captured or sent to the bottom.

In Italy and Spain, there was unrestrained rejoicing (indeed, more than was merited, since the victory was not followed up, and the Turks remained a menace in Mediterranean waters). Yet Philip was not among the celebrants. Though his reign was a magnificent success to this point, the bizarre madness and death of his son and heir, Don Carlos, followed closely by the death of his wife, Elizabeth Valois, in childbirth (1568) extinguished what little sense of merriment the monarch might theoretically have possessed.[248] Increasingly, he sequestered himself in the Escorial, a palace as drab and oppressive as it was massive and imposing. There, with the corpses of his ancestors close at hand (since the building was also the family mausoleum), he donned black clothing and spent his days immersed in government documents, which he perused in maddening detail.[249] Besides, he now had another problem on his hands; for, like so many other European rulers, the religious war had finally reached his own dominions—not, to be sure, in Spain, but in the Netherlands.

The Dutch War

The Netherlands had come into the possession of the Hapsburgs in 1477 with the marriage of Mary of Burgundy to the future Hapsburg emperor, Maximilian. Maximilian's son, Philip the Handsome served as king of the Netherlands from 1494 until his death in 1506, at which time the throne passed to Maximilian's grandson Charles V (the future Hapsburg emperor). During his tenure, Charles imposed strict anti–Protestant laws. In the first two decades of his reign, thousands of Dutchmen were executed on charges of heresy, and as late as 1550, the emperor was still prescribing death—"the men [to be killed] by the sword, the women by being buried alive."[250] Needless to say, the local populace resented such treatment, and by the mid–1550s many of the Netherlands' provincial councils were ignoring Charles' decrees.[251]

A year before his abdication, Charles bequeathed the Netherlands to his son, Philip II of Spain, who not only pursued his father's anti–Protestant laws with great obstinacy but also issued decrees infringing upon local prerogatives in matters both secular and religious. To enforce his will, he introduced the Inquisition to the Netherlands—that horrid institution that "arrested on suspicion, tortured till confession, and then punished by fire."[252] By 1566, the Inquisition's deadly persecutions and the violation of their own traditional privileges provoked the Netherlands' lesser nobility—Catholic and Protestant alike—to sign the so-called "Compromise," establishing a confederacy pledged to resistance. As an initial act, they petitioned the king to recall the Inquisition and temper his heavy handedness ("Petition of the Confederates," April 1566).[253] In response, they were derided as "beggars"—a name that they promptly appropriated as their rallying cry.

At the grassroots level the opposition was less subtle. Protestant crowds consoled their fellows as they were led to the stake by singing Protestant hymns in the presence of the inquisitors.[254] Far from being extirpated, the Protestant heresy spread. Calvinist preachers held sermons in open fields attended by tens of thousands of congregants.[255] In August 1566, defiance gave way to violence. Goaded by religious radicals and criminal elements, mobs of commoners staged a two-week uprising in the streets ransacking hundreds of Catholic churches across the country. (Because they smashed religious images in the process, they are remembered in history as the "iconoclasts"[256]). Although the local authorities put down the riots, Philip believed a stronger hand was required for the maintenance of order. He deputed the task to the commander of his armies, Fernando Álvarez de Toledo, 3rd Duke of Alva. Once arrived, the "Iron Duke" established a so-called, "Council of Troubles"—or as the Dutch preferred to call it, "Council of Blood"—which instituted a reign of terror that claimed upwards of fifty Dutch lives per day.[257] Not even a façade of justice or legality accompanied the council's proceedings. Of twelve ostensible members, only four had the power to pronounce judgment—all of them Spaniards. The other eight were local collaborators, one of whom habitually slept through testimony, waking only to cry for the death penalty. So plentiful were the victims that the tribunal frequently found it expedient to try them en bloc rather than individually.[258] Two of the Netherlands' highest-ranking noblemen, Counts Egmont and Hoorne, were publicly beheaded in Brussels without having been allowed to present evidence in their own defense.

Resolved to fight back, the Protestants rallied to the banner of the popular nobleman William the Silent, Count of Nassau and Prince of Orange. The son of a Lutheran, William had spent much of his youth at the imperial court as a ward of Charles V. There he received Catholic instruction and was groomed to be a supporter of Philip II in the Netherlands. At the abdication ceremony held for Charles in the Netherlands, the gouty emperor had leaned on the shoulder of William while delivering an address to those assembled. Serving briefly as a hostage to France for the fulfillment of the treaty of Câteau-Cambrésis, however, William learned that kings Philip and Henry were plotting the extermination of all heretics in France and the Netherlands. The French king revealed the secret while riding with William through the forest of Vincennes. He had assumed that William already knew. William by his silence and unchanged demeanor concealed that he did not, thereby by earning his famous moniker, "the Silent."[259] Alienated by the plot, he was determined thereafter to thwart it. For several years, he pursued his ends by moderate means, but Alva's appointment as governor-general convinced him that armed resistance was the only viable option.

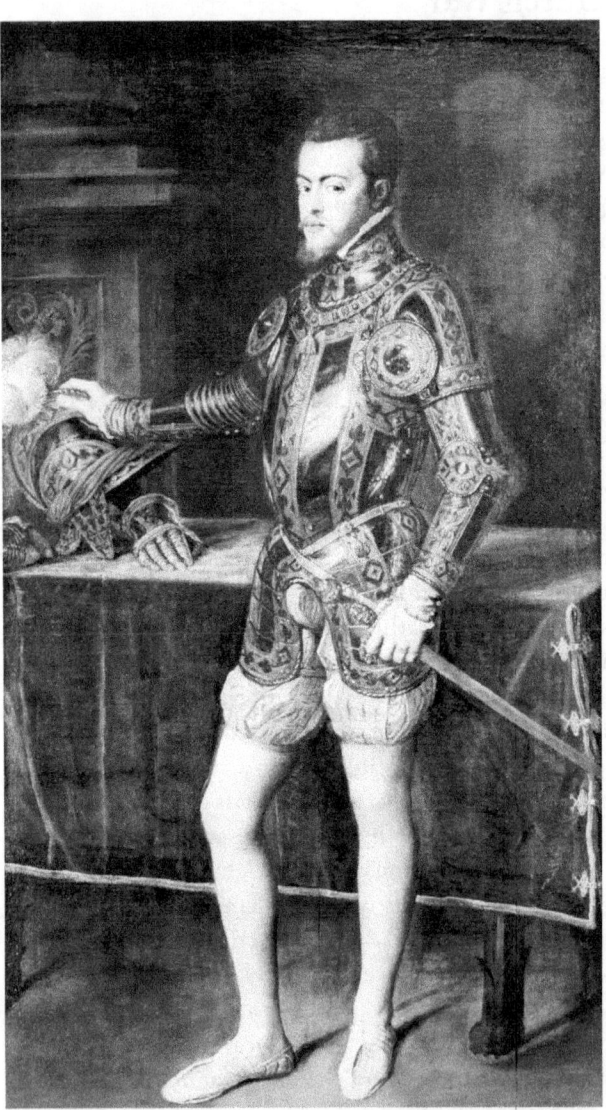

Philip II of Spain, portrait by Titian (1551) currently housed at the Prado Museum (Wikimedia Commons). (http://commons.wikimedia.org/wiki/File:Philip_II.jpg)

For his first military campaign (1568), he raised an army of 30,000 men—among them many German Protestants and French Huguenots. Alva, however, thwarted his designs by leading him on a wild goose chase across the length and breadth of Holland until William's supplies and money ran out without having fought a major battle. Nor would the cities open their gates to the prince, fearing Alva's vengeance should he be defeated. In the end, William was forced to disband his army, selling his worldly possessions to pay what he could to the troops and pledging himself as hostage for what was still owed.[260]

Having failed on land, William altered his strategy with a privateering campaign against Spanish shipping. The viability of this policy ultimately depended on securing a safe harbor for the privateering vessels (whose crews—comprised of Dutch refugees—were popularly celebrated as "Sea Beggars"). When this goal was unexpectedly achieved with the seizure of Brille (1572), it proved the spark of a national rebellion; for, by this time, Alva's rule had become too odious to bear no matter what the risk. In addition to his continuing persecutions, Alva had attempted to impose a new tax system whereby he intended to extract from the Netherlanders a revenue "stream fathoms deep" that would flow into the coffers of Spain.[261] A ruinous impost of 10% was placed on the sale of all goods—to be paid and repaid at every step from raw material to finished product. In city upon city, merchants and tradesman closed their shops rather than comply, bringing business to a standstill. In Brussels, where he was headquartered, Alva determined that he would hang 18 of the most prosperous merchants in front of their shops as an inducement to the resumption of commerce, but on the morning that this was intended, news of the capture of Brille monopolized the governor's attention.[262] Electrified by the event, city after city repudiated their unwilling allegiance to Alva and declared in favor of William the Silent. It would not be the prince's fate this time to roam the country with the gates closed to him. Hereafter, the rebellious cities of the Netherlands recognized him as their lawful governor or "stadtholder"—an office nominally beholden to King Philip, but which in tangible effect, gave William command of the provincial armies and assemblies.

William the Silent, leader of the Dutch revolt against Spain, 19th century engraving (© Deposit photos.com/Georgios Kollidas).

Alva quickly dispatched his son, Don Fadrique, to put down the revolution. The town of Zutphen was captured with excessive cruelty—the corpses of its garrison being hung upside down from the town ramparts.[263] The example convinced the populace of Naarden to submit without a fight. A feast was prepared for the conquering Spaniards, after which the citizenry was summoned to the town church, purportedly to hear the terms of reconciliation. Instead, 500 of them were cut down in cold blood. The town was then set ablaze, while "laughing [Spanish] soldiers, intoxicated not with wine but with blood" murdered everyone in sight. Says the historian Motley, "Some of the burghers were for a time spared that they might witness the violation of their wives and daughters, and were then butchered in company with these still more unfortunate victims."[264]

Haarlem sustained a siege of seven months. At one point, spirits were lifted by word of a Dutch relieving force, but it was annihilated en route—the head of one of its officers being cast into the city with the cruel message, "This is the head of Captain de Koning, who is on his way with reinforcements for the good city of Haarlem."[265] By July 1573, the city had reached the last extremity. The populace was beyond starvation and the only contact with the outside was by carrier pigeon. Word came from Prince William that relief was on its way. The Spanish, unfortunately, shot down another pigeon carrying the same message, and routed the relief army before it reached the walls. Bereft now of food and of hope, the defenders surrendered at discretion after assurances of "forgiveness." On entering the city, the Spanish besiegers (who had lost 12,000 dead in the contest out of an initial force of 30,000) demonstrated their notion of "forgiveness" by summarily executing 2,300 soldiers and civilians. The remaining citizens only preserved their lives by paying a crippling fine.[266]

Alva next invested Alkmaar, boasting that here too he would conduct a general massacre.[267] The city's garrison was tiny. Its anxious commander sent a note to William asking the stadtholder if he had yet secured the alliance of a foreign king to assist in the Dutch cause. William replied "that before I ever took up the cause of the oppressed Christians in these provinces, I had entered *into a close alliance with the King of kings*; and I am firmly convinced that all who put their trust in Him shall be saved by His almighty hand."[268] After a vicious cannonade on September 18, 1573, the veteran Spanish infantry attempted to storm Alkmaar only to be thrown back three times by the unseasoned militia who defended the town walls with cauldrons of boiling pitch, pistol shot and cannon fire.[269] Ordered to attack again, the Spanish soldiery refused saying the town was under Satan's protection. The siege was then halted in its tracks by the opening of the local dikes.[270]

Soon thereafter, Alva learned from captured documents that the Dutch intended to open more dikes and flood the entire countryside if he continued his advance—and before he could recover from this ill news, he learned that the Sea Beggars had destroyed his fleet off the coast of Enkhuizen at the outlet of the Zuyder Zee (Holland's North Sea bay). Despairing of further success, Alva proffered his resignation, advising Philip that the burning of cities might be the next logical strategy.[271] As he had incurred a great deal of personal debt during his tenure, he set a date for his creditors to meet him in Amsterdam for the settling of accounts. On assembling, they learned that he had eloped with his retinue the previous night.[272]

His successor, Don Luis de Requesens promptly invested Leiden (1574), but the Dutch proved good to their word. They opened the dikes, and the city held out defiantly until a fortuitous storm raised the encroaching waters sufficiently for a flotilla of light ships to bring relief. Despite plague and famine, the Spaniards had been held at bay for four months and now had to withdraw. The city's famous university was founded in celebration.[273]

The war had literally become a quagmire. More than this, Spain was now bankrupt. Unpaid, her troops ran riot in Antwerp—sacking the city in an episode known as "The

Spanish Fury" (1576). According to an eyewitness who managed twice to get himself trampled by fleeing crowds, the Spaniards "spared neither friend nor foe.... Within three days Antwerp, which was one of the richest towns in Europe, had now no money nor treasure to be found therein, but only in the hands of murderers or strumpets."[274] In 1578, the situation was eased by Philip's appointment of a new governor-general for the Netherlands—Allesandro Farnese, Duke of Parma, who, by arms and diplomacy, effected a reconciliation with the Netherlands' ten southernmost provinces on the basis of their Catholicism (1579–1583). But the seven northern provinces were Protestant and refused to yield, forming instead the "Union of Utrecht," whereby they became known as the "United Provinces" (1579). William made a final bid to reunite the whole Netherlands by forging the Treaty of Plessis Le Tours (1580), whereby the Catholic French duke, Francis of Anjou, was named "Prince of the Netherlands" (1580). In this way, William hoped to appease the southern Catholics and, with luck, obtain the backing of France against Spain.[275] But the distrust and intolerance between Catholic and Protestant had now surmounted the hatred between Spaniard and Netherlander. In 1581, the United Provinces renounced their allegiance to Spain and declared their independence. Thus was the Netherlands cleaved into two separate states: Protestant Holland and Catholic Belgium.

In the meantime, Spanish fortunes and finances had been restored by events in the Iberian Peninsula. In 1578, the heirless king of Portugal was killed in a madcap effort to seize Morocco. Two years later, under the prodding of a Spanish army commanded by Alva, the Portuguese handed their entire empire over to Philip II—colonies and all.[276] The unexpected windfall gave renewed impetus to the Dutch War. A price was placed on the head of Prince William, and in 1582, an assassin shot him below the right ear from point blank range—the ball emerging from his jaw on the left.[277] Miraculously, he survived, while the half-wit who shot him was beaten to death on the spot. In 1584, however, he was shot again—this time fatally—while tending to a group of petitioners after a dinner party. (In a cruel irony, the assassin, Balthasar Gérard, had finagled the money for his pistol out of William's own pocket by posing as a loyal, but needy, admirer.[278]) In the previous year the duke of Anjou had provoked an uprising in Antwerp by attempting a coup against William ("The French Fury," 1583). Anjou likewise died in 1584.

Without capable leadership or the hope of a French alliance, the Dutch cause seemed lost. In short order, Bruges and Ghent fell to the forces of Parma, and in 1585 Antwerp submitted as well, leaving the Spanish on the threshold of total victory.

But the war was now to assume an international flavor. Spanish military rule in the Netherlands was not just an imposition on the Dutch. It also threatened the interests of France, Germany and—most of all—England.[279] For this reason, England's Elizabeth I had secretly authorized piracy against Spanish shipping for more than ten years—her campaign reaching a crescendo in 1577, when the swashbuckling Sir Francis Drake circumnavigated the globe, attacking every Spanish vessel in sight. When he returned to England with a rich cargo of pirated gold and silver, Elizabeth knighted him. Four years later, in a provocative violation of Spain's New World claims, England established a colony at Roanoke, Virginia.

The Spanish were hardly amused. Several plots were hatched—apparently with Philip's connivance—to assassinate the English queen and place the still imprisoned Mary Stuart on her throne. One conspirator intended to approach Elizabeth's coach on horseback, level a pistol at her head and fire off a ball that had been consecrated in Rome.[280] Another conspirator, stretched on the rack, directly implicated Spain's ambassador to England, Bernadino de Mendoza. When Elizabeth, fittingly enough, handed the ambassador his diplomatic papers, Philip answered with an embargo against English goods, and the seizure of all English ships in Spanish harbors (1584).

Abandoning all pretense of friendly relations, Elizabeth now gave open sanction to raids on Spanish ports, and concluded the Treaty of Nonesuch (1585) with the Dutch, providing much needed reinforcement to the embattled rebels.[281] Although she stopped short of accepting the sovereignty of the United Provinces when it was offered to her, war with Spain was now a virtual certainty. A last attempt to dethrone Elizabeth—the so-called Babington Plot (1587)—directly implicated Mary Stuart at the cost of her head. She went to her death in a black cloak, which she removed at the last moment to reveal a crimson dress, the color of blood. The three hundred in attendance gasped and fell silent. A few moments after the axe struck, the fallen queen's pet dog emerged from her clothing where it had taken refuge and lay down between her head and torso.[282] With the failure of the Babington plot, Philip decided to force a decisive encounter.

1588

Legend would have us believe that the Spanish Armada was "invincible," but such was not the case. Before it even set sail, it had suffered a series of blows. In April 1587, Drake "singed the King of Spain's beard" with another of his famous raids—this time at Cadiz, where he destroyed some three dozen vessels being outfitted for the Armada. The disaster at least taught the Spanish that the galleys used at Lepanto were entirely unsuited to ocean warfare. They were blown out of the water by Drake's guns.[283] But the lesson was a bitter one, since the financially strapped Philip was hard-pressed to recoup his losses. Next, on the eve of the Armada's departure, came the premature death of its able commander, the Marquis of Santa Cruz, and his replacement by the hesitating and inexperienced Duke of Medina Sidonia. Finally, a lack of wind followed by a violent gale delayed the departure of the fleet for weeks, so that by the time it set sail most of its on-board victuals had spoiled—only a fraction being replaced from the local ports.[284]

While it is true that Spain's ships were larger than England's, they were slower and less maneuverable, and they carried guns of significantly lower range. In all, one hundred and thirty vessels set sail in May 1588 with a general notion of braving the Channel to reach the Netherlands where they would link with reinforcements from the duke of Parma's Army of Flanders. The combined force would then re-cross the Channel and make for the Thames estuary and London. On paper, it was a menacing plan, but there were some notable defects. First of all, since the Armada had put to sea with absolutely no secrecy, the English knew they were coming and were making ready for them. Even worse, neither Medina Sidonia, commanding the Armada, nor the duke of Parma, stationed with the army in Flanders, had any notion as to how the pivotal union between their forces was to be achieved.[285] The shallow Netherlands ports could not accommodate the large Spanish ships. Nor could Parma hope to put to sea in his cumbersome transport vessels, since these would be sitting ducks for Justin of Nassau, commanding the new Dutch navy, who awaited them off the coast.[286] When these facts were brought to King Philip's attention, he replied that the expedition was in God's hands, and that the commander of the fleet would do well to get on with his work.[287]

Reaching the entrance to the Channel, near Plymouth, on July 30, the Spanish fleet arrayed itself in a crescent with the fighting ships on the periphery and supply ships protected in the center.[288] When they were first sighted, the British fleet commanders were having a game of bowls at Plymouth Hoe, and Drake insisted that they finish it before dispersing to their ships. The rival forces clashed four times—July 31, August 2, 3 and 4 (New Calendar)—and each time they adhered to the same script. The English vessels kept their distance, relying on the superior range of their guns to chastise the Spanish, whose return fire consistently splashed harmlessly into the sea well short of its mark. The Spaniards were bewildered by the new English tactic of sailing like ducks in a row, firing broadsides as they went. Yet the damage sustained was quite modest, and on August 6, the Armada put in safely at Calais—a haven flawed only in that it was in France, while Parma's reinforcing army and supplies, as we have already noted, were in the inaccessible Netherlands.

Medina Sidonia was given little time to ponder this dilemma. On the night of August 8th, the English floated fire ships into Calais harbor scattering his fleet in all directions. At daybreak, as the decisive battle began at Gravelines, only a portion of the Armada had returned to the battle line. Since fire from a distance had not inflicted the damage necessary to bring outright victory, the English were finally willing to come to close quarters. But the Spaniards were unable to exploit this long-awaited opportunity. Historians have variously argued that they had expended the bulk of their ammunition during the encounters of the previous week,[289] or that their fire passed harmlessly over the English ships whose decks were built much lower to the water.[290] But exploration of sunken and shipwrecked Armada vessels have conclusively shown that a large proportion of their cannonballs went unused—a finding which has prompted Martin and Parker, coauthors of a modern work on the expedition, to conclude that the Spanish were simply overwhelmed by the new English tactic of sailing in line with sustained broadside fire. The Spaniards had counted on discharging their guns once as a prelude to grappling and boarding, and were not trained in the art of rapid reloading for prolonged artillery duels.[291] Another theory—gleaned from the Armada's provisions list—is that the Spaniards had only brought enough powder to fire off a quarter of their projectiles.[292] But this may be a moot point, since most of the Spanish shot was so poorly cast that it probably shattered on impact without inflicting much damage.[293]

As the decisive battle raged, England's deft Lord Admiral, Charles Howard, and his Vice Admiral, Sir Frances Drake, kept enough distance to avoid the Armada's grappling hooks while steering close enough to fire devastating broadsides into the Spanish hulls at point blank range. Without losing a single vessel, the English sunk one Spanish ship, drove four others aground, and crippled many more. The Armada labored to recover her crescent formation, brought it together, and saw it dissolve again amidst the English onslaught.[294] Spanish casualties were in the thousands, and there are reports of blood pouring off the decks.[295] Thoroughly outclassed, the Spaniards took advantage of a sudden squall to make their escape into the North Sea.

The battle was over, but for the Armada the nightmare had just begun. A return passage through the heavily guarded English Channel was out of the question. The only option was to press forward around the northern coasts of Scotland and Ireland before setting course for Spain—an onerous detour, indeed, for a fleet whose supplies of food and water were near exhaustion. But the journey was far more horrible in practice than it was in theory, for the Spaniards encountered a hostile "Protestant Wind" while attempting to get west of Ireland. Seventeen vessels were swept against the rocky shore and smashed to pieces. Three of them had sought shelter in Donegal Bay near Sligo only to be torn from their anchorage and battered against the coast.[296] Some 1,100 corpses eventually washed onto the beach, and those who got there alive were scarcely more fortunate, for the Irish inhabitants robbed and butchered them almost to a man. Elsewhere, starving crews came ashore as beggars. Some were murdered on the spot,[297] but the Irish, being Catholic, were not uniformly hostile, and much of the actual killing was done later by the island's English overlords, whose search parties either slaughtered their quarry in the fields or brought them in to be interrogated and hanged.[298]

Roughly half of the fleet eventually hobbled back to Spain bearing sick, starving, and wounded crewmen, the majority of whom died during the ensuing months. When news of the disaster reached the Escorial, Philip stoically remarked that he could raise a new armada whenever he pleased. But the myth of Spain's invincibility was at an end. Moreover, Elizabeth I had further torments in store.

The Edict of Nantes and the End of the French Religious Wars

Throughout the 1570s and 1580s the Protestants and Catholics of France had continued their intermittent civil war, graced by such truces as the "Peace of Monsieur" (1576), and by such new outbreaks as "The Lovers' War" (1580). The crisis point was reached in 1585, by which time it had become apparent that the French king, Henry III, would not produce an heir. As he had no surviving brothers, his brother-in-law, Henry of Navarre, became heir to the throne. This latter Henry was the same man who had married Princess Margot just prior to the St. Bartholomew's Day Massacre (1572), which is to remind the reader that he was a Protestant. Lest the throne pass to a heretic, the Catholics threw their support behind yet a third Henry—the ultra–Catholic Duke of Guise, who also had the enthusiastic support of Philip II of Spain.

France now embroiled herself in a hot contest known as "the War of the Three Henrys" (1585–1589). Three years into this fracas, on the so-called "Day of the Barricades" (May 1588), a Catholic mob erected barricades against the troops of King Henry III, and handed the city over to his rival, Henry, Duke of Guise. Taking refuge outside Paris, King Henry repaid this usurpation by summoning Guise to his new apartments, and having him stabbed to death outside the door.[299] This reduced the number of Henrys to two, but it did not preserve the king's throne. Eight months later, while attempting to retake Paris, Henry III was assassinated by a fanatical Dominican friar (August 1589).

There was now but one Henry left—namely, the rightful heir, Henry of Navarre, who promptly claimed the throne as Henry IV. With clever use of his cavalry and musketeers, the new king won unlikely victories at Arques and Ivry against armies twice the size of his own. But his effort to take Paris was thwarted by Philip II, who sought to unseat the pretender and hand France back to the Catholics. Predictably, Elizabeth I of England dispatched five thousand troops to help sustain the opposite cause. The struggle continued for years, with King Henry's Protestants and their English allies being barred from Paris by the capital's Catholics and their Spanish allies. Although the Parisians suffered grisly privations—at one point they had to pulverize human bones as a substitute for flour[300]—they showed no signs of capitulating. Indeed, the battle might still be going on today had it not occurred to Henry IV to convert to Catholicism. Declaring that, "Paris is well worth a Mass," he won the favor of the majority of the nation's Catholics (1593), and was officially anointed king at Chartes the following year.

Aided by Spain, a few Catholic extremists and self-seeking nobles held out against Henry until 1598. Having defeated them all and made peace with Spain, he propagated the famous Edict of Nantes (1598) giving legal protection to the Huguenots. No retribution was allowed to either side, although Henry was not above taking a subtle personal revenge on occasion, as when he feigned friendship for Henry of Guise's brother, the duke of Mayenne, inviting the obese opposition leader to join him for very long walks on very hot days, just to watch him huff and puff.[301] As a matter of policy, however, bloodshed gave way to toleration, and the likeable Henry went on to become one of the most revered kings in French history. He reigned until 1610, when a fanatical Catholic leaped into his carriage and murdered him amidst rumors that he was planning to unite the Protestants of Europe for a war against the Hapsburgs. According to Henry's able finance minister, the duke of Sully, who had placed the state on a stable economic footing in anticipation of such a venture, Henry ultimately intended to establish a cooperative European confederation on the ruins of the Hapsburg Empire[302]—a rather utopian notion for the time, but perhaps not impossible for the man who had finally brought peace to France.

King Henry IV of France, whose accession brought an end to the French religious wars of the 16th century, 1859 engraving by T. Kuhner (© Deposit photos.com/Georgios Kollidas).

While none of the three Henrys escaped assassination, Philip II and Elizabeth I survived to torment one another for the rest of their natural lives. At sea, the English resumed their raids, and, in 1597, Philip launched a massive new armada against them, replete with a reasonably well-conceived plan of operations. Alas, the enterprise was thwarted by weather before battle could be joined, and the Spanish king died the following year. His campaign to stamp out heresy had thrice bankrupted the Spanish nation, and had purchased nothing but the undying enmity of England, France and his own Dutch subjects.

Though the sun still did not set on the Spanish empire when Philip was entombed in the Escorial, there was an eclipse from time to time. The loss of the Great Armada had dealt a fatal blow to Spanish prestige, while irrevocably shattering her naval supremacy. Worse still, the king's royal successors were not of his caliber. His son, Philip III (1598–1621), reigned but did not rule—leaving the details to the duke of Lerma, who enriched himself from the failing Spanish treasury while the nation meandered from one catastrophe to the next. In the Netherlands, the war dragged on at massive expense. At Nieuwpoort (1600), Maurice of Nassau (son of William the Silent) and his cousin, William Louis, employed new tactics to obtain a major victory—Holland's first over the supposedly "invincible" Spanish infantry. For the first time, Dutch musketeers had fired their volleys in alternating ranks, thus sustaining a consistent barrage against the advancing *tercios*. (William Louis had improvised the tactic after reading a description of ancient slingers in Aelian's classical military text, *Tactics*.[303])

Bankrupt again, Spain made peace—first with England (1604) and then with the United Provinces (1609). Yet there was no economic recovery, since Lerma used the respite to deport Spain's Moriscos (i.e., Christianized Moors)—contriving to make them the scapegoats for his own failed economic policies. In expelling them, Spain lost the most consistently productive segment of her society. They were deposited without ceremony on the Barbary Coast of North Africa, where the locals made them suffer piteously for their abjuration of Islam.

Dutch musketeer, illustration by Jacob de Gheyn (II), circa 1565–1629 (Wikimedia Commons). (http://commons.wikimedia.org/wiki/File:Jacob_de_Gheyn_-_Wapenhandelinge_4.jpg)

The Thirty Years' War

At the dawn of the 17th century, it appeared that the Peace of Augsburg might spare Germany further religious calamity. The liberal Holy Roman Emperor, Maximilian II (ruled 1564–76), openly tolerated Lutheranism, while the "*cuius regio, eius religio*" provided reasonably well for Catholics and Lutherans alike. True, a prince might convert or be succeeded by a member of the opposite religion, but for those who didn't wish to be uprooted each time this happened, there was always the option of moving to one of the empire's sixty "Free Cities" where, in the absence of a ruling prince, both religions were tolerated simultaneously.

Sadly, the apparent calm was a mirage. Far from resolving the religious controversy, the Augsburg Peace had only swept it under the rug.[304] Chief amongst its defects was its failure to sanction Calvinism, the fastest growing Protestant sect in Europe. Additionally, there was the so-called *Ecclesiastical Reservation*, requiring the return of all church properties seized by the Protestants after 1552, and forbidding prelates from carrying their church lands with them into the Protestant fold if they themselves converted. These provocative clauses had been inserted into the Peace of Augsburg despite Lutheran protests, and without the consent of the imperial diet. The result was simmering discontent, which, owing to events at Donauwörth in 1607, increased to a boil.

Donauwörth was one of the imperial "Free Cities," and as such, should have tolerated both Lutheranism and Catholicism. But when the city's Catholics sought to flaunt their freedom with an ostentatious religious procession, the Protestants chased them into a monastery.[305] In response, the reigning emperor, Rudolf II (ruled, 1576–1612), an arch-Catholic, ordered his loyal supporter, Duke Maximilian of Bavaria, to intervene. Maximilian's troops promptly occupied Donauwörth, whereat the duke himself announced that the city was now his personal possession, which meant that it now had a ruling prince and was subject to the "*cuius regio, eius religio*." The city's Protestants were duly informed that they had either to convert or emigrate.[306]

To the empire's Protestant princes, the episode seemed a very disagreeable precedent, and to guard against further encroachments, they organized themselves into a Protestant Union under the leadership of Frederick IV, the imperial elector from the Palatinate. Not to be outdone, the Catholic princes formed a Catholic League under Bavaria's Duke Maximilian (1609). Tensions eased briefly when Emperor Rudolf died and was succeeded by his more conciliatory brother, Matthias (1612). But Matthias, being elderly and without heir, felt constrained to name a successor, and to the chagrin of the Protestants, he chose his cousin, Ferdinand, Archduke of Styria, an ardent Catholic who openly promised to rid the realm of "heresy."

Ferdinand's nomination had to be ratified by the seven imperial electors, three of whom were Protestant princes who might be counted upon to vote no. Unfortunately for them, of the four remaining electors, three were Catholic archbishops who were certain to support Ferdinand's candidacy, and the fourth—the king of Bohemia—was none other than Ferdinand himself.[307] The election, in other words, was a done deal. Indeed, Ferdinand saw no reason to wait for Emperor Matthias' death before enacting an anti–Protestant program. In 1618, he dispatched five imperial deputy-governors to Bohemia with a mandate to curb Protestant freedoms. Twice, the Bohemian Protestants tried to convene assemblies in protest, but they were dispersed both times, and their leaders were arrested.

Bohemia, however, was a land still proud with the heritage of Jan Hus. During the 13th and 14th centuries, her ruling princes had been powerful enough to challenge the Hapsburgs for the imperial throne, and despite her subsequent incorporation into the Hapsburg domains in 1526, she had lost little of her independent spirit. On May 23, 1618, a Protestant throng led by Count Heinrich von Thurn barged into Prague's Hradschin Castle, seizing two imperial deputy-governors, Jaroslav Borzita von Martinitz and Wilhelm Slawata, and their secretary, Fabricius. The deputies were hurled forthwith from a window fifty feet above ground. The secretary offered spirited reasons why he ought not to be thrown, but the Protestants informed him that the time for discussion had passed, and commended him to the Earth's gravitational field as well. Miraculously, all three escaped harm owing (at least in Protestant legend) to the cushioning of their fall by a large dung heap beneath the window. The secretary is said to have sought pardon from the deputies for having landed on top of them, when his proper station was beneath them.[308]

These proceedings, known to history as the "Defenestration of Prague," inaugurated the Thirty Years' War—the last and most devastating of Europe's religious wars, encompassing the destruction of 30,000 German towns and villages,[309] and the death of one-third of the empire's population (which declined from an estimated twenty-one millions to less than fourteen).[310]

The Bohemian Phase (1618–1623)

Having deposited the imperial deputy-governors in the dung heap beneath the window of Hradschin Castle, the Bohemian rebels declared Emperor-Elect Ferdinand deposed, and conferred the Bohemian crown on their own candidate, Frederick V of the Palatinate. Although he was head of the Protestant Union, Frederick's fellow Unionists considered his enthronement illegal, and would not subscribe to his cause. Nor would the aloof elector of Saxony (who had been bought off by imperial assurances for the rights of his own Lutheran subjects). In contrast, the Catholic League rallied unanimously to the imperial banner—not the least because of a promise that, once Frederick was defeated, his Palatine electorship would be awarded to the league's ruling prince, Maximilian of Bavaria. Consequently, Frederick's disorganized Bohemians were without allies when they clashed with the combined Catholic armies of Count Tilly (Johan Tserclaes) and Duke Maximilian at the Battle of the White Mountain (1620). Unaware that the battle had even begun, Frederick was riding in his carriage to a midday banquet when he encountered his troops in panicked flight.[311] By scampering after them, he earned the contempt of the Catholics who dubbed him the "Winter King" to mock his fleeting reign.

Unfortunately, Frederick had nowhere to run. While he was in Bohemia, his old home, the Palatinate, had been seized by Spain as a link in the so-called "Spanish Road" (i.e., the crucial supply route between Lombardy and the Netherlands, which Spain required for a renewal of its war with the Dutch after a twelve years' truce). The only ray of hope for the defeated Protestants was evolving friction in the victorious imperialist camp over the emperor's award of the Palatinate to Maxmilian of Bavaria—a pledge that not only upset the Spanish, who needed the territory for their "Spanish Road," but also the other imperial electors, who did not feel that their offices should be redistributed at the emperor's whim.[312]

While this was being sorted out, Emperor Ferdinand reestablished himself on the Bohemian throne, and outlawed Protestantism throughout the kingdom. Twenty-seven vanquished rebels were sent to the executioner to be hanged or beheaded, while tens of thousands more were deported for refusing conversion to Catholicism.[313] Protestant properties were confiscated and sold at bargain rates to the emperor's Catholic supporters—the biggest buyer being the ambitious Czech nobleman, Count Albrecht von Wallenstein, who now emerges as an important figure in our story.

The Danish Phase (1624–1629)

The war ought to have ended at this juncture, but the resounding Catholic victory at the White Mountain had made all Protestant Europe uneasy. So much so, in fact, that Denmark's Lutheran king, Christian IV, now entered the mêlée on the Protestant side (1624). There were, at this time, two other Protestant armies in the field—one led by the irrepressible mercenary captain, Ernst von Mansfeld, the "Atilla of Christendom,"[314] who had gathered in the fugitives from the White Mountain and molded them into a first-rate force of plunderers, and the other by the Transylvanian prince, Bethlen Gabor, "a semi-barbarous ... chieftain, who hoped, with Turkish support, to make himself master of all Hungary, if not of Austria as well."[315] Hoping to counter this little coalition without indebting himself further to Maximilian of Bavaria (who had finally received the coveted Palatinate in 1623), Emperor Ferdinand turned to Albrecht von Wallenstein.[316]

While the emperor held the crown of Bohemia, Wallenstein may rightfully be said to have been its landlord. He had profited so much from his purchase of confiscated Protestant lands, that he was now able to hire and outfit his own private army, which he maintained, after Mansfeld's example, by plundering the innocent (albeit by less brutish means, consisting mainly of semi-legal, orderly "requisitions").[317] Protestant by birth, Wallenstein had converted to Catholicism, but he was no religious zealot. Protestant recruits were welcome in his army, provided only that their spiritual needs did not impair their sense of military duty. In April 1626, Wallenstein put his army in motion, crossing the Elbe at Dessau Bridge, covering the structure with ship sails to cloak his movements.[318] Mansfeld engaged him on the far bank, but was sharply defeated and withdrew in the direction of Bohemia hoping to rendezvous with Gabor. Wallenstein pursued him, leaving behind a rearguard under Count Tilly. Perceiving his chance to strike a blow, Christian IV led forth his Danes against Tilly. Before he could force an encounter, however, Wallenstein perceived the threat and reinforced Tilly's position. With the odds having shifted against him, Christian attempted an about-face, but Tilly caught him at Lutter, and put his army to rout (August 1626)—the Danish king only narrowly escaping the field with his life after his horse was killed under him.[319]

Albrecht von Wallenstein (Waldstein), generalissimo of the imperial armies (© Deposit photos.com/Oprea Nicolae).

The Protestant coalition now came apart—Gabor making a separate peace, while Mansfeld, ill with tuberculosis, fled to Bosnia, where he perished. (It is reported that in his last days he defiantly stood next to his sickbed in full armor daring Death to take him—a challenge from which Death did not shrink.)[320] Believing that his armies had now dealt the deathblow to the Protestant cause, Emperor Ferdinand issued the so-called "Edict of Restitution" (1629), declaring his intent to enforce the hated Ecclesiastical Reservation clauses of the Peace of Augsburg. "Never," says the historian Wakeman, "was [a] greater mistake made. To resume lands in the name of the law, which had been from fifty to eighty years in the undisputed possession of Protestant holders was in itself a straining of the letter of the law in violation of its spirit.... In itself it armed the public opinion of all Germany against the Emperor."[321] Hitherto, many German Protestants had held aloof from the fight, seeing the emperor as the symbol of order in the midst of an unnecessary revolution. Now they could not but see him as a reactionary despot.[322]

Wallenstein thought it precisely the wrong policy. He had in the meantime harried Christian's remaining Danes out of Germany and had begun occupying the old Hanseatic trading ports on the Baltic coastline in a bid to fashion the empire into a Baltic power. Towards this end, plans were laid to join Spain in subjugating the Netherlands whose lucrative Baltic trade routes might then be usurped.[323] Alone among the emperor's advisors, Wallenstein perceived that the overriding purpose of the war ought to be an imperial victory rather than a Catholic one—a victory that would make the rebellious Protestants subservient to their emperor rather than to a religious doctrine. It would be naïve, however, to assume that Wallenstein was motivated by selfless devotion to the emperor. More likely, as the military historian, J. F. C. Fuller has surmised, he intended to have Ferdinand play the role of "Merovingian king," while he himself became "mayor of the palace."[324]

Whatever Wallenstein's motivations, his entire program received a serious check at the Baltic port of Stralsund, which successfully resisted an imperialist siege with help from the Danish and Swedish navies. In the aftermath of this setback, Wallenstein defeated the Danes at Wolgast, and offered them such liberal peace terms that they abandoned their war effort and signed the Peace of Lübeck (1629). His leniency was born of necessity, for he now believed it was imperative to secure the Baltic coast—not just to enhance the power of the emperor, but also to guard against enemy landings; for Sweden had Baltic ambitions of its own, and after Stralsund, it seemed increasingly likely that that nation would enter the war on the Protestant side.[325]

Nor was this Wallenstein's only problem. The empire's myriad princelings secretly feared a policy that would enhance the power of the emperor and his military commander at their own expense. At the Diet of Regensburg (1630), the electors complained that Wallenstein was flaunting his power, and that the burdensome expropriations made to keep his army in being were devastating the countryside. Lest there be any confusion about what they were driving at, they announced their refusal to elect Ferdinand's son as "King of the Romans" (i.e., putative heir to the imperial throne) until Wallenstein had been sacked. Unwilling to jeopardize his son's succession, Ferdinand dismissed Wallenstein from the imperial service, and agreed to subject the Edict of Restitution to princely review.[326] Wallenstein tactfully withdrew knowing that if Sweden were to enter the war, the emperor would have no alternative but to restore him to his post.

The Swedish Phase (1629–1635)

Gustavus Adolphus, the yellow-bearded "Lion of the North," had ruled Sweden since 1611 and had already acquired the Baltic states of Finland and Estonia in wars against the Russians and Poles. More than a king and general, he was an innovator in strategy and tactics, and was among the first to employ a telescope to survey the field of battle (a necessity, actually, since he was woefully nearsighted).[327] The acquisition of Finland and Estonia had given Gustavus control of most of the Baltic coastline. Were he to capture the German shoreline as well, the Baltic Sea would become a "Swedish lake." On the other hand, if these lands fell to Wallenstein and the emperor, Sweden would come face-to-face with a hostile titan. Clearly, Gustavus had abundant motivation to enter the war. What he lacked was money—a problem that was to be solved by a most unlikely benefactor.

By the mid–1620s, the pre-eminent political voice in France was that of Cardinal Armand Jean du Plessis, Duc de Richelieu. As chief councilor to the French king, Louis XIII (reigned 1610–1643), Cardinal Richelieu was initially preoccupied with domestic affairs. In his opinion, the Edict of Nantes, passed by Henry IV in 1598, had gone too far. Not only did it grant religious toleration to French Huguenots, but it allowed them to fortify their towns, thus placing them in a position to defy the king. Accordingly, the cardinal took steps to disarm them in a campaign so deficient in subtlety that it provoked a rebellion (1624). Richelieu suppressed the uprising mercilessly. By 1628, the Huguenots were besieged even in their chief stronghold—the Atlantic port of La Rochelle. For fourteen months, the city resisted defiantly, until the construction of a royalist jetty blocked access to her harbor and starved her populace into submission. (Ironically, a week after the heroic defense ended, a storm leveled the jetty and reopened the harbor.[328]) There followed the Decree of Alais, whereby the political power of the Huguenots was erased, leaving them only their religious privileges.

Even while he subdued the Huguenots, Richelieu made inroads against the other threat to royal authority: i.e., the entrenched power of the nobility. Symbolic of this campaign was the outlawing of the duel, which hitherto had allowed rival nobles to square accounts by "chivalrous" murder without being subject to prosecution. A popular young aristocrat promptly decided to put the new decree to the test by fighting a duel beneath Richelieu's window, for which Richelieu promptly had him beheaded.[329] Another statute mandated the destruction of fortresses located in the interior of France, lest they become foci of resistance to the crown. Finally, Richelieu dispatched a body of inspectors, known as "*intendants*," to the far corners of the realm to ensure the enforcement of royal edicts.

But the destruction of Huguenot opposition and the consolidation of the king's domestic authority comprised only part of Richelieu's program, for he was also intent on elevating the status of France in the international arena.[330] Far from improving French prospects, however, the sweeping victories of Ferdinand II and the resumption of the Spanish onslaught in the Netherlands had raised the specter of a renewed Hapsburg policy of encirclement. Richelieu worked tirelessly to forestall this outcome. In Italy, he conspired with Savoy and Venice to seize the Valtelline Pass—a vital link allowing overland military cooperation between the Spanish and Austrian Hapsburgs (1626). Failing in this, he sought other means to promote his anti–Hapsburg policy. From 1627 to 1631, he tied down imperial forces in Italy in a contested succession over Mantua. In the latter year, however, he discerned a far superior opportunity to disrupt Hapsburg designs in the impending entry of Sweden into the Thirty Years' War. As financing alone stood in the way of this boon, the Catholic cardinal agreed to bankroll Sweden's entry into the war on the Protestant side.

Even before his fiscal dilemma had been solved, Gustavus Adolphus had been forced by events to act. Harboring no illusions as to the magnitude of the task before him or the potential danger to his person, he bade farewell to the Swedish Estates in a moving address.

Left: King Gustavus Adolphus of Sweden, military innovator. Painting attributed to Jacob Hoefnagel (1575–1630), a Flemish painter (Google Art Project via Wikimedia Commons). (http://commons.wikimedia.org/wiki/File:Attributed_to_Jacob_Hoefnagel_-_Gustavus_Adolphus,_King_of_Sweden_1611-1632_-_Google_Art_Project.jpg) *Right:* Jean du Plessis, Duc de Richelieu, cardinal and chief councilor of the French king (© Depositphotos.com/Georgios Kollidas).

"Though, for the Swedish kingdom, I have already gone through many dangers ... without bodily harm," he told the assembly, holding his four-year-old daughter, Christina, in his arms, "yet the time will come when all is over for me and I must say farewell to life. Therefore I have desired before my departure to see you all ... that we may together commend ourselves and each other ... to our all-gracious God."[331] He arrived in Germany with a small army in May 1630, nearly a year before France committed itself to subsidize him. Distrusting his territorial aims, the Protestant principalities gave him a tepid reception. But their countenance changed after Magdeburg (1631). Having defied the Edict of Restitution, this strategically located town on the Elbe had come under siege by Count Tilly's army.[332] Its capture threatened to expose all northern Germany to Hapsburg domination.[333] For two days after the siege-works were complete, the city's defenders cast irreverent taunts at the imperialists while keeping them at bay with chain shot. On the third day, however, Tilly's forces breached the walls, and subjected the city to fire and sword. Defenders and civilians alike were beaten, raped, murdered or cast alive into the flames. Says one chronicler:

> "When a marauding party entered a house, if its master had anything to give he might thereby purchase respite and protection for himself and his family till the next man, who also wanted something, should come along. It was only when everything had been brought forth and there was nothing left to give that the real trouble commenced.... [T]housands of innocent men,

women, and children, in the midst of a horrible din of heartrending shrieks and cries, were tortured and put to death in so cruel and shameful a manner that no words would suffice to describe, nor tears to bewail it."[334]

Some 20,000 inhabitants perished by murder, fire or drowning. Another 5000 survived—most of them women who were taken as war brides unless their freedom could be purchased.[335] The Protestants never forgot this slaughter. In subsequent battles, should the imperial troops request quarter, they were invariably answered with the roar of muskets and the cry, "Magdeburg quarter!"[336] Even Wallenstein was shocked by the barbarity. When a messenger brought him the news, he cast a piece of furniture at him, crying: "It is a lie!"[337]

Enraged by the Magdeburg atrocity, Saxony and Brandenburg, the key states of north Germany, ceased wavering and rallied to the Swedish banner.[338] Thus reinforced, Gustavus confronted the emperor's forces at Breitenfeld (1631). The battle's opening moves went entirely in the imperialists' favor. Attacking on both flanks simultaneously, the imperialist commander, Count Tilly, drove Gustavus' Saxon allies from the field and moved to envelop the center of his line. Yet Tilly lost and Gustavus won, and to understand why, we must briefly discuss the tactical innovations adopted by the Swedish king in the preceding years.

To begin with, he deployed his cavalry in smaller units than was typical for the period, thus giving it an advantage in maneuverability over its imperial counterpart. Moreover, since the Swedish horsemen employed the saber in addition to the single-shot pistol used by their opponents, they could continue their attack after discharging their handguns, which the imperialists could not.[339] As regards his infantry, Gustavus boasted a like superiority.

The Sack of Magdeburg, 1631, by Johann Philipp Abelin, c. 1634 (Wikimedia Commons). (http://commons.wikimedia.org/wiki/File:Sack_of_Magdeburg_1631.jpg)

He had refined the technique of volley-fire pioneered by Maurice and William Louis of Nassau at the battle of Nieuwpoort (1600)—arraying his musketeers three-deep, with the front rank firing while the rear ones reloaded. More than this, he interspersed his musketeers with his pikemen in a brilliantly conceived "inverted-T" formation, such that the pikemen could either stand firm as a bulwark of defense, or advance to lead the attack, supported in either circumstance by musket fire that struck the incredulous enemy from multiple directions simultaneously.[340] Finally, the Swedish lion limited his artillery to a few standardized calibers so that each gun of a given class could utilize the same ammunition.[341] Particularly effective at Breitenfeld was a maneuverable light gun that could be repositioned by three artillerists or by one horse.[342]

Thus, as Tilly's men bore down on Gustavus' exposed flank, the ever-maneuverable Swedes were able to wheel about and pummel them with musket and artillery fire. As the imperialists began to waver, Gustavus' lieutenant, Johan Baner, led a counterattack that drove a wedge between Tilly's center and left. Gustavus then sealed the victory by leading his reserves into the breach.[343]

The Protestants had won a major battle for the first time in the war, and it appeared as though their victory might be decisive. The road to Vienna lay open, and though the Swedes chose instead to invade Bavaria (the Catholic heartland), a panicked Ferdinand begged Wallenstein to return to the colors and raise a new army. The invitation was extended none too soon, for Tilly suffered a new disaster on the banks of the river Lech, incurring mortal wounds in a failed attempt to prevent the Swedes from crossing the Bavarian border. (Gustavus sent his "court barber ... a good and famous surgeon" into the enemy camp to offer his services, but Tilly's life could not be saved.[344])

Gustavus continued as far as Munich, and for a time was master of southern Germany. But Wallenstein soon rendered his position untenable by threatening his lines of communication.[345] Nor were the locals willing to provide succor. A chilling report was forwarded to Gustavus from Swabia, where an ill-mannered body of peasants ambushed some Swedish stragglers, "cutting off their noses and ears, hands and feet, [and] pulling out their eyes...."[346] Little wonder that Gustavus abandoned the south in search of more congenial ground. At Zirndorf, outside Nuremburg, he tried to push Wallenstein out of his path, but Wallenstein had dug himself in, and the Swedes suffered five casualties for every one they inflicted.[347] The armies drew off, but by forced marches, Gustavus caught up with the imperialists again at Lützen (November 16, 1632), where a surprised Wallenstein had already divided his forces with thoughts of encamping for the winter.[348] As Gustavus' army approached, Wallenstein implored his lieutenant, Count Gottfried Heinrich zu Pappenheim, to muster every available unit and march to his support. Gustavus, meanwhile, sought to envelop Wallenstein's undermanned left flank. Fog delayed his attack, but when the sun finally broke through, Gustavus very nearly drove the imperialist left from the field. He was thwarted by Pappenheim's reinforcements.

Though those who commanded him frequently cursed his impetuosity, Pappenheim was the idol of his men. According to C. V. Wedgwood, the soldiery recounted his legendary feats of courage around their evening campfires.[349] His arrival stabilized the collapsing flank. Unfortunately, he was shot in the chest at the first charge. Twice before—at White Mountain and Breitenfield—he had been wounded badly enough to be thought dead.[350] But this time there was to be no miraculous resurrection. He was taken, gasping, to his coach, where he soon expired,[351] but not before expressing satisfaction over news from another part of the field: The Swedish king was dead.[352]

Gustavus had been wounded in his bridle arm while leading the charge against the imperial left. With Pappenheim's demise, that flank had again begun to waver, but word now reached the Swedish king that Wallenstein had launched a counterattack against the Swedish center, and that the Swedes had given ground. Hoping to steel the courage of his men, Gustavus rode off in the direction of the threatened quarter.[353] But the fog was now so dense that the nearsighted commander strayed into the midst of the enemy. Struck in the back by a pistol shot, he had time to say to a comrade, "Brother, I have enough. Look to your own life," before toppling to the ground.[354] Catholic soldiers surrounded him with swords drawn, demanding that he identify himself. He replied: "I am the King of Sweden, who do seal the Religion and Liberty of the German nation with my blood."[355] He spoke no more but was stabbed to death on the spot. A loyal page who had dismounted to be with him[356] survived the battle long enough to dictate an account of the king's final moments before succumbing to his own wounds.[357]

The truth of Gustavus' fate was revealed to the Swedes by the sight of his horse galloping out of the fog, wounded, bloodied and without a rider.[358] Furious, they ran amok—driving the Catholics from the field and taking solace in the recovery of their beloved champion's mangled corpse.

The Demise of Wallenstein

For the Swedes, Lützen was a victory narrowly won and not worth winning, for it cost them their hero king. Nor did Wallenstein benefit. After the battle his intentions became suspect. The imperial court demanded a new offensive, but Wallenstein put out peace-feelers instead—using Count Thurn (the notorious instigator of the Defenestration of Prague) as an intermediary. In Wallenstein's view, the death of the popular Gustavus might be the empire's last chance to rid itself of foreign armies. Denmark and Sweden had already intervened, and France could not be far behind. The time for compromise had come. The empire's Protestants must be lured back into the imperial fold. In return for their allegiance, Wallenstein would coax the emperor into granting them religious freedom. It would be the means to a greater end. For in surrendering the chimera of religious hegemony, the emperor would so enhance his secular authority that Germany might at last become a centralized state.[359] Even better, Sweden, deprived of her Protestant allies, could be counted upon to quit on favorable terms, and the war would end before France could throw her weight into the scales.

In short, Wallenstein was pursuing his original policy of seeking an imperial, rather than a Catholic, victory. But Emperor Ferdinand was so blinded by Catholicism that he could see neither the shrewdness of his general's program nor the dangers of his own. He ordered Wallenstein to take the field. Wallenstein obliged—netting 8000 Swedish prisoners with a brilliant maneuver at Steinau, and clearing Silesia of Protestant forces (1633). When he established winter quarters instead of exploiting his successes, however, the court became openly hostile. In retaliation, Wallenstein extracted a written statement of loyalty from his officers, and resumed his secret negotiations. Rumors abounded that he would seize the Bohemian throne and destroy the war effort with a separate peace.[360] Amidst these allegations, the emperor dismissed him again in February 1634—this time ordering the confiscation of his property.

The extraction of loyalty oaths notwithstanding, Wallenstein's army had no intention of defying the emperor. Fearing for his life, the deposed general fled to the friendly fortress of Eger on the Bohemian frontier with a force of 1000 men. But his entourage included a body of imperial spies, and while Wallenstein slept, these infiltrators lured four of his chief lieutenants to a dinner party. Toasts were drunk until the four had been plied with wine, whereupon armed dragoons burst into the room, demanding to know who was loyal to the emperor. All but the startled guests of honor rose to affirm their allegiance. Swords were unsheathed, and in an instant two of the officers were cut down where they sat. A third was laid low after scrambling into the kitchen. The fourth—Wallenstein's brother-in-law, Adam Terzka—fled to the adjacent courtyard, killing three of his assailants before he, too, was dispatched by musket butt and dagger.[361]

The conspirators now made their way to Wallenstein's lodging. Bursting in, they killed his servants, and clambered up the stairs to his bedroom. Infirm from gout and unable to defend himself, Wallenstein feebly requested quarter. He did not receive it. By one account one of the attackers ran him through with such force, that the halberd-point protruded fully twelve inches out of his back.[362] The assassins then dragged him feet first down a flight of steps, before laying him out unceremoniously alongside the other victims.[363]

The Last Hurrah of the Imperialists

In the aftermath of this gory episode, Emperor Ferdinand appointed his son (the future Ferdinand III) to Wallenstein's former post as commander of the army. His next move, however, was of dubious merit; for he betrothed young Ferdinand to his cousin, Maria—the sister of Spain's King Philip IV—in an effort to buttress his ties to the Spanish House of Hapsburg.

It is said that Philip IV of Spain was incapable of laughter, though it is conceded that he did manage three smiles during his lifetime.[364] Otherwise, he wore an inscrutable expression that would have served him well in diplomacy had his attentions not been entirely absorbed by a compulsive sexual promiscuity, made worse by an obsessive need for atonement after each transgression.[365] Occupied thus, the king deferred in matters of state to his willful advisor, Gaspar de Guzman, Duque du Olivares,[366] whose chief aspiration was to reestablish Spain's mastery over the Netherlands. In Olivares' view the death of Gustavus Adolphus had left the Swedes vulnerable. If they could be expelled from Germany, a decisive victory over the Protestants would follow, and Spain would at last be free to move her troops overland to the rebellious Netherlands via the "Spanish Road." Toward this end, he dispatched King Philip's brother, Cardinal Ferdinand, to Germany to aid in operations against the Swedes. The Spanish and Austrian Ferdinands—simultaneously cousins and brothers-in-law[367]—linked forces, and engaged a combined army of Swedes and German Protestants at Nördlingen, where, amidst outcries of "Viva Espana," they emerged with a stunning victory (1634).

Giddy with success, Emperor Ferdinand cynically offered Saxony and Brandenburg what Wallenstein would have granted them in earnest—an exchange of religious freedom for imperial allegiance. To obtain peace, the Edict of Restitution would be rescinded, but the Protestant princes must accept the territorial boundaries as they existed towards the end of the Danish phase before Gustavus and his Swedes had extended them. Chastened by the death of Gustavus and the defeat at Nördlingen, John George of Saxony and George William of Brandenburg eagerly put their signatures to the Peace of Prague (1635). In so doing, they sold their souls; for the treaty's fine print obligated the Protestant signatories to fight on the side of the emperor if the war continued—and there was now little question that it would.[368]

At Lützen, the Swedes had lost their king but won the battle. If a religious settlement had robbed them of their Protestant allies at that juncture, they might have made peace—but on favorable terms, since they had won the victory. After Nördlingen, they had no bargaining power, and would face a dictated peace. Make no mistake—Sweden's predicament was tenuous in the extreme. Her domination of southern Germany had been undone at a blow, her prestige lay in ruins, her treasury was in a state of exhaustion, and she was possessed of precious few German allies. But there was simply no chance that she would abandon, on demeaning terms, a struggle in which so much had already been invested. Besides, as the state's new regent, Axel Gustafsson Oxenstierna, well knew, Germany was not the only place one could find friends.

The French or "Balance of Power" Phase (1635–1648)

Had religion been the sole motivating force in European politics, Protestantism might have been swept from the continent. The Swedes would have been driven out of Germany, the Protestant princes squashed beneath the imperial thumb, and the Dutch overrun by the combined armies of the Austrian and Spanish Hapsburgs. But Emperor Ferdinand had lost sight of a far weightier principle than religion—one that had been only too familiar to his great ancestor, Charles V—namely, the "balance of power" principle.

No one had more to fear from an overwhelming Hapsburg victory than France. With Spanish troops marching to-and-fro along the Spanish Road skirting her eastern border, and with the emperor a hair's breadth from consolidating his authority in the whole of Germany, France was more vulnerable to Hapsburg encirclement than at any time since the reign of Charles V. An end to the war at this point would have been disastrous.

Following the Hapsburg victory at Nördlingen, Louis XIII's chief minister, Cardinal Richelieu, could no longer afford to remain uncommitted. He formed an alliance with the Dutch and declared war on Spain, bringing French soldiers directly into the conflict for the first time. Then, by the Treaty of Compiègne (1635), he pledged active support to the Swedes—both countries swearing never to make peace with the emperor without the other's consent. To soothe the sensibilities of Germany's Protestant princes, overall military command was given to a German, Bernard of Saxe-Weimer, who had been defeated along with the Swedes at Nördlingen, and who only agreed to remain in the anti-imperialist fold if the prize of Alsace were to be awarded to him in the event of victory.

The battle lines were thus drawn. On the one side, a French Catholic cardinal allied to the Protestants of Sweden, Germany and the United Provinces; on the other, the Catholic Hapsburgs of Spain and Germany, and the duped Protestant signatories of the Peace of Prague. Religion and idealism had been eclipsed by nationalism and the balance of power principle.[369] The metamorphosis that Wallenstein would have used to rid Germany of foreign armies, had—by Ferdinand's misguided hand—transformed the fatherland into the battleground for an ever-widening European war. For Germans, this could hardly be counted an improvement.

Although Richelieu had wrested military authority from the factious French nobility during the previous decade, and had provided the crown with its first standing army and navy, the French intervention initially did little to arrest the tide of imperialist victory. Disorganized French armies were cut to pieces in the Rhineland, while an invading force from the Spanish Netherlands drove south to within eighty miles of Paris. Usually a rock of stability, Richelieu seems to have lost his nerve as the enemy approached—urging the king to flee the capital. But with equally uncharacteristic steadfastness, the king refused to do so under any circumstances.[370] Mastering his anxieties in the face of the king's tenacity, Richelieu rode through the Paris streets in an unguarded carriage to rally the populace. In the end, the capital never came under attack.

In February 1637, Emperor Ferdinand II died, believing the problems of his empire to be at an end. In truth, however, they had barely begun. Before the emperor breathed his last, Sweden's Johan Baner, the hero of Breitenfeld, marched against a larger imperialist army at Wittstock (October 1636). Like Lee at Chancellorsville, he dangled half his army as bait, while the other half executed a daring march around the enemy's flank. Baner was clinging to the field by his very fingertips when at day's end the flanking force finally reemerged to snatch victory from the jaws of defeat.[371]

Whether their putative champions on the field of battle won or lost, the war had become an unceasing source of catastrophe for the inhabitants of Germany. Armies marched hither and yon, feeding themselves at the countryside's expense. On capturing a town, soldiers considered it their God-given right to rape, murder and plunder. And in their train came legions of dispossessed women and children—the victims of previous calamities—hoping to share in their expropriations. Beset by murder and mayhem, the German populace resorted to every extremity—including cannibalism. Cemeteries had to be guarded lest the freshly buried be exhumed.[372] Bodies of criminals disappeared from the gallows, and people knew better than to ask what had become of them. In at least one instance—at Zweibrüken—a mother devoured her own child.[373]

On the imperial side, the new emperor, Ferdinand III, the victor of Nördlingen, was quickly learning that his alliance with tottering Spain was more a burden than a blessing. In Madrid, Olivares' attempts at economic reform had all come to naught. With some difficulty, he managed to abolish the flamboyant "ruff" collar worn at court, replacing it with the starched "*golilla*" collar, which was less costly to maintain.[374] Sadly, the savings therefrom did not suffice to run a war economy. Olivares embarked, therefore, on an ambitious plan to "Castilianize" the provinces of Aragon and Catalonia. But this proved exceedingly unpopular, since the Catalans and Aragonese, saw it as an effort to make them help pay for policies that profited Castile alone.[375] Needing money from somewhere, Olivares bypassed the recalcitrant Castilian Cortes to impose unpopular taxes of doubtful legality on Castile itself. Although his chief military commander, Cardinal Ferdinand, provided Olivares with a victory in Flanders in 1636, the Dutch countered with a victory of their own at Breda in the following year. The disasters now came in rapid succession. In 1638, Bernard of Saxe-Weimer besieged and captured Breisach, on the upper Rhine, thereby severing the "Spanish Road."[376] Olivares' subsequent attempt to supply Cardinal Ferdinand by sea resulted in the

The Hanging Tree by Jacques Callot (c. 1630–1635) depicting soldiers being hanged by their superiors for plundering, one of the iconic images from the Thirty Years' War (Wikimedia Commons). (http://commons.wikimedia.org/wiki/File%3AHanging_Humans.JPG)

destruction of the Spanish navy at the Battle of the Downs (1639), where the Dutch Admiral, Maarten Tromp, sank seventy out of seventy-seven Spanish ships, inflicting 15,000 casualties on a total force of 24,000.[377]

The disaster marooned Cardinal Ferdinand in Flanders. Desperate to relieve him, Olivares continued his economic experiments. Among these was the decision to billet troops in Catalonia. In response, Catalonia's peasants ran riot, burning a royal functionary alive.[378] Philip IV and Olivares led an army into the province to restore order. Not only was this venture unsuccessful, but it allowed the Portuguese to stage their own rebellion at the opposite end of the peninsula.

Portugal had suffered grievously since the unification of the monarchies in 1580. Seeing Spain's current difficulties as an opportunity to sever the Spanish tie, the Portuguese enthroned Duke John of Braganza (a member of Portugal's former ruling house), and reestablished the independence that they had lost sixty years before. Aghast at the calamity, Spain's Queen Isabel prevailed upon her husband, King Philip IV, to dismiss Olivares, whom she had long despised (1643).[379] The result of her intercession was to leave Spain without any guiding hand at all at a moment of supreme crisis.

While Spain teetered on the brink of collapse, her Austrian cousins were defeated in the second battle of Breitenfeld by Gustavus Adolphus' former general of artillery, Count Lennart Tortensson (November 1642). So severe was this setback that the emperor's brother, Leopold, cited an entire regiment for cowardice, hanged or beheaded its officers, and condemned every tenth man in the ranks to be shot.[380] Breitenfeld, however, was not to be the worst of it, for an even ghastlier defeat for the imperialist coalition had been prophesied in a dream. In 1642, Cardinal Richelieu died despite the ministrations of his royal master, Louis XIII, who attempted to spoon-feed him back to health. Unable to exist without his chief minister, King Louis took to his own deathbed within the year. In his last days, he awoke from sleep to see the Prince of Condé at his bedside, and related to him a dream that the latter's son had gained a magnificent triumph in the field.[381] Even as he spoke, the young man in question, Louis, Duc d'Enghein, was marching toward Rocroi and a fateful clash with the forces of Spain.

The Spanish army of the Netherlands, led by Don Francisco de Melo, had just reached the French border for a planned attack on Paris. En route, the Spaniard decided to invest the town of Rocroi, but was intercepted by a smaller French force under d'Enghein. The cards were clearly stacked against the latter, since the Spanish *tercio* infantry phalanxes were generally reputed to be invincible in a fair fight on open ground.[382] D'Enghein's officer corps advised against battle—one asking, "What will become of us if we are defeated?" "That," replied d'Enghein, "will not concern me, for I shall be dead."[383] In the battle's first actions, d'Enghein led a cavalry charge that drove the Spanish left wing from the field. But his own left was routed at the same moment, and d'Enghein's center was soon being pressed, front and flank, by the *tercio* infantry and the victorious cavalry of the Spanish right.

To relieve his center of this double burden, d'Enghein made the daring decision to lead his horsemen on an end-around behind the Spanish *tercios*, decimating the enemy's dumbstruck infantry reserves, and then falling upon their right wing cavalry from behind. The successive targets of this onslaught fled in shock, leaving d'Enghein and his disburdened infantry to focus their attention on the *tercios*. Twice their attacks were repulsed, but under the strain of a third assault, the "invincible" Spanish squares finally broke.

The Spanish attempted to surrender, but in the confusion, some of their number fired their muskets at d'Enghein. At this, the French went berserk. A few terrified Spaniards obtained sanctuary by grasping the stirrups of d'Enghein's horse, but the commander was no longer in control of his troops. By day's end, the Spanish infantry had lost eight thousand dead and seven thousand captured. A mere three thousand escaped. Spain's status as a world power was forever broken.[384]

Five weeks later, Emperor Ferdinand convoked a peace conference in the Westphalian towns of Münster and Osnabrük. Unfortunately, the negotiations would plod along for four years. Each side still felt strong enough to play for time in order to secure political advantage. Pompous delegates from both camps expended more effort squabbling over matters of protocol (who should sit where, who should enter a room first, etc.) than they did discussing peace terms. And as the delays continued so did the battles, privations, plague and famine. Bavaria produced an able commander in Franz von Mercy, who defeated French armies near the Black Forest on three separate occasions—even seizing the French baggage train at Tuttlingen in 1643. But by 1645, the imperialists were again reeling in defeat. When Tortensson and his Swedes pressed into Bohemia and routed an imperial army at Jankau, the emperor abandoned Prague and raced to Vienna, while Brandenburg and Saxony deserted him for a separate peace. On the Rhine, at Allerheim, d'Enghein and Turenne won a costly victory in which von Mercy was killed—and now even the stalwart Maximilian of Bavaria threatened to make his own peace. Clearly, it was time for Ferdinand III to make concessions.

The Treaty of Westphalia (1648)

Sweden's Queen Christina, had been pressing for peace since reaching her majority in 1644. Her delegation, however, would not consider any terms that did not include the cession of Pomerania—a territory on the Baltic coastline to which Brandenburg held the legal claim. Brandenburg's Prince Frederick William absolutely refused to relinquish this province without compensation. In the end, he only parted with the western half—receiving the bishoprics of Magdeburg, Halberstadt and Minden from the emperor in return. Thus, the Swedes achieved their long-sought dream of Baltic supremacy, but at a cost of allowing Brandenburg to become the leading power in northern Germany. Over the next sixty years, Sweden's power in the Baltic would be broken, while Brandenburg would rise to become the kingdom of Prussia—the foundation stone of modern Germany (1701).

There were other winners, too. Dutch independence was at last recognized by Spain. Likewise, Swiss independence was formally conceded by Austria. French control of Metz, Toul and Verdun (held since the time of Charles V) was reconfirmed, but France refused to ratify the peace until she received the Alsace as well. Ferdinand balked. Together with Maximilian of Bavaria he attempted to piece together a serviceable army. But the effort came apart at Zusmarshausen on the Bavarian frontier, when the new force was surprised by Franco-Swedish troops and routed with loss of its entire baggage train (1648). Afterwards, the emperor not only had to surrender jurisdiction (though not dominion) over the Alsace, but he had to pledge his neutrality while France beat Spain to a pulp. The Franco-Spanish conflict dragged on until 1659, when, by the Peace of the Pyrenees, France achieved her goal of making the Pyrenees not just the natural, but also the legal boundary between the two nations. The subsequent fifty years of French history would be spent in an effort to reach her other natural boundaries—the Alps and the Rhine.

The Peace of Westphalia exposed the hypocrisy of the war. Amidst all the jockeying for position, the religious revolt of 1618 had become a dim memory. When reminded that the religious question still needed to be addressed, the peacemakers unimaginatively dusted off the same answer made ninety-three years earlier at the Peace of Augsburg: "*Cuius regio, eius religio*" or "whose realm, his religion." The same rule was already in force in 1618, and had been since 1555. The only modifications were (i) the inclusion of Calvinism on the list of princely options; (ii) the abandonment of the Edict of Restitution; and (iii) the restoration of church lands within Germany to the status of 1624.

The war had begun as a religious struggle—the last great effort to drive Protestantism from the Holy Roman Empire. But the devastation perpetrated in the name of God spoiled the reputation of religion. When Pope Innocent X angrily declared the Peace of Westphalia "invalid, iniquitous, unjust, condemned, rejected, frivolous, [and] without force or effect" no one so much as stirred.[385] The last and most destructive of the religious wars had ended as a battle of nations—and Europe had stumbled into a new era, wherein the concerns of God would be as nothing in comparison to the concerns of state.[386]

Societal Achievements

Between 1350 and 1648, a conceptual revolution took root in Europe. It has been termed the "Renaissance," or in its Anglicized form, "Renascence" meaning "rebirth." What was reborn, in a phrase, was the Greek outlook toward life.[387] It was a rebirth that would herald the West's transformation from a world of faith to a world of reason.

The underlying thrust of the movement was "humanism." By the 14th century, there was a growing sentiment in Europe that men possessed the intelligence and ability to discern *for themselves* the difference between right and wrong, without having to pay blind obedience to the Church. Simultaneously, there came a shift in focus from the *hereafter* to the *here and now*. Like the Greeks before them, the humanists began to sense the beauty of the earthly world, and sought fulfillment in an earthly life.[388] In so doing, they bade fair to make humankind what the Greek Sophist, Protagoras, had said it was: namely, "the measure of all things."[389]

The Renaissance in Literature

The ideas of humanism were to be found in literature as early as the 13th century, with Dante's masterpiece, the *Divine Comedy*. Though its subject matter is medieval, the work qualifies as a product of the Renaissance since the author displays a clear humanistic emphasis in describing the plight of the individuals he encounters on an imaginary tour of Heaven and Hell.[390]

But as Charles Van Doren relates, the movement really got going in the 14th century—and was spurred almost exclusively by the efforts of two Florentine writers: Francesco Petrarch (1304–1374) and Giovanni Boccaccio (1313–1375).[391] The humanism of these authors is obvious in their literary works—Petrarch's *Letters* to his beloved, and possibly mythical, Laura,[392] and Boccaccio's *Decameron*, a collection of bawdy tales concentrating on the joys and sorrows of being human as told by ten Florentines seeking sanctuary from the Black Death. Their main contribution to the Renaissance, however, is not to be found in their own writings, but in their almost single-handed rediscovery of the classics of antiquity.

Beginning in the late 11th century, when the fall of Toledo and the First Crusade began to make these writings available again, interest in the classical world had been on the rise. Petrarch, however, was among the first to realize that the ideas of humanism had already been fully contemplated in this all-but-lost universe.[393] To him, the revered works of Cicero and Aristotle gave a voice of authority to humanism, and he was determined to spread the gospel.

Relying on the reputation of the ancients, Petrarch hoped to stimulate a rebirth of learning throughout Europe. In 1350, he enlisted the assistance of Boccaccio, and together they began mining monastic libraries for classical manuscripts. Petrarch found letters of Cicero, lost for a millennium, and produced an authoritative version of Livy's histories.[394] Although Boccaccio's pilgrimage to Monte Cassino, (the monastery founded in the 6th century AD by St. Benedict) netted him a copy of the works of Tacitus, his errand had been heartbreaking. It is said that he departed in tears after finding the cloister's library in a state of dilapidation—its volumes covered in dust and missing entire pages.[395] Afterwards, Boccaccio met Leonzio Pilato, a scholar sufficiently versed in ancient Greek to produce the first modern translation of Homer's *Iliad*. The work was presented to Petrarch (who had failed in his own attempt to learn Greek owing to a lack of materials and the loss of his tutor[396]), and it is said that he knelt before the translator in gratitude.[397]

Nor was the unearthing of long-lost classics Petrarch's sole contribution. To increase the circulation of ideas, he followed Dante's precedent, and promoted the use of the vernacular in popular literature.[398] Afterwards, it was not uncommon for Renaissance authors to write in their native tongues: Rebalais' *Inestimable Life of Gargantua, Father of Pantagruel* heralded the French literary Renaissance, while Chaucer's *Canterbury Tales*—equally ribald—ushered in the new period of vernacular writing in England. (The latter would culminate in the works of Shakespeare, whose treatment of the human condition has touched the soul of every succeeding generation down to our own.)

Some humanists, however, continued to write in Latin. Two of these deserve brief mention. The first, Poggio Bracciolini spent the first half of the 15th century tracking down ancient works for the Holy See.[399] Chief among his finds was Lucretius' lost treatise *De Rerum Natura* ("On the Nature of Things"), which exemplifies the worldview of the Greek Epicurean school. The second was the Dutchman, Desiderius Erasmus, known as the "Prince of Humanists" (1466–1536). Erasmus' most famous work, *In Praise of Folly*, ridicules the self-righteous posturing of the era's politicians, churchmen and intellectuals. "As for the theologians," he wrote of the schoolmen, who continued to dominate education, "perhaps the less said the better ... since they are a style of man who show themselves ... supercilious and irritable unless they can heap up six hundred conclusions about you and force you to recant; and if you refuse, they brand you as a heretic.... It must be confessed that no other group of fools are so reluctant to acknowledge Folly's benefits toward them...."[400] A devout man, Erasmus nonetheless believed the Church had erred in concentrating too intensely on its own forms and ritual at the expense of the actual substance and teachings of Christianity. Hoping to guide the religion back to its intended path, he produced a more accurate Latin translation of the New Testament from the original Greek text (1516). But by exposing the diverse flaws of the Church-authorized Vulgate version, the new edition did less to effect a tranquil return to Christian piety than it did to embolden those who sought a more radical program of reform. In the following year, Luther attached his ninety-five theses to the church door at Wittenburg, thus inaugurating the Reformation—a movement much more extreme in its objectives than the mortified Erasmus had ever intended or desired.[401]

The Renaissance in Art and Architecture

In art, the interest in things human stimulated a desire for more accurate portrayal of the human form. Giotto (1270–1317), a Florentine artist, was among the first to bring his painted human subjects to life (figuratively speaking). His works represent a revolutionary departure from the medieval disdain for the human body, but his figures appear two-dimensional when compared to the works of subsequent Renaissance artists, who took advantage of two new opportunities to enhance the realism of their work.

The first was the chance to study human anatomy. By the 15th century, many artists were attending cadaver dissections at Europe's leading medical schools. For most, the experience was a huge disappointment: The lessons were dominated by the flawed teachings of Galen—the great, if self-deluded, 2nd century physician and anatomist who had never himself dissected a human being. According to the physician-historian, Sherwin Nuland, such deficiencies hardly mattered to the medical students, who were benumbed by the tedious lectures; but for the artists, the lack of accuracy was disheartening. Consequently, the majority remained after class to pursue their own investigations—foremost among them, Leonardo da Vinci, who made a book of drawings derived from dissections that he himself had performed.[402]

More important than anatomy lessons, however, was the development of perspective—an artistic technique that allowed artists to create the illusion of three-dimensional depth on a flat canvas. The details are beyond the scope of this text. Suffice to say that perspective artworks draw the viewer's attention to a so-called "vanishing point," where the main lines of the drawing intersect (or would do if extended by ruler and straightedge). The technique, which is easier to demonstrate by example than to describe in words, not only allowed Renaissance artists to create a sense of three dimensions, it also made it possible to abandon the awkward medieval contrivance of exaggerating those aspects of a drawing to which the artist hoped to attract attention. For example, in a medieval drawing, a king might be depicted as a veritable giant in comparison with his attendants so that the observer would be able to identify him. In contrast, by employing perspective, the artist could simply superimpose the essential person or object on the vanishing point, and the viewer's eye would be drawn to it automatically.[403]

Surprisingly enough, "perspective" was not introduced to Western art by an artist, but by the Florentine architect, Filippo Brunelleschi, who had learned its principles from an Arabic work on optics. In hopes of gaining important architectural commissions, Brunelleschi made himself the only architect in the world who could supply his prospective employers with three-dimensional drawings of what he proposed to build.[404] His first perspective drawing was a one-foot-square exact mirror image of the Baptistery that stands opposite the Florence Cathedral. Realizing that his audience had never seen "perspective art," and that they might have difficulty seeing things "in perspective" for the first time, he devised a fascinating teaching exercise: He brought his prospective client to the actual Baptistery, and situated him facing the building's doors. The observer was then told to study Brunelleschi's perspective painting of the building—but in a peculiar way. Rather than look at the work directly, he was instructed to gaze through a small peephole the architect had cut in the back of canvas, and then to view the painting's reflection in a mirror held in the opposite hand a foot or so away. Once the observer had familiarized himself with the painted Baptistery's appearance, the mirror was removed, and the observer—still gazing through the peephole—saw the true Baptistery from the exact same vantage point. The images were identical—and to perfect the illusion, Brunelleschi used burnished silver to represent the sky in his painting, so that moving clouds would reflect off of it, and could be seen in the viewing mirror.[405]

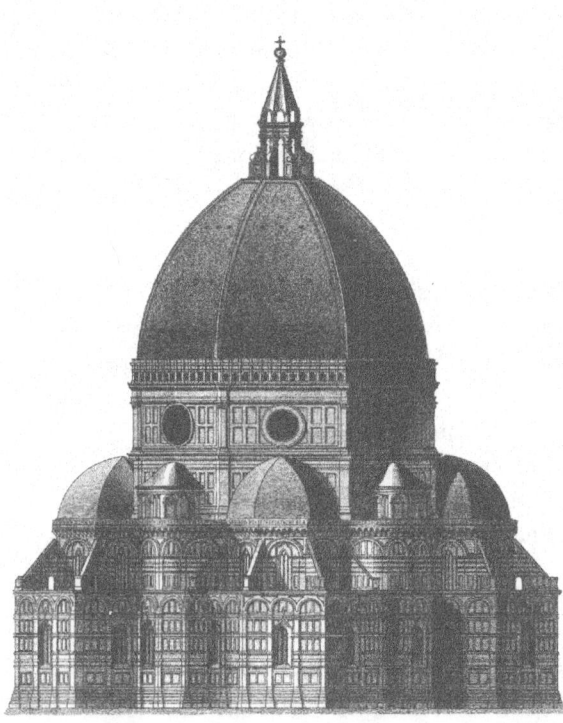

The Duomo (or Florence Cathedral) crowned by Brunelleschi's Dome. The baptistery is actually located across from the cathedral entrance and is not pictured here. (© Depositphotos.com/Pietro Ballardini).

Brunelleschi's reputation soared, but to win his greatest commission, he needed to play a comedic trick on his competitors. He was sought after to construct the famous dome atop the Florence Cathedral, but refused to submit a model of his proposed design. When, on this account, his competitors denounced him as a charlatan and attempted to gain the commission for themselves, he put forth the challenge that "he who could make an egg stand upright on a piece of smooth marble, should be appointed to build the cupola, since in doing that, his genius would be made manifest. They took an egg accordingly, and all those masters did their best to make it stand upright, but none discovered the method of doing so. Wherefore, Filippo, being told that he might make it stand himself, took it daintily into his hand, gave the end of it a blow on the plane of the marble, and made it stand upright. Beholding this, the artists loudly protested, exclaiming, that they could all have done the same; but Filippo replied laughing, that they might also know how to construct the cupola, if they had seen [his] model and design."[406] Having made his point, Brunelleschi was commissioned to build his masterpiece.

The Renaissance in Medicine

Two transcendent figures may be said to personify the Renaissance in medicine: Andreas Vesalius (1514–1564) and Ambroise Paré (1510–1590). Vesalius single-handedly inaugurated the accurate study of anatomy. His childhood home in Belgium overlooked the local executioner's grounds, and the sight of decaying bodies in his backyard drew him to his life's work. The flawed teaching of anatomy at his Paris medical school provoked unsanctioned visits to the city charnel houses and cemeteries, where the nimble student and his fellows evaded terrifying stray dogs and possessive crows in the quest for a worthy specimen to study.[407] (Vesalius later related how he and his companions donned blindfolds and identified the various bones they had scavenged by touch alone.[408]) As guest Professor of Anatomy at Bologna in 1540, he publicly challenged the mistaken teachings of Galen for the first time—backing up his allegations with accurate dissection.[409] Despite strong opposition from Galen's adherents, he refused to back down, and in 1543 he published his masterful anatomical treatise, *De Humani Corporis Fabrica* (*On the Fabric of the Human Body*). A fellow Belgian, Jan van Calcar, used woodcuts to provide the volume with a wealth of revolutionary anatomical illustrations.[410] After publication of his work, Vesalius left academic medicine and became court physician to the Holy Roman Emperor, Charles V.

Ambroise Paré was likewise destined to be a court physician, but in the rival court of France. He was a surgeon whose humanism helped bring a sense of humanity to a still-primitive profession. The firearm was in widespread use by Paré's time, and he loathed its devastating impact—voicing his disapproval in vernacular prose worthy of Shakespeare: "Thunder, as a thing natural, falls by chance, one while upon a high oak, another while upon the top of a mountain ... but seldom upon man. But this hellish Engine, tempered by the malice and guidance of man, assails man only, and takes him for his only mark, and directs his bullets against him. The Thunder by its noise as a messenger sent before, foretells the storm at hand; but, which is the chief mischief, this infernal Engine ... roars as it strikes, and strikes as it roars, sending at one and the same time the deadly bullet into the breast and the horrible noise into the ear."[411]

Because they were felt to be inherently poisonous, gunshot wounds were disinfected in that era by the application of boiling oil—a barbaric treatment, more noxious to its recipients than the original injury.[412] Paré was a man of his time and dutifully followed the prescription until the siege of Turin (1537), when the number of the wounded caused him to exhaust his supply of oil. Desperate, he dressed the remaining wounds with a "digestive" containing egg yolk, rose oil and turpentine. He awoke early the next morning in a state of anxiety, expecting to find the patients thus treated already dead. Instead they were faring far better than those treated with the boiling oil.[413]

By publicizing the episode, he averted agony for untold numbers of battlefield wounded. Likewise, he pioneered the use of ligature to tie off exposed blood vessels, thereby saving soldiers the torture of cauterization by hot iron, and he developed a gentler method of extracting teeth in an era when the art of dentistry was primitive, indeed. According to Professor Howard Haggard, Paré sometimes took matters a step further—grafting a healthy tooth, purchased from a willing donor, in place of the extracted one. As the wound healed, the new tooth took root and could serve its host indefinitely.[414]

The Renaissance in the Sciences

As Renaissance men learned anew how to view and depict their world, they developed a burning desire to investigate it through experiment. The experimental method had been laid out in ancient Greece by the likes of Pythagoras and Aristotle, but was scarcely used in the Middle Ages when its lone champion was the 13th century Franciscan Monk, Roger Bacon of Oxford (see Section II). After Bacon's demise, we hear nothing more of observational experiment until the critical year 1543. This was the year in which Vesalius published his *De Humani Corporis Fabrica*, but in the same 12-month span the book of a Polish priest named Nicolas Copernicus caused an even greater stir. It was entitled *De Revolutionibus Orbium Coelestium* (*On the Revolution of the Celestial Spheres*). Prior to its publication, the universe had been viewed as "geocentric" or "earth-centered"—a medieval conception based almost entirely on Aristotle's cumbersome notion that the planets and sun were embedded in crystalline spheres moving in perfectly circular orbits around the earth. Though satisfactory in some ways, the model's glaring defects created havoc with the calendar, since the latter's accuracy depended on a precise charting of celestial motions. As James Burke tells it, Copernicus had merely hoped to smooth out the system's rough edges, but his observations led him to scrap the Aristotelian paradigm altogether in favor of a "heliocentric" (i.e., sun-centered) hypothesis.[415] In 1514, he circulated a summary of his ideas, but it was so ill-received that he did not publish the work in its entirety until he was on his deathbed in 1543. (Durant and Durant relate that on being handed a published copy, he smiled at the title page and died within the hour.)[416]

At first, there was no protest on the part of the Church—partly because Copernicus' friend, Osiander, who took the manuscript to be published, inserted a preface saying that the contents were not necessarily to be taken as literal truth, but merely as workable "hypotheses,"[417] and partly because the work accomplished its purpose: i.e., it allowed for a more exact calculation of the calendar.[418] But by the end of the century, the Church's mood had changed. In 1577, Tycho Brahe (1546–1602) raised new doubts about Aristotle's perfect spheres by demonstrating that the comet of 1577 had an oblong or "elliptical" orbit.[419] More damaging still was the work of his assistant, the Austrian mathematician, Johannes Kepler (1571–1630), who used his mentor's data to prove that the planets themselves moved in elliptical orbits, and that the sun, not the earth, was located at one focus of the ellipse.[420]

Finding this all rather difficult to swallow, the Church attempted to suppress further inquiry. In 1600, Giordano Bruno went to the stake for embellishing the new heliocentric theory with ideas about an infinite universe. As he burned, Bruno cried out that the earth moves nevertheless[421]—an act of defiance that has since been attributed, apocryphally, to another adherent of Copernicus: Galileo Galilei (1564–1642). Galileo's most famous experiment proved the uniform acceleration of falling bodies, which he demonstrated (at least in legend) by dropping differently weighted objects from the leaning tower of Pisa to show that they landed at the same time. He coupled this finding with other experiments to produce the birth of modern physics. But he also made use of a new invention, the telescope, to discover the moons of Jupiter—the first time another planet was shown to have satellites. In his *Dialogue on the Two New Sciences* (1632), he pits a Copernican in debate against an Aristotelian, depicting the latter as an imbecile named Simplicio. The Church, clinging to Aristotle and his doctrines, failed to see the humor. Galileo was forced to recant or face Bruno's fate. He died in broken health under house arrest in 1642.[422]

Isaac Newton is regarded as England's greatest man of science, but in Galileo's time the honor belonged to Francis Bacon (1561–1626). Like his predecessor and namesake, Roger Bacon, Francis Bacon was a firm believer in the potential of the experimental method. (In his book, *The New Atlantis*, he adds submarines to the cars and flying machines already envisioned by the monk.[423]) Before delving into the sciences, he had been an energetic and successful politician in the service of King James I, but in 1621, he was banished from public life for taking bribes. His downfall was a boon to the English Renaissance. Bacon used his newfound leisure to immerse himself in scientific pursuits. In so doing he became the consummate Renaissance man. He was absolutely insistent on the use of inductive reasoning, saying, in the *Novum Organum*, which he published in 1620, that nothing could be regarded with certainty unless it could be observed.[424] He died in the midst of an inductive inquiry—contracting a fever after buying a chicken and packing it with snow to see if it might thus be preserved. He survived just long enough to see his hypothesis borne out.[425]

The Renaissance in Mathematics

Prior to the 17th century, the very best mathematicians were not inclined to share their knowledge—a major reason being that one could earn a lucrative wage solving economic problems for tradesmen, and if the secret formulae and computations got out, there would be too much competition and very little work.[426] In the 1630s, however, a certain Father Mersenne, residing at a cloister near Paris, convinced some of the best minds in the field to participate in a network for the exchange of mathematical ideas, thus to foster progress in the sciences. Over the ensuing two decades, Father Mersenne's network came to boast three of the giants of modern mathematics: René Descartes, Blaise Pascal and Pierre de Fermat.

René Descartes (1596–1650) may be best remembered today as the philosopher who uttered the famous phrase "I think, therefore I am." But to mathematicians, he is the creator of "Cartesian" or "analytical" geometry—i.e., the branch of geometry wherein algebraic equations, including those of the form "$y = mx + b$," are graphed onto x- and y-axes. I hesitate, of course, to dredge up disagreeable memories from the reader's schooldays, but Descartes' system was a great milestone in the history of mathematics, establishing as it did the first bridge between algebra and geometry. Legend says that Descartes dreamed it all up while gazing at a fly buzzing about the intersection of the walls and ceiling of his room during one of his morning meditations.[427] For the first five decades of his life, it had been his habit to lie in bed for hours contemplating his various theories before rising. In the midst of his sixth decade, however, Sweden's Queen Christina (the daughter of Gustavus Adolphus) ultimately gave him a rude awakening from these slumbers. Hearing of his genius, she summoned him to Sweden to be her tutor. He reluctantly obliged, only to learn that she expected the tutoring sessions to occur at 5 a.m. Under so harsh a taskmaster, he succumbed to pneumonia within the year.[428]

Blaise Pascal (1623–1662) was a mathematical prodigy. An arithmetical triangle of numbers that bears his name is still used as a shortcut by math students who cannot quite master Newton's binomial theorem.[429] Even more practical was his idea for a horse-drawn shuttle-bus service in Paris,[430] and his invention of a gear-driven mechanical calculator that could add and subtract. (Leibniz soon built a better one that could also multiply, divide and extract roots.[431]) His brilliant career in mathematics was cut short at age thirty-one, when the horses pulling his carriage stumbled off the side of a bridge. The carriage got stuck just in time to save Pascal from plummeting to his death (1654), but he interpreted the experience as God's way of directing his attentions to religious matters.[432] Thereafter, under the tutelage of his sister, a Jansenist nun, he became the leading literary voice of Jansenism—a movement within Catholicism that accepted the notions of original sin and predestination. His famous *Pensées*, on which basis he is credited with taking French prose out of the ribald hand of Rabelias and delivering it into its modern formal eloquence, was not published until after his death, but their composition marked his abandonment of secular pursuits. Indeed, it is recorded that he sometimes scourged himself with a whip for turning his mind from devout matters.[433] Thus was French eloquence purchased at the expense of mathematics.

Pierre de Fermat (1601–1665) has ties both to Descartes and Pascal. He did Descartes one better by adding a z-axis to Descartes' original x and y, thus moving Cartesian geometry from its two-dimensional plane into three-dimensional space[434]; and he actually collaborated with Pascal to create the branch of mathematics known as "probability theory." The breakthrough came when a notorious gambler, the Chevalier de Méré, had to quit a gambling contest in mid-game, and asked the mathematicians whether they could predict by mathematical methods what the chances of winning were for each competitor so that the purse could be fairly divided. Fermat and Pascal solved the problem by inventing this entirely new branch of mathematics.[435]

In general, however, Fermat did not enjoy working with his fellow mathematicians nearly as much as he enjoyed baffling them. With Father Mersenne acting as a go-between, he published a host of difficult mathematical riddles, but would not supply the proofs to go with them.[436] His most famous riddle, however, was one that he didn't publish: Fermat's Last Theorem, which was found after his death jotted in the margin of his copy of Diophantus' *Arithmetica*. Building on the familiar Pythagorean Theorem of right triangles: ($a^2 + b^2 = c^2$), Fermat proposed that if the exponent was changed to any whole number greater than "2," there could be no solution for a, b and c that could satisfy the equation.

Next to this assertion, he recorded that he possessed a proof, but that it would not fit in the margin.[437] Nor, apparently, did he write it down elsewhere, for it was never found. A solution proved elusive for three centuries, before Andrew Wiles of Princeton University finally produced a proof in 1994—and *he* required mathematical techniques not developed until the late 20th century in order to do it.[438]

The Renaissance in Warfare and Politics

In nearly every aspect, the Renaissance was a source of beauty, but in warfare and politics the case was decidedly otherwise. In warfare, the Renaissance bore witness to the introduction of hand-held firearms, which brought an end to the armored knight just as the cannon had done to the castle wall. The iron ball could pierce armor with much greater efficiency than the longbow's arrow. Uncouth as it must have seemed, the most gallant man-at-arms could now be shot dead by a "cowardly" commoner standing well beyond the reach of his lance.[439]

In politics, the classic treatise of the period was Niccolò Machiavelli's *The Prince*—a tome declaring that the best politician is the most unscrupulous one. For ten years, Machiavelli (1469–1527) served as advisor to the Florentine despot, Soderini. Exiled after Soderini's deposition (1512), he wrote *The Prince* in hopes of obtaining a government commission under the Medici, who had taken power in Soderini's wake. He wasn't hired, but this did not stop the majority of European rulers from adopting his advice.[440] Indeed, it was not until the 17th century that political philosophers extricated themselves from the gory quagmire of Machiavellian diplomacy. One of the first to make a clean break was the Dutchman, Hugo Grotius, whose treatise, *On the Law of War and Peace* (published in 1625), put forth the unfathomable proposition that justice and negotiation, rather than war, ought to be the basis of relations between states.

The Dissemination of a New Worldview

The dissemination of the new ideas of the Renaissance would have been a difficult task, indeed, had it not been for an invention made around 1450, which is popularly credited to Johann Gutenberg of Mainz—namely, the printing press.[441] Utilizing mass-produced, durable typeset letters, the new press greatly increased the availability of books, thereby facilitating the spread of the era's burgeoning wisdom. (It should be noted that this occurred over the protests of many Renaissance men who considered penmanship to be an art form, and derided the printed word as a laughable invention of German "barbarians."[442])

For the first time since antiquity, knowledge was wrested from the hands of the priests, and placed within reach of the populace at large.[443] Here, as in other respects, the Renaissance represents a fundamental rebirth of Western Civilization; for the dissemination of knowledge was among the crucial factors separating Ancient Greece—the first Western society—from its Eastern predecessors. To be sure, the Roman Church had not been so jealous in protecting her knowledge as the priesthoods of Mesopotamia or Egypt—indeed, her monastic orders had long been the leaders in European education. But one finds it difficult to argue with Wells' contention that the Church's idea of education—whether her purpose was malevolent or not—was to control minds rather than enlighten them.[444] We have seen how bitterly she could struggle to prevent the spread of ideas that might compromise her authority. Her treatment of the Hussites and Lollards, of Bruno and Galileo, serve as ready examples. Now, she had to contend with the printed word; and the very first book off the press nearly toppled her at a blow.

What was this dangerous volume? Some heretical Renaissance tome? Not at all. Rather, it was a work with which the Church was all too familiar: the Bible. Perhaps the decorative Gutenberg edition cannot take credit, but later versions, such as those of Erasmus and Luther, well may. Personal copies of these Bibles were distributed to a world, still devout, but now imbued with the humanist spirit that had taught man faith in his own competence to understand the Word of God without the supervision of an overbearing clergy. Just over a half a century later, inexpensive printed copies of the Bible were to play an instrumental part in the successful launching of the Reformation.[445]

Screw printing press, vintage engraving (© Depositphotos.com/Patrick Guénette).

The Renaissance spurred Western Civilization's transition from the medieval to the modern period, laying the foundation for mankind's current worldview, most notably its belief in progress. Between that era and the present day, technological advances have come at an unprecedented pace bringing untold benefit to humankind while simultaneously increasing our capacity for destructiveness—a paradox, alas, that is likely to persist in the imperfect hands of the human race. Yet the great game is not over. Through much of the Middle Ages, the civilization of the West sought and expected the return of universal monarchy as the harbinger of a utopian city of god on earth. The Renaissance, Reformation and Thirty Years' War exploded that illusion forever. As consolation prizes go, mankind might have done far worse than to emerge from the wreckage with a belief in the possibility of progress and the desire to make said progress the object of his pursuit.

Notes

Abbreviations for frequently used sources are found in the bibliography.

Section I

1. Rostovtzeff, 179; Fuller, vol. 1, 243–4.
2. While Aurelius still lived the legions began to recover, but the advantage was ruined first by the attempted coup of Aurelius' lieutenant, Avidius Cassius, in Parthia, and then by Aurelius' death and the accession of his useless son, Commodus.
3. From Tacitus' *Germania* in Botsford and Botsford, 547; F. Ogg, p. 27.
4. Munro, *TMA*, 23–4 and 41.
5. Bury, *LRE*, vol. 1, 411.
6. Oman, 62 (*BE*). Strabo's actual name was Theodoric "One Eye." Notably, the modern term "strabismus" refers to misaligned eyes.
7. Bury, *LRE*, vol. 1, 413–421; Charles W. C. Oman, 62–63. (*BE*).
8. Bury, *LRE*, vol. 1, 423.
9. Norwich, *SHB*, 56.
10. Brownworth, 70.
11. Durant and Durant, vol. 4, 101; Gibbon, XXXIX, vol. 3, 24–6. Falsely implicated, Boethius uttered a treasonous reply at his interrogation, for which crime he was half-strangled with a cord and then clubbed to death.
12. Procopius, *Wars*, 141–43; 146–47; Gibbon, XLI, vol. 3, 101–04.
13. Gibbon, XLI, vol. 3, 103; Procopius, *Wars*, 147–49.
14. Bury, *LRE*, vol. 1, 317–20, 389.
15. Bury, *LRE*, vol. 1, 430–33.
16. Bury, *LRE*, vol. 1, 434–35.
17. Bury, *LRE*, vol. 1, 435–36.
18. Bury, *LRE*, vol. 2, 15.
19. Bury, *LRE*, vol. 2, 16–18.
20. Vitalian was subsequently murdered under mysterious circumstances.
21. Brownworth, 67–69.
22. Gibbon, XL, vol. 3, 34.
23. We relegate the lurid details to a footnote: "Slaves," writes Procopius, the era's leading historian, "would then scatter grains of barley from above into the calyx of this passion flower, whence geese, trained for the purpose, would next pick the grains one by one with their bills and eat" (Procopius, *Secret History*, 103). In an adjoining passage he reports that, "On the field of pleasure she was never defeated. Often she would go picnicking with ten young men or more, in the flower of their strength and virility, and dallied with them all, the whole night through. When they wearied of the sport, she would approach their servants, perhaps thirty in number, and fight a duel with each of these.... And though she flung wide three gates to the ambassadors of Cupid, she lamented that nature had not similarly unlocked the straits of her bosom, that she might there have contrived a further welcome to his emissaries" (*Secret History*, 101–2). Procopius reported these things, however, after he had been spurned in his desire for a promotion at court, and the same *Secret History* contains information that is obviously fantastical, as when he describes the emperor as a demon who secretly roamed the palace at night without his head (Bury, *LRE*, vol. 2, 421–24).
24. Gibbon, XL, vol. 3, 34–35.
25. Bury, *LRE*, vol. 2, 26.
26. Previté-Orton, vol. 1, 188; Brinton, et al., vol. 1, p. 144.
27. Oman, *BE*, 75.
28. Gibbon, XL, vol. 3, 37–40. Gibbon places this event at the Ides of January races themselves, but in a 12 volume edition of Gibbons *Decline and Fall* published in 1906 (for which he served as editor) J. B. Bury notes that it occurred at the rehearsal for the races two days earlier and that the Blues and Greens united against him on the Ides. See *The Nika Riot*, http://oll.libertyfund.org/?option=com_staticxtandstaticfile=show.php%3Ftitle=1374andchapter=90214andlayout=htmlandItemid=277. Accessed 3/18/14.
29. Brownworth (77) offers this version, but the condemned men may have been in custody prior to the verbal altercation at the Hippodrome due to factional violence perpetrated at an earlier date.
30. Bury, *LRE*, vol. 2, 40.
31. T. T. Rice, 100; Gibbon, XL, vol. 3, 37–41; Dahmus, *HMA*, 117–18.
32. Gibbon, XL, vol. 3, 41; Bury, *LRE*, vol. 2, 41. Brownworth, 78–79.
33. Bury, *LRE*, vol. 2, 82.

34. Haldon, 30–32; Goodenough, 107–10; Procopius, *Wars*, 31–2 and 37–9; Gibbon, XLI, vol. 3, 79.
35. Oman, *BE*, 79–80.
36. Norwich, *SHB*, p. 64.
37. Gibbon, XLI, vol. 3, p. 83.
38. Gibbon, vol. 3, XLI, pp. 83–5.
39. Larousse, vol. 1, 252. (The defeated Gelimer was apprehended and sent back to Constantinople, where he lived in forced retirement on a private estate.)
40. Quotes: Gibbon, XLI, vol. 3, pp. 81 and 95. Spain was not taken until 554, when the weaker of two Gothic factions contesting the throne appealed to Justinian for deliverance. Answering the call, Byzantine troops garrisoned Spain's coastal strongholds, thereby delivering the peninsula (or at least its southern coastline) into imperial hands.
41. Procopius, *Wars*, 150; Gibbon, XLI, vol. 3, 105.
42. Norwich, *SHB*, 70.
43. Gibbon, XLI, vol. 3, 113–14; Procopius, *Wars*, 180–1, and 190.
44. Gibbon, XLI, vol. 3, 119; see also Procopius, *Wars*, 212.
45. Gibbon, XLI, vol. 3, 120.
46. Norwich, *SHB*, 73.
47. Norwich, *SHB*, 74–5.
48. As the daughter of a charioteer and a theatre wench, Antonina was a kindred soul to Theodora. On hearing of his reprieve, Belisarius is said to have kissed Antonina's feet and promised to live as her slave (Procopius, *Secret History*, 53–9; Gibbon, XLI, vol. 3, 132). According to Procopius' *Secret History*, she had already been treating him as such—carrying on multiple infidelities behind his back—including an incestuous affair with their adoptive son (Procopius, *Secret History*, 27–30; Gibbon, XLI, vol. 3, 128–9).
49. Gibbon, XLIII, vol. 3, 179–80.
50. Bury, *LRE*, vol. 2, 388.
51. Obolensky, 44.
52. Gibbon, XLII, vol. 3, 134–5.
53. Gibbon, XLII, vol. 3, 136–7.
54. Oman, *BE* 105.
55. Luttwak, 92.
56. Procopius, *HWEJ*, II.16 (spelling updated by author).
57. Procopius, *Wars*, II.23, 120; *HOW*, II.23, 467*fn*.
58. Intent on retaining her position when Justin died (578), Empress Sophia pressed Tiberius to accept her hand in an incestuous marriage. Fond as he was of his adoptive mother, Tiberius chose instead to elevate Anastasia, to whom he was already married. In anger, Sophia conspired to oust him, but her plot was exposed, and she spent her last years in confinement (Gibbon, XLV, vol. 3, 271; see also, Oman, *BE*, 116–17).
59. Maurice was engaged to Tiberius' daughter just prior to Tiberius' expiration and married her on ascending the throne (T. Gregory, 163–64).
60. Oman, *BE*, 72. Carrhae had been a devastating defeat for Rome in which Caesar's contemporary, the triumvir, Marcus Crassus, lost first his army and then his life.
61. Luttwak, 56–59; Haldon, 43.
62. Oman, *BE*, 61, 72.
63. Ravenna's Church of San Vitale boasts the famous mosaics of Justinian and Theodora.
64. Ostrogorsky, 80 and 96; Jenkins, 16–17.
65. Theophylact, 24.
66. Gibbon, XLVI, vol. 3, 301.
67. Theophylact, 155–61.
68. Gibbon, XLVI, vol. 3, 303–4; Theophylact, 179*fn* and 218.
69. Gibbon, XLVI, vol. 3, 305–6; also Theophylact, 227.
70. Gibbon, XLVI, vol. 3, 307.
71. Theophanes, 7; Durant and Durant, vol. 4, 423–4.
72. See Larousse, vol. 1, 258.
73. Gibbon, XLVI, vol. 3, 308–09.
74. Oman, *BE*, 133–34.
75. Oman, *BE*, 132–33.
76. Norwich, *SHB*, 91; Gibbon, XLVI, vol. 3, 317–18.
77. T.T. Rice, 154–5.
78. Alas, the Avars and Slavs continued to wreak havoc in Illyria and Greece, robbing the Byzantine army of its Illyrian recruiting grounds, and severing the land bridge with the West—a circumstance that caused Latin to fall into disuse in the Empire (Obolensky, 58).
79. Theophanes, 24.
80. Jenkins, 24; Oman, *BE*, 139.
81. See Wells, p. 611.
82. Wells, 604.
83. Gibbon, L, vol. 3, 526.
84. Watt, 136–40; Wells, p. 605.
85. Watt, 167.
86. Wells, 606–7.
87. The name derives from the Greek trading town of Byzantium, which later became the metropolis of Constantinople.
88. Gibbon, XLVI, vol. 3, 313.
89. Norwich, *SHB*, 96; Jenkins, 34.
90. Wells, 615.
91. Gibbon, LI, vol. 3, 581.
92. Stark, 17.
93. Gibbon, LI, vol. 3, 581.
94. Treadgold, 92; Norwich, p. 96.
95. T. E. Gregory, 179.
96. Gibbon, LI, vol. 3, 595; Beckmann, 74.
97. Bémont and Monod, 152. Given Christian antipathy to pagan writings, many authors, Gibbon included, find it extremely doubtful that another library had truly been established.
98. Wells, 615.
99. Gibbon, LI, vol. 3, 561.
100. Gibbon, LI, vol. 3, 562–6. Another tradition says that Yezdegerd was assassinated.
101. A widow of Mohammed on camelback had been their leader (Durant, vol. 4, 191).
102. Durant and Durant (vol. 4, 192) say it was a sword; Gibbon (L, vol. 3, 548) says a dagger.
103. Theophanes, 44; Ostrogorsky, 116; Jenkins, 38; Gibbon, LI, vol. 3, 588.
104. Theophanes, 45; Ostrogorsky, 116*fn*.
105. Gibbon, XLVIII, vol. 3, 387; Theophanes, 50–1; Norwich, *SHB*, 100–1.

Notes—Section I

106. Treadgold, 95–6. (The *theme system* may actually have developed under Maurice.)
107. Jenkins, 53; Ostrogorsky, 98 and 132–4.
108. G. Holmes, *OME*, 13.
109. See Ostrogorsky, 125; Norwich, *SHB*, 101.
110. T. E. Gregory, 188–89.
111. Ostrogorsky, 133–40.
112. Gibbon, XLVIII, vol. 3, 390–1; Theophanes, 72.
113. Norwich, *SHB*, 105–08.
114. Initially, Anastasius was banished to a monastery and his life was spared, but later, he made a failed attempt to recover the throne and was put to death.
115. Jenkins, 62–4.
116. Gibbon, LII, vol. 4, 7; Durant and Durant, vol. 4, 425.
117. *Encyclopædia Britannica*, vol. 7, 5.
118. Gibbon, LII, vol. 4, 9–10.
119. Gibbon, LII, vol. 4, 9–10; Durant and Durant, vol. 4, 424–5.
120. Treadgold, 105; Theophanes, 89.
121. Fuller, vol. 1, p. 338–9.
122. Jenkins, 25; see also, Diehl, *BGD*, 238.
123. Jenkins, 84–5.
124. Theophanes, 97.
125. See Asimov, 124; Gibbon, XLVIII, vol. 3, 394; Norwich, *SHB*, 113.
126. Dahmus, *HMA*, 136. Owing to a breakdown in communications amidst the turmoil of the 7th century, the law code of Justinian fell into disuse in much of the empire. Leo compiled the *Ecloga* as a handbook to facilitate the reintroduction of imperial legal precepts as communications were restored in the wake of his great victory (Finlay, vol. 1, 32).
127. Theophanes, 113.
128. Jenkins, 70; Von Grunebaum, 78.
129. Gibbon, LII, vol. 4, 17; Durant and Durant, vol. 4, 196.
130. Theophanes, 130–3.
131. Diehl, *HBE*, 55; Theophanes, 138.
132. Finlay, vol. 1, 75; Ostrogorsky, 180–1.
133. Oman, *BE*, 199.
134. Theophanes, 155; T. T. Rice, 38; Diehl, *BGD*, 136; Ostogorsky, 181.
135. Theophanes, 158–61.
136. Oman, *BE*, 199.
137. Jenkins, 92 and 117.
138. Gibbon, LII, vol. 4, 27.
139. Theophanes, 163; Ostrogorsky, 195; Dahmus, *SMK*, 72.
140. Norwich, *SHB*, 124.
141. According to Jenkins (125–6), "mania" had kept him in his tent even when he was winning.
142. Gibbon, LV, vol. 4, 93; see also Theophanes, 171.
143. Gibbon, LV, vol. 4, 93.
144. Jenkins, 126.
145. Dahmus, *SMK*, 72.
146. Jenkins, 118–20.
147. Theophanes, 158; Gibbon, XLVIII, vol. 3, 399.
148. Finlay, vol. 1, 100.
149. Gibbon, XLVIII, vol. 3, 399–400.
150. Finlay, vol. 1, 108.
151. Finlay, vol. 1, 109; Oman, *BE*, 205.
152. Finlay, vol. 1, 113*fn*1.
153. Oman, *BE*, 206; Norwich, *SHB*, 131–2; Finlay, vol. 1, 116–18; Gibbon, XLVIII, vol. 3, 401–2; Jenkins, 137–8.
154. Jenkins, 141.
155. T. T. Rice, 175–6.
156. Gibbon, XLVIII, vol. 3, 402; Finlay, vol. 1, 121–22.
157. Jenkins, 143–4.
158. Byzantium had retained Venice by terms of the *Pax Nicephori*—the agreement signed with the Franks in 812 recognizing Charlemagne's status as "Holy Roman Emperor."
159. Finlay, vol. 1, 134–35.
160. Finlay, vol. 1, 140–41; Oman, *BE*, 208–10.
161. Finlay, vol. 1, 144–47; Oman, *BE*, 210.
162. Diehl, *HBE*, 66–7; see also, Ostrogorsky, 220.
163. Ostrogorsky, 217–18.
164. The last conversion, however, necessitated the decapitation of fifty-two recalcitrant Bulgarian boyars who had fought Christianization tooth and nail (Ostrogorsky, 230).
165. Treadgold, 132.
166. Gibbon, XLVIII, vol. 3, 405.
167. Finlay, vol. 1, 161. The actual patriarch, meanwhile, was illegally deposed. The pope—who would have approved this usurpation in return for the restoration of the lands taken from the papacy a century earlier—excommunicated Uncle Bardas' handpicked patriarchal successor when this expectation was not met. The quarrel did not end until Emperor Michael had publicly derided the pope as a barbarian since the latter did not know Greek. In reply, the pope asked how Michael could be emperor of "the Romans" when he did not know Latin (Finlay, vol. 1, 168–69).
168. Norwich, *SHB*, 148, says he was not from Macedonia. Finlay, vol. 1, 214, says he was a servant of the Macedonian governor before embarking for Constantinople.
169. Finlay, vol. 1, 178.
170. Finlay, vol. 1, 181–82.
171. Gibbon, XLVIII, vol. 3, 408.
172. Fuller, vol. 1, 396–7.
173. T. T. Rice, 113.
174. Oman, *BE*, 219. The prize seems to have been received only after a defeat. Apparently, rescue of the wounded in the midst of victory was not felt to be as dangerous an enterprise.
175. Finlay, vol. 1, 262.
176. Norwich, *SHB*, 167; Gibbon, XLVIII, vol. 3, 412.
177. Leo the Deacon, cited by Jenkins, 235; Liudprand, 123.
178. Finlay, vol. 1, 273.
179. Finlay, vol. 1, 286.
180. Finlay, vol. 1, 317.
181. Liudprand, 185–6.
182. Liudprand, 186.
183. Liudprand, 193; Gibbon, XLVIII, vol. 3, 413.
184. Gibbon, XLVIII, vol. 3, 413–14; Ostrogorsky, 279.

185. Gibbon, XLVIII, vol. 3, 414.
186. Oman, *BE*, 226–27.
187. Finlay, vol. 1, 295.
188. Norwich, *Apogee*, 178.
189. Ostrogorsky, 286.
190. Finlay, vol. 1, 311.
191. Gibbon, LII, vol. 4, 43.
192. Norwich, *SHB*, 194–95; Ostrogorsky, 286.
193. Finlay, vol. 1, 310.
194. Oman, *BE*, 229–30, 232.
195. Finlay, vol. 1, 308–10; Oman, *BE*, 231–33.
196. Diehl, *BGD*, 136.
197. Finlay, vol. 1, 312*fn*2. (Gibbon, XLVIII, vol. 3, 416–17 mistakes this Basil for Theophano's son of the same name.)
198. Norwich, *Apogee*, 215.
199. Obolensky, 130; Ostrogorsky, 296; Jenkins, 298.
200. Finlay, vol. 1, 333.
201. Psellus, 31.
202. Ostrogorsky, 303.
203. Gibbon, LV, vol. 4, p. 110; Obolensky, p. 191; Jenkins, p. 307. Happily for Anna, Vladamir faithfully embraced his new religion—and gave up his 800 concubines to boot.
204. Finlay, vol. 1, 339.
205. Finlay, vol. 1, 339; Psellus, 36–37.
206. See for example Treadgold, 210 (seizure), Jenkins, 310 (stroke) and Ostrogorsky, 304 (heart attack). Basil's brother and co-emperor, Constantine, capitalized on the confusion to claim that he personally had killed Phocas (Psellus, 36).
207. Psellus, 37.
208. Brinton, et al., vol. 1, 150–1; Jenkins, 319–20; Ostogorsky, 306–7.
209. Haldon, 161.
210. Psellus, 53–4; Among the victims were members of the Sclerus, Phocas, Burtzes and Comnenos families (Finlay, vol. 1, 362–63).
211. Gibbon, XLVIII, vol. 3, 419.
212. Psellus, 82.
213. Finlay, vol. 1, 375.
214. Among the Norsemen was Harald Hardrada who would later vie for the British throne (Norwich, *SHB*, 221).
215. Norwich, *SHB*, 217; Ostrogorsky, 323.
216. Finlay, vol. 1, 383.
217. Norwich, 227–28.
218. Jenkins, 343; Ostrogorsky, 325.
219. Psellus, 115.
220. Psellus, 139.
221. The figure comes from Cedrenus (see Psellus, 203*fn*).
222. Obolensky, 225.
223. Norwich, *SHB*, 228.
224. Psellus, 198.
225. Psellus, 206–19.
226. Finlay, vol. 1, 400.
227. Diehl, *HBE*, 108–09; Previté-Orton, vol. 1, 277.
228. Jenkins, 346–47; Treadgold, 167–68; Ostrogorsky, 331–32.
229. Brinton, et al., vol. 1, p. 146; Gibbon, LX, vol. 4, 257; Durant, vol. 4, 544.
230. Michael VI was allowed to return in peace to the house in which he had lived prior to his elevation (Finlay, vol. 1, 420).
231. Norwich, *SHB*, 234–35.
232. Finlay, vol. 2, 9.
233. Finlay, vol. 1, 394.
234. Finlay, vol. 1, 406–09.
235. Oman, *BE*, 251–52.
236. Gibbon, LVII, vol. 4, 161.
237. Gibbon, LVII, vol. 4, 161.
238. Jenkins, 373.
239. Gibbon, LXVI, vol. 3, 424.
240. Finlay, vol. 2, 36.
241. Diehl, *HBE*, 107.
242. Michael, the son and heir of Constantine × Ducas, is chiefly remembered for having cheated the people on government grain sales during a time of want (Oman, *BE*, 256).
243. Anna Comnena, p. 142.
244. Gibbon, LVI, vol. 4, 133; Norwich, *SHB*, 251–2. The figure of 70,000 men is drawn from Gibbon. A modern researcher estimates it 18–20,000 (Haldon, 189).
245. Gibbon, LVI, vol. 4, 134–5; Anna Comnena, 147.
246. Anna Comnena, 148–9.
247. Diehl, *HBE*, 114.
248. Norwich, *SHB*, 265.
249. Finlay, vol. 2, 63.
250. Norwich, *SHB*, 263.
251. Oman, *BE*, 257.
252. Finlay, vol. 2, 144.
253. Finlay, vol. 2, 161–62 and 170–71.
254. Finlay, vol. 2, 172–73, 178.
255. Diehl, *HBE*, 118–19; Previté-Orton, vol. 1, 539–41; Norwich, *SHB*, 288–90.
256. Ostrogorsky, 391–4.
257. Previté-Orton, vol. 1, 541; Ostrogorsky, 394. The man she chose was the boy-emperor's cousin, Alexius, a conceited and unpopular mediocrity.
258. Geanakoplos, 365–6.
259. Gibbon, XLVIII, vol. 3, 432–7; Finlay, vol. 2, 201–08.
260. Gibbon, XLVIII, vol. 3, 439.
261. Ostrogorsky, 397; Previté-Orton, vol. 1, 542.
262. Ostrogorsky, 396–8; Previté-Orton, vol. 1, 541–2.
263. Finlay, vol. 2, 201 and 208.
264. Gibbon, XLVIII, vol. 3, 441.
265. Diehl, *BGD*, 144–5; Norwich, *SHB*, 294.
266. Gibbon, XLVIII, vol. 3, 441.
267. Gibbon, LX, vol. 4, 260.
268. Oman, *BE*, 275–76.
269. Finlay, vol. 2, 231.
270. In contrast, Alexius' talented (and conceited) wife, Euphrosyne, was an accomplished rider who dazzled the capital, cantering with a falcon on her wrist and her dogs in tow. Finlay, vol. 2, 242–44.
271. Diehl, *HBE*, 133–5.
272. Norwich, *SHB*, 301; Gibbon, LX, vol. 4, 272.
273. Gibbon, LX, vol. 4, 275.
274. Durant and Durant, vol. 4, 605; Joinville and Villhardouin, 91–2.

275. Gibbon, LX, vol. 4, 287.
276. The bronze horses seen above the doors today are replicas—the originals are on display in an upstairs museum within the cathedral.
277. Gibbon, LXI, vol. 4, 292; Norwich, *SHB*, 306.
278. Reprisal for Basil II's epithet "Bulgar-slayer" (Ostrogorsky, 429; Diehl, *HBE*, 142).
279. Diehl, *HBE*, 144–5.
280. Finlay, vol. 2, 302, 310, 312, 316–17.
281. Finlay, vol. 2, 315–16.
282. Oman, *BE*, 303–04; Finlay, vol. 2, 348.
283. Norwich, *SHB*, 315; Runciman, *SV*, 62.
284. Oman, *BE*, 305.
285. Gibbon, LXI, vol. 4, 308–9; Norwich, *SHB*, 315–16.
286. Diehl, *HBE*, 151–2; Norwich, *SHB*, 317–18.
287. Oman, *BE*, 310–11.
288. Nor would his predecessor Urban IV—see Ostrogorsky, 452.
289. Nicol, 17.
290. Norwich, *SHB*, 317.
291. Runciman, *SV*, 207.
292. Ostrogorsky, 454–5; Norwich, 318, 329–30.
293. Ostrogorsky, 457–59.
294. Norwich, *SHB*, 328; Ostrogorsky, 464; Nicol, 30, Treadgold, 205.
295. T. T. Rice, 118; Ostrogorsky, 485.
296. Finlay, vol. 2, 386.
297. Runciman, *FOC*, 27–33; Ostrogorsky, 491–92.
298. Nicol, 24–25, 27–8; Norwich, *SHB*, 332–33, 336.
299. Gibbon, LXIII, vol. 4, 347.
300. Gibbon, LXII, vol. 4, 338–42; Finlay, vol. 2, 399–407; Ostrogorsky, 493–96; Nicol, 26–27; Oman, *BE*, 317–19.
301. Norwich, *SHB*, pp. 339–40; Oman, *BE*, 323–24.
302. Finlay, vol. 2, 426.
303. Nicol, 33–35.
304. Norwich, *SHB*, 342. Many authorities disagree with this assessment.
305. Norwich, *SHB*, 343; Ostrogorsky, 515.
306. Oman, *BE*, 328.
307. Gibbon, LXIII, vol. 4, 353.
308. Finlay, vol. 2, 443.
309. Gibbon, LXIII, vol. 4, 353; Finlay, vol. 2, 439; Norwich, *SHB*, 344.
310. Finlay, vol. 2, 446.
311. Runciman, *FOC*, 4.
312. Ostrogorsky, 523–5.
313. Gibbon, LXIII, vol. 4, 361.
314. Kinross, 41.
315. Gibbon, LXIV, vol. 4, 387.
316. Froissart (*COF*), 446–7. (Froissart, admittedly, claims only 300 were victimized, but other chroniclers put the figure at 10,000—see Kinross, 69.)
317. Weatherford, 13; Larousse, vol. 1, 346.
318. Gibbon, LXIV, vol. 4, p. 364. (Weatherford, disagrees, saying that Genghis was actually defeated in this battle and that seventy of his own followers were boiled alive [41].)
319. Liddell Hart, 13–16; Chambers, 9–14.
320. Gibbon, LXIV, vol. 4, 373; see also Chambers, 99.
321. Weatherford, 156–7; Chambers, 105.
322. Weatherford, 158.
323. Liddell Hart, 18–20; Chambers, 24–5.
324. Liddell Hart, pp. 9–10 and 28; Chambers, 59–63.
325. Chambers, 55–6; Livesey, 31.
326. Reischauer, et al., vol. 1, 266.
327. Gibbon, LXIV, vol. 4, 374.
328. Gibbon, LXV, vol. 4, 396.
329. Larousse, vol. 1, 393 (Herat); Gibbon, LXV, vol. 4, 401–2 (Siwas).
330. Wells, 726.
331. Kinross, 76.
332. Kinross, 76; Goodwin, 27. (According to Gibbon, she was not nude, but merely exposed without a veil—LXV, vol. 4, 408.)
333. Goodwin, 27.
334. Gibbon, LXV, vol. 4, 410.
335. Fuller, vol. 1, 502.
336. Oman, *BE*, 341.
337. Gibbon, LXVII, vol. 4, 469.
338. Gibbon, LXVII, vol. 4, 467.
339. Kinross, 91.
340. Another survivor was the Prince of Wallachia, Vlad Dracul ("the Dragon"), the original "Count Dracula," who, contrary to legend, was no vampire, but a former worker in the Hungarian mint. (His more infamous son, Vlad the Impaler—upon whom the Dracula myth is based—wasn't a vampire either, though he did impale a disproportionate number of people on wooden stakes while ridding Wallachia of the Turks in the 1450s.)
341. Nicol, 83; Ostrogorsky, 567.
342. The Greeks called the fort "*Rumeli Hisar*" or Romeland Castle (Kinross, 98).
343. Runciman, *FOC*, 66–7; Goodwin, 31; Gibbon, LXVIII, vol. 4, 481.
344. Gibbon, LXVIII, vol. 4, 483.
345. Runciman, *FOC*, 96.
346. Fuller, vol. 1, 516; Runciman, *FOC*, 119; also Gibbon, LXVIII, vol. 4, 490–1.
347. Finlay, vol. 2, 511.
348. Runciman, *FOC*, 108; Gibbon, LXVIII, vol. 4, 494–5; Goodwin, 37.
349. Norwich, *SHB*, 377; Runciman, *FOC*, 114–20.
350. Finlay, vol. 2, 514; Gibbon, LXVIII, vol. 4, 497.
351. Gibbon, LXVIII, vol. 4, 497–8.
352. Oman, *BE*, 348.
353. Gibbon, LXVIII, vol. 4, 499.
354. Runciman, *FOC*, 143–4.
355. Finlay, vol. 2, 518; Oman, *BE*, 349.
356. Oman, *BE*, 349–50.
357. Kinross, 113–20; Runciman, *FOC*, 158–9.
358. See Jenkins, 383; Runciman, *FOC*, 190; Brinton, et al., vol. 1, 151. The Western detractor of Byzantium would do well to recall that the culture of the empire did not descend to its nadir until the period of the Latin conquest, when Western "crusaders," rather than Byzantines, ruled the empire.
359. Diehl, *BGD*, 227.
360. Brinton, et al., vol. 1, 140–3; T. T. Rice, 132–4.

361. Brinton, et al., vol. 1, 139.
362. T. T. Rice, 52.
363. Diehl, *BGD*, 54.
364. Liudprand, 207–8.
365. T. T. Rice, 57–8; Brinton, et al., vol. 1, 145.
366. The West, in AD 968, considered its own ruler, Otto I, to be the Holy "Roman" Emperor.
367. Liudprand, 263–4. (*Embassy to Constantinople*, chapter 47.)
368. Frank, 583.
369. Diehl, *BGD*, 233.
370. Diehl, *BGD*, 21. (The first two were heroes of 5th century BC Athens, the third of 4th century BC Thebes.)
371. Durant and Durant, vol. 4, 442–3; C. H. King, vol. 1, 268–71.
372. Durant and Durant, vol. 4, 434.
373. Diehl, *BGD*, 262–3.
374. Diehl, *BGD*, 261.
375. For a more intriguing description, see De Camp, 285–86.
376. C. H. King, vol. 1, 272–5; Durant, vol. 4, 130–1.
377. De Camp, 309–10.
378. Singer, 156–7.
379. Durant and Durant, vol. 4, 241. One of his treatises is entitled *On the Numerals of the Indians*.
380. Dahmus, *HMA*, 188.
381. Durant and Durant, vol. 4, 246–47.
382. Durant and Durant, vol. 4, 249.
383. Ja. Burke, *DUC*, 36–44.
384. Stark, 60.
385. Durant and Durant, vol. 4, 330.
386. Durant and Durant, vol. 4, 236–37.
387. Wells, 632 and 750–1; Van Doren, 154.

Section II

1. J. B. Bury, *LRE*, vol. 2, 280.
2. Gibbon, XLIII, vol. 3, 196–7.
3. Gibbon, XLIII, vol. 3, 197; J. B. Bury, *LRE*, vol. 2, 280*fn*2.
4. Oman, *BE*, 119.
5. Gibbon, XLV, vol. 3, 265.
6. Munro, *TMA*, 56; Gibbon, XLV, vol. 3, 268.
7. The Byzantines were delighted to receive the princess, but not her lover. Confident that she could make new friends, Rosamond served her unwanted companion a cup of poison. The act undid them both: He recognized the potion for what it was after imbibing just half, and insisted at knife point that she drink the rest (Gibbon, XLV, vol. 3, 267–69).
8. Gibbon, XLV, vol. 3, 281.
9. C. H. King, 244–5 and 401–8.
10. Munro, *HMA*, 4.
11. Ja. Burke, *DUC*, 20.
12. C. H. King, 399–401.
13. C. H. King, 411–12.
14. Hollister, *SH*, 58–60; C. H. King, 248–9; Durant and Durant, vol. 4, 58–60. One of Simeon's disciples surpassed this record (T.T. Rice, 76), but originality ought to count for something.
15. F. Ogg, 87; Durant and Durant, v. 4, 518.
16. Durant and Durant, vol. 4, 517; O'Sullivan and Burns, 276.
17. Gibbon, XLV, vol. 3, 284–85.
18. Hollister, *SH*, 64.
19. Wells, 644; Hollister, *SH*, 65.
20. Asimov, 127.
21. So-named after his grandfather, Merowig, who fought alongside Aetius at Chalons against Attila (Gibbon, vol. 2, XXXV, 497; Fuller, vol. 1, 341).
22. Gregory of Tours, II.27, 140.
23. Thatcher and Swill, 84.
24. Gregory of Tours, II.30, 143.
25. Gregory of Tours, II.42, 158. (The quote is from Guizot, *France*, vol. 1, 122.)
26. Previté-Orton, v. 1, 152.
27. Gregory of Tours, IV.20, 216.
28. Guizot, *France*, vol. 1, 139.
29. Guizot, *France*, vol. 1, 140–42.
30. Thatcher and Schwill, 90.
31. Guizot, *France*, vol. 1, 142.
32. Thatcher and Schwill, 91–92.
33. Hollister, *SH*, 84–85.
34. i.e., "Rock of Tarik" (Gibbon, vol. 3, 609; Durant and Durant, vol. 4, 291; Brinton, vol. 1, 161).
35. Creasy, 170–71.
36. Creasy, 173; Fuller, vol. 1, 345.
37. Creasy, 175.
38. Fuller (vol. 1, 347), however, argues that the triumph of Leo III at Constantinople fifteen years earlier was far more decisive in this regard.
39. Gibbon, LII, vol. 4, 15. This report may be overstated, however, since Charles was also a generous patron of "the Apostle of Germany," Saint Boniface of Fulda—the famed Benedictine whose lifework wrought close ties between the mayors and the papacy.
40. Asimov, 125.
41. Einhard, II, 18–19.
42. Einhard, I (Turner's translation, 16–17).
43. Einhard, I (Turner's translation, 16).
44. Winston, 22.
45. Winston, 22.
46. The same Benedictine monk who had been courted by Charles Martel (see note 39).
47. Durant and Durant, vol. 4, 525; C. H. King, vol. 1, 308.
48. *Encyclopædia Britannica*, vol. 8, 408–09.
49. Thatcher and Schwill, 248–51.
50. Wells, 555–56.
51. Wells, 556.
52. Gibbon, XLIX, vol. 3, 474.
53. Winston, 29–31; O'Sullivan and Burns, 373; Previté-Orton, vol. 1, 303–4.
54. F. Ogg, 115 and 131–2.
55. Previté-Orton, vol. 1, 306.
56. Winston, 70.
57. Winston, 123.
58. Lamb, 37–8.
59. Durant and Durant, vol. 4, 462; Winston, 45–6.
60. Lamb, 64.
61. Winston, 52.
62. Gibbon, XLIX, vol. 3, 475–6.
63. Hollister, 109; Winston, 141.

Notes—Section II

64. C. H. King, 321; Thatcher and Schwill, 125.
65. Thatcher and Schwill, 127.
66. Bemont and Monod, 187; Gibbon, XLIX, vol. 3, 470; Einhard, XXVIII, 65; Wells, 652.
67. Einhard, XXVIII, 66. (Modern historians argue that he did not object to the crown, but to the notion that the authority to confer one rested with the Pope rather than with himself.)
68. O'Sullivan and Burns, 378; Winston, 93–5; Previté-Orton, vol. 1, 313.
69. Winston, 98–102; Previté-Orton, vol. 1, 313 and 328.
70. Durant and Durant, vol. 4, 469.
71. Scholz, 87; Einhard, XVI, 43–4.
72. Hollister, *SH*, p. 94.
73. F. Ogg, 108–9; Einhard, XVII; De Camp, 341; Dahmus, *SMK*, 137.
74. Winston, 86; Gibbon, XLIX, vol. 3, 476; Previté-Orton, 325; Dahmus, *SMK*, 137.
75. Dahmus, *SMK*, 113–19.
76. Dahmus, *SMK*, 134.
77. Einhard, XXV (Turner's translation, 62).
78. Hollister, *SH*, 98; Ja. Burke, *DUC*, 24–5; Winston, 59–60; Dahmus, *SMK*, 136; Lamb, 192.
79. Hollister, *SH*, 93; Previté-Orton, vol. 1, 319.
80. Bémont and Monod, 185.
81. Thatcher and Schwill, 123.
82. Munro, *TMA,* 116 (also, Dahmus, *HMA,* 209; Previté-Orton, vol. 1, 342).
83. Hollister, *SH*, 104–6; C. H. King, vol. 1, 317.
84. Bémont and Monod, 218.
85. Thatcher and Schwill, 147.
86. Hollister, *SH,* 108.
87. The name "Russia" derives from the term applied to the Swedes by the indigenous population (see Brinton, et al., vol. 1, 156).
88. Scholz (introduction), 23.
89. Duckett, 17.
90. Bémont and Monod, 234; F. Ogg, 166; Durant and Durant, vol. 4, 474; C. H. King, 329.
91. Wells, 637–38; Brinton, et al., vol. 1, 123; C. H. King, 325–26.
92. Wells, 638.
93. *Encyclopædia Britannica*, vol. 10, 300. (Also quoted in Wells, 638.)
94. Thatcher and Schwill, 218–19.
95. Munro, *TMA,* 121; Previté-Orton, vol. 1, 348.
96. Munro, *TMA,* 123.
97. The quoted passages are from the *Chronicle of St. Denys*, in Guizot, *France,* vol. 1, 210.
98. Bémont and Monod, 245.
99. Munro, *TMA,* 151. In 896, Arnulf was crowned emperor by Pope Formosus—an act that was so resented in Italy that when Formosus died, the next pope exhumed his corpse and put it on trial at a church synod. Though clad in his papal attire, Formosus was unable to offer an effective defense. Convicted on all counts, his body was cast into the Tiber (Thatcher and Schwill, 177).
100. Gibbon, LV, vol. 4, 97–8.
101. Bémont and Monod, 230.
102. Thatcher and Schwill, 167.
103. Asimov, 135; Dahmus, *HMA*, 218; Bémont and Monod, p. 270.
104. Thatcher and Schwill, 167–68.
105. Thatcher and Schwill, 169.
106. Thatcher and Schwill, 170.
107. O'Sullivan and Burns, 420.
108. Gibbon, LV, vol. 4, p. 100; see also Liudprand, 85.
109. Liudprand, 86.
110. Thatcher and Schwill, 171.
111. Larousse, vol. 1, 287–8.
112. Hollister, *SS*, 102–3.
113. Gibbon, LV, vol. 4, 101.
114. Hollister, *SS*, 104.
115. Liudprand, 93.
116. Liudprand, 132.
117. Gibbon, XLIX, vol. 3, 482. (Marozia rose to become Senatrix of Rome, and had she not been unseated by a disinherited son from a previous marriage, she and her last husband, Hugh of Provence, might have been crowned Emperor and Empress [Chamberlin, 32 and 35–7].)
118. See Theophylact family tree in Chamberlin, 24 and text, 64–5.
119. Gibbon, XLIX, vol. 3, p. 482.
120. Gibbon, XLIX, vol. 3, p. 482.
121. Chamberlin, 50–8; Liudprand, 216–29.
122. Liudprand, 231.
123. Hollister, *SH*, 127.
124. Previte-Orton, v. 1, 443.
125. Munro, *TMA*, 159.
126. Ja. Burke, *DUC*, 33; Durant and Durant, vol. 4, 539 and 989; Singh, 55.
127. Bémont and Monod, 280.
128. Gibbon, XLIX, vol. 3, 484; Durant and Durant, vol. 4, 513 and 539.
129. Previte-Orton, vol. 1, 449.
130. C. H. King, vol. 1, 381 and 405.
131. Thatcher and Schwill, 220.
132. Munro, *TMA*, 163–4.
133. Durant and Durant, vol. 4, 546–47; Hollister, *SH*, 221–22; Munro, *TMA*, 168.
134. J. H. Robinson, *Readings*, vol. 1, p. 279.
135. Munro, *TMA*, pp. 170–1.
136. Thatcher and Schwill, 262; J. H. Robinson, *History*, 194–95.
137. Thatcher and Schwill, 262–64.
138. Thatcher and Schwill, 264–65.
139. J. H. Robinson, *History*, vol. 1, 199.
140. Thatcher and Schwill, 261, 265.
141. Indeed, according to Churchill, a larger fraction of the population had central heating by hypocaust in AD 300 than by modern equipment in 1900 (Churchill, vol. 1, 35).
142. Churchill, vol. 1, 52–4.
143. Bede, I.15 (Giles translation in *EHEN*, 31).
144. Previte-Orton, vol. 1, 169; Durant and Durant, vol. 4, 81; Giles, p. 408; Churchill, vol. 1, 58–61.
145. Durant and Durant, vol. 1, 81.
146. Churchill, vol. 1, 85.
147. F. Ogg, p. 181; Churchill, vol. 1, 95.
148. Swanton, 69.
149. Jo. Burke, 29–30.
150. Thatcher and Schwill, 197.
151. Duckett, 79; Asser, 84.

152. *Anglo-Saxon Chronicle* for the year 896, in Asser, 118–19.
153. Churchill, vol. 1, 119; see also *Anglo-Saxon Chronicle* for the year 896.
154. Previte-Orton, v. 1, 398.
155. *Encyclopædia Britannica*, vol. 12, 935.
156. D. Howarth, *1066*, 108–15.
157. *Encyclopædia Britannica*, vol. 28, 659.
158. Thorpe (*Bayeaux Tapestry,* plate 20, not paginated).
159. Guizot, *England*, vol. 1, 98.
160. Brooke, 86; Swanton, 195–7.
161. D. Howarth, *1066,* 135.
162. Goodenough, 15; D. Howarth, *1066,* 169–70.
163. Thorpe, 29 (citing the Norman chronicler, Robert Wace).
164. Thatcher and Schwill, 208; *Encyclopædia Britannica*, vol. 28, 660.
165. Munro, *TMA*, 186; Newhall, 17; Previte-Orton, vol.1, 507.
166. The same who sacked Rome in 1084 (vide infra).
167. Previte-Orton, vol. 1, 519.
168. Gibbon, LVIII, vol. 4, 178.
169. Thantcher and Schwill, 219.
170. J. H. Robinson, *Readings*, vol. 1, 313–15.
171. Funck-Brentano, 102.
172. S. Howarth, 30.
173. Funck-Brentano, 102.
174. Mills, 40*fn.*
175. Gibbon, LVIII, vol. 4, 183–4.
176. Stark, 126.
177. Tuchman, *BAS,* 57–8; Runciman, *HC* vol. 1, 134–40.
178. Wells, 672–3.
179. Runciman, *Crusades,* vol. 1, 124; Brinton, et al., vol. 1, 226; Funck-Brentano, 105.
180. Funck-Brentano, 105.
181. *Encyclopædia Britannica,* vol. 7, 526.
182. Funck-Brentano, 106.
183. Runciman, *HC,* vol. 1, 128; Funck-Brentano, 106; Anna Comnena, 311.
184. Anna Comnena, 313. (Anna says Peter was among the rescued but most authorities agree that Peter returned to Constantinople before the battle—see, for example, Gibbon, vol. 4, LVIII, 188, Durant, vol. 4, 589; and Runciman, *HC*, vol. 1, 130–1.)
185. Anna Comnena, 312–13 (see also Funck-Brentano, 107 and Gibbon, LVIII, vol. 4, 188).
186. S. Howarth, 36; Runciman, *HC*, vol. 1, 179.
187. Funck-Brentano, 111.
188. Funck-Brentano, 114.
189. Funck-Brentano, 116 (source: *La Chanson d'Antioche,* ed. P. Paris, 1848).
190. Some believe it was a Saracen lance head that Bartholomew himself had secretly contrived to bury there (Gibbon, LVIII, vol. 4, 209).
191. D. Wright, 91.
192. William of Tyre, 238 (spelling and punctuation updated for clarity).
193. Stark, 155–57; Runciman, *HC*, vol. 1, 279–85.
194. Runciman, *HC*, vol. 1, 286–87.
195. J. H. Robinson, *Readings*, vol. 1, p. 327.
196. William of Tyre, 273–4 (spelling modernized by the author).
197. Funck-Brentano, 122; see also Mills, 153*fn.*
198. Anna Comnena, 366–7.
199. Thatcher and Schwill, 393–94.
200. C. H. King, vol. 1, 465–7 and 491–8.
201. Hollister, *SH,* 153–4; Funck-Brentano, 144; Dahmus, *HMA*, 263.
202. Ja. Burke, *DUC*, 40–4.
203. Thatcher and Schwill, 161–62.
204. Thatcher and Schwill, 484–85.
205. Funck-Brentano, 127 and 131.
206. J. H. Robinson, *Readings*, vol. 1, p. 203.
207. Funck-Brentano, 136–8.
208. Bémont and Monod, 401–2.
209. Durant and Durant, v. 4, 595; Thatcher and Schwill, 403.
210. Runciman, *HC*, vol. 2, pp. 281–4; Munro, *TMA*, 254.
211. Dahmus, *SMK*, p. 138; Funck-Brentano, p. 139.
212. Munro, *HMA,* 214.
213. Durant and Durant, vol. 4, 828.
214. C. H. King, vol. 1, 368–9.
215. Brooke, 183–4.
216. Thatcher and Schwill, 517.
217. Bémont and Monod, 456.
218. So named, say most authorities, because he was born in August, though Previté-Orton (vol. 2, 703) believes it to be a corruption of the Latin "augere," since he greatly augmented the royal domains during his reign.
219. Funck-Brentano, 254; O'Sullivan and Burns, 403.
220. Possibly the site of Jesus' Sermon on the Mount (S. Howarth 153).
221. Newhall, 64; S. Howarth, 153.
222. Bémont and Monod, 314–15; Previté-Orton, vol. 1, 574–5.
223. England's Plantagenet Kings had formerly been Dukes of Anjou—thus the adjective "Angevin" is frequently used to designate their continental holdings.
224. Joinville and Villehardouin, 183; Joinville, 109; Munro, *TMA*, 302.
225. Tuchman, *BAS*, 72; Churchill, vol. 1, 233; S. Howarth, 174–5.
226. Bémont and Monod, 405.
227. Guizot, *England*, vol. 1, 202; see also Funck-Brentano, 259.
228. Funck-Brentano, 259.
229. Brinton, et al., vol. 1, 195; *Encyclopædia Britannica*, vol. 15, 439; Durant and Durant, vol. 4, 674.
230. Hollister, *SH,* 231.
231. O'Shea, 10–11; Hollister, *SH*, 205; Previté-Orton, vol. 2, 662. Their tolerance of the Jews was another black mark against them (O'Shea, 53).
232. Brinton, et al., vol. 1, 180; Hollister, *SH*, 232.
233. Allshorn, 34.
234. Funck-Brentano, 281–2.
235. F. Ogg, 302–3.
236. De Camp, 346.
237. Jo. Burke, 56; Brooke, 223; Previté-Orton, vol. 2, 723.
238. O'Shea, *PH,* 112–6.

239. O'Shea, *PH*, 130–1.
240. Funck-Brentano, 272.
241. O'Shea, *PH*, 133–49; Funck-Brentano, 273–4.
242. From the *Chanson de la Croisade* (Funck-Brentano, 276).
243. F. Ogg, 314; Joinville and Villehardouin, 182; Joinville, 108.
244. Joinville and Villehardouin, 191; Joinville, 116.
245. Joinville, 123.
246. Joinville and Villehardouin, 201–03; Joinville, 123–25.
247. The same itinerary had been employed once before: during the ill-fated Fifth Crusade (1217–1221), wherein the Christian host had been lured forward and trapped—their route of retreat being flooded by the opening of the Nile dikes. Had it not been for the mercy of the Egyptian Sultan, Al-Kamil, those crusaders would not have lived to tell the tale.
248. Joinville and Villehardouin, 209; Joinville, 130.
249. Funck-Brentano, 310; Joinville and Villehardouin, 219; Joinville, 140.
250. Gibbon, LIX, vol. 4, 250.
251. Joinville, 158–9; see also Joinville and Villehardouin, 236–7.
252. Joinville and Villehardouin, 239–46; Joinville, 161–71.
253. Dahmus, *SMK*, 246–47, 250.
254. Durant and Durant, vol. 4, 693; Dahmus, 247.
255. Durant and Durant, vol. 4, 692; Asimov, 166.
256. Bémont and Monod, 433.
257. Bémont and Monod, 433.
258. Graetz, vol. 3, 571.
259. Thatcher and Schwill, 495–99.
260. Thatcher and Schwill, 495–96.
261. Bémont and Monod, 462.
262. Churchill, vol. 1, 273.
263. Churchill, vol. 1, 278.
264. Churchill, vol. 1, 280–2.
265. Jo. Burke, 58.
266. C. H. King, vol. 1, 387–8.
267. Durant and Durant, vol. 4, 718–20; Dahmus, *SMK*, 207 and 220.
268. Wells, 683.
269. Dahmus, *SMK*, 221.
270. Dahmus, *HMA*, 304.
271. Larousse, vol. 1, 325.
272. Dahmus, *HMA*, 304.
273. Dahmus, *SMK*, 206.
274. Dahmus, *SMK*, 221.
275. Dahmus, *SMK*, 224; Larousse, vol. 1, 325.
276. Allshorn, 65–6.
277. Dahmus, *HMA*, 304; Allshorn, 93 and 122; Runciman, *SV*, 34.
278. Burckhardt, 5–6.
279. Dahmus, *SMK*, 211–12.
280. C. H. King, vol. 1, 387.
281. Durant and Durant, vol. 4, 717.
282. In 1242, the hapless youth fell, or jumped, into a gorge while in transit to another jail.
283. Dahmus, *SMK*, 230; Allshorn, 153–5.
284. Allshorn, 158.
285. Allshorn, 122 and 259–62; Previte-Orton, vol. 2, 693.

286. Previte-Orton, vol. 2, 701. (Lucera was a colony of transplanted Saracens founded in southern Italy by Frederick II after he pacified the island of Sicily at the outset of his reign.)
287. Runciman, *SV*, 118–25.
288. Runciman, *SV*, 127–31.
289. See Section I.
290. The name derives from the family domicile "Habichtsburg" or "Hawk's Castle" (*Encyclopædia Britannica*, vol. 12, 787).
291. Brinton, et al., vol. 1, 275.
292. Thatcher and Schwill, 306.
293. Previte-Orton, v. 2, 658.
294. Durant and Durant, vol. 4, 606.
295. Wells, 692.
296. Brinton, et al., vol. 1, 209.
297. Jo. Burke, 58; Dahmus, *HMA*, 355; C. H. King, 375.
298. The Welsh Prince, Llewellyn the Last, was killed in ambush in that year. Thenceforth, heirs to the English throne assumed the title "Prince of Wales."
299. Churchill, vol. 1, 301–2; Scott, 16.
300. D. Ross, *Wallace*, pp. 20–1; Scott, p. 35; Mackay, p. 74.
301. The story may be apocryphal, but the Wright family nicknamed their first-born sons "Pin," ever after (D. Ross, *WW*, 72).
302. D. Ross, *WW*, 72–3.
303. D. Ross, *WW*, 97. (The *schiltrons* were of Wallace's own devising, and served as a prototype for the British square of a later age—Mackay, 178.)
304. Oman, *AWMA*, 120–1; Mackay, 194–9; D. Ross, *WW*, 96–9.
305. Lodge, 49.
306. Lodge, 29; Larousse, vol. 1, 332–33.
307. Wells, 692.
308. *Encyclopædia Britannica*, vol. 4, 207.
309. Dahmus, *HMA*, 361.
310. Oman, *AWMA*, 77–88; Waley, 91–94.
311. The parade of rulers were of varying caliber. One broiled his chef on a spit for serving an unsatisfactory meal (L.B. Smith, *EW*, p. 19).
312. Lodge, 102.
313. Thatcher and Schwill, 556–57.
314. *Encyclopædia Britannica*, vol. 12, 207–08.
315. From James Bryce, *The Holy Roman Empire* (new ed., New York, 1904), 234 (quoted in F. Ogg, 410).
316. Thatcher and Schwill, 559*fn*.
317. Lodge, 118–19.
318. Funck-Brentano, 364–70.
319. Previté-Orton, vol. 2, 789–90; Funck-Brentano, 392–5; Asimov, 176.
320. Lodge, 53.
321. Funck-Brentano, 402–3.
322. The order held all goods in common, thus the initiate's wealth was forfeit.
323. O'Sullivan and Burns, 605.
324. S. Howarth, 258–9; Funck-Brentano, 410.
325. D. Ross, *RB*, 87–91; Scott, 158–61; Churchill, vol. 1, 313–15.
326. Froissart, translated by Bourchier in *COF*, 11; see also *FC*, 44; *CEFS*, I.13, 18.

327. Seward, *HYW*, 20; D. Ross, *RB*, 117; Churchill, vol. 1, 319; Scott, 216.
328. Fuller, vol. 1, 444.
329. Thatcher and Schwill, 510; Lodge, 66–67.
330. Lodge, 68.
331. Seward, *HYW*, 30, Lodge, 67.
332. Thatcher and Schwill, 529.
333. Seward, *HYW*, 31.
334. Lodge, 70–71. Some Flemish cloth makers moved their operations to England.
335. Lodge, 71.
336. Seward, *HYW*, 36.
337. Tuchman, *DM*, 70–1; Seward, *HYW*, 47.
338. Seward, *HYW*, 53–5; Tuchman, *DM*, 70.
339. The prohibition was issued in 1337 by Edward III (Tuchman, *DM*, 70).
340. Previte-Orton, vol. 2, 876–7 and 889.
341. Lodge, 75.
342. Froissart, *CEFS*, I.128, 81.
343. Froissart, *CEFS*, I.129, 82.
344. Tuchman, *DM*, 91.
345. Froissart, *CEFS*, I.144, 90.
346. The original source is Gabriel de Mussis of Piacenza; excerpts can be found in Gasquet, 4–6 and *JAMA*, 196:179–82. See also: Ziegler, 15–16; Cartwright and Biddiss, 36–7; Sutcliffe and Duin, 30; McNeill, 147; Bray, 55 and Margotta, 61.
347. Gasquet, 140; see also, Carey, 48.
348. Cartwright, 37; Ross and McLaughlin, 174.
349. Gasqet, 67; Tuchman, *DM*, 93–4; Ziegler, 111–12.
350. Tuchman, *DM*, 92; see also Ziegler, 19–20.
351. Churchill, vol. 1, 352.
352. Ziegler, 198; Ross and McLaughlin, 219–20; Tuchman, *DM*, 97; Gasquet, 160.
353. Ziegler, 85.
354. Boccaccio, 8; see also Ziegler, 48.
355. Gardner, 25–6 (see also Ziegler, 58; Sutcliffe and Duin, 30).
356. Sutcliffe and Duin, 31; Cartwright and Biddiss, 30–1; Ziegler, 19–29; Tuchman, *DM*, 92; Durant and Durant, vol. 5, 30; Haggard, 178–9.
357. Cartwright and Biddiss, 50.
358. Sutcliffe and Duin, 31. (Healthy family members were confined with the sick.)
359. Cartwright and Biddiss, 37; Haggard, 176; Tuchman, *DM*, 94–5; Carey, 48.
360. Ziegler, 67; Tuchman, *DM*, 105; Hecker, 53–4.
361. Durant and Durant, vol. 6, 244; Tuchman, *DM*, 100; Haggard, 178.
362. Ziegler, 114; Sutcliffe and Duin, 31; Hecker, 27.
363. Tuchman, *DM*, 113; Ziegler, 103; Hecker, 40.
364. Hecker, 42; see also Ross and McLaughlin, 174–6.
365. Hecker, 42; Durant and Durant, vol. 6, 730; Cartwright and Biddiss, 46; Ziegler, 106.
366. Cartwright and Biddiss, 46–7; Ziegler, 95 and 106.
367. Gasquet, 29–30 (also, Tuchman, *DM*, 99; Ziegler, 45).
368. Seward, *HYW*, 87.
369. Froissart, *CEFS*, I.161, 104.
370. Tuchman, *DM*, 149–50.
371. Ross and McLaughlin, 108.
372. Ross and McLaughlin, 111.
373. Froissart, *CEFS*, I.163, 106.
374. Tuchman, *DM*, 151.
375. Guizot, *France*, vol. 2, 104.
376. Froissart, *CEFS*, I.163, 106.
377. Denis de Morbecque, a French knight who had enlisted with the English after being exiled from France.
378. Froissart, *CEFS*, I.163, 106.
379. Froissart, *FC*, 147–50; *CEFS*, I,169–178, 109–12; Durant and Durant, vol. 6, 66–7.
380. Froissart, CEFS, I.181–3, 113.
381. Previté-Orton, vol. 2, 881; O'Sullivan and Burns, 695–6.
382. Froissart, *FC*, 160; *CEFS*, I.187, 115.
383. Seward, *HYW*, 81–2.
384. Lodge, 88–89; Thatcher and Schwill, 530–31.
385. The 14th century epic poet, Cuvelier, said of du Guesclin that "there was none so ugly from Rennes to Dinant" (quoted in Tuchman, *DM*, 226).
386. Lodge, 95.
387. Froissart, *FC*, 178; *CEFS*, I.288–90, 199–200.
388. Seward, *HYW*, 110.
389. Durant and Durant, vol. 6, 39–40.
390. Froissart, *CEFS*, II.73, 283. (Punctuation slightly altered for clarity.)
391. Froissart, *CEFS*, II.73, 283.
392. Froissart, *CEFS*, II.73, 284.
393. Froissart, *FC*, 217; *CEFS*, II.75, 285.
394. Froissart, *CEFS*, II.75, 285.
395. *Encyclopædia Britannica*, vol. 27, 495–96.
396. Froissart, *CEFS*, II.76, 287.
397. Guizot, *England*, 349.
398. Fuller, vol. 1, 469.
399. This practice of purchasing military loyalty with cash is considered by historians to be so burlesque a caricature of the old feudal loyalties that historians now refer to it as "bastard feudalism."
400. Froissart, *FC*, 426–32; *CEFS*, IV.88–92, 596–602.
401. Churchill, vol. 1, 387–8.
402. Churchill, vol. 1, 388–9.
403. Guizot, *England*, vol. 1, 357.
404. Guizot, *England*, vol. 1, 358; Froissart, *CEFS*, IV. 112, 617.
405. Lodge, 318–19.
406. Gordon, 32; Seward, *HYW*, 143. (Froissart says none were killed.)
407. Seward, *HYW*, 143; Gordon, 32.
408. Lodge, 322.
409. Seward, *HYW*, 148.
410. Thatcher and Schwill, 532; Guizot, *England*, vol. 1, 383.
411. A complete farce at this stage, since the claim (through Isabel, daughter of Philip the Fair and mother of Edward III), if it had any validity, belonged rightfully not to Henry but to the Earl of March (Guizot, *England*, vol. 1, 383).
412. Seward, *HYW*, 163; Keegan, *FOB*, 88; Tuchman, *DM*, 584.
413. Guizot, *England*, vol. 1, 388.

Notes—Section II

414. Wavrin, 203; see also Carey, 70.
415. Keegan, *FOB*, 91, see also Livesey, 42; Seward, *HYW*, 166.
416. Wavrin, 211; Carey, 73. Keegan suggests a better explanation for the head bowing: the curved top-surface of the helmet would deflect the arrows (*FOB*, 98).
417. Livesey, 41.
418. Livesey, 41–2; Wavrin, 212; Carey, 74.
419. Wavrin, 215; Carey, 76.
420. Lodge, 332.
421. Guizot, *England*, vol. 1, 394.
422. Thomas Basin, quoted in J. H. Robinson, vol. 1, *Readings*, 475.
423. See Pernoud and Clin, 10.
424. Creasy, 227.
425. Creasy, 232.
426. Thatcher and Schwill, 534.
427. Guizot, *France*, vol. 2, 279; see also Pernoud and Clin, 135; Durant, vol. 6, 86.
428. Pernoud and Clin, 136; Gordon, 129.
429. Guizot, *France*, vol. 2, 279; see also Durant and Durant, vol. 6, 86; Fuller, vol. 1, 493; Pernoud and Clin, 137.
430. Lodge, 351.
431. Lodge, 353–53.
432. Tuchman, *DM*, 594.
433. Thatcher and Schwill, 535.
434. Froissart, *CEFS*, II.12, 235.
435. Froissart, *CEFS*, II.12, 236.
436. Lodge, 196.
437. Lodge, 197–201.
438. Asimov, 182; Durant and Durant, vol. 6, 36*fn*.
439. Lodge, 219–20.
440. Lodge, 220; Thatcher and Schwill, 581.
441. Tuchman, *A DM*, 591; Previté-Orton, vol. 2, 967.
442. Asimov, 195 (plague as the cause of death). Durant and Durant, vol. 6, 169 (war drum).
443. Wells, 745.
444. Durant and Durant, vol. 6, 170.
445. Previté-Orton, vol. 2, 968–9.
446. Wells, 449–52, 476–78.
447. Durant and Durant, vol. 4, 991; *Encyclopædia Britannica*, vol. 5, 249. It may be added that it is false to accuse the learned men of the Middle Ages of believing the world to be flat, for Aristotle thought the sphere to be perfect, and the scholars of medieval times, taking his cue, assumed the earth to be spherical (Singer, 176).
448. Singer, 138.
449. Brinton, et al., vol. 1, 126.
450. Ja. Burke, *DUC*, 104–7.
451. *Encyclopædia Britannica*, vol. 8, 954–55.
452. The example of the horse is taken from Thatcher and Schwill, 592.
453. Thatcher and Schwill, 593.
454. *Encyclopædia Britannica*, vol. 8, 955. (The quote is by Ernest Renan.)
455. Ja. Burke, *DUC*, 44–5; Durant and Durant, vol. 4, 939–40; Dahmus, *HMA*, 329.
456. Bémont and Monod, 518–19.
457. C. H. King, vol. 1, 423–4.
458. Hollister, *SH*, 213 and 298.
459. Hollister, *SH,* 208; Walsh, 267.
460. J. H. Robinson, vol. 2, 43.
461. Munro, *HMA*, 163.
462. Thatcher and Schwill, 598.
463. Munro, *HMA*, 166.
464. The supplanted German tribal law, which reigned for much of the period, stands out as a glaring example of unenlightened thinking. An accused person could, as a first and reasonable step, attempt to clear himself through a process known as compurgation, wherein he simply brought forward witnesses to testify to his innocence. But if he was unable to produce the requisite "compurgators," or if the testimony of his witnesses was not believed, the issue got a good deal thornier. The defendant would now have to clear his name by ordeal, which might include recovering a small object from a kettle of boiling water (ordeal by hot water), walking across hot charcoal or through a column of fire (ordeal by fire), or undergoing the ordeal by cold water. At first glance, this last option might seem preferable, but an explanation of the rules prompts reconsideration: The defendant was hurled into a body of water with his hands and feet tied. If he sank, his innocence was proclaimed. The happy man would be dragged from the depths, coughing and sputtering, and if he survived, he was free to go. If, however, in his effort to avoid drowning, he managed to stay afloat, he was declared guilty, since it was reasoned that the "pure" water had rejected him as impure (F. Ogg, 196–7; Durant and Durant, vol. 4, 89). The best option of all was the ordeal by bread and cheese, wherein the accused was made to swallow bits of bread and cheese without gagging (F. Ogg, 197). Alas, this alternative was not available in all areas.
465. De Camp, 347.
466. *Encyclopædia Britannica*, vol. 8, 956.
467. Gibbon, vol. 4, 578; quoted also in Gies and Gies, 1.
468. Singh, 55.
469. Newhall, 115.
470. Van Doren, 179.
471. Van Doren, 152–4.
472. De Camp, 342.
473. Robinson, *Readings*, vol. 1, 492.
474. Singer, 171; Durant, vol. 4, 1015.
475. J. H. Robinson, *Readings*, vol. 1, 461; see also Durant and Durant, vol. 4, 1010.
476. Although he loses points when he claims that Ethiopians fly around on winged dragons, and that dragon meat, properly cooked, can prolong life (see Ross and McLaughlin, 634).
477. Fuller, vol. 1, 469. The rumor that he "invented" gunpowder remains unsubstantiated (see Durant and Durant, vol. 4, 1011).
478. De Camp, 351.
479. Durant and Durant, vol. 4, 1007.
480. Gies and Gies, 162–63. The tie to chemistry is self-evident, but alchemists also sought the discovery of "the elixir of immortality"—hence the tie to pharmacology.
481. Hollister, *Short History*, 280–5; C. H. King, vol. 1, 430–2; Durant and Durant, vol. 4, 865–873. On

the inside, both Gothic and Romanesque churches were gloriously decorated with scenes from the Bible. This was a touchy point between East and West, ultimately giving rise to the Iconoclast Controversy, but fewer people in the West were literate, and the visual depictions in these museum cathedrals were an obvious boon to comprehension (C. H. King, vol. 1, 430).

482. De Camp, 360–65.
483. De Camp, 372.
484. Gies and Gies, 44–47.
485. Gies and Gies, 111–12. The field under cultivation was square, but the plots carved out by individual farmers were long narrow strips extending from one end of the field to the other and directly adjacent to similar strips on either side within the square field. The system was known as an "open field" system.
486. Stark, 69–70.
487. Gimpel, 4–5.
488. Gies and Gies, 212.

Section III

1. Montross (187) notes that by 1453 he was the only living general from that battle.
2. Seward, *HYW*, 262.
3. See Fuller, vol. 1, 496.
4. See for example the family trees provided by Churchill (vol. 1, 435) and Neillands (*WOR*, 18–19).
5. Neillands, 17.
6. Neillands, 15–17.
7. Neillands, 26.
8. Neillands 17–20.
9. Seward, *WOR*, 30; Churchill, vol. 1, 438.
10. Neillands, 98; Churchill, vol. 1, 444–6; St. Aubyn, 44; Seward, *WOR*, 62.
11. Churchill, vol. 1, 450.
12. Seward, *WOR*, 152.
13. Churchill, vol. 1, 470; Seward, *WOR*, 180–1.
14. Neillands, 154.
15. Lander, 155–6; Seward, *WOR*, 222–3.
16. Dahmus, *SMK*, 320–21.
17. Dahmus, *SMK*, 320–21.
18. Oman, *AWMA*, 96.
19. Oman, *AWMA*, 97–100.
20. Oman, *AWMA*, 100–3; quoted phrase is by a certain Molinet (in Commynes, vol. 1, 338*fn*).
21. Dahmus, *SMK*, 324; Durant and Durant, vol. 6, 136; Guizot, *France*, vol. 2, 359–60.
22. Dahmus, *SMK*, 324–5.
23. Lander, 155.
24. Neillands, 170–81.
25. C. Markham's *Richard III, A Doubtful Verdict Reviewed*, in Littleton and Rea, 112–15.
26. Neillands, 196–7.
27. Neillands, 191.
28. Croyland Chronicle in Seward, *WOR*, 277–8; Littleton and Rea, 92–3.
29. See C. Markham's *Richard III, A Doubtful Verdict Reviewed*, in Littleton and Rea, 116–21—or better still, see the same evidence presented stirringly (if inadmissibly, given that the source is literary) in Josephine Tey's, *Daughter or Time* (wherein a fictional Scotland Yard detective named Grant and his eager young research assistant, Carradine, prove the king's innocence beyond doubt).
30. See Neillands, 198.
31. Croyland Chronicle in Lander, 187–8; C. Ross, 122–4.
32. Polydore Vergil, 164 (spelling updated). See also Seward's similar quote, *WOR*, 207.
33. The claim was bolstered (if not by much) by the fact that Henry's mother, Margaret Beaufort, was descended illegitimately from John of Gaunt, Edward III's third son and founder of the Lancastrian line.
34. C. Ross, 222–3.
35. Polydore Vergil, 224; Lander, 197; St. Aubyn, 214.
36. Polydore Vergil, 225; St. Aubyn, 214–15; C. Ross, 224.
37. Buck, 99.
38. Fabyan, 238 (Spelling updated); see also, Seward, *WOR*, 307; St. Aubyn, 216.
39. Cook, 98; Neillands, 214.
40. Durant and Durant, vol. 6, 108–9.
41. Jo. Burke, 84.
42. See L. B. Smith's discussion of "Morton's Fork" in *TRE*, 91–2.
43. Brinton, et al., vol. 1, 277–8; E. F. Rice, 114.
44. J. Wright, 46 and 69.
45. Polo had already completed his celebrated travels, but was not yet famous. To pass the time in his Genoese captivity, he recounted to a scribe his sundry adventures at the court of Kublai Khan where, over the course of sixteen years, he had been a great favorite and had served as an official in the Mongol government. His trek had taken him through China, India and the Mongolian province of Persia (where he was charged with the task of bringing a "purebred" Mongol bride to the local ruler). These fascinating stories were initially regarded as fiction, but the inclusion of a tale about a wondrous priest named Prester John who allegedly lived and proselytized amongst the Mongols, piqued the curiosity of the devout and led to Polo's fame (Wells, 711–14; Durant and Durant, vol. 4, 993).
46. Brinton, et al., vol. 1, 277.
47. Burckhardt, 56–7.
48. Durant and Durant, vol. 5, 109; see also Schevill, 105.
49. Durant and Durant, vol. 5, 158–61; Burchard, 153–9.
50. Gilmore, 10–11; Durant and Durant, vol. 6, 187.
51. E. F. Rice, 31.
52. Brinton, et al., vol. 1, 372; Asimov, 199.
53. C. H. King, vol. 1, 559.
54. At least after Cortez conquered the Mexican Aztecs (1521) and Pizarro thrashed the Peruvian Incas (1532).
55. E. F. Rice, 53–4; Harbison, 12–13.
56. See E. F. Rice's discussion, 46–7.
57. Harbison, 14–15.
58. E. F. Rice, 11.
59. Harbison, 15.
60. A. H. Johnson, 5–6.
61. A. H. Johnson, 7.
62. A. H. Johnson, 19.
63. Burckhardt, 109.

Notes—Section III

64. Durant and Durant, vol. 5, 407.
65. Burckhardt, 110.
66. Burchard, 100 and 106; Durant and Durant, 407. Pope Alexander was the unintended beneficiary of Charles' good manners; for several years later, fifty of these unharmed courtesans are said to have competed in a fornication contest at his daughter Lucrezia's wedding reception—Burchard, 194; Manchester, 79; Durant and Durant doubt this story (vol. 5, 427–8).
67. Durant and Durant, vol. 5, 410–11.
68. Burckhardt, 37.
69. Commines, vol. 1, 214; see also Parker, *HOW*, 153.
70. Brinton, et al., vol. 1, 343; Asimov, 202.
71. The Sforzas had conspired with Charles VIII to depose Pope Alexander, which helps explain the latter's willingness to join in Louis' attack on Milan (Chamberlin, 184–5).
72. Durant and Durant, vol. 5, p. 422.
73. Manchester, p. 84. Chamberlin, 192. (Chamberlin says the charge is false.)
74. Burckhardt, 109–10.
75. Burckhardt, 116; Chamberlin, 202–3; Burchard, 220. (Durant and Durant, vol. 5, 433 says the illness was malaria, while the others cite only a fever common to Rome.)
76. Chamberlin, 204; Burchard, 225–6; Durant and Durant, vol. 5, p. 433.
77. Burckhardt, 117.
78. A. H. Johnson, 54–55.
79. Durant and Durant, vol. 5, 438–9; Burchard, 228.
80. Thatcher and Schwill, 59; Hallam, 197–98.
81. Gibbon, LI, vol. 3, 608.
82. Gibbon, LI, vol. 3, 610.
83. *Encyclopædia Britannica*, vol. 25, 541.
84. *Encyclopædia Britannica*, vol. 25, 542.
85. G. Jackson, 48–53.
86. Hallam, 200–01.
87. G. Jackson, 62.
88. *Encyclopædia Britannica*, vol. 25, 544–45.
89. Hallam, 202.
90. Hallam, 202.
91. Durant and Durant, vol. 6, 197.
92. Graetz, vol. 4, 116.
93. Froissart, *COF*, 177.
94. Froissart, *CEFS*, I.241, 166. ("Spaniards" here refers to Henry's forces.)
95. Thatcher and Schwill, 531.
96. H. S. Williams, 91. To make sure of the matter, Henry personally struck off Pedro's head.
97. J. H. Elliott, 15.
98. Fuller, vol. 1, 531.
99. Durant and Durant, vol. 6, 208–14.
100. G. Jackson, 194.
101. A. H. Johnson, 41.
102. Durant and Durant, vol. 5, 615.
103. J. H. Elliott, 133–4.
104. Goodenough, 113.
105. A. H. Johnson, 39–40.
106. Durant and Durant, vol. 5, 616.
107. Durant and Durant, vol. 5, 442–4.
108. Durant and Durant, vol. 5, 443.
109. Guizot, *France*, vol. 2, 428.
110. By marrying Catherine of Aragon, the widow of his dead brother, Arthur, Henry had become the son-in-law of Ferdinand of Spain.
111. Gilmore, 158.
112. J. H. Robinson, *Readings*, vol. 2, p. 18.
113. Gilmore, 157.
114. Gilmore, 160; A. H. Johnson, 127–28.
115. Langdon-Davies, 27.
116. Durant and Durant, vol. 6, 226–7.
117. Knecht, 76.
118. Armstrong, vol. 1, 62; Durant and Durant, vol. 6, 358; Hare, 63.
119. Elliott, 144.
120. Durant and Durant vol. 6, 357.
121. Watson, 5.
122. C. H. King, vol. 1, 573; Durant and Durant, vol. 6, 358.
123. Knecht, 74; Rady, 15.
124. E. F. Rice, 108.
125. J. H. Robinson, *Readings*, vol. 2, 19–20; F. Hackett, 154–8; Knecht, 42–5.
126. J. H. Robinson, *Readings*, vol. 2, 20–1.
127. J. H. Robinson, *Readings*, vol. 2, 22.
128. F. Hackett, 160.
129. F. Hackett, 161; Knecht, 46.
130. McKendrick, 104.
131. A. H. Johnson, 142.
132. F. Hackett, 226.
133. Abbott, *HC*, 421; Durant and Durant, vol. 6, 338; Manchester, 133–5.
134. Abbott, *HC*, 421.
135. Manchester, 136; Durant and Durant, vol. 6, 340.
136. A. H. Johnson, 153.
137. Harbison, 47–50; A. H. Johnson, 153–54.
138. Elton, 17.
139. Manchester, 139.
140. J. H. Robinson, *Readings*, vol. 2, 59–60 (Theses 28, 39 and 40).
141. Harbison, 52; Elton, 20; Durant and Durant, vol. 6, 350.
142. Rady, 23.
143. Durant and Durant, vol. 6, 359–61; Manchester, 170–3.
144. Abbott, *A*, 111–12; see also Durant and Durant, vol. 6, 361.
145. Manchester, 133–6; Durant and Durant, vol. 6, 338 and 345.
146. Armstrong, vol. 1, 70.
147. J. H. Robinson, *Readings*, vol. 2, 87.
148. Clark, 71; Durant and Durant, vol. 6, 369; Wallbank and Taylor, 524.
149. J. H. Robinson, *Readings*, vol. 2, 107.
150. A. H. Johnson, 177–79.
151. A. H. Johnson, 147.
152. Hare, 97.
153. F. Hackett, 290.
154. A. H. Johnson, 175.
155. Kinross, 174.
156. New, 105; Durant and Durant, vol. 6, 512.
157. Manchester, 197–8; F. Hacket, 337.

Notes—Section III

158. F. Hacket, 349–50.
159. Goodwin, 84; Durant and Durant, vol. 6, 440–1.
160. Kinross, 186–7.
161. Rady, 46.
162. Durant and Durant, vol. 6, 442; Bainton, 148; Wallbank and Taylor, vol. 1, 524–5.
163. Bainton, 99–101; Harbison, 63–5.
164. Elton, 100–1.
165. Durant and Durant, vol. 6, 401.
166. New, 131–2.
167. *Encyclopædia Britannica*, vol. 6, 275.
168. Voltaire (1993), 33–4; (1864), 202–3.
169. A. H. Johnson, 202.
170. *Encyclopædia Britannica*, vol. 28, 1063.
171. Durant and Durant, vol. 6, 467–8; J. H. Robinson, *Readings*, vol. 2, 130.
172. Durant and Durant, vol. 6, 469.
173. See Durant and Durant, vol. 6, 469–71; J. H. Robinson, *Readings*, vol. 2, 131–3; Elton, 224–5.
174. Durant and Durant, vol. 6, 472*ff*; Elton, 213, 229; Bainton, 121.
175. J. H. Robinson, *Readings*, vol. 2, 134.
176. C. H. King, vol. 1, 639.
177. A. H. Johnson, 274.
178. Elton, 108; Brinton, et al., vol. 1, 328; Bainton, 134.
179. Durant and Durant vol. 6, 480–1; Osler, 121 and 157–9; Nuland, 122; Haggard, 244–5.
180. Durant and Durant, vol. 6, 482–4; Elton, 108–9 and 230.
181. F. Hackett, 216–17; Knecht, 81–2.
182. Lacey, 92.
183. E. F. Rice, 134. To be sure, Luther was not actually locked in Satan's bowels, but since he has been portrayed as something of a hero in our story, it is rightful to note that in his spare time, he was a loathsome, intolerant, superstitious anti–Semite, who denounced Copernicus as a dunce for his celestial theories, and accused Jews of using the blood of Christian children in their rituals. (See Durant and Durant, vol. 6, 727 and 858.)
184. Neillands, 217.
185. Jo. Burke, 102.
186. Bainton, 199; Durant and Durant, vol. 6, 572.
187. Henry referred to her as "the Flanders Mare" (Churchill, vol. 2, 79).
188. Wells, 755.
189. See Durant and Durant, vol. 6, 906.
190. Harbison, 85; Durant and Durant, vol. 6, 915; Brinton, et al., vol. 1, 332–35.
191. A. H. Johnson, 269.
192. Rady, 58–63; A. H. Johnson, 212–13.
193. Hare, 189–91.
194. Knecht, 365.
195. Knecht, 370–2.
196. Lacey, 203–6. Henry's alliance agreement with Charles at the outset of the war had pledged the parties to continue the fight until Charles had captured Burgundy and Henry Normandy, Guienne and the French crown (A. H. Johnson, 215).
197. Rady, 75.
198. A. H. Johnson, 229.
199. Rady, 82.
200. A. H. Johnson, 236–37.
201. Hare, 247–8; Armstrong, vol. 2, 255; Durant and Durant, vol. 6, 455.
202. A. H. Johnson, 242.
203. Rady, 92.
204. Abbott, *A*, 140–1.
205. *Encyclopædia Britannica*, vol. 17, 814–15.
206. *Encyclopædia Britannica*, vol. 17, 815.
207. *Encyclopædia Britannica*, vol. 17, 815–16.
208. Durant and Durant, vol. 6, 597.
209. Durant and Durant, vol. 6, 598; Larousse, vol. 2, 24.
210. Haggard, 219; Durant and Durant, vol. 6, 522; Asimov, 230.
211. Haggard, 219–21; Saunders and O'Malley, 36–7.
212. A. H. Johnson, 394.
213. Durant and Durant, vol. 7, 112 and 116.
214. Durant and Durant vol. 7, 119; L. B. Smith, *EW*, 171.
215. *Encyclopædia Britannica*, vol. 17, 818 and vol. 7, 837.
216. *Encyclopædia Britannica*, vol. 17, 818.
217. Durant and Durant, vol. 7, 121–24; *Encyclopædia Britannica*, vol. 17, 818–21.
218. Durant and Durant, vol. 7, 334.
219. A. H. Johnson, 391–95.
220. *Encyclopædia Britannica*, 864–65. The gate of King Hugo is dedicated to Hugh Capet, founder of France's Capetian dynasty.
221. Durant and Durant, vol. 7, 334–6.
222. Her wedding to Henry had been arranged in 1534 by Francis I who desired the backing of the Medici pope, Clement VII, for one of his ubiquitous schemes to regain Milan (A. H. Johnson, 207).
223. New, 168. Francis II had technically been of age to rule and had not required a regency.
224. L. B. Smith, *EW*, 129; Durant and Durant, vol. 7, p. 342.
225. Neale, 66; L. B. Smith, *EW*, 130.
226. L. B. Smith, *EW*, 131–2; Neale, 71–2.
227. Arnold, 191–4; Durant and Durant, vol. 7, 345.
228. L. B. Smith, *EW*, 134.
229. Guizot, *France*, vol. 3, 296.
230. J. H. Robinson, *Readings*, vol. 2, 181.
231. Abbott, *HC*, 458.
232. Durant and Durant, vol. 7, 351.
233. Abbott, *HC*, 459.
234. Durant and Durant, vol. 7, 351–2.
235. Durant and Durant, vol. 7, 351; Neale, 79; L. B. Smith, *EW*, 135.
236. Weber, 362–3; Asimov, 230; Fletcher, 168.
237. Baird, vol. 2, 459–60 and 497.
238. Durant and Durant, vol. 7, 355; Guizot, *France*, vol. 3, 311; L. B. Smith, *EW*, 136; A. H. Johnson, 420.
239. A. H. Johnson, 279.
240. Arnold, 40–2.
241. Arnold, 129–31.
242. A. H. Johnson, 287–92.
243. Fuller, vol. 1, 564; Durant and Durant, vol. 7, 523; Goodwin, 160.
244. Among the combatants was Miguel Cervantes,

Notes—Section III

author of Don Quixote, who emerged from the contest with his left hand crippled by a gunshot wound. (See Durant and Durant, vol. 7, 298; O. Warner, 23; Kinross, 270.)

245. Fuller, vol. 1, 565.
246. O. Warner, 21. (Kinross says the shot killed him outright, 270.)
247. Durant and Durant (vol. 7, 523) say they ran it up the dead Admiral's own flagpole. O. Warner, 21, Kinross, 270 and L. B. Smith, *EW*, 153, all opt for the pike.
248. See L. B. Smith, *EW*, 153–5.
249. L. B. Smith, *EW*, 143–7; Martin and Parker, 75–9; A. H. Johnson, 304.
250. J. H. Robinson, *Readings*, vol. 2, 173. Such mercy, however, was reserved for the repentant. The recalcitrant were to be burnt at the stake (Edict of 1550).
251. Rady, 29–30.
252. Motley, 104.
253. A. H. Johnson, 324–28.
254. Motley, 111.
255. Motley, 181.
256. *Encyclopædia Britannica*, vol. 19, 417–18; Barnouw, 68–69.
257. Wallbank and Taylor, vol. 1, 553–4; Brinton, et al., vol. 1, 348.
258. Motley, 266–68; A. H. Johnson, 333.
259. Motley, 68–69; Barnouw, 65.
260. Motley, 309–13.
261. A. H. Johnson, 337–38.
262. Motley, 338–39.
263. Wedgwood, *WS*, 126.
264. Motley, 362–64.
265. Motley, 370. The defenders answered by casting a barrel filled with eleven Spanish heads from the ramparts.
266. Motley, 374–77; A. H. Johnson, 342–43.
267. Wells, 808.
268. Motley, 383.
269. Wells, 809–10.
270. Motley, 384.
271. Wedgewood, *WS*, 135; *Encyclopædia Britannica*, vol. 19, 419; (Alva's idea of burning cities, A.H. Johnson. 346).
272. Motley, 392.
273. Wedgwood, *WS*, 141-3 and 147–8; *Encyclopædia Britannica*, vol. 19, 419.
274. George Gascoigne quoted in Carey, 119–21.
275. A. H. Johnson, 361; *Encyclopædia Britannica*, vol. 13, 596.
276. As Motley reports, Alva returned from Portugal with a fever "and was only kept alive by milk which he drank from a woman's breast. Such was the gentle second childhood of the man who had almost literally been drinking blood for seventy years" (Motley, 393).
277. *Encyclopædia Britannica*, vol. 13, 596.
278. Wedgwood, *WS*, 248–50.
279. Martin and Parker, 41 and 44.
280. N. Williams, 267; L. B. Smith, *EW*, 177.
281. Fuller, vol. 2, 6–7; Martin and Parker, 70–71.
282. Churchill, vol. 2, 119; Mattingly, 5; Carey, 138.
283. Marx, 39–41.

284. Mattingly, 251–6.
285. Martin and Parker, 91. D. Howarth, *VA*, 53–4.
286. L. B. Smith, *EW*, 183; Fuller, vol. 2, 28–9.
287. Martin and Parker, 130.
288. L. B. Smith, *EW*, 194; D. Howarth, *VA*, 124.
289. Fuller, vol. 2, 30; Mattingly, 310–11.
290. Durant and Durant, vol. 7, 35.
291. Martin and Parker, 163–70.
292. Marx, 54; Mattingly, however, says the Armada had powder in abundance, since it had brought extra for a land campaign in England, 310.
293. Howarth, *VA*, 190.
294. Mattingly, 332–4.
295. Durant and Durant, vol. 7, 36; Mattingly, 333; Marx, 101.
296. Martin and Parker, 195–6; Howarth, *VA*, 225.
297. Durant and Durant, vol. 7, 36–7.
298. Marx, 116; Martin and Parker, 200; D. Howarth, *VA*, 215–19; Mattingly, 369.
299. Mattingly, 382–4.
300. Larousse, vol. 2, 52; L. B. Smith (*EW*, 272) says the bones were mixed with flour.
301. L. B. Smith, *EW*, 273; Durant and Durant, vol. 7, 365.
302. Friedrich, 126–9; Wakeman, 27–30.
303. Parker, *HOW*, 154 and *TYW*, 205; Arnold, 57.
304. Watson, 9–10.
305. Langer, 20.
306. Parker, *TYW*, 23.
307. Ferdinand had gained his throne by promising (falsely) to uphold Bohemian religious freedoms.
308. Watson, 73; Wedgwood, *TYW*, 79.
309. Liddell Hart, 160.
310. Brinton, et al., vol. 1, 368; Wedgwood, *TYW*, 516.
311. Watson, 98.
312. Steinberg, 42.
313. Watson, 101–2; Liddell Hart, 169; Durant and Durant vol. 7, 557.
314. Fuller, vol. 2, 45.
315. Gardiner, *TYW*, 40.
316. Steinberg, 45.
317. Gardiner, *TYW*, 91–92; Wakeman, 70.
318. Liddell Hart, 176.
319. Wedgwood, *TYW*, 211–12.
320. D. Ogg, 140fn; Watson, 204.
321. Wakeman, 77.
322. Wakeman, 75–77.
323. Watson, 243; Brinton, et al., vol. 1, 363.
324. Fuller, vol. 2, 66.
325. Wedgwood, *TYW*, 250–2; Liddell Hart, 179–81.
326. Wedgwood, *TYW*, 262–5.
327. Livesey, 52 (telescope); Liddell Hart, 97 (nearsighted).
328. Friedrich, 212.
329. Wedgwood, *RFM*, 49–50; Watson, 272.
330. Friedrich, 198.
331. J. H. Robinson, *Readings*, vol. 2, 208. (Daughter in his arms, *Encyclopædia Britannica*, vol. 12, 735.)
332. Durant and Durant, vol. 7, 563.
333. D. Ogg, 143.
334. J. H. Robinson, *Readings*, vol. 2, 211–12.

335. Wedgwood, *TYW*, 290.
336. Wedgwood, *TYW*, 291.
337. Fletcher, 168.
338. Lee, 6; J. H. Robinson, *Readings*, vol., 2, 211; Friedrich, 181. (We should not, however, discount the effect on the electors' decision made by Tilly's invasion of Saxony or Gustavus' march on Berlin.)
339. Liddell Hart, 120–1; Montross, 269; Goodenough, 73; Lee, 42.
340. Liddell Hart, 118–19; Goodenough, 71–2.
341. Fuller, vol. 2, 55; Livesey, 55.
342. Goodenough, 72; Montross, 273; Lee, 42; Liddell Hart, 121–2.
343. Fuller, 62–3.
344. Fletcher, 246 (The word "surgeon" has been substituted for the archaic "chirurgeon" by the author.)
345. Liddell Hart, 190–1; Steinberg, 59; Livesey, 55.
346. Fletcher, 243.
347. Watson, 358–9.
348. Fuller, vol. 2, 67.
349. Wedgwood, *TYW*, 346–7.
350. Watson, 324 and 332.
351. Durant and Durant, vol. 7, 564; Wedgwood, *TYW*, 326.
352. Stevens, 419.
353. Livesey, 58; Fuller, vol. 2, 71; Liddell Hart, 148.
354. Stevens, 416.
355. Fletcher, 284 (see also Watson, 368; Durant and Durant, vol. 7, 564.)
356. Fletcher, 284; Watson, 368 (By some accounts, the fatal blow was a gunshot wound to the head.)
357. Stevens, 416.
358. Wedgwood, *TYW*, 326; Livesey, 59; Watson, 368.
359. Watson, 272 and 373.
360. Durant and Durant, vol. 7, 565.
361. Watson, 406–7; Wedgwood, *TYW*, 358–9.
362. Watson, 408.
363. Wedgwood, *TYW*, 360 (from a description by the English mercenary, Poyntz).
364. Langdon-Davies, 39.
365. Langdon-Davies, 36–7.
366. Durant and Durant, vol. 7, 288.
367. Steinberg, 67.
368. Wedgwood, 387–91.
369. Wedgwood, *TYW*, 383.
370. Wedgwood, *RFM*, 81–2.
371. Goodenough, 115–18; Wedgwood, *TYW*, 414–15.
372. Wedgwood, *TYW*, 412; Abbott, *A*, 300.
373. Wedgwood, *TYW*, 412; Durant and Durant, vol. 7, 568.
374. Trevor Davies, 8–9; Elliott, 327.
375. Elliott, 329.
376. All of the Alsace fell into Bernard's hands, and in accordance with the agreement of 1635, he claimed the prize as his own. As France likewise coveted this territory, the fulfillment of the agreed terms would have created a degree of embarrassment for her long-term plans. Bernard, however, was carried away by a fever before the matter could be further discussed, and the Alsace was incorporated into France.
377. Durant and Durant, vol. 7, 461.
378. Trevor Davies, 25–7; Elliott, 343–4.
379. Trevor Davies, 20–1.
380. Durant and Durant, vol. 7, 566; Wedgwood, *TYW*, 450.
381. Wedgwood, *TYW*, 453–4.
382. A royal personage, known as an *infanta*, was assigned to each *tercio* as an ex-officio colonel. The foot-soldiers were thus called "*infantaria*"—the genesis of the modern term "infantry" (Fuller vol. 2, 50).
383. *Encyclopædia Britannica*, vol. 26, 859.
384. For Rocroi, see Wedgwood, *TYW*, 457–8; Montross, 288; Goodenough, 103–6.
385. J. H. Robinson, *Readings*, vol. 2, 216; see also Durant and Durant, vol. 7, 571.
386. Wedgwood, *TYW*, 525; Durant and Durant, vol. 7, 572.
387. C. H. King, vol. 1, 506.
388. C. H. King, vol. 1, 506 and 510; Ja. Burke, *DUC*, 68.
389. See Van Doren, 166–7; Brown, 63; Durant and Durant, vol. 5, 77.
390. Brinton, et al., 1, 298; Schevell, 43; New, 64–5; Plumb, 13.
391. See Van Doren, 130–4 for further discussion.
392. Durant and Durant, however, identify her as the very real wife of Hugues de Sade, and the mother of twelve children. (Durant and Durant, vol. 5, 6; see also Gibbon, *EB*, LXX, footnote 3.)
393. Schevill, 45.
394. Brinton, et al., vol. 1, 299.
395. Brinton, et al., vol. 1, 299; Brown, 17; New, 70.
396. Durant and Durant, vol. 5, 43.
397. Van Doren, 132–3.
398. Van Doren, 133.
399. New, 70; Plumb, 90; Durant and Durant, vol. 5, 82–3.
400. J. H. Robinson, *Readings*, vol. 2, 43.
401. Brinton, et al., vol. 1, 302–3.
402. Nuland, 64–9; Vasari (*LA*), 264; Had Da Vinci but published his work, he, and not Vesalius, might today be hailed as the "Father of Anatomy" (W. J. Bishop, 76–7; Margotta, 73; Osler, 161–3).
403. See the discussion of Frayling et al., in their chapter on perspective.
404. Ja. Burke, *DUC*, 70–2.
405. Manetti, 42–4; Ja. Burke, *DUC*, 72–74; Edgerton, 152; R. King, 34–36.
406. Vasari (Foster's translation in *LPSA*, vol. 1, 431).
407. Nuland, 72–3; Saunders and O'Malley, 14.
408. Saunders and O'Malley, 14; Haggard, 213.
409. Nuland, 77–80.
410. The original woodcuts survived in Munich until 1944, when they were destroyed in an Allied bombing raid (Nuland, 85; Saunders and O'Malley, 10). There is controversy concerning Calcar's role. He was a student of Titian, and some attribute the drawings to the latter on account of their beauty. Others say Calcar and others drew them under Titian's guidance, but that Calcar's friend Giorgio Vasari exaggerated his (Calcar's) role owing to their friendship (See Saunders and O'Malley, 27–8).

Notes—Section III

411. Paré, 308–9 (spelling updated); see also Nuland's longer excerpt (Nuland, 97).
412. Nuland, 97–8; Haggard, 224–5; Sutcliffe and Duin, 34–5.
413. C. W. Eliot, ed., p. 11; F. Packard, 162–3; Nuland, 98–9.
414. Haggard, 227–8.
415. Ja. Burke, *DUC*, 131–4.
416. Durant and Durant, vol. 6, 857–60.
417. Durant and Durant, vol. 6, 859–60.
418. Ja. Burke, *DUC*, 136; Durant and Durant, vol. 6, 859.
419. Ja. Burke, *DUC*, 143–4; Singer, 216.
420. Ja. Burke, *DUC*, 149–50; Singer, 240.
421. Beckmann, 87.
422. Ja. Burke, *DUC*, 147–9; Singer, 230–49; Durant and Durant, vol. 7, 600–11.
423. Durant and Durant, vol. 7, 179.
424. Durant and Durant, vol. 7, 175.
425. Durant and Durant, vol. 7, 180.
426. Singh, 38.
427. Singer, 226–7.
428. Bell, 49–51; Durant and Durant, vol. 7, 644–5; D. Ogg, 388.
429. Bell, 87–8; Beckmann, 121–2.
430. Brinton, et al., vol. 1, 420; Durant and Durant, vol. 8, 61.
431. Bell, 125; Durant and Durant, vol. 8, 662.
432. Bell, 83; Beckmann, 123; Durant and Durant, vol. 8, 58.
433. Beckman, 123; Durant and Durant, vol. 8, 66.
434. Bell, 63.
435. Bell, 86–7; Singh, 40–4.
436. Singh, 39–40 and 59–60.
437. Singh, 61–2; Bell, 71–2; Durant and Durant, vol. 8, 499.
438. The quest for the proof is brilliantly recounted in *Fermat's Engima* by Simon Singh.
439. E. F. Rice, 14–16; see also, Fuller, vol. 1, 470.
440. Durant and Durant, vol. 5, 564.
441. If Gutenberg was not the actual inventor, he can at least be numbered amongst the very first to successfully cast type—the others being (i) his fellow townsman and creditor, Fust, who absconded with his printer, Schoffer, and his first printing press after a successful lawsuit, and (ii) Laurens Coster who may have been printing professionally in the Netherlands as early as 1430. (Durant and Durant, vol. 6, 158–9; Ja. Burke, *DUC*, 112.)
442. Burckhardt, 194.
443. Durant and Durant, vol. 6, 160.
444. Wells, 563 and 740–1.
445. Durant and Durant, vol. 6, 160; Wells, 753–4; G. Clark, 61–2.

Bibliography

Abbott, John S. C. *Austria: Its Rise and Present Power*. New York: P. F. Collier, 1898. (*A*)

Abbott, John S. C. *The History of Christianity*. Portland, Maine: George Stinson and s., 1885. (*HC*)

Ahnlund, Nils. *Gustavus Adolphus the Great*. New York: History Book Club, 1999.

Albright, William Foxwell, et al. *The Jewish People, Past and Present*. New York: Jewish Encyclopedic Handbooks, 1955.

Allshorn, Lionel. *Stupor Mundi*. London: Martin Secker, 1912.

Ammianus Marcellinus. *The Later Roman Empire*. Trans. by Walter Hamilton. London: Penguin Books, 1986. (*LRE*)

Ammianus Marcellinus. *The Roman History of Ammianus Marcellinus*. Trans. by C. D. Yonge. London: George Bell and Sons, 1887. (*RHAM*)

Anna Comnena. *The Alexiad of Anna Comnena*. Eng. Trans. by E. R. A. Sewter, New York: Penguin Books, 1969.

Armstrong, Edward. *The Emperor Charles V*. 2 vol. London: Macmillan and Co., 1902.

Arnold, Thomas F. *The Renaissance at War*. London: Cassell and Co., 2001.

Asimov, Isaac. *Asimov's Chronology of the World*. New York: HarperCollins, 1991.

Asprey, Robert. *War in the Shadows*. Vol. 1. Garden City, New York: Doubleday, 1975.

Asser. *Alfred the Great: Asser's Life of Alfred and other Contemporary Sources*. London: Penguin Books, 1983.

Atchity, Kenneth, ed. *The Renaissance Reader*. New York: HarperPerennial, 1997.

Auchincloss, Louis. *Richelieu*. New York: The Viking Press, 1972.

Bainton, Roland H. *The Reformation of the Sixteenth Century*. Boston: Beacon Press, 1952.

Baird, Henry Martyn. *History of the Rise of the Huguenots*. 2 vol. New York: Charles Scribner's Sons, 1879.

Barbaro, Nicolo. *Diary of the Siege of Constantinople*. Trans. by J. R. Jones. New York: Exposition Press, 1969.

Barnouw, A. J. *The Making of Modern Holland*. New York: W. W. Norton and Company, 1944.

Beckmann, Petr. *A History of π*. New York: St. Martin's Press, 1971.

Bede. *The Ecclesiastical History of the English Nation*. Temple Edition: Eng. Trans. by J. A. Giles. London: J. M. Dent, 1903. (*EHEN*)

Bede. *A History of the English Church and People*. Trans. by Leo Sherley-Price, revised by R. E. Latham. London: Penguin Books, 1968. (*HECP*)

Bell, E. T. *Men of Mathematics*. New York: Simon & Schuster, 1965.

Bémont, Charles, and Monod, G. *Medieval Europe from 395 to 1270*. Translated by Mary Sloan, with notes and revisions by George Burton Adams. New York: Henry Holt and Company, 1902.

Bennett, Michael. *Lambert Simnel and the Battle of Stoke*. New York: St. Martin's Press, 1987.

Berlinski, David. *A Tour of the Calculus*. New York: Vintage Books, 1995.

Bickerman, E. and Smith, M. *The Ancient History of Western Civilization*. New York: Harper and Row, 1976.

Bishop, Jim. *The Day Christ Died*. San Francisco: Harper, 1977.

Bishop, W. J. *The Early History of Surgery*. New York: Barnes and Noble, 1995.

Boccaccio, Giovanni. *The Decameron*. Trans. by J. M. Rigg. London: Navarre Society Ltd., 1921.

Botsford, George Willis and Lillie Shaw Botsford. *A Source-Book of Ancient History*. New York: Macmillan, 1913.

Bowen, Marjorie. *Sundry Great Gentlemen*. Freeport: Books for Libraries Press, 1968.

Bray, R. S. *Armies of Pestilence: The Impact of Disease on History*. New York: Barnes and Noble, 1996.

Brinton, C. Christopher, J. B. Wolff, R. L. *A History of Civilization: 2 Volumes*. Englewood Cliffs, New Jersey: Prentice Hall, 5th Edition, 1976.

Brooke, Christopher. *From Alfred to Henry III: 871–1272*. New York: The Norton Library, 1961.

Brown, Alison. *The Renaissance*. London and New York: Longman, 1988.

Brownworth, Lars. *Lost To The West*. New York: Three Rivers Press, 2009.

Buck, Sir George. *The History of Richard the Third*. Gloucester: Alan Sutton, 1982.

Burchard, Johann. *At the Court of the Borgia*. Ed. and trans. by Geoffrey Parker. London: The Folio Society, 1963.

Burckhardt, Jacob. *The Civilization of the Renaissance in Italy*. Eng. Trans. by S. G. C. Middlemore. London: Swan Sonnenschein and Co., 1893.

Burke, James. *Connections*. Boston: Little, Brown and Company, 1995. (*C*)

Burke, James. *The Day the Universe Changed*. Boston: Little, Brown and Company, 1995. (*DUC*)

Burke, John. *An Illustrated History of England*. London: William Collins and Sons, 1985.

Burke, Peter. *The Renaissance*. Atlantic Highlands, New Jersey: Humanities Press International, 1987.

Bury, J. B. *History of the Later Roman Empire*. 2 vol. New York: Dover Publications, 1958. (*LRE*)

Bury, J. B. *The Invasion of Europe by the Barbarians*. New York: W. W. Norton and Company, 1967. (*IEB*)

Carey, John, ed. *Eyewitness to History*. Cambridge: Harvard University Press, 1987.

Carr, Raymond, ed. *Spain: A History*. Oxford: Oxford University Press, 2000.

Cartwright, Frederick F. and Michael D. Biddiss. *Disease and History*. New York: Barnes and Noble, 1972.

Chamberlin, E. R. *The Bad Popes*. New York: Barnes and Noble Books, 1993.

Chambers, James. *The Devil's Horsemen*. New York: Barnes and Noble Books, 2003.

Choniates, Niketas. *O City of Byzantium, Annals of Niketas Choniates*. Eng. Trans. by Harry J. Morgan. Detroit: Wayne State University Press, 1984.

Churchill, Sir Winston. *History of the English-Speaking Peoples*. 4 vol. New York: Dodd, Mead and Co., 1956.

Clark, Sir George. *Early Modern Europe*. New York: Oxford University Press, 1960.

Commines, Philip de. *The Memoirs of Philip de Commines, Lord of Argenton*. 2 vol. Ed. By Andrew R. Scoble. London: Henry G. Bohn, 1855.

Cook, David R. *Lancastrians and Yorkists: The Wars of the Roses*. New York: Longman, 1984.

Crampton, R. J. *A Concise History of Bulgaria*. Cambridge: Cambridge University Press, 1997.

Creasy, Edward Shepherd. *Decisive Battles of the World*. New York: D. Appleton and Company, 1904.

Dahmus, Joseph. *A History of the Middle Ages*. New York: Barnes and Noble Books, 1995. (*HMA*)

Dahmus, Joseph. *Seven Medieval Kings*. New York: Barnes and Noble Books, 1994. (*SMK*)

De Camp, L. Sprague. *The Ancient Engineers*. New York: Ballantine Books, 1963.

Defoe, Daniel. *Memoirs of a Cavalier*. Oxford: Oxford University Press, 1991.

Dickens, A. G. *The Counter Reformation*. New York: W. W. Norton, 1968.

Diehl, Charles. *Byzantium: Greatness and Decline*. Eng. Trans. by Naomi Walford. New Brunswick: Rutgers University Press, 1957. (*BGD*)

Diehl, Charles. *History of the Byzantine Empire*. Princeton: Princeton University Press, 1925. (*HBE*)

Ducket, Eleanor Shipley. *Alfred the Great: The King and His England*. Chicago: University of Chicago Press, 1956.

Durant, Will. and Ariel Durant. *The Story of Civilization*. 11 vol. New York: Simon & Schuster, 1954–75.

Earle, Peter. *The Life and Times of Henry V*. London: Wiedenfeld and Nicolson, 1972.

Edgerton, Samuel Y. *The Renaissance Rediscovery of Linear Perspective*. New York: Basic Books, 1975.

Einhard (Eginhard). *Life of Charlemagne*. Eng. Trans. by Samuel Epes Turner. New York: American Book Company, 1880.

Einhard and Notker the Stammerer. *Two Lives of Charlemagne*. Eng. trans. by Lewis Thorpe. Middlesex: Penguin Classics, 1969.

Eliot, C. W. ed. *Scientific Papers*, vol. 38. New York: P. F. Collier and Son, Co., 1897.

Elliott, J. H. *Imperial Spain 1469–1716*. London: Penguin Books, 1963. (Reprinted, 1990)

Elton, G. R. *Reformation Europe: 1517–1559*. New York: Harper Torchbooks, 1963.

Encyclopædia Britannica. 11th ed. 29 vol. Cambridge (England): University Press, 1911.

Fabyan, Robert. *Great Chronicle of London*. ed. by A. H. Thomas and I. D. Thornley. London: G. W. Jones, 1938.

Fair, Charles. *From the Jaws of Victory*. New York: Simon & Schuster, 1971.

Falls, Cyril, ed. *Great Military Battles*. London: Spring Books, 1964.

Finlay, George. *A History of Greece: The Byzantine and Greek Empires, Pt. 2, A.D. 1057–1453*. Oxford: Clarendon Press, 1877. (Referred to in endnotes as "vol. 2.")

Finlay, George. *History of the Byzantine Empire From 717 to 1057*. London: J. M. Dent, 1906. (Referred to in endnotes as "vol. 1.")

Fisher, George Park. *Outlines of Universal History*. New York: Ivison, Blakeman, Taylor, and Company, 1885.

Fletcher, C. R. L. *Gustavus Adolphus and the Struggle of Protestantism for Existence*. New York and London: G. P. Putnam's Sons, 1901.

Frayling, Christopher, Helen Frayling, and Ron Van Der Meer. *The Art Pack.* New York: Alfred A. Knopf, 1992.
Friedrich, Carl J. *The Age of the Baroque, 1610–1660.* New York: Harper Torchbooks, 1962.
Froissart, John. *Chronicles.* Translated by Geoffrey Brereton. London: Penguin Books, 1978. (*FC*)
Froissart, John. *Chronicles of England, France, Spain and the Adjoining Countries.* New York: Leavitt, Trow and Co., 1849. (*CEFS*)
Froissart, John. *The Chronicles of Froissart.* (Globe edition). Translated by John Bourchier. New York: Macmillan, 1904. (*COF*)
Fuller, J. F. C. *A Military History of the Western World: 3 Vols.* London: Minerva Press, 1956.
Funck-Brentano, Fr. *The Middle Ages.* New York: G. P. Putnam and Sons, 1926.
Galbert of Bruges. *The Murder of Charles the Good.* Toronto: University of Toronto Press, 1982.
Gardiner, Samuel Rawson. *The Thirty Years' War.* New York: Charles Scribner's Sons, 1906. (*TYW*)
Gardner, Edmund G. *The Story of Siena and San Gimignano.* London: J. M. Dent and Co., 1902.
Gasquet, Francis Aidan. *The Great Pestilence (AD 1348-9), Now Commonly Known as the Black Death.* London: Simpkin Marshal, Hamilton, Kent, and Co., Ltd., 1893.
Geanakoplos, Deno John, ed. *Byzantium: Church, Society, and Civilization Seen through Contemporary Eyes.* Chicago: University of Chicago Press, 1984.
Gibbon, Edward. *Decline and Fall of the Roman Empire.* 5 volumes. New York: American Book Exchange, 1880. (All entries unless *EB* is specifically noted)
Gibbon, Edward. *Decline and Fall of the Roman Empire.* 2 vol. Chicago: Encyclopædia Britannica, 1952. (*EB*)
Gies, Frances and Joseph. *Cathedral, Forge, and Waterwheel. Technology and Invention in the Middle Ages.* New York: HarperPerennial, 1995.
Gilbert, Martin ed. *The Illustrated Atlas of Jewish Civilization.* New York: Macmillan Publishing Company, 1990.
Giles, J. A. ed. *Six Old English Chronicles.* London: H. G. Bohn, 1848.
Gilmore, Myron P. *The World of Humanism.* New York: Harper Torchbooks, 1962.
Gimpel, Jean. *The Medieval Machine.* New York: Barnes and Noble, 1976.
Goodenough, Simon. *Tactical Genius in Battle.* London: Phaidon Press, 1979.
Goodwin, Jason, *Lords of the Horizons*, New York: Henry Holt and Company, 1998.
Gordon, Mary. *Joan of Arc.* New York: Viking, 2000.
Graetz, Heinrich Hirsch. *History of the Jews.* 6 volumes. Philadelphia: Jewish Publication Society of America, 1894.
Gregory of Tours. *The History of the Franks.* Eng. trans. by Lewis Thorpe. Middlesex: Penguin Books, 1974.
Gregory, Timothy. *A History of Byzantium.* 2nd Ed. Chichester: Wiley-Blackwell, 2010.
Guizot, Francois. *The History of France.* 8 vol. English translation by Robert Black. New York: John B. Alden, Publisher, 1885. (*France*)
Guizot, Francois. *A Popular History of England.* 5 vol. Eng. Trans. by M. M. Ripley. Boston: Estes and Lauriat, 1874–81. (*England*)
Hackett, Francis. *Francis the First.* New York: The Literary Guild, 1934.
Hackett, Neil. *The World of Europe: The Ancient World to 800.* St. Louis: Forum Press, 1979.
Haggard, Howard W. *The Doctor in History.* New York: Barnes and Noble Books, 1996.
Haldon, John. *The Byzantine Wars.* Stroud: The History Press, 2001.
Hall, Gordon Langley. *William, Father of the Netherlands.* Chicago: Rand McNally and Company, 1969.
Hallam, Henry. *View of the State of Europe during the Middle Ages.* 6th London edition, complete in one volume. New York: Harper and Brothers, 1837.
Harbison, E. Harris. *The Age of Reformation.* Ithaca: Cornell University Press, 1955.
Hare, Christopher (pseudonym of Marian Andrews). *A Great Emperor, Charles V, 1519–1558.* New York: Charles Scribner's Sons, 1917.
Hecker, J. F. C. *The Epidemics of the Middle Ages.* Eng. Trans. by B. G. Babington. London: Trübner and Co., 1859.
Hill, Christopher. *The Century of Revolution: 1603–1714.* New York: W. W. Norton and Co., 1961.
Hollister, C. Warren. *Medieval Europe: A Short History.* 5th Ed. New York: Alfred A. Knopf, 1982. (*SH*)
Hollister, C. Warren, Joe W. Leedom, Marc A. Meyer, and David S. Spear. *Medieval History: A Short Sourcebook.* New York: Alfred A. Knopf, 1982. (*SS*)
Holmes, George. *The Later Middle Ages: 1272–1485.* New York: W. W. Norton, 1962. (*LMA*)
Holmes, George. *The Oxford Illustrated History of Medieval Europe.* Oxford: Oxford University Press, 1988. (*OME*)
Holmes, Richard. *Epic Land Battles.* Secaucus: Chartwell Books, Inc., 1976.
Howarth, David. *1066: The Year of Conquest.* New York: Penguin Books, 1977. (*1066*)
Howarth, David. *The Voyage of the Armada.* New York: Penguin Books, 1982. (*VA*)
Howarth, Stephen. *The Knights Templar.* New York: Barnes and Noble Books, 1982.
Jackson, Gabriel. *The Making of Medieval Spain.* Norwich: Harcourt Brace Jovanovich, Inc., 1972.

Jenkins, Romilly. *Byzantium: The Imperial Centuries, AD 610–1071*. New York: Vintage Books, 1966.

Johnson, A. H. *Europe in the Sixteenth Century*. London: Rivingtons, 1903.

Joinville, Jean de. *Memoirs of John, Lord de Joinville, Grand Seneschal of Champagne*. Eng. Trans. by Thomas Johnes. 2 vol. Hafod: Hafod Press, 1807.

Joinville and Villehardouin. *Chronicles of the Crusades*. Eng. Trans. by M.R.B. Shaw. Middlesex: Penguin Classics, 1982.

Jones, Prudence, and Nigel Pennick. *A History of Pagan Europe*. New York: Barnes and Noble, 1995.

Jones, Terry and Alan Ereira. *Crusades*. London: BCA, 1995.

Keegan, John. *The Face of Battle*. New York: Barnes and Noble Books, 1993. (*FOB*)

Keegan, John. *The Mask of Command*. New York: Viking Press, 1987. (*MOC*)

Kenyon, J. P. *Stuart England*. 2nd Ed. London: Pelican Books, 1985.

King, C. Harold. *A History of Civilization*. 2nd Edition. Volume I. New York: Charles Scribner's Sons, 1964.

King, Ross. *Brunelleschi's Dome*. New York: Walker and Company, 2000.

Kinross, Lord J. P. D. B. *The Ottoman Centuries*. New York: Morrow Quill Paperbacks, 1977.

Knecht, R. J. *Francis I*. Cambridge: Cambridge University Press, 1982. (Paperback ed., 1984.)

Kubovy, Michael. *The Psychology of Perspective and Renaissance Art*. Cambridge: Cambridge University Press, 1986.

Lacey, Robert. *The Life and Times of Henry VIII*. New York: Welcome Rain, 1998.

Lamb, Harold. *Charlemagne: The Legend and the Man*. New York: Bantam Books, 1954.

Lamonte, John L. *The World of the Middle Ages*. New York: Appleton Century Crofts, 1949.

Lander, J. R. *The Wars of the Roses*. London: Grange Books, 1997.

Langdon-Davies, John. *Carlos, The King Who Would Not Die*. Englewood Cliffs: Prentice-Hall, Inc., 1962.

Langer, Herbert. *The Thirty Years' War*. Poole: Blandford Press, 1978.

Larousse Encyclopedia of Ancient and Medieval History. Marcel Dunan, ed. London: Paul Hamlyn, 1966. (Vol. 1)

Larousse Encyclopedia of Modern History. Marcel Dunan, ed. London: Paul Hamlyn, 1967. (Vol. 2)

Lee, Stephen J. *The Thirty Years War*. London: Routledge, 1991.

Lewis, Jon E., ed. *The Mammoth Book of Eye-Witness History*. New York: Carrol and Graf Publishers, Inc., 1998.

Lewis, W. H. *The Splendid Century*. Prospect Heights: Waveland Press, 1997.

Liddell Hart, B. H. *Great Captains Unveiled*. New York: De Capo Press, 1996.

Limm, Peter. *The Thirty Years War*. London: Longman, 1984.

Littleton, Taylor and Robert R Rea. *To Prove a Villain*. New York: Macmillan, 1964.

Liudprand. *The Works of Liudprand of Cremona*. Eng. Trans. by F. A. Wright. London: George Routledge and Sons, 1930.

Livesey, Anthony. *Great Commanders and their Battles*. Philadelphia: Courage Books, 1987.

Lodge, R. *The Close of the Middle Ages, 1273–1494*. London: Rivingtons, 1904.

Luttwak, Edward N. *The Grand Strategy of the Byzantine Empire*. Cambridge: The Belknap Press of Harvard University Press, 2009.

Mackay, James. *William Wallace: Braveheart*. Edinburgh: Mainstream Publishing, 1995.

Magill, Frank. *Masterpieces of World Philosophy*. New York: HarperCollins, 1991.

Major, Ralph A. *Classic Descriptions of Disease*. Springfield; Baltimore: Charles C. Thomas, 1932.

Manchester, William. *A World Lit only by Fire*. Boston: Little, Brown and Company, 1992.

Manetti, Antonio di Tuccio. *Life of Brunelleschi*. University Park: Pennsylvania State University Press, 1970.

Manetti, Antonio di Tuccio. Excerpt from *The Life of Brunelleschi*. In *Brunelleschi in Perspective*. Isabelle Hyman, ed. Englewood Cliffs: Prentice-Hall, Inc., 1974 (p. 66 describes different painting, Temple of San Giovanni in Florence).

Margotta, Roberto. *The History of Medicine*. New York: Smithmark Publishers, 1996.

Markov, Walter, ed. *Battles of World History*. New York: Hippocrene Books, 1979.

Martin, Colin and Parker, Geoffrey. *The Spanish Armada*. New York: W.W. Norton and Company, 1988.

Marx, Robert F. *The Battle of the Spanish Armada, 1588*. Cleveland: The World Publishing Company 1965.

Mattingly, Garrett. *The Armada*. Boston: Houghton Mifflin Company, 1987.

May, Arthur J. *A History of Civilization*. 2nd Edition. Volume 2. New York: Charles Scribner's Sons, 1964.

Maynard, Theodore. *Queen Elizabeth*. Milwaukee: The Bruce Publishing Company, 1954.

McKendrick, Melveena. *The Horizon Concise History of Spain*. New York: American Heritage Publishing, Co., Inc., 1972.

McNeill, William H. *Plagues and Peoples*. New York: Anchor Books, 1976.

Mehring, Franz. *Absolutism and Revolution in Germany, 1525–1848*. London: New Park Publications, 1975.

Mills, Charles. *History of the Crusades*. Philadelphia: H. C. Carey and I. Lea, 1826.

Montross, Lynn. *War Through the Ages*. New York: Harper and Brothers Publishers, 1960.

Motley. John Lathrop. *The Rise of the Dutch Republic*. (*The Student's Motley*) New York: Harper and Brothers, 1898.

Munro, Dana Carleton. *A History of the Middle Ages*. New York: D. Appleton and Company, 1902. (*HMA*)

Munro, Dana Carleton. *The Middle Ages: 395–1272*. New York: The Century Co., 1923. (*TMA*)

Neale, J. E. *The Age of Catherine de Medici*. New York: Harper Torchbooks, 1962.

Neillands, Robin. *The Wars of the Roses*. London: Cassell Books, 1992.

New, John F. H. *The Renaissance and Reformation: A Short History*. New York: Alfred A. Knopf, 1977.

Newhall, Richard A. *The Crusades*. New York: Holt, Rinehart and Winston, Inc., 1963.

Nicol, D. M. *The End of the Byzantine Empire*. London: Edward Arnold, 1979.

Norwich, John Julius. *Byzantium: The Apogee*. Alfred A. Knopf, 1992. (*Apogee*)

Norwich, John Julius. *Byzantium: The Early Centuries*. Alfred A. Knopf, 1989. (*EC*)

Norwich, John Julius. *A Short History of Byzantium*. New York: Alfred A. Knopf, 1997. (*SHB*)

Nowell, Charles E. *The Great Discoveries and the First Colonial Empires*. Ithaca: Cornell University Press, 1954.

Nuland, Sherwin. *Doctors: The Biography of Medicine*. New York: Vintage Books, 1988.

Obolensky, Dimitri. *The Byzantine Commonwealth*. London: Phoenix Press, 1971.

Ogg, David. *Europe in the Seventeenth Century*. New York: Collier Books, 1960.

Ogg, Frederic Austin., ed. *A Sourcebook of Medieval History*. New York: American Book Co., 1907.

Oman, C. W. C. *The Art of War in the Middle Ages*. Ithaca: Great Seal Books, 1960. (*AWMA*)

Oman, C. W. C. *The Byzantine Empire*. Yardley: Westholme Publishing, 2008. (*BE*)

O'Shea, Stephen. *The Perfect Heresy*. New York: Barnes and Noble Books, 2000.

Osler, William. *The Evolution of Modern Medicine*. New Haven: Yale University Press, 1913.

Ostrogorsky, George. *History of the Byzantine State*. New Brunswick: Rutgers University Press, 1969.

O'Sullivan, Jeremiah and Burns, John F. *Medieval Europe*. New York: Appleton-Century-Crofts, 1943.

Packard, Francis R. *The Life and Times of Ambroise Pare*. New York: Paul B. Hoebber, Inc. 1926.

Paré, Ambroise. *The Workes of that Famous Chirurgeon Ambrose Parey*. Eng. Trans. by Thomas Johnson. London: Richard Cotes, 1649.

Parker, Geoffrey, ed. *The Cambridge Illustrated History of Warfare*. Cambridge: Cambridge University Press, 1995. (*HOW*)

Parker, Geoffrey. *The Thirty Years' War*. New York: Military Heritage Press, 1987. (*TYW*)

Pernoud, Regine and Clin, Marie-Veronique. *Joan of Arc: Her Story*. New York: St. Martin's Griffin, 1998.

Plumb, J. H. Ed. *The Italian Renaissance*. New York: American Heritage Press, 1961.

Previté-Orton, C. W. *The Shorter Cambridge Medieval History*. 2 Volumes. Cambridge: Cambridge University Press, 1953.

Procopius. *The History of the Warres of the Emperour Justinian in eight books*. "Englished" by Sir Henry Holcroft. London: H. Moseley, 1653. (*HWEJ*)

Procopius. *Procopius: History of the Wars*. Vol. 1 (Books I and II). Eng. Trans. by H. B. Dewing. London: William Heinemann, 1914. (*HOW*)

Procopius. *History of Wars, Secret History and Buildings*. Eng. Trans. by Averil Cameron. New York: Twayne Publishers, 1967. (*Wars*)

Procopius. *Secret History*. Eng. Trans. by Richard Atwater. New York: Covici Friede, Publishers, 1934. (*Secret History*)

Psellus, Michael. *Fourteen Byzantine Rulers*. Eng. trans. by E. R. A. Sewter. Baltimore: Penguin Classics, 1966.

Rady, Martin. *The Emperor Charles V*. London: Longman, 1988.

Reilly, Bernard F. *The Medieval Spains*. Cambridge: Cambridge University Press, 1993.

Reischauer, Edwin O., John K Fairbank, and Albert M. Craig. *East Asia, The Great Tradition*. 2 Vol. Boston: Houghton Mifflin, 1958–65.

Reither, Joseph, ed. *Masterworks of History*. Garden City, New York: Doubleday, 1948.

Rice, Eugene F. *The Foundations of Early Modern Europe, 1460–1559*. New York: W. W. Norton, 1970.

Rice, Tamara Talbot. *Everyday Life in Byzantium*. New York: Dorset Press, 1967.

Robinson, James Harvey. *History of Western Europe*. 2 volumes. Boston: Ginn and Company, 1934. (*History*)

Robinson, James Harvey. *Readings in European History*. 2 volumes. Boston: Atheneum Press, 1906. (*Readings*)

Rogers, P. G. *The Dutch in the Medway*. London: Oxford University Press, 1970.

Ross, Charles. *Richard III*. Berkeley: University of California Press, 1981.

Ross, David R. *On the Trail of Robert the Bruce*. Edinburgh: Luath Press Limited, 1999. (*RB*)

Ross, David R. *On the Trail of William Wallace*. Edinburgh: Luath Press Limited, 1999. (*WW*)

Ross, James Bruce and McLaughlin, Mary Martin.

The Portable Medieval Reader. New York: Penguin Books/Viking Press, Inc., 1977.

Rostovtzeff, M. *Rome.* New York: Oxford University Press, 1960.

Runciman, Steven. *The Fall of Constantinople, 1453.* Cambridge: Cambridge University Press, 1965. (*FOC*)

Runciman, Steven. *A History of the Crusades.* Vol. 1. New York: Harper Torchbooks, 1964. (*HC*, vol. 1)

Runciman, Steven. *A History of the Crusades.* Vol. 2. Cambridge: Cambridge University Press, 1951. (*HC*, vol. 2)

Runciman, Steven. *The Sicilian Vespers.* Baltimore: Penguin Books, 1958. (*SV*)

St. Aubyn, Giles. *The Year of Thee Kings: 1483.* New York: Atheneum, 1983.

St. Jerome. *Letters and Select Works.* Vol. 6, of *A Select Library of Nicene and Post-Nicene Fathers of the Christian Church.* Translated by Philip Schaff and Henry Wace. New York: The Christian Literature Company, 1893.

Saunders, J. B. deC. M. and Charles D. O'Malley. *The Illustrations from the Works of Andreas Vesalius of Brussels.* New York: Dover Publications, 1950.

Schevill, Ferdinand. *The Medici.* New York: Harper Torchbooks, 1960.

Scholz, Bernhard Walter (translator). *Carolingian Chronicles* (*Royal Frankish Annals*; Nithard's *Histories*). Ann Arbor: University of Michigan Press, 1972.

Scott, Ronald McNair. *Robert the Bruce.* New York: Carroll and Graf Publishers, Inc., 1992.

Sellar, W. C. and Yeatman, R. J. *1066 and All That.* New York: E. P. Dutton and Co., 1931.

Seward, Desmond. *The Hundred Years War: The English in France, 1337–1453.* New York: Atheneum, 1978. (*HYW*)

Seward, Desmond. *The Wars of the Roses.* New York: Penguin Books, 1995. (*WOR*)

Singer, Charles. *A Short History of Scientific Ideas to 1900.* Oxford: Oxford University Press, 1959.

Singh, Simon. *Fermat's Enigma.* New York: Anchor Books (Doubleday), 1997.

Smith, Lacey Baldwin. *The Elizabethan World.* Boston: Houghton Mifflin Company, 1966. (*EW*)

Smith, Lacey Baldwin. *This Realm of England, 1399 to 1688.* 4th Ed. Lexington: D. C. Heath and Co., 1983. (*TRE*)

Smith, Preserved. *The Life and Letters of Martin Luther.* Boston: Houghton Mifflin, 1914.

Somers, Baron John. *Somers tracts.* 13 vol. London: T. Caldwell, W. Daves [etc], 1809–1815.

Sphrantzes, George. *The Fall of the Byzantine Empire.* Eng. Trans. by Marios Philippides. Amherst: University of Massachusetts Press, 1980.

Stark, Rodney. *God's Battalions: The Case for the Crusades.* New York: HarperOne, 2009.

Steinberg, S. H. *The Thirty Years' War and the Conflict for European Hegemony, 1600–1660.* New York: W. W. Norton and Co., 1966.

Stevens, John L. *History of Gustavus Adolphus.* New York: G. P. Putnam's Sons, 1884.

Sutcliffe, Dr. Jenny and Nancy Duin. *A History of Medicine.* New York: Barnes and Noble Books, 1992.

Swanton, M. J., translator and editor. *The Anglo-Saxon Chronicle.* New York: Routledge, 1996.

Taylor, A. J. P. *The Habsburg Monarchy.* Harmondsworth, Middlesex: Peregrine Books, 1964.

Thatcher, Oliver J., and Schwill, Ferdinand. *Europe in the Middle Age.* New York: Charles Scribner's Sons, 1907.

Theophanes Confessor. *The Chronicle of Theophanes Confessor.* Translated by Harry Turtledove. Philadelphia: University of Pennsylvania Press, 1982.

Theophylact Simocatta. *The History of Theophylact Simocatta.* Translated by Michael and Mary Whitby. Oxford: Clarendon Press, 1986.

Thorpe, Lewis. *The Bayeaux Tapestry and the Norman Invasion.* London: The Folio Society, 1973.

Thubron, Colin. *The Venetians.* Alexandria: Time-Life Books, 1980.

Treadgold, Warren. *A Concise History of Byzantium.* New York: Palgrave, 2001.

Trevelyan, G. M. *A Shortened History of England.* Middlesex: Penguin Books, 1982.

Trevor Davies, R. *Spain in Decline: 1621–1700.* London: Macmillan and Company, 1965.

Tuchman, Barbara. *Bible and Sword.* New York: Ballantine Books, 1984. (*BAS*)

Tuchman, Barbara. *A Distant Mirror.* New York: Ballantine Books, 1979. (*DM*)

Tuchman, Barbara. *The March of Folly.* New York: Alfred A. Knopf, 1984. (*MOF*)

Twiss, Miranda. *The Most Evil Men and Women in History.* New York: Barnes and Noble Books, 2002.

Van Doren, Charles. *A History of Knowledge.* New York: Ballantine Books, 1991.

Vasari, Giorgio. *Lives of the Artists.* Eng. Trans. by George Bull. New York: Penguin Books, 1965. (*LA*)

Vasari, Giorgio. *Lives of the Most Eminent Painters, Sculptors, and Architects.* Six volumes. Eng. Trans. by Mrs. Jonathan Foster. London: George Bell and Sons, 1890. (*LPSA*)

Vergil, Polydore. *Three Books of Polydore Vergil's English History, Comprising the Reigns of Henry VI, Edward IV., and Richard III.* London: The Camden Society, 1844.

Viorst, Milton. *The Great Documents of Western Civilization.* New York: Barnes and Noble Books, 1994.

Voltaire, François Marie Arouet de. *The History of Charles XII.* Edited from the 1762 translation of

Tobias Smollet by O. W. Wight. New York: Hurd and Houghton, 1864.

Voltaire, Francois Marie Arouet de. *The History of Charles XII King of Sweden*. Eng. Trans. by Antonia White. New York: Barnes and Noble Books, 1993.

Von Grunebaum, G. E. *Classical Islam*. New York: Barnes and Noble Books, 1996.

Wakeman, Henry Offley. *Europe, 1598–1715*. New York: Macmillan and Co., 1895.

Waley, Daniel. *Later Medieval Europe: from St. Louis to Luther*. London: Longmans, 1964.

Wallbank, T. W. and Taylor, A. M. *Civilization Past and Present*. 3rd Ed. Chicago: Scott Foresman and Company, 1954.

Walsh, James Joseph. *The Thirteenth, Greatest of Centuries*. New York: Catholic Summer School Press, 1913.

Warner, Oliver. *Great Sea Battles*. New York: The Macmillan Company, 1963.

Watson, Francis. *Wallenstein, Soldier under Saturn*. London: Chatto and Windus, 1938.

Watt, W. Montgomery. *Muhammad: Prophet and Statesman*. London: Oxford University Press, 1961.

Wavrin, Jehan de. *A Collection of the Chronicles and Ancient Histories of Great Britain, Now Called England*. Eng. Trans. by William Hardy and Edward L. C. P. Hardy. London: Eyre and Spottiswoode, 1887.

Weatherford, Jack. *Genghis Khan and the Making of the Modern World*. New York: Three River Press, 2004.

Weber, Eugen. *The Western Tradition. From the Ancient World to the Atomic Age*. Boston: D. C. Heath and Company, 1965.

Wedeck, Harry E. ed. *Putnam's Dark and Middle Ages Reader*. New York: G. P. Putnam's Sons, 1964.

Wedgwood, C. V. *Richelieu and the French Monarchy*. New York: Collier Books, 1962. (*RFM*)

Wedgwood, C. V. *The Spoils of Time*. Garden City: Doubleday and Company, Inc., 1985. (*SOT*)

Wedgwood, C. V. *The Thirty Years War*. New Haven: Yale University Press, 1939. (*TYW*)

Wedgwood, C. V. *William the Silent*. New York: W.W. Norton and Company, 1968. (*WS*)

Wells, H. G. *The Outline of History*. New York: Garden City Books, 1949.

William, Archbishop of Tyre. *Godeffroy of Boloyne or the Siege and Conquest of Jerusalem*. Eng. Trans. by William Caxton, London: Keegan, Paul, Trench, Trübner and Co., 1893.

Williams, Henry Smith. *The Historians History of the World*. Vol. 10. New York: The Outlook Company, 1904.

Williams, Neville. *Elizabeth I, Queen of England*. London: Sphere Books Limited, 1971.

Winston, Richard. *Charlemagne*. New York: Harper and Row, 1968.

Woodruff, Douglas. *The Life and Times of Alfred the Great*. London: Wiedenfeld and Nicolson, 1974.

Wright, Desmond, ed. *The Medieval and Renaissance World*. Secaucus: Chartwell Books, 1979.

Wright, John (translator). *The Life of Cola di Rienzo*. (Anonymous). Toronto: Pontifical Institute of Medieval Studies, 1975.

Xenophon. *Xenophon's Anabasis or Expedition of Cyrus and the Memorabilia of Socrates*. Eng. Trans. by Rev. J. S. Watson. New York: Harper and Brothers, 1875. (*Anabasis*)

Yonge, Charlotte. *A Pictorial History of the World's Great Nations*. 3 volumes. New York: Selmar Hess, 1882.

Zeigler, Philip. *The Black Death*. New York: Harper Torchbooks, 1969.

Index

Numbers in ***bold italics*** indicate pages with illustrations.

Aachen 76, 81, 108, 170
abacus 83, 99, 140
Abbasids 24, 40, 62, 75, 91, 158
Abd al-Rahman I 158
Abd al-Rahman III "the Great" 158
Abd-ar-Rahman 70–71
Abelard, Peter 138–39
Abrittus 3
Abu Bekr 17
Abul Abbas 81, 83
Abydos 20, 36
Acre 101, 110, 117
Act of Supremacy 174
Adams, G. B. 79
Adolph I of Naussau 115
Adoptionism 75
Adrianople 34, 48, 52–53, 56, 58
Adriatic Sea 42–43, 101
Aegean Sea 49, 59
Aelian 194
Age of Discovery 155
Agincourt 129–30, ***131***, 145–46
Agnedello 162
agriculture 4, 19, 66, 109, 127; medieval innovations in 142
Aistulf 71–72
Aix-la-Chapelle *see* Aachen
Akroinos 24
al-Aqsa Mosque 95
Al-Hazen 63
Al-Kamil 110, 227*n*247
Al-Khwarizmi 62
al-Mansur 158
Alais, Decree of 199
Alaric the Bold 3, 137
Albert I of Hapsburg 115
Albigensians 102–04, 108, 112, 115
Alboin 66
Alchemy 63, 141
Alcuin 75, 138
Aleander, Girolamo 164
Alemanni 3, 10
Alexander (uncle of Constantine VII) 31
Alexander III 101
Alexander V 135
Alexander VI (Rodrigo Borgia) 156–57, 231*n*66, 231*n*71
Alexander the Great 14, 51
Alexandria 17–18, 106

Alexandrian Library 17, 62
Alexiad 44, 62
Alexis Branas 46
Alexius I Comnenus 42–45, 91, 93–94, 96
Alexius II Comnenus 45
Alexius III Angelus 46–47, 222*n*270
Alexius IV Angelus 47
Alexius V Ducas Murzuphlus 47
Alfonso VI 158–59
Alfonso VIII 159
Alfonso X, "the Wise" 160
Alfonso XI 160
Alfonso, Duke of Bisceglia 157
Alfonso "the Slobberer" 159
Alfred the Great 87, ***88***
algebra 62, 215, 216
Algiers 176
Ali (son-in-law of Mohammed) 18
Ali Pasha 184
Aljubarotta 159
Alkmaar 188
Allah 15–18, 61, 86
Allerheim 208
Almohads 159
Almoravids 159
Alousianus 38
Alp Arslan 41–42
Alps 73, 165, 177, 209
Alsace 78, 149, 205, 209, 234*n*376
Alva, Fernando Álvarez de Toledo, 3rd Duke of 185–89
Amalasuntha 5, 9
Ambien Hill 151
Amboise, Edict of 182
Amiens 120, 149
Amorion 29
Amsterdam 188
Anabaptists 170–71
Anagni 115
Anastasius I 5, 6, 11
Anastasius II 20, 24, 221*n*114
Anatolia 28, 35, 37–38
anatomy 211, 213, 234*n*402
Anchiolos 25
Andronicus I Comnenus 45, 47
Andronicus II Palaeologus 50–51
Andronicus III Palaeologus 51–52
Andronicus IV Palaeologus 53
Andronicus Kontosthephanos 44

Angeloi dynasty 46–48
Angevin claim: English in France 101–05, 114, 226*n*223; French in Sicily 50, 111, 153, 155, 158, 169
Angles 86
Anglicanism, Anglicans 174–75, 178–79
Anglo-Saxons 42, 67, 86–89
Angora *see* Ankara
Ani 41
Anjou 99, 102, 226*n*223
Ankara 56
Ann of Cleves 175
Anna (sister of Basil II) 36, 222*n*203
Anna Comnena 62
Anne (sister of Charles VIII) 155
Anne (wife of Charles VIII, Louis XII) 155–57
Antioch (city) 14, 17, 34, 43–45, 94, 98
Antioch (principality of) 95
Antonina 10, 220*n*48
Antwerp 188–89
Apokaukos, Alexius 52
Aquinas, St. Thomas 139
Aquitaine 70, 73, 97–99, 102–03, 107, 114, 116, 126
arabesque 63
Arabian Nights 63
Arabic numerals 62, 83, 140
Arabs 16–22, 25, 27, 29–30, 32–33, 35, 62, 63, 83, 91, 95, 106, 109, 111, 117, 227*n*286; *see also* Islam; Muslims
Aragon 50, 104, 153, 158–59, 161, 206
Arcadiopolis 28, 34–35, 46
architecture 11, 62, 68, 141–42, 212–13
Aristotle 63, 97, 137–38, 140, 210, 214, 229*n*447
Arithmetica 216
Armada, Spanish 190–92, 194, 233*n*292
Armagnacs 129, 131–33
Armenia 14, 31, 40–41
armor 12, 32, 44, 65, 104, 115, 152, 162, 197; gunpowder and 134, 136, 140, 142, 217; longbow and 119, 130
Arno River 154

Index

Arnold of Brescia 101
Arnulf 80, 225*n*99
arquebus 162, 169, 182
Arques 192
Arras, Treaty of 133
art 62–63, 211–12
Artevelde, Jacob van 119
Arthur (Artorius) 86
Arthur (son of Henry VII of England) 152, 174, 231*n*110
Arthur of Brittany 102
artillery 136, 145, 155–56, 162, 165, 169, 184, 188, 191, 202, 207; and demise of the castle 134, 155, 217; and fall of Constantinople 57–59, 133, 145
Artois 104, 118
Ascalon 101
Asia Minor 14, 18–20, 25–26, 28–30, 33, 36, 40–45, 47–48, 51–52, 54, 56, 61, 91, 98, 101
Aspar 5
Assertio Septem Sacramentum 173
Asses Hill 88
Assyria 15
astronomy 76, 137, 214–15
Athalaric 5
Athens 51, 224*n*370
Atlantic Ocean 19, 73, 199
Attalia 98
Attila the Hun 4–5, 68
Augsburg 82
Augsburg, Diet of: 1530 170; 1548 177
Augsburg Interim 177
Augsburg, Peace of 175, 177, 195, 198, 209
Augustine, St. 3, 76
Augustus 3, 76
Austrasia 70
Austria, Austrians 115, 170, 197, 199, 204–05, 207, 209, 214
auto da fé 184
Auvergne 97
Auwa 122
Auxerre 182
Avars 13–14, 74, 77, 226*n*78
Averroës 138
Avicenna 63, 140; *Canon of Medicine* 63
Avignon 115, 134–35, 153

Babington Plot 190
Babylonian Captivity 153
Bacon, Francis 214–15
Bacon, Roger 141, 214–15
Badajoz 115
Badon Hill 86
Badr 16
Baghdad 62–63, 91
Bajazet 54, 56
Baker, Geoffrey Le 125
balance of power principle 163, 205
Baldwin I 47–48
Baldwin II 49
Balkans 13, 19, 25, 27, 43, 48, 66
Ball, John 127–28
Balliol, John 113
Baltic Sea 198–99
Baltic States 62

Baner, Johan 202, 206
Bannockburn 117
Baptistery (of Florence Cathedral) 212
Barbary Coast 194
Bardas (uncle of Michael III) 30, 221*n*167
Bardas Phocas *see* Phocas, Bardas
Bardas Sclerus *see* Sclerus, Bardas
Bari 30, 37, 42, 109, 134
Barletta 162
Barnet 149–50
Bartholomew, Peter 94
Basil I (the Macedonian) 30–31, 221*n*168
Basil II (the Bulgar-Slayer or the Great) 33, 35–37, 39–40, 60, 222*n*206, 223*n*278
Basil Lecapenus 34–35, 222*n*197
Basilica 31, 62
Basilica Thermia 35
Basle 123
Basle, Council of 136
Bavaria, Bavarians 73–74, 80–81, 115, 175, 195–97, 202, 208–09
Becket, Thomas 100
Bede 68, 86–87
beggars (Dutch War) 185; *see also* Sea Beggars
Beirut 35, 154
Belgium 69, 78, 149, 179, 189, 213
Belgrade 13, 57, 169
Belisarius 8–11, 32, 220*n*48
Beltran de la Cueva 161
Benedict XI 115
Benedict XIII 135
Benedict of Nursia, St. 67, 210
Benedictine Rule 67
Benedictines 68, 70, 72, 137, 224*n*39, 224*n*46
Benevento 111
Beowulf 143
Bernard (nephew of Louis the Pious) 77
Bernard of Armagnac 129
Bernard of Clairvaux, St. 98, 139
Bernard of Saxe-Weimer 205–06, 234*n*376
Berrhoa 46
Berwick 113
Berzem 42
Béziers 104
Bible 57, 135, 218, 230*n*481; *see also* Gutenberg Bible; New Testament; Scripture; Vulgate
binomial theorem 216
Birgu bastion 184
Black Death *see* bubonic plague
Black Forest 168, 208
Black Prince *see* Edward, the Black Prince
Black Sea 6, 20, 27, 31, 47, 49, 53–54, 56–57, 78, 121–22
Blanche de Bourbon 160
blast furnace 142
Bloody Meadow 149
Blues 7, 219*n*28
Boccaccio, Giovanni 122, 142, 210
Boethius 4, 137–38, 219*n*11; *Consolations of Philosophy* 87

Boghza Kesen (the "Throat Cutter") 57
Bohemia, Bohemians 115–16, 120, 135–36, 163, 168, 170, 195–97, 203–04, 208, 233*n*307
Bohemond 94–96
Boïlas 39
Boleyn, Ann 174–75, 179–80
Bologna 219; law school 62, 99, 142
Boniface VIII 114–15
Boniface of Fulda, St. 72, 224*n*39
Borgia, Cesare 157
Borgia, Giovanni 157
Borgia, house of 158, 162
Borgia, Rodrigo *see* Alexander VI (Rodrigo Borgia)
Borgia, Lucrezia 157
Bosnia 197
Bosphorus 14, 18, 20, 25, 42–43, 47, 51–52, 56–57, 61, 93, 145
Bosworth Field 151
Bothwell, James Hepburn, Lord 180–81
Boulogne 176
Bourbon, Blanche de 160
Bourges 132
Bouvines Bridge 103
Bracciolini, Poggio 211
Braganza, John, Duke of (John IV of Portugal) 207
Brahe, Tycho 214
Brandenburg 81, 116, 201, 204–05, 208–09
Braveheart *see* Wallace, William
Breda 206
Breisach 206
Breitenfeld 201–02, 206–07
Brescia 111
Bretigny, Treaty of 126
Brille 187
Britain, Britons 6, 67, 86, 109; *see also* England
Brittany 102, 116, 138, 155, 157
Bruce, Robert 117–18
Bruges 189
Brunanburh 87
Brunelleschi, Filippo 212–13
Brunhilde 69–70
Bruno, Giordano 215, 218
Brussels 186–87
bubonic plague 24, 53, 58, 127–28, 140, 142, 160; Black Death (1347) 121–22, 123, 124, 210; at Constantinople in Justinian's reign 11–12
Buda 55, 176
Bulgaria, Bulgarians (Bulgars) 5, 11, 19, 22, 25, 27–29, 31–32, 34–38, 46, 48, 50–51, 54–55, 75, 99, 221*n*164
Burckhardt, Jacob 109, 157
Bureau of Barbarians 61
Burgundy, Burgundians 68, 70, 129, 131–33, 148–50, 163, 169, 185
Burtzes 34
Bury, J. B. 6
Bythinia 32, 51
Byzantium 1, 3 *passim*, 65, 72, 75, 96, 112, 133, 136, 145, 220*n*87, 221*n*158

Cairo 106
Calabria 30

Calais 118, 120–21, 126, 130–31, 133, 149, 179, 181–82, 191
Calcar, Jan van 213
calendar 16, 214
Calixtus II 85
Callinicus 22
Calvin, John 171–72, *173*, 175, 180
Calvinism, Calvinists 172, 177, 180–81, 185, 195, 209
Cambrai, League of 162
Cambrai, Peace of 169
Camel, Battle of the 18
Candia 33
Cannae (battle, 216 BC) 10, 150
Cannae (battle, AD 1018) 36
cannibalism 94, 98, 206
cannon *see* artillery
Canon Law 66, 100
Canon of Medicine 63
Canossa 84
Canterbury 68, 100, 103, 174
Canterbury Tales 210
Canute 88
Cape of Good Hope 155
Capella, Martianus 137–38
Capetian dynasty 79–80, 118, 232*n*220
capitalism 155
capitularies 76
Capua 65
Carberry Hill 180
Carloman (brother of Charlemagne) 72–73
Carloman (brother of Pippin the Short) 71
Carlos, Don 179
Caroline Books 75
Carolingian miniscule 76, 138
Carolingians 72–80, 83
Carrhae 12, 220*n*60
Carthage 5, 8–9, 12–14, 19, 137, 158
Casilinum 10, 65, 68
Casket Letters 181
Cassel 118
Cassiodorus 4, 137–38
Castile 123, 158–160, 165, 206
Castillon 133–34, 145, 147, 149
Castle Santangelo 156, 169
castles 90, 94, 99–100, 102, 132, 142, 147, 157, 195–96, 223*n*342, 227*n*290; architecture of 141–42; demise of 134, 140, 155, 217
Catalonia, Catalans 51, 206–07
Câteau-Cambrésis, Treaty of 179, 181, 186
Cathars *see* Albigensians
Catherine (wife of Henry V) 132
Catherine de Medici 182–83
Catherine of Aragon 152, 174, 178, 231*n*110
Catholic League 195–96
Catholicism *see* Church, Catholic
cavalry 3, 8–9, 17, 23, 27, 31, 41, 50, 55–56, 79, 89–90, 106, 108, 114–15, 117, 124, 133, 156, 159, 162, 165, 169, 180, 192, 201, 208
Cerignola 162
Cerularius, Michael 40
Chalcedon 13–14
Chalcedon, Council of 6, 22

Châlons 4
Chancellorsville 206
Charlemagne 26, 72, *74*, 77–79, 81, 83, 86–87, 108, 138, 142; *filioque* thesis 75, 221*n*158; imperial schemes of 74–76; learning and 76; military campaigns of 73–74
Charles (son of Charlemagne) 77
Charles IV (France) 118
Charles IV (Germany) 115–16, 120
Charles V (Germany, also Charles I of Spain) 163, *164*, 171, 174, 178–79, 184–86, 205, 209, 213; character and imperial election of 164–65; and Francis I 168–69, 173, 176; and Henry VIII 173–74; and Luther 167–68; war with Schmalkaldic League 170, 176–77
Charles V the Wise (France) 125–27, 129
Charles VI the Mad (France) 129, 132
Charles VII the dauphin (France) 131–34, 146
Charles VIII (France) 155–56
Charles IX (France) 182–83
Charles de Guise (Cardinal of Lorraine) 181
Charles Martel 70–71, 224*n*39, 224*n*46
Charles of Anjou 49–50, 111, 155
Charles of Flanders 97
Charles the Bald 77–79
Charles the Fat 79–80
Charles the Great *see* Charlemagne
Charles the Rash 148–50, 163
Charles the Simple 79–80
Chartres 193
Chaucer, Geoffrey 210
Chauliac, Guy de 123
chemistry 141, 229*n*480
Childeric III 71
China 11, 54–56, 140, 230*n*45
Chinon 100, 132
Chios 52
Chippenham 87
Chosroes I 8, 10
Chosroes II 12–15, 17–18
Christian III 171
Christian IV 197–98
Christians, Christianity 3, 22, 43, 54–55, 66, 74–76, 78, 107, 112, 121, 137, 139, 143, 184, 188, 194, 197–98, 211, 220*n*97, 221*n*164, 227*n*247, 232*n*183; Byzantine 15, 50, 56, 58–59; conversions to 31–32, 36, 67–68, 73, 81, 86; and Crusades 43, 57, 92–96, 98, 100, 106, 109–10, 117; in Muslim world 17, 51, 63; Protestant Reformation and 167, 171–72; and reconquest of Spain 97, 158–59, 161
Christina, Queen of Sweden 200, 208, 216
Chrysocheir 30
Chrysopolis 36, 42
Church, Catholic 1, 43, 50, 66–68, 72, 75, 80, 81, 83–85, 91–92, 96–97, 100–03, 109, 112, 124, 135–39, 143, 153–54, 166–68, 170–71, 175, 177–78, 181, 210–11, 214–15, 217–18

Church, Eastern (Greek) Orthodox 14, 26–30, 40, 50, 75, 91
Church of England *see* Anglicanism, Anglicans
Cimbalongus 36
Circus Gate 59
Cistercians 108, 139, 142
Cistern of 1001 Columns 14
City of God (papal aspiration) 1, 72, 85, 112, 137, 165, 177, 218
City of God (Saint Augustine) 3–4, 76
Civitate 91
Clarence, George, Duke of 148–49, 152, 174
Clarendon, Constitutions of 100
Clement IV 50, 141
Clement V 115
Clement VII (anti-pope) 135
Clement VII (Medici pope) 169, 232*n*222
Clericis Laicos 114
Clermont, Council of 43
clock, invention of 142
Clothar I 69
Clovis 4, 68–69, 73, 158
Cluniac Reforms 84, 112
Codex Justinianus 11, 99, 140, 221*n*126
Cognac, League of 169
Coligny, Gaspard 181–83
College of Cardinals 66, 84–85, 111, 134–35
Cologne 92, 116
Colonna, Oddo *see* Martin V
Colossus of Rhodes 18
Columbus, Christopher 155, 161
comet of 1577 214
commerce 60, 79, 96, 109, 115, 121, 140, 154, 187; Byzantine 37, 45, 49–50, 53; Flemish 116, 119, 129; Mediterranean 153, 155
Common Law 99
Comnena, Anna *see* Anna Comnena
Comnenian dynasty 41–46
Compiègne 133
Compiègne, Treaty of 205
Comprehensive Book 63
"Compromise" 185
Comunero Revolt 165
conciliar movement 135–36
Condé, Henry I, Prince of 183
Condé, Henry II, Prince of (father of d'Enghein) 207
Condé, Louis I de Bourbon, Prince of 181–82
Condé, Louis II de Bourbon, Prince of (Duc d'Enghein) 207–08
condottieri 153
Conrad III 98
Conrad IV 111
Conrad of Franconia 80–81
Conrad of Montferrat 46
Conrad the Red 82
Conradin 111
consistory 172
Consolations of Philosophy 87
Constance, Council of 135
Constance of Sicily 101
Constans II 18–19
Constantine (son of Basil I) 30
Constantine I the Great 21, 72

Index

Constantine IV Pogonatus 19
Constantine V Copronymus 24–25
Constantine VI 25–26
Constantine VII Porphyrogenitus 31–33
Constantine VIII 33, 36, 222n206
Constantine IX Monomachus 38, *39*, 40
Constantine X Ducas 40–41, 222n242
Constantine XI Palaeologus 58–60
Constantinople 4, 6, 10, 13–15, 17, *21*, 24, 27, 30–35, 37, 40–42, 45, 50, 52–54, 61–63, 67, 72, 75, 91, 99, 103, 111, 143, 184; besieged by Moawiyah (AD 674) 19; besieged by Moslemah (AD 717) 20–22, 224n38; besieged by Murad II (AD 1421) 56; besieged by Thomas the Slav 28; First Crusade 43, 93–94, 226n184; Fourth Crusade and Latin conquest (AD 1204–1261) 47–49, 112; Muslim conquest by Mehmet II (AD 1453) 57–60, 145, 154; *Nika* riots 7–8; Russian naval attacks on 30, 32; as town of Byzantium 220n87
Constitution of Melfi 110
Copernicus, Nicolas 137, 214–15, 232n183
Cordova, caliphate of 158
Cordova, city 159
coronelia 162
Cortenuova 110
cortes 161, 168, 206
Cotyaeum 5
Council of Blood (Council of Troubles) 185–86
Counter-Reformation 175–76, 179
Courtrai 116
Cranmer, Thomas 174, 179
Crécy 118–20, *121*, 140, 146
Cremona 110
Crépy, Peace of 176
Crescentius 83
Crete 29, 31, 33, 37
Crimea 18
Cromwell, Thomas 174–75
crossbow 95, 119, *120*, *121*, 142
Crusades, crusaders 22, 45, 49, 54, 57, *93*, 106–12, 117, 121, 129, 136, 142, 153, 159, 161; Albigensian 103–05, 115; Fourth (Constantinople) 47, 223n358; Holy Land—First 43–44, 90–97, 210, Second 98, Third 46, 100–01
Ctesiphon 15, 18
cuius regio, eius religio 177, 194–95, 209
Cunimund 66
Cyclades fleet 24
Cyprus 34, 46, 184
Cyrillic alphabet 62
Czechs 81; *see also* Bohemia, Bohemians

Dagobert 70
Dalmatia 42, 44, 76
Damascus 24, 35, 98, 158
Damietta 106–08
Dandolo, Henry 47

danegeld 88
Danelaw 87
Dante Alighieri 143, 165, 210
Danube River 10–11, 13, 25, 35, 54, 76, 93; Rhine-Danube salient 3
Daphnusia 49
Daras 6, 8, 12
Dardanelles 20
Darnley, Henry 180–81
Dastagerd 15
Day of the Barricades 192
De Humani Corporis Fabrica 213–14
De Nuptiis Philologiae et Mercurii 137
De Rerum Natura 211
De Revolutionibus Orbium Coelestium 214
De Trinitatus erroribus 172
Deacon John 20
Decameron 122, 210
Decius 3
deductive method 140
Defender of Peace 141
Deliverance 147
Delyan, Peter 38
d'Enghein, Louis, Duc *see* Condé, Louis II de Bourbon, Prince of (Duc d'Enghein)
Denmark, Danes 77–78, 80–81, 87–88, 171, 176, 196–98, 203, 205
Descartes, René 215–16
Dessau Bridge 197
Dialogue of the Two New Sciences 215
Diaz, Bartholomew 155
Digests 11, 62, 140
Dijon 150
dikes 188, 227n247
Diocletian 61
Diophantus 216
Dispenser, Hugh 118
Dissolution of the Monasteries 174
Divine Comedy 210
Domesday Book 90
Dominicans (Black Friars) 139, 166, 192
Domrémy 132
Donation of Constantine 72, 85
Donation of Pippin 72–73, 83
Donauwörth 195
Donegal Bay 192
Dorylaeum 43, 94, 98
Downs, battle of 207
Dracul, Vlad 223n340
Drake, Sir Francis 189–91
Dreux 117
Drin River 44
Ducas, Andronicus 41
Ducas, Constantine (imposter) 32
Dunbar 180
Duomo *see* Florence Cathedral
Durazzo 42, 91, 96
Dushan, Stephen 53
Dutch War 185–90, 194, 196
Dyle River 80

Ebro 73–74
Ecclesiastical History of England 68, 87
Ecclesiastical Reservation 195, 197
Ecloga 24, 221n126
Ecumenical Council (AD 842) 29

Edessa 95, 98
Edgecote 148
Edict of January 182
Edict of Restitution 197–98, 200, 204, 209
Edinburgh 180–81
Edington 87
Edmund Ironside 88
Edmund of East Anglia 87
education 4, 137–39, 211, 217
Edward I 108, *113*, 114, 116–17, 119
Edward II 117–18
Edward III 118–19, 120–21, 126–27, 145, *146*, 147, 228n339, 230n33
Edward IV 148–50
Edward VI 175, 178
Edward, Prince of Wales (prince of the tower) 150–51
Edward, Prince of Wales (son of Henry VI) 148–49
Edward, the Black Prince 120, 124–27, 145–46, 160
Edward the Confessor 88
Egbert 87
Eger 204
Egfrid 86
Egmont, Count 186
Egypt 11, 14, 17, 19, 22, 40, 49, 55, 63, 82, 91, 95, 105–06, 109–10, 140, 217, 227n247
Einhard 71, 75–76, 142
El Cid *see* Vivar, Rodrigo Diaz de
Elbe 3, 76, 197, 200
Eleanor of Aquitaine 97–100
electoral college (imperial) 116, 163–64, 176, 195–96, 198
Elizabeth I 179–82, 189, 192
Emico of Leningen 92
England 68, 78, 95, 97–105, 107–08, 111–14, 117, 124, 126–29, 131–33, 135, 155, 164, 172–82, 189, 193–94, 211, 215; and Armada 190–92; Black Death in 122; conquered by invaders 85–90; in Hundred Years' War 118–21; in War of the Roses 145–52
English Channel 98, 117, 119–20, 190–91
Enkhuizen 188
Epaminondas 62
Epicurean school 211
Epirus 42, 47–50, 52–53
Erasmus, Desiderius 139, 211, 218
escadron volant 182
Escorial 185, 192, 194
Estates General 114–15, 124–25, 133
Estonia 198–99
Estramadura 178
Ethelbert 68
Ethelred (brother of Alfred the Great) 87
Ethlered the Unready 87–88
Eudes (Count) *see* Odo
Eudes, Duke of Aquitaine 70–71
Eudocia 41
Eugenius IV 136
Euphrates River 30, 33, 41, 56
Euprepia 39
Eustace 99
Everlasting Peace 8, 10

Index

Evesham 108
Exarchate of Africa 12
Exarchate of Ravenna 12, 72
exchequer 99
excommunication 24, 84–85, 100, 110, 112, 114, 167

Fabricius 195–96
Fadrique, Don 187
Faenza 162
fainéant (do-nothing) kings 70
Falkirk 114, 117, 119
Fariskour 106
Farmer's Law 19
Farnese, Allesandro *see* Parma, Allesandro Farnese, Duke of
Fatimids 40–41, 91
Felix V 136
Ferdinand (Cardinal) 207
Ferdinand I (Castile) 158
Ferdinand I (Germany) 168–170, 176, 178
Ferdinand II (Aragon, husband of Isabella) 147, 158, 161–64, 174
Ferdinand II (Germany) 195–99, 202–06
Ferdinand III (Germany) 198, 204, 206, 208–09
Fermat, Pierre de 215–17, 235n438
Fermat's Last Theorem 216–17
Ferrand, Count of Flanders 103
Ferrante I 156
Ferrara, Council of 57, 136
feudalism 78, 80, 92, 96, 104, 128, 134, 143, 155, 228n399
Fibonacci, Leonardo 109
fief 78, 84, 128
Field of the Cloth of Gold 173
filioque controversy 75
Finland 198–99
firearms 217
flagellants 123–24
Flanders 103–04, 116, 118–19, 129, 190, 206–07
flayers 133
Florence 57, 153–54, 156, 163, 169
Florence Cathedral 57, *212*, 213
Florence, Council of 57
Foix, Andre de 165
Foix, Gaston de 163
Fontenoy 77
Fornovo 156
France 49, 69, 78–81, 91, 96–97, 99–105, 107, 109, 112–17, 135, 138, 145–50, 160, 164–65, 171–73, 176–77, 179–80, 186, 189, 191, 213, 238n220, 234n376; in Hundred Years' War 118–20, 124–33; Italian invasions 154–56, 161–63; in Thirty Years' War 199–200, 203, 205, 209–10; Wars of Religion 181–83, 192–94; *see also* Frankland, Franks
Franche Comté 149–50, 155, 163
Francis I 164–66, 168–69, 173, 176–77, 232n222
Francis II 179–82, 232n223
Francis, Duke of Guise 181
Francis of Anjou 189
Francis of Assisi, St. 109, 139

Franciscans (Grey Friars) 139
Franconia 80–81
Frankfurt 75, 124
Frankfurt, Council of 75
Frankland, Franks 10, 24, 29, 43, 65, 68–76, 78–79, 87, 94, 158, 221n158
Frederick I Hohenstaufen (Barbarossa) 46, 100–01, 108–09
Frederick II Hohenstaufen 103–04, 108–12, 227n286
Frederick III (Germany) 163
Frederick III (Palatine elector) 176
Frederick IV (Palatine elector) 195
Frederick V (Palatine elector, "Winter King") 196
Frederick the Wise (Saxon elector) 168
Frederick William (Brandenburg elector) 208
Free Cities 194–95
Free Companies 125
Freiberg 124
French Fury 189
Freteval 102
Frisians 70
Froissart, John 119, 121, 125, 127, 142, 160
Fuggers 164, 167
Fulcher 92
Fulda 70, 72, 224n39
Fuller, J. F. C. 198

Gabor, Bethlen 197
Gabriel, archangel 15
Gaita 42
Galata 12, 20, *21*, 53 58
Galen 63, 140, 211, 213
Galilei, Galileo 215, 218
galleys 9, 14, 22, 32, 46, 49, 59–60, 106, 184, 190
Gallipoli 51, 53, 56
Gama, Vasco da 155
Garigliano 162
Gascony 107, 114
Gaul 6, 69, 77–78, 158
Gaveston, Piers 118
Gebel al-Tariq 70, 158
Gelimer 8, 220n40
Genghis Khan 54–55, 223n318
Genoa, Genoese 49–51, 53, 55, 95–96, 111, 119–22, 153, 155; defenders at fall of Constantinople 58–60
geocentric theory 214
geometry 215–16
George William (Brandenburg elector) 205
Gepids 66
Gérard, Balthasar 189
Gerbert of Aurillac *see* Sylvester II (Gerbert of Aurillac)
Germany, Germans 3–5, 10, 42, 46, 70, 73, 76–81, 83–86, 91–92, 101, 103–04, 108–12, 115–16, 135, 155–56, 166–70, 175, 177, 178, 186, 189, 194, 217; in the Thirty Years' War 196, 198–206, 209
Ghent 189
Ghibellines 153, 156
Gibbon, Edward 1, 6, 9, 11, 13, 16, 22, 24, 27, 30, 33–34, 46, 52, 54–56, 58, 66, 71, 82, 92, 140, 143, 158

Gibraltar 70, 158, 160
Giotto 211
Giustiniani, Giovanni 59
Glendower, Owen 146
Gold Coast 154
Golden Bull 116, 120
golden gate 49
Golden Horn 20, *21* (labeled "Port"), 47, 53, 58, 60
golilla 206
Gonzalo de Córdoba 162
Gothic architecture 141
Goths 3–5, 9–11, 19, 65, 86, 220n40; *see also* Ostrogoths; Visigoths
Gottschalk 92
Granada 159, 161–62, 184
Granada, Treaty of 161–62
Grand Company *see* Catalonia, Catalans; Roger de Flor
Grand Ordinance 125
Grandson 150
Gravelines 191
Great Schism 134–35, 153
Great Theatre of Constantinople 39
Greece 24, 47, 49–50, 57, 62, 141, 184, 214, 217, 220n78
Greek Fire 19, 22, *23*, 24, 32, 42, 106
Greens 7, 219n28
Gregorian chant 67
Gregory I the Great, St. 67, *69*, 86; *Pastoral Care* 87
Gregory II 24
Gregory III 24
Gregory VII (Hildebrand) 43, 83–85, 91
Gregory IX 110–11
Gregory X 50
Gregory XI 134
Gregory XII 135
Gregory XIII 183
Gregory of Nyssa, St. 22
Gregory of Tours 69
Grey, Lady Jane 178
Grotius, Hugo 217
Guelphs 153, 156
Guesclin, Bertrand du 126, 228n385
Guienne 107–08, 114, 118, 129, 133, 232n196
guilds 92, 139, 142, 155
Guinegate 150, 163
Guiscard, Robert *see* Robert Guiscard
gunpowder 58, 140–42, 180, 229n477
Gustavus I Vasa 171
Gustavus II Adolphus 198–99, *200*, 201–05, 207, 216, 234n338
Gutenberg, Johann 63, 217, 235n441
Gutenberg Bible 218
Guthrum 87

Haarlem 188
Hadrian I 73–75
Hadrian IV 101
Hadrianic Code 11
Hadrianopolis 3
Hadrian's Mausoleum 9, 156
Hadrian's Wall 86
Hagia Sophia *see* Saint Sophia, church
halberd 115, 150, 183, 204

Halberstadt 101, 209
Halidon Hill 118–19
Hallam, Henry 159–160
Hammurabi 153
Hanseatic ports 198
Hapsburg, House of 112, 115, 150, 155, 163–65, 168–69, 175–77, 179–81, 185, 193, 195, 199–200, 204–05
Hapsburg-Valois Wars 165, 169, 175, 179, 181
Harald Hardrada 88–89, 222*n*214
Harfluer 130
harnessing 142
Harold of England 88–90
Harun al-Raschid 25–26, 75
hashishin 96
Hastings (battle) 42, 89, **90**
Hastings, Lord William 150
Hattin 100
Hegira 16, 18
Helena 32
heliocentric theory 137
Heliopolis 22
Hellespont 20, 36
Henrician Reformation 174–75
Henry (son of Frederick II Hohenstaufen) 110
Henry I (England) 98
Henry I (France) 97
Henry II (England) 98, **99**, 100–102, 104
Henry II (France) 179, 182, 186, 232*n*222
Henry II "of Trastamara" (Castile) 160–61, 231*n*94, *n*96
Henry III (England) 104–05, 107, 108, 111, 113
Henry III (France) 192
Henry III "the Sufferer" (Castile) 160
Henry IV (Germany) 42–43, 83–85, 91, 112
Henry IV "Bolingbroke" (England) 128–29, 146
Henry IV "of Navarre," (France) 183, 192, **193**, 199
Henry IV "the Impotent" (Castile) 160
Henry V (England) 129–32, 146, 228*n*411
Henry V (Germany) 85
Henry VI (England) 132, 146–49, 151
Henry VI (Germany) 46, 101, 103
Henry VII (England) 151–52, 155, 230*n*33
Henry VII (Germany) 115
Henry VIII (England) 152, 162–64, 173–80, 231*n*110, 232*n*187, *n*196
Henry, Duke of Guise 192
Henry of Flanders 48
Henry of Navarre *see* Henry IV "of Navarre" (France)
Henry of Trastamara *see* Henry II "of Trastamara" (Castile)
Henry the Fowler 80, **81**
Henry the Lion 101
Henry the Navigator 154
Heraclian dynasty 13–15, 17–20
Heraclius (emperor) 13–15, 17–19
Heraclius (exarch) 13
Herat 56

heresy 24, 117, 133, 154, 161, 166–67, 174, 176, 178, 183, 185, 193, 195; Adoptionist 75; Albigensian 102–03; Hussite and Lollard 135–36; Monophysist 6–7, 22; Paulician 30
Heruls 71
Hexamilion Wall 57
Hildegard 77
Hilderic 8
Hippocrates 63, 140
Hippodrome 7–8, 13, 20, 29, 219*n*29; bronze horses of 47, 62
Hohenstaufen, House of 49, 101, 103, 107–08, 111, 116, 153, 165
Holland 78, 149, 186, 188–89, 194; *see also* Netherlands
Holy League 156, 162
Holy See *see* Papacy
Holy Sepulcher 75, 92
Homer 62, 210
Honorius III 108, 110
Hoorne, Count 186
housecarls 89–90
Howard, Catherine 175
Howard, Charles 191
Hradschin Castle 195–96
Hugh Capet 80, 97, 232*n*220
Huguenots 172, 181–83, 186, 193, 199
humanism 143, 209–10, 213
Humber River 86
Hunayn Ibn Ishaq 63
Hundred Years' War 118–21, 124–27, 129–34, 142, 145, 147–49, 153, 160, 179
Hungary, Hungarians 31, 44, 55, 57, 62, 81–82, 92, 163, 168–70, 175–76, 197; *see also* Magyars
Huns 4–5, 8, 12, 68
Hunyadi, John 57
Hus, Jan **135**, 136, 195
Hussites 136, 218

Ibrahim Inal 41
Iceland 78
Iconoclasm 20, 24–29, 72, 230*n*481
Iconoclasts (Netherlands) 185
Iliad 210
In Praise of Folly 211
inductive method 140, 215
indulgences 166–67
Inestimable Life of Gargantua, Father of Pantagruel 210
Inferno 143
Ingeborg 102
Innocent III 102–03, 112
Innocent IV 111
Innocent X 209
Innsbruck 177
Inquisition 107, 176, 185; Spanish 161, 183
Institutes 11
Institutes of the Christian Religion 171–72
intendants 199
interdict 102, 110, 154, 162
Investiture Controversy 83–85, 112
Ireland 78, 191–92
Irene (wife of Alexius I) 44
Irene (wife of Leo IV) **25**, 26–27, 75
Irminsul 73

Isaac I Comnenus 40
Isaac II Angelus 45–47
Isabeau 132
Isabel of France (wife of Philip IV of Spain) 207
Isabella I of Castile 152, 161, 163, 174
Isabella of Portugal 168
Isabelle (mother of Edward III) 118, 228*n*411
Isaurian dynasty 20, 22, 25–26
Isaurians 5, 12
Islam, Muslims 24, 33–34, 37, 40, 51, 61, 73–74, 98, 100–01, 106, 109, 112, 121–23, 155, 158–59, 172, 184, 194; birth of 15–18; Charles Martel defeats at Tours 70–71; Constantinople—final conquest 57–60, first siege 19, second siege 20–22; Crusades and 43, 91–96; intellectual legacy of 62–63, 140; *see also* Arabs
Isle of Wight 87
Ispahan 56
Issus 14
Istanbul 60, 62
Italy 24, 50, 66–67, 96, 115, 135, 137, 141–43, 153, 175, 184, 199, 225*n*99; Byzantine rule in 9–10, 25, 29, 36–38, 65; Frankish rule in 77–79; French invasions 154–58, 161–63, 165, 168–69, 179; Gothic rule in 4–5, 11; Hohenstaufen rule in 101, 103, 109–11, 227*n*286; Lombard depredations in 12, 19, 71–73; Norman depredations 40, 42–43, 90–91; Otto I campaigns in 82–83
Ivry 192

Jabir 63
Jacquerie 126–27
Jaffa 95, 101
Jaffa, Treaty of 110
Jagatai Khanate 55
James I 180, 215
James, St. 158
Janibeg 121–22
Jankau 208
Jansenism 216
Jarnac 182
Jaxarta River 18
Jerusalem (city) 15, 17, 43, 95–96, 100–01, 110–11
Jerusalem, kingdom of 95
Jesuits 175–76
Jewish Temple 17
Jews *see* Judaism, Jews
jihad 17, 100
Joan of Arc, St. 132–33, **134**
John I Lackland (England) 100, 102–04, 112
John I Tzimisces 33–35
John II (France) 124–26, 129
John II (Portugal) 154
John II Comnenus 44
John III Vatatzes 48
John IV Lascaris 48
John V Palaeologus 52–54
John VI Cantacuzenus 52–53
John VIII Palaeologus 56–57, 136
John X (pope) 82

John XII (pope) 82–83
John XXII (pope) 115
John George (Saxon elector) 205
John of Gaunt 146, 230n33
John of Luxembourg 120
John the Fearless 129, 131
John, the "Orphanotrophos" 37
John the Red Comyn 117
Joinville, Jean de 106, 142
Juan of Austria, Don 184
Juana la Beltraneja 161
Juana the Mad 163–64
Judaism, Jews 4, 7, 13, 15–16, 18, 60, 107, 109, 160, 172, 183; expulsions of 116–17, 161; pogroms against 55, 92, 95, 123–24
Judith (wife of Louis the Pious) 77
Julian, Count 158
Julian the Apostate 3, 69
Julius II (Giuliano della Rovere) 157, 162–63
Jupiter 215
Justin I 6
Justin of Nassau 190
Justinian I (Peter Sabbatius) 5–6, 7, 8–12, 14, 29–30, 36, 62, 65, 137, 220n63
Justinian II Rhinotmetus 19–20
Justinian Code *see* Codex Justinianus
Jutes 86

Kadessia 17
Kadija 15
Kaffa 53, 121–22
Kalmar, Union of 171
Kaloyan 48
Kappel 171
Kepler, Johannes 214
Ketboga 55
Khalid 17
Kiev 45, 54, 78
Kilij Arslan 44
King's Bench 100
Kipchak Khanate 56, 121
Kirk o' Field 180
kismet 16
Kismian dynasty 54
Kizyl Kum Desert 54
Klokotnika 48
Knighton, Henry 122
Knights Hospitaller 96, 117
Knights of St. John 159, 184
Knights Templar 96, 117, 159
Knight's War 168
knowledge 62–63, 137–38, 140, 217–18
Knox, John 180
Koning, Captain de 188
Koraidha 16
Kosmas 24
Kossovo 54, 57
Krum 27
Kublai Khan 55, 230n45
Kurkuas, John 32

La Rochelle 182, 199
Ladies' Peace *see* Cambrai, Peace of
Ladislas 57
Lake Ascania 43, 94
Lake Tiberias 100

Lancaster, House of 128, 145–49, 151–52, 230n33
Landriano 169
Langside 181
Lateran 43, 82, 138
Latin Empire of Byzantium 47–50
Laupen 150
Lavaur 104
Le Havre 182
League of the Public Weal 148
Lech River 82, 202
Lechfeld 82
Lee, Robert E. 206
Leibniz, Gottfried Wilhelm 216
Leicester 152
Leiden 188
Leo I (emperor) 5
Leo III (emperor) 20, 22, 24, 224n38
Leo III (pope) 74–75
Leo IV (emperor) 25
Leo V the Armenian (emperor) 27–29
Leo VI the Philosopher (emperor) 31, 62, 221n126
Leo IX (pope) 91
Leo X (pope) 164, 166, 169, 173
Leon 158–59
Leonardo da Vinci 154, 157, 211
Leopold (brother or Ferdinand III) 207
Leopold of Austria 101
Lepanto 184, 190
Lerma, Francisco Gómez de Sandoval, Duke of 194
Lesbos 26, 52
Letters (Petrarch) 210
Levant 49
Lewes 108
Libernion Hill 43
Lignitz 54–55
Limoges 126
Lincolnshire 174
Liudprand 61
Livy 210
Lochleven Castle 181
logic 97, 137–40
Logroño 165
Loire River 70, 132, 181
Lollards 135, 218
Lombard, Peter 139
Lombard League 101
Lombards 12, 19, 24, 66–67, 71–73, 75, 82, 109–10
London 87, 127–28, 149–50, 190
London Bridge 174
long-ships 87
longbow 119–20, *121*, 124, 130, *131*, 134, 145, 217
Longobardia 30, 42
Lorraine 78, 132, 149, 177, 181
Losecoat Field 148
Lothar (grandson of Louis the Pious) 79
Lothar (son of Charlemagne) 77
Lothar (son of Louis the Pious) 77–79
Loudon Hill 117
Louis II (Frankland) 79
Louis II Jagiellon (Hungary) 169–70
Louis III (Frankland) 79

Louis V (Frankland) 80
Louis VI the Fat 97
Louis VII 97–100
Louis VIII (Louis of France) 104–05
Louis IX (Saint Louis) *105*, 106–08, 111–12, 181
Louis XI (Spider King) 148–50, 155
Louis XII 156–58, 161–63, 166
Louis XIII 199, 205, 207
Louis, Count of Flanders 118
Louis, Duc d'Enghein *see* Condé, Louis II (Duc d'Enghein)
Louis of Orleans 129
Louis the Bavarian 115
Louis the Child 80
Louis the German 79
Louis the Pious 77
Louis the Stammerer 79
Lovers' War 192
Low Countries *see* Netherlands
Loyola, Ignatius 175, *176*
Lübeck, Peace of 198
Lucretius 211
Ludford Bridge 147
Luther, Martin 166, *167*, 168, 171, 173–75, 211, 218, 232n183
Lutheranism, Lutherans 167–68, 170–72, 176–77, 186, 194–97
Lutter 197
Lützen iv , 202–03, 205
Lyons, Council of 50, 111

Macedonia 48, 53, 221n168
Macedonian dynasty 30–36, 40
Machiavelli, Niccolò 154, 157, 161, 217
Mad Parliament 107
Madelaine, Church of the 104
Madrid 206
Madrid, Treaty of 169
Magdeburg 81, 200, *201*, 209
Magna Carta 104, 108, 113
Magyars 31, 80–82, 92
Maine 99, 102
Mainz 63, 76, 92, 116, 167, 217
malaria 101, 115, 157, 231n75
Malek Shah 42–43
Malta 184
Mamelukes 55, 106
Manfred of Sicily 49–50, 111
Maniakes, George 37–39
Mansfeld, Ernst von 197
Mansourah 106
Mantua 199
Manuel I Comnenus 44–45
Manuel II Palaeologus 54, 56
Manzikert 41, 91
Marburg, Colloquy of 171
Marcel, Etienne 125–26
Marcus Aurelius 3
Margaret (Queen of Norway) 171
Margaret, Lady 174
Margaret of Anjou 147–48
Margaret of Burgundy 148
Margot of Valois 182, 192
Maria Anna of Spain (wife of Ferdinand III) 204
Maria de Padilla 160
Maria of Antioch 45
Marignano 165

Index

Maritza River 54
Markham, Sir Clements R. 151
Marozia 82, 225n117
Marsiglio of Padua 141
Martel, Charles *see* Charles Martel
Martin IV 50
Martin V 136
Martinitz, Jaroslav Borzita von 195
Mary I (Mary Tudor) 174, 178–79
Mary of Burgundy 150, 163, 185
Mary of Guise 181
Mary, Queen of Scots (Mary Stuart) 180–81
Masts, Battle of the 18
mathematics 109, 140, 215–16
Matilda 98–99
Matthias I 195
Maurice (Byzantium) 12–13, 220n59, 221n106
Maurice of Nassau 194, 202
Maurice of Saxony 177
Maxmilian I 116, 155, 162–64, 185
Maxmilian II 194
Maximilian of Bavaria, Duke 195–97, 208–09
Mayenne, Charles de Lorraine, Duke of 193
mayor of the palace (*major domus*) 70
Mecca 15–16, 18, 61
Medici, Cosimo 154
Medici, Piero de' 156
Medici family 154, 163, 169
medicine 63, 140, 172, 213–14
Medina 15–16
Medina Sidonia, Alonzo Pérez de Guzmán, Duke of 190–91
Mediterranean Sea 20, 49, 61, 70, 82, 96, 105, 109, 111–12, 153–54, 176, 184
Mehmet I 56
Mehmet II 57–58, *59*, 60, 154
Melo, Francisco de, Don 208
Memmingen 168
Mendoza, Bernadino de 190
Merchants' Treaty *see* Picquigny, Treaty of
Mercia 86–87
Mercy, Franz von 208
Méré, Chevalier de 216
Merovingians 68–73, 158, 198
Merowig 68–69, 224n21
Merseberg 81
Mersen, Edict of 78
Mersen, Treaty of 79
Mersenne, Father Marin 215–16
Mesembria 27
Mesopotamia 14–15, 35, 217
Messina 9, 37, 103, 122
Metz 177, 179, 209
Meux 126
Michael I Rhangabé 27
Michael II (of Epirus) 49
Michael II the Phrygian (the Stammerer) 27–29
Michael III, the Drunkard 29–30
Michael IV 37–38
Michael V Calaphates 38
Michael VI Stratioticus 40
Michael VII Ducas 42
Michael VIII Paleologus 48–51

Middle Ages 7, 61, 65 *passim*, 155, 214, 218, 229n447
Milan 101, 110, 123, 153–54, 156–58, 161, 163, 165, 168–69, 176, 231n71, 232n222
Minden 209
Minerve 104
Mirabello 168
missi dominici 76
Moawiyah 18–20
Model Parliament 113
Mohács 169
Mohammed 15–18, 60, 86, 220n101
monasticism, monasteries 7, 22, 25, 32, 35, 38, 40, 53, 63, 67, 70–71, 74, 76–77, 83, 96, 122, 137–39, 142, 159, 166, 174–75, 182, 195, 210, 217, 221n114
Monenergism 22
Mongols 48, 54–56, 121, 230n45
Mongonmery, Gabriel, Comte de 179
Monophysite heresy 6, 22
Monotheletism 22
Mons-en-Pevele 116
Monte Cassino 67, 71, 210
Montlhéry 148
Moors 19, 73, 104, 159, 161, 194
Morat 150
Moravians 29
More, Thomas 174
Morea 53
Morgarten 115, 150
Moriscos 184, 194
Morocco 159, 189
Mortimer, Roger 118
mosaic art 7, *25*, *39*, 62, 220n63
Moscow 48
Moslemah 20, 22
Mosynopolis 46
Motley, John Lathrop 188
Mount Oreste 71
Mountain of Leo 27
Mühlberg 176–77
Münster 170–71, 208
Münzer, Thomas 168
Murad I 53–54
Murad II 56–57
Musa 56
musket, musketeer 58, 155, 162, 184, 192, *194*, 201–02, 204, 208
Muslims *see* Islam, Muslims
Mussis, Gabrielle de 142
Myriocephalus 44

Naarden 187
Nancy 150
Nantes, Edict of 192–93, 199
naphtha see Greek Fire
Naples 9, 66, 109–11, 153, 155–56, 161–63, 165, 169, 172
Narses 8–11, 65–66, 68
Navarre 157–59, 183, 192; Lower Navarre (north of the Pyrenees) 182; Spanish Navarre (south of the Pyrenees) 163, 165
Nennius 86
nepotism 157
Nestorian Christians 63
Netherlands 148–50, 163–64, 175, 190, 196, 208, 211, 217, 235n441; revolt of 185–89; Spanish attempts to regain 193–94, 196, 198–99, 205–07, 209
Neustria 70, 73
New Atlantis 215
New Testament 168, 211
New World 155, 189
Newton, Isaac 215
Nicaea (city) 40, 43, 51, 93–94
Nicaea (empire) 47–49
Nicaea, Council of 75
Nicephorus I 26–28, 75
Nicephorus II Phocas 33–36
Nicephorus III Boteniates 42
Nicholas I Mystikos (patriarch) 31
Nicholas III (pope) 50
Nicopolis 54, 129
Nika riots 7, 8, 11, 219n28
Nile River 106, 227n247
Ninety-five Theses 166, 211
Nineveh 15
Nish 3, 57, 93
Nithard 78
Nogaret, Guillaime de 115
Nominalism 138
nomisma 61
Nonesuch, Treaty of 190
Nördlingen 204–06
Norfolk, John Howard, 1st Duke of 151–52
Normandy, Normans 37, 40, 42–46, 88–91, 97–99, 102, 131, 133, 226n163, 232n196; founded by Rollo 79
Norsemen *see* Denmark, Danes; Normandy, Normans; Vikings
North Africa 8, 19, 158–59, 194
North Sea 188, 199
Northampton 147
Northumberland, Henry Percy, Earl of 152
Northumbria , 68, 70, 72, 75, 86–87, 89
Northumbrian Renaissance 68, 87
Norway, Norwegians 78, 88–89, 122, 171
Novum Organum 215
Nuland, Sherwin 211
Nuremburg 202

Odo 79–80
Odoacer 4
Offa 86
Olivares, Gaspar de Guzman, Duque du 204, 206–07
Oman, C. W. C. 60
Omar I 17–18
Omayyads 18, 24, 82–83, 158
On the Law of War and Peace 217
Opsikion Theme 24
optics 63, 141, 212
Opus Maius 141
Ordinance of 1439 133
Orkhan 52
Orleans 129, 132–33
Osiander, Andreas 214
Osnabrük 208
Ostrogoths 3–4, 9, 65, 137
Oswy 86

Othman (founder of Ottoman dynasty) 51
Othman (Omayyad caliph) 18
Otranto 40, 154
Otto I the Great 80–84
Otto II 83
Otto III 83
Otto IV 100, 103–04, 108, 112
Ottoman Turks *see* Turks
Oxenstierna, Axel Gustafsson 205
Oxford, John de Vere Earl of 152
Oxford, Provisions of 107–08
Oxus River 18

Padua 141, 162
Palace of Justice 183
Palaeologus, George 42
Palaeologus, John 49
Palatinate 116, 176, 195–97
Palermo 50
Palestine 14
Pamplona 175
Pancalia 35
Pannonia 31
Papacy 10, 22, 40, 86, 91, 97, 102, 105, 108, 112–14, 116, 136, 139, 154, 156–57, 161, 167, 177, 184, 211, 221*n*167; at Avignon 115, 134–35, 153; and Crusades 90–91, 96, 100; and Franks 70–73; and Hohenstaufen 101, 109–11, 165, 174; and Investiture Controversy 83–85
Papal States 73, 110–11, 153, 156–57, 162
paper manufacture 63, 140
Pappenheim, Gottfried Heinrich zu, Count 202–03
papyrus 63
Paré, Ambroise 179, 183, 213
Paris 69, 78–79, 97, 105, 107, 119, 126, 130, 132–33, 138–39, 172, 176, 182–83, 192–93, 206, 208, 213, 215–16
Paris, Treaty of 107
parlement 107
parliament: English 107–08, 113, 126–28, 147, 152, 174; other states 7, 109, 114, 167, 180–81, 199
Parliament of Devils 147
Parma 111
Parma, Allesandro Farnese, Duke of 189–91
Parthians 12
Pascal, Blaise 215–16
Pastoral Care 87
Patay 133
Paul, St. 30
Paul III 175–76
Paulician heresy 30
Pavia 73, 168–69
Peace of Monsieur 192
Peasants' Revolt 127–28
Pechenegs 31, 35, 40, 43
Pedro the Cruel 160, 231*n*96
Peking 54
Peloponnesus 29, 53–54, 57
pendentive base 62
Pensées 216
People's Crusade 92, 94
Pericles 62

perspective 211–12, 234*n*403
Peter (brother of Emperor Maurice) 13
Peter (officer under Nicephorus II) 34
Peter, St. 82
Peter II (Aragon) 104–05
Peter III (Aragon) 50
Peter the Hermit 92–94, 96
Petition of the Confederates 185
Petrarch, Francesco 124, 210
Petronas 29
phalanx 10, 41, 71, 87, 119, 162, 165, 208
Philip I (France) 97
Philip II (Spain) 178–79, 183–85, *186*, 187–90, 192–94
Philip II Augustus (France) 100–04, 107, 112
Philip III (Spain) 194
Philip IV (Spain) 204, 207
Philip IV the Fair (France) 113–18, 228*n*411
Philip VI of Valois (France) 118–20, 124
Philip of Macedonia 51
Philip of Swabia 103
Philip the Bold 125, 129
Philip the Good 131
Philip the Handsome 163–64, 185
Philipopolis 53
Philippicus Bardanes 20
Philomelion 43
Phocas (emperor) 12–13, 222*n*206
Phocas, Bardas 35–36
Phrygia 41
Phrygian dynasty 27–30
physics 63, 215
Piacenza, Council of 43, 91
Picardy 171
Picquigny, Treaty of 149
Picts 86
Pilato, Leonzio 210
Pillar of Theodosius 47
Pippin (son of Charlemagne by Hildegard) 77
Pippin I the Short 24, 71–72
Pippin of Heristhal 70
Pippin the Hunchback 76
piracy 37, 79, 87, 116, 176, 187, 189
Pisa 156, 215
Pisa, Council of 135
Pius III 157
plague *see* bubonic plague
Plantagenet dynasty 98–99, 152, 174, 226*n*223
Plato 63
Plessis Le Tours, Treaty of 189
plow, medieval improvements in 142
Plymouth 191
Po River 66, 153
Poitiers 71, 124–25, 129, 158
Poland, Poles 54–55, 175, 199
Polo, Marco 55, 153, 230*n*45
Polyeuctus 34
polygamy 171
Pomerania 208
Ponthieu 126
Pontus 45
Portsmouth 119

Portugal, Portuguese 154, 159, 168, 189, 207
Powerful 34, 36–37, 40, 42, 45
Prague 81, 92, 203, 208; Defenestration of 195–96
Prague, Peace of 205
predestination 16, 171, 175, 216
Presbyterians 172
Preslav 34
The Prince 217
Princeton University 217
printing press 63, 140, 143, 217, *218*, 235*n*441
probability theory 216
Procopia 27
Procopius 6, 11, 219*n*23
Prokop the Bald 136
prostitutes 6, 109, 149, 156, 172, 231*n*66
Protagoras 210
Protestant Wind 192
Protestantism, Protestants 170–73, 175–79, 181–83, 185–86, 189, 192–93, 195–205, 209
Prussia 203
Psellus, Michael 38
Pseudo-Isidorean Decretals 72, 85
Publius Quinctilius Varus 3
Puritans 172
Pyrenees 70, 73–74, 182, 209
Pyrenees, Peace of 209
Pythagorean Theorem 216

quadrivium 137–38
quarantine 123
Quo Warranto 113

Radcot Bridge 128
Ratisbon 82, 92
Ravenna 4, *7*, 9–10, 12, 24, 62, 66, 72, 162, 220*n*63
Raymond VI 103
realism (medieval philosophy) 138
Rebalais, François 210
Reformation 163, 166–67, 169, 171–75, 211, 218
Reformation Parliament 174
Regensburg, Diet of 176, 198
Religion, French Wars of 181–83, 192–94
Renaissance 60, 139, 143, 154, 209–18; Gothic 4; Northumbrian 68, 87
Rense 115
Requesens, Don Luis de 188
Restitution of Christianity 172
Rhazes 63
Rheims 72, 83, 133
Rhine River 3, 76, 78
Rhineland 206
Rhodes 18, 20, 184
Rhone River 70, 123
Ribalds 94
Richard I the Lion-Hearted 100–02
Richard II 127–28, 146
Richard III 150, *151*, 152, 160
Richard of Cambridge 146–47
Richard of York (Lord Protector) 146–48
Richard of York (prince of the Tower) 150–51

Richelieu, Armand Jean du Plessis, Cardinal 199, **200**, 205–07
Rienzo, Cola di 153
Rimini 162
Rizzio, David 180
Roanoke 189
robber barons 97
Robert (brother of Odo), Duke 80
Robert II the Pious 97
Robert Curthose 94, 98
Robert Guiscard 42–43, 45, 85, 91, 94, 101
Robert of Artois 118
Robert the Strong 79
Rocroi 207–08
Roderic 158
Roger I 91
Roger II the Great 44, 101
Roger de Flor 51
Rollo 79
Romagna 157
Roman Empire (Ancient) 1, 3, 4, 11–12, 61, 68, 74–76, 86, 95, 137, 158, 177, 220n60
Roman Empire (Eastern) *see* Byzantium
Romanesque architecture 141
Romanus I Lecapenus 32, 34, 36
Romanus II 33–35
Romanus III Argyrus 37
Romanus IV Diogenes 41–42
Romany 61
Rome (city) 5–6, 9–10, 40, 42–43, 53, 62, 66–67, 71–73, 75, 82–86, 91, 101, 112, 114–15, 134, 137, 162, 166, 183, 189; besieged by Frederick II Hohenstaufen 111; sacked by imperialists under Charles V 169; sacked by Normans 43, 85, 226n166; under Cola di Rienzo 153; under the Borgias 156–57
Rome (seat of Catholicism) 174–75, 178
Romulus Augustulus 4, 9
Roncesvalles 74
Rosamond 66, 224n7
Rouen 79
Roussillon 155
Rovere, Giuliano della *see* Julius II (Giuliano della Rovere)
Rubaiyat of Omar Khayyam 63
Rudolf (Capetian king) 80
Rudolf II 195
Rudolph of Hapsburg 112, 115
Rule of Harlots 82, 84
Runnymede 104
Russia, Russians 30–32, 34–36, 38, 56, 62, 78, 88, 198, 225n87
Rustam 17–18

Sabbatius, Peter *see* Justinian I, emperor
Sacraments 67, 166, 171, 173, 175
Saint Albans 147
Saint Bartholomew's Day Massacre 183, 192
Saint-Denis 182
Saint-Dizier 176
Saint-Germain, Treaty of 182
Saint Gothard Pass 115

Saint Gregory *see* Gregory of Nyssa, St., Gregory I the Great, St
Saint Jacob-en-Birs 149
Saint Louis *see* Louis IX
Saint Mark's Cathedral 47, 62
Saint Peter, church of (Antioch) 94
Saint Peter's Cathedral 75, 166
Saint Sophia, church (Hagia Sophia) 11, **25**, *39*, 60, 62
Saint Vitale, church 7, 62, 220n63
Saladin 100–01
Salerno 85, 90–91, 109, 140
Salian dynasty 83
Samarkand 54, 140
Samosata 33
Samuel 35–36, 38
Sancho II 158–59
Sancho IV 160
Sangate Hill 120
Santa Cruz, Álvaro de Bazán, Marquis of 190
Santiago de Compostela 158
Saphrantzes, George 60
Saracens *see* Arabs
Sarzana 156
Savonarola, Girolamo 154, 156
Savoy 172, 199
Saxon dynasty 81–83
Saxony, Saxons 73–75, 77, 80–83, 86, 116, 177, 196, 201, 204–05, 208, 234n338
Scandinavia, Scandinavians 74, 78, 122, 171, 175
Scheherazade 63
schiltrons 114, 117, 227n303
Schism of 1054 40, 43, 47, 50, 57, 75, 91
Schleswig 81
scholasticism, schoolmen 139, 211
science 62–63, 140–42, 160, 214–15
the Sclerena 38
Sclerus, Bardas 34–36, 38
Sclerus, Romanus 38
Scotland, Scots 78, 113–14, 117–19, 122, 129, 135, 172–73, 180, 191
Scripture 135, 137, 166–67
Sea Beggars 187–88
Sea of Marmora 6, 20–21, 30, 58
Seine River 69, 79, 91, 119, 130
Seljuk Turks *see* Turks
Sempach 150
Sens, Council of 138
Sentences 139
Serbia, Serbians 44, 46, 52–54
serfdom 37, 127
Serres 48
Servetus, Michael 172
Seville 159
Sforza family 154, 157, 165, 231n71
Shakespeare, William 151, 211, 213
Shiites 18, 82, 91, 95
Sic et Non 138–39
Sicilian Vespers 50, 112
Sicily 19, 24, 29, 37, 40, 50, 82; Hohenstaufen rule in 49, 107–11, 227n286; Justinian's conquest of 5, 9; Norman rule in 44–45, 91
Sidon 110
Silesia 203

Simnel, Lambert 152
Simon de Montfort, Count of Toulouse 104–05
Simon de Montfort, Earl of Leceister 108
simony 84–85, 157
Singer, Charles 62
Sirmium 13, 44
Siroes 15
Siwas 56
Six Articles 174–75
Slawata, Wilhelm 195
Sligo 192
Sluys 119, 145
smallpox 63, 180
Society of Jesus *see* Jesuits
Soderini, Piero 154, 217
Soderini family 163
Sofia 57
solar system 137
Somerset, Edmund Beaufort, Duke of 147
Song of Roland 74, 143
Sophia 12, 65
Sophists 210
Southampton 119
Spain, Spaniards 9, 13, 50, 69–70, 73–74, 82–83, 97, 104, 135, 152–53, 155–56, 164–65, 168, 170, 175, 178–79, 181–84, 193–94, 220n40, 231n94; and Armada 190–92; in Dutch War 185–90; early history summarized 158–63; in Thirty Years' War 196, 198–99, 204–209
Spanish (Gothic) March 74
Spanish Fury 188–89
Spanish Inquisition *see* Inquisition
Spanish Navarre *see* Navarre
Spanish Road 196, 204–05
Speyer 92, 124, 170
Speyer, Diet of 170
Spider King *see* Louis XI (Spider King)
spinning wheel 142
Spiritual Exercises 175
Spurs, Battle of the 163
Stamford Bridge 89
Stanley, Thomas 152
Stanley, William 152
Star Chamber, Court of 152
Statute of Laborers 127
Staurakios 27
Steinau 203
Stephen (Byzantine admiral) 37
Stephen I (Hungary) 93
Stephen I "of Blois" (England) 98–99
Stephen II (pope) 24, 72
Stephen Langton 103
Stilicho 86
Stilo 83
Stirling Bridge 114
Stockholm Massacre 171
Stoke 152
Strabo 4, 219n6
Strassbourg 3, 124, 171
Strassbourg, Oaths of 77
Strategopoulos, Alexius 49
Straw, Jack 128

Index

Stuart, Mary *see* Mary, Queen of Scots (Mary Stuart)
Studion (Studite) Monastery 38, 40
Stylites, Simeon 67
Suffolk, William de la Pole, 1st Duke of 147
Suleiman (Saracen naval commander) 27
Suleiman (son of Bajazet) 62
Suleiman the Magnificent 169, 184
Sully, Maximilien de Béthune, Duke of 193
Sultanate of Roum 43
Summa Theologica 139
Sunnites 18, 91
Suntel Mountain 73
Svyatoslav 35
Swabia 80, 202
Swabian League 168, 170
Sweden, Swedes 78, 171, 198–206, 208–09, 216, 225n87
Switzerland, Swiss 78, 115, 149–50, 162–63, 165, 171, 209
Sylvester II (Gerbert of Aurillac) 83, 140
Symeon 31, 32, 35
Synod of Whitby 68, 86
syphilis 163
Syracuse 19, 37
Syria 14–15, 18, 20, 22, 37, 40, 49, 63, 67, 91, 107, 110, 117

Taborites 136
Tacitus 210
Tactica 31
Tactics 194
Tafur 94, 98
Tagina 10
Tagliacozzo 111
Taillebourg 105
Talas 63
Tamarlane 55–56
Tariq 70, 158
Tarsus 33
Taurus Mountains 14, 18
technology 140, 142, 218
Teias 10
telescope 141, 198, 215
Teletzes 25
Temple of Solomon 95
Ten Articles 181
Tenchebrai 98
Tephrike 30
tercio 162, 194, 208, 234n382
Tertry 70
Terzka, Adam 204
Tettenhall 87
Tetzel, Johann 166–67
Teutoburger Forest 3
Teutonic Knights 54, 108
Tewksbury 149–50
Thames River 87, 190
Thebes 44, 224n370
theme (military district) 12, 19, 24–25, 28, 40–41, 221n106
Themistocles 62
theocracy 172
Theodora (daughter of Constantine VIII) 38, 40
Theodora ("Harlot") 82

Theodora (mistress and niece of Manuel I) 45
Theodora (wife of Justinian I) 6, 8, 10, 62, 220n48
Theodora (wife of Theophilus I) 29
Theodore Ducas Angelus 48
Theodore II 48
Theodoric ("One-Eye") *see* Strabo
Theodoric (Ostrogoth) 4–5, 9–10, 65, 137
Theodoric IV (Merovingian) 71
Theodosius I 13
Theodosius II 21
Theodosius III 20
Theophanes Confessor 25, 27–28
Theophano 33–34, 222n197
Theophilus I 29
Theophobus 29
Thessalonica 31, 42, 45, 48–49, 52–54, 56
Thessaly 47, 49–50, 52–53
Thirty Years' War 194–206, *207*, 208–09; Bohemian phase 196; Danish phase 196–98; French "Balance of Power" phase 205–08; Swedish phase 198–203
Thomas, duke of Gloucester 128
Thomas the Slav 28
Thrace 14, 19, 28, 32, 34, 48, 53
three-field system 142
Throat Cutter *see* *Boghza Kesen*
Thurn, Heinrich von, Count 195, 203
Tiber River 9, 153, 156, 169, 225n99
Tiberias 100
Tiberius (son of Justinian II) 20
Tiberius II 12, 220n58–59
Timur the Lame *see* Tamarlane
tithes 66, 117
Titian 234n410
Toledo 97, 158–59, 210
Tornikius, Leo 39
Tortensson, Lennart, Count 207–08
Tostig 88
Totila 10
Toul 177, 179, 209
Toulon 176
Toulouse 102–03, 105
Touraine 99, 102
Tourelles 132–33
Tours 69, 71, 181, 189
Tours, Cathedral of *93*
Tower of London 127, 149–51
Towton 148
Trajan's Gate 35–36
Trebizond 47, 49
trebuchet 142
Trent, Council of 175–77
Tribonian 11
Trier 116
trigonometry 62
Tripoli 18
Tripoli, county of 95
trivium 137–38
Troyes, treaty of 132, 146
Truce of God 92
True Cross 14–15, 17, 20, 100
Tudor, Henry *see* Henry VII (England)
Tudor dynasty, founding of 152–53
Tura, Agnolo di 122, 142

Turenne, Vicomte Henri 208
Turkish War (Lepanto) 183–84
Turks 18, 50, 55, 93–94; Ottoman 51–60, 133, 136, 145, 154–55, 169–70, 176–77, 183–84, 191, 223n340; Seljuk 40–45, 48, 91–92, 95–96, 98
Tuttlingen 208
Twelve Articles 168
Tyler, Wat 127–28
Tyre 100
Tyrol 115

Uhud 16
Unam Sanctum 114
Unitarianism 172
United Provinces 189–90, 194, 205
university (medieval conception of) 139
University of Constantinople 38
University of Leiden 188
University of Naples 109–10
University of Paris 63, 139
University of Wittenburg 166
Unstrutt 84
Urban (artillery engineer) 57–58
Urban II (pope) 43, 91–92
Urban IV (pope) 223n288
Urban VI (pope) 134–35
Utrecht, Union of 189

Val d'Or 173
Valley of Thorns *see* Roncesvalles
Valois, Elizabeth 184
Valtelline Pass 199
Van Doren, Charles 140, 210
Vandals 4, 8–9, 11, 86, 169
vanishing point 212
Varna 57
Vassy 182
Vatican 134–35, 138, 156, 183
Venice, Venetians 29, 42–47, 56–57, 59, 62, 76, 111, 154, 156–57, 162, 169, 184, 209, 221n158; rivalry with Genoa 49–51, 53, 55, 153
Verdun 177, 179, 209
Verdun, Treaty of 77–78
Verneuil 132
Versinikia 27
Vesalius, Andreas 172, 179, 213–14, 234n402
Vespers *see* Sicilian Vespers
Vienna 55, 170, 202, 208
Vienne 172
Vikings (Norsemen) 37, 74, 78–80, 87, 96, 143, 222n214
Villafranca 165
Villalar 165
Vincennes 132, 186
Visconti family 154, 157
Visigoths 3–4, 19, 70, 137, 158
Vitalian 6, 219n20
Vitry 98
Vittoria 111
Vladamir 36, 222n203
volley-fire 194, 202
Vortigern 122
Vulgate 211

Wakefield 147
Wakeman, Henry Offley 198

Wales, Welsh 86, 113, 120, 146, 227*n*298
Wallace, William 113–14
Wallachia, Wallachians 57, 223*n*340
Wallenstein, Albrecht von, Count 196, *197*, 198–99, 201–05
War of the Roses 145–53
War of the Three Henrys 192–93
Warbeck, Perkin 152
Warwick, Richard Neville, Earl of 148–49
Wedgwood, C. V. 202
Welfs 103
Wells, H. G. 1, 16, 56, 72, 137, 217
Weser River 73
Wessex 87–89
Westphalia, Peace of 1, 208–09
Whitby, Synod of 68, 86
Widukind 73
Wiles, Andrew 217
William I the Conqueror 88–90, 94, 97, 98–99
William II 98
William Louis of Nassau-Dillenburg 194
William of Champeaux 138
William of Malmsbury 92
William of Tyre 95
William of Villehardouin 49
William the Good 45
William the Silent 186, *187*, 188–89, 194
Wilton 87
Winwaed River 86
witan 89
Wittenburg 166, 211
Wittstock 206
Wolgast 198
Wolsey, Thomas 173–74
Woodville, Elizabeth 148
Woodville family 148, 150
Worms 92
Worms, Concordat of 85
Worms, Diet of 167–68
Worms, Edict of 167–68
Wright, John "Pin" 114
Wycliffe, John 124, 135, 137, 167

Yarmuk River 17
Yersinia pestis 122; *see also* bubonic plague
Yezdegerd 18, 220*n*100
York (city) 89, 152
York, House of 145–48, 150, 152
Yorkshire 174
Yusuf 159

Zacharias 71–72
Zapetra 29
Zápolya, John 170
Zautses, Stylian 31
Zeno 4–5
zero 62
Zeugmin 44
Zirndorf 202
Zizka, Jan 136
Zoë (wife of Romanus III, Michael IV and Constantine IX) 37–38, *39*, 40
Zoë Carbonopsina (mother of Constantine VII) 31–32
Zusmarshausen 209
Zutphen 187
Zuyder Zee 188
Zweibrüken 206
Zwingli, Ulrich 171

www.ingramcontent.com/pod-product-compliance
Lightning Source LLC
Chambersburg PA
CBHW081549300426
44116CB00015B/2806